Music Drama at the Paris Odéon, 1824–1828

Music Drama
at the Paris Odéon,
1824–1828

Mark Everist

UNIVERSITY OF CALIFORNIA PRESS
Berkeley   Los Angeles   London

I am grateful to, respectively, Bärenreiter Verlag and the University of California Press for permission to use extracts from two previously published articles in this book: "Lindoro in Lyon: Rossini's *Le Barbier de Séville,*" *Acta musicologica* 44 (1992): 50–85; and "Giacomo Meyerbeer and Music Drama at the Paris Odéon during the Bourbon Restoration," *19th-Century Music* 16 (1993): 124–48.

Figures 1–28 are used by permission of Bibliothèque nationale de France, Paris.

University of California Press
Berkeley and Los Angeles, California

University of California Press, Ltd.
London, England

Library of Congress Cataloging-in-Publication Data

Everist, Mark.
    Music drama at the Paris Odéon, 1824–1828 / Mark Everist.
        p.   cm.
    Includes bibliographical references and index.
    ISBN 0-520-23445-6 (alk. paper).
        1. Opera—France—Paris—19th century.   2. Odéon (Theater :
Paris, France)—History.   I. Title.
ML1727.8.P2 E93   2002
782.1'0944'36109034—dc21   2002018842

Manufactured in the United States of America
11   10   09   08   07   06   05   04   03   02
10   9   8   7   6   5   4   3   2   1

The paper used in this publication is both acid-free and totally chlorine-free (TCF). It meets the minimum requirements of ANSI/NISO Z39.48-1992 (R 1997) *(Permanence of Paper).* ♾

For Jeanice, who arrived at this book's beginning,
and for Amelia, who arrived at its end

Il est un air, pour qui je donnerais
Tout Rossini, tout Mozart et tout Wèbre [sic],
Un air très vieux, languissant et funèbre,
Qui pour moi seul a des charmes secrets.

GÉRARD DE NERVAL, Fantaisie, Odelettes *(1832)*

CONTENTS

LIST OF ILLUSTRATIONS / *xi*

ACKNOWLEDGMENTS / *xv*

ABBREVIATIONS / *xvii*

INTRODUCTION / *1*

PART I: THE INSTITUTION

1. *Un délassement honnête et instructif*—Music Drama
   in Restoration Paris / *13*
   The City • *The Maison du Roi* • *Music Drama in Paris*

2. *L'obligation de jouer le répertoire du premier ordre*—Repertory and
   Management at the Odéon / *44*
   Regulating the Odéon • *Claude Bernard* • *Frédéric du Petit-Méré* •
   Thomas Sauvage

3. *Cet ensemble si harmonieux et si parfait*—The Odéon's Personnel / *73*
   Soloists • *The Orchestra* • *Composers* • *Literary Collaborators* • *Patterns
   of Dispersal*

4. *La férule sévère et souvent capricieuse*—Control
   and Consumption / *112*
   The jury de lecture • *Censorship* • *The Audience* • Les chevaliers de lustre •
   Benefit Performances • *Publishers*

PART II: THE REPERTORY

5. *Une heure à l'opéra-comique*—Occasional Works / *143*
   Opening the Theater: Les trois genres • *The Monarchy and the Theater* •
   The Monarch's Name Day • *Crowning Charles X* • *Command Performances*

6. *Rendre service à notre scène lyrique*—The Pasticcio / *171*
   *The Pasticcio in Paris • The 1826 Plan • Single-Composer Pasticci •
   Castil-Blaze*

7. *Le fruit défendu*—Opéra Comique and the French Tradition / *199*
   *The ancien répertoire • Opéra Comique • Berlioz • French Origins
   of Odéon Compositions*

8. *Les heureux étrangers*—Italian Music Drama / *227*
   Rossini • Meyerbeer • Mozart

9. *Une leçon de morale*—German Music Drama / *250*
   Weber • Beethoven • Viennese Musicians and the Kärntnertortheater

CONCLUSION / *283*

APPENDIX 1 / *291*
APPENDIX 2 / *301*
BIBLIOGRAPHY / *303*
INDEX / *317*

ILLUSTRATIONS

FIGURES

(Cliché Bibliothèque nationale de France, Paris.)

1. The eleventh arrondissement of Paris in 1826 / *16*

2. Montano in the role of Rosine (*Le barbier de Séville*) / *23*

3. Jacques-Alexandre-Bernard Law, marquis de Lauriston / *27*

4. Jean-Henri Dupin / *37*

5. Daniel-François-Esprit Auber / *38*

6. Michele Carafa / *39*

7. Giacomo Meyerbeer / *40*

8. Charles-Louis Huguet, marquis de Sémonville / *49*

9. Sir Walter Scott / *58*

10. Campenaut in the role of Almaviva (*Le barbier de Séville*) / *74*

11. Lecomte in the role of Almaviva (*Le barbier de Séville*) / *75*

12. Letellier in the role of Nancy (*Robin des bois*) / *76*

13. Coeuriot in the role of MacGregor (*La dame du lac*) / *79*

14. Valère in the role of Richard (*Robin des bois*) / *87*

15. Florigny in the role of Anna (*Robin des bois*) / *88*

16. Lemoule in the role of Marguerite (*Marguerite d'Anjou*) / *91*

17. Lemoule in the role of Lélia (*Ivanhoé*) / *92*

xi

18. François-Adrien Boieldieu / *98*

19. Jean-François-Alfred Bayard / *107*

20. Antoine-Chrysostome Quatremère de Quincy / *115*

21. Hector Berlioz / *122*

22. Eugène Delacroix / *125*

23. Anne-Honoré-Joseph Duveyrier (pseud. Mélesville) / *178*

24. Émile Deschamps / *180*

25. Set design for act II of Grétry's *Richard Coeur-de-Lion*
    at the Odéon / *200*

26. Gioachino Rossini / *228*

27. Carl Maria von Weber / *253*

28. Set design for act II of Weber's *Robin des bois* / *262*

TABLES

1. Repertory at royal theaters, 1 October to 7 October 1825 / *32*

2. Operatic repertory during Claude Bernard's management / *55*

3. Operatic repertory during Frédéric du Petit-Méré's
   management / *60*

4. Operatic repertory during Thomas Sauvage's management / *66*

5. Repertory during first week of Théâtre anglais / *68*

6. Repertory during Christmas period 1827–28 / *69*

7. Sources of *Ivanhoé* / *183*

8. Comparison of *Il barbiere di Siviglia* and *Le barbier de Séville* / *230*

9. Comparison of *Robin des bois* and *Der Freischütz,* act II finale / *261*

10. Cast changes for 1824 performances of *Robin des bois* / *263*

11. Viennese compositions at the Théâtre-Royal de l'Odéon,
    1824–28 / *280*

MUSIC EXAMPLES

1. Rossini/Castil-Blaze, *Le barbier de Séville,* "C'est d'abord rumeur légère" / *86*

2. Auber/Boieldieu, *Les trois genres,* "La belle chose qu'un tournois" / *147*

3. Auber/Boieldieu, *Les trois genres,* "La belle chose qu'un tournois" / *148*

4. Mozart, *Die Entführung aus dem Serail,* "Singt dem großen Bassa Lieder" / *162*

5. Mozart/Vergne, *Louis XII ou La route de Reims,* "Allez, laissez-moi" / *163*

6. Mozart/Vergne, *Louis XII ou La route de Reims,* "Allez, laissez-moi" / *164*

7. Mozart/Vergne, *Louis XII ou La route de Reims,* "Près de ma belle" / *166*

8. Beginning of "Si par hasard à travers la campagne" and "Oui, malgré votre mésaventure" (*Les noces de Gamache*) / *191*

9. Reconstruction of "Si vous voulez nous plaire" (*Les Français au sérail*) / *204*

10. Context for "Non più, tacete" (*Il barbiere di Siviglia*) and "Pensez-vous qu'il soit" (*Le barbier de Séville*) / *232*

11. Comparison of "Largo al factotum" (*Il barbiere di Siviglia*) and "Place au factotum" (*Le barbier de Séville*) / *233*

12. Ornamentation in "Je suis donc" (*Le barbier de Séville*) and "Dunque io son" (*Il barbiere di Siviglia*) / *236*

13. "Non plus d'alarmes" from *Euryanthe* (*Robin des bois*) / *260*

ACKNOWLEDGMENTS

In any study that depends to such a large extent on primary sources, debts are incurred on a large scale to libraries and their staff: British Library, London; Staatsbibliothek, Berlin; Bibliothèque nationale de France, Paris (sections *musique* and *manuscrits*); Bibliothèque-Musée de l'Opéra, Paris; Archives nationales, Paris; Bibliothèque de l'Arsenal, Paris; Bibliothèque historique de la ville de Paris, Paris; Archives des la ville de Paris, Paris; Bibliothèque municipale, Rouen.

Support for publication of this book was received from the Arts and Humanities Research Board and the University of Southampton.

I would like to thank colleagues who have provided direct assistance to the research for this book or who have read parts of the work: Michael Wittman (Freie Universität, Berlin); Roger Parker (University of Cambridge); Philip Gossett (University of Chicago); M. Elizabeth Bartlet (Duke University); Janet Johnson (University of Southern California); David Charlton (Royal Holloway, University of London); Nicole Wild (Paris); Herbert Schneider (Universität Saarlandes); Steven Huebner (McGill University); Hervé Lacombe (Université de Metz); Joachim Veit (Universität Detmold), Julian Rushton and Clive Brown (University of Leeds), Donald Gíslason (University of British Columbia), Sieghart Döhring (Forschungsinstitut für Musiktheater, Universität Bayreuth), Corinne Schneider (Université de Tours), Nicholas Cook and Jeanice Brooks (University of Southampton).

It is always a great pleasure to acknowledge the support of the editorial team, but in this case the staff of the University of California Press has made editing this book even more of a delight than it would normally have been. I am grateful to Lynne Withey, Lynn Meinhardt, and their staff, who supervised and coordinated operations in Berkeley, and especially to Edith

Gladstone, who copyedited the manuscript superbly and who also taught me some Louisiana French. Sarah Hibberd took a long list of names and turned it into the index with great skill and ingenuity.

Finally, the book's dedicatees call for acknowledgment and thanks for—quite simply—everything. They both know what I mean.

ABBREVIATIONS

D-Bds   Berlin, Staatsbibliothek zu Berlin—Preußischer Kulturbesitz, Musikabteilung mit Mendelssohn-Archiv

FétisB   Fétis, François-Joseph, *Biographie universelle des musiciens et bibliographie générale de la musique*, 2d ed., 8 vols. (with supplement in two vols.) (Paris: Firmin Didot, 1860–65)

F-Pan   Paris, Archives nationales

F-Pn   Paris, Bibliothèque nationale de France

F-Po   Paris, Bibliothèque nationale de France, Bibliothèque-Musée de l'Opéra

LDD-NS   Larousse, Pierre, *Grand Dictionnaire universel du XIXe siècle français, historique, géographique, biographique, mythologique, bibliographique, littéraire, artistique, scientifique, etc.*, 15 vols. (with supplements) (Paris: Grand Dictionnaire Universel, 1866)

MGG   *Die Musik in Geschichte und Gegenwart: allgemeine Enzyklopädie der Musik*, 16 vols. (Kassel: Bärenreiter-Verlag, 1949–79)

Introduction

In the years after the battle of Waterloo, music drama was very unlike what it is today. As much entertainment as art, it was a central element in court and civic recreation across Europe and the New World. National styles of composition and performance—far more diverse in the nineteenth century than in the twenty-first—characterized much stage music in an age where the locomotive and the telegraph were yet to accelerate communication across continents. Balances of power in music drama were also different: librettists were considered at least as important as composers, and the producer was only just beginning to emerge as a creative voice. Although some soloists continued to be treated as celebrities, their position was much more akin to that enjoyed by eighteenth-century figures in that composers still adjusted works to suit them and continued to do so for much of the century. At the same time, however, soloists also depended to a significant degree on the goodwill of impresarios and patrons.

Definitions of what constituted opera in the early nineteenth century were much more inclusive than those of the early twenty-first, when a preference for the Wagnerian-Verdian operatic paradigm focuses critical attention on continuous opera at the expense of such works with spoken dialogue as singspiel or opéra comique. At the beginning of the nineteenth century, librettists and composers moved effortlessly between various types of music drama: they used recitative or spoken dialogue to drive a work's narrative and wrote incidental music. Spohr could write *Faust* with spoken dialogue, through-compose *Jessonda* as continuous music drama, and then return to the use of spoken dialogue in *Pietro von Albano* and *Der Alchymist*. Rossini provided *Elisabetta, regina d'Inghilterra* with continuous accompanied recitative and returned to *recitativo semplice* the year after. Weber, likewise, could write *Der Freischütz* with spoken dialogue, through-compose *Euryanthe*, and return to spoken dialogue in *Oberon*. All three composers contributed incidental music to spoken drama. In Paris, despite the institutional segregation of genres, composers through-composed works for the Académie royale de musique (the Opéra), used spoken dialogue at the Opéra-Comique, and wrote incidental music for the stage. To take two examples, between 1828 and 1834 Auber wrote *La muette de Portici*, *Le serment*, *Le philtre*, and *Gustave III* for the Académie royale de musique, and *La fiancée*, *Fra Diavolo*, and *Lestocq* for the Opéra-Comique; his librettist, Eugène Scribe, not only worked for both theaters but also wrote plays and comédies-vaudevilles for other institutions. Hérold moved among a different range of genres during the same period: opéra comique, ballet music, and incidental music for a play at the Odéon. This multi-faceted nature of Parisian stage music explains why this book treats the term "opera" as a generic term with a degree of caution and prefers the more neutral term "music drama" to encompass a wider range of music for the stage.[1] The term encourages the inclusion of various genres and styles of stage music: in France, for example, opéra comique and grand opéra, as well as mélodrame and comédie-vaudeville; or in German-speaking lands, *Singspiel*, *romantische Oper* with continuous recitative, or incidental music. This is not to rule out such formulations as "the opera-going public" or the idea of an opera house, but for a study such as this, where continuous opera on the Verdian-Wagnerian model is very far from the surface of the institution's activity or any discussion of it, such terminological inclusiveness is a valuable reminder that much stage music in nineteenth-century Europe was similarly far removed from what is today thought of as opera.

Nineteenth-century France (which meant then and still means to many, nineteenth-century Paris) arranged its music drama in ways that were regimented and bureaucratic; three institutions mounted productions of different types: the Académie royale de musique put on productions of grand

1. Recent studies apply the term to stage works and repertories before Wagner as varied as Handel's *Hercules* (Todd S. Gilman, "Handel's *Hercules* and Its Semiosis," *The Musical Quarterly* 81 [1997]: 449–81), Gluck's stage music (Thomas Betzwieser, "Der in Bewegung gesetzte Chor: Gluck und der *choeur dansé*," in *D'un opéra à l'autre: hommage à Jean Mongrédien*, ed. Jean Gribenski, Marie-Claire Mussat, and Herbert Schneider [Paris: Presses de l'Université de Paris-Sorbonne, 1996], 45–54), Mozart's *Mitridate, rè di Ponto* (Philipp Adlung, *Mozarts Opera Seria "Mitridate, rè di Ponto"* [Hamburg: Wagner, 1996]), Kuhlau (Gorm Busk, "Friedrich Kuhlau's Operas and Theatre Music and Their Performances at the Royal Theatre in Copenhagen [1814–1830]: A Mirror of European Music Drama and a Glimpse of the Danish Opera Tradition," *Musik & Forskning* 21 [1996]: 93–127), and Verdi's *Macbeth* (Daniel Brandenburg, "Musikdrama, das Traditionen änderte: zu Verdis *Macbeth*," *Österreichische Musikzeitschrift* 55 [2000]: 21–24).

opéra, the Théâtre italien produced Italian music drama in the original language, and the Opéra-Comique mounted works of the same name as the institution. Each type of composition was governed by different conventions, was heard in different locations, and was subject to different administrative and budgetary pressures. Parisian bureaucracy may also however have been one of the city's strengths. In the three principal opera houses, vocal, instrumental, and scenic resources were deployed generously, and such generosity acted like a magnet on composers from all over Europe. The list of foreign composers who took up residence in Paris reads like a *Who's Who* of music drama in the fifty years either side of 1800 and includes Gluck, Sacchini, Piccini, Spontini, Cherubini, Rossini, Reicha, Paër, and Meyerbeer. The list of composers who spent shorter periods of time in Paris, for the production of particular works, is even longer with Bellini, Donizetti, Wagner, and Verdi at its head.

For a period in the 1820s, a fourth lyric theater joined the three official ones and—at a time when all three (for various reasons) were facing difficulty—succeeded in shifting the balance of Parisian operatic power in its favor. The Théâtre-Royal de l'Odéon was technically the Second Théâtre-Français, designed to prepare actors for the Comédie-Française, the most prestigious venue for spoken drama in the capital. As soon as it received a license in 1824 to promote music drama, it set about producing the most imaginative and far-reaching seasons that had been seen— or would be seen—in Paris for many years. During four and a half years, the management put on fifty-six operatic productions at the rate of slightly more than one a month. The Odéon was allowed to produce, in addition to the spoken drama that had always been its standard repertory, public-domain opéras comiques, pasticci and occasional works, and translations of foreign music drama. The result was the importation of music by Mozart, Rossini, Weber, Winter, Weigl, Mercadante, Conradin Kreutzer, Carafa, Cimarosa, and Meyerbeer. Although Mozart and Rossini were known from the Théâtre italien, the arrival of these works at the Odéon changed the landscape of Parisian stage music. Other composers whose works were associated with, but were never mounted at, the Odéon included Berlioz, Beethoven, and Spohr. The Odéon contributed to the internationalization of music drama in a way that the Académie royale de musique and the Théâtre italien did not. The arrival of foreigners at the these two opera houses was, if not haphazard, the result of ad hoc arrangements that sometimes worked well but were sometimes spectacularly unsuccessful. By contrast, the Odéon's license to mount foreign stage music meant that it had to seek out works for the theater and to convince foreign composers to work there. For the years that it was active in the field of music drama, its business was purposeful and its outcomes positive, as the list of foreign composers represented at the Odéon—and those it enticed to work there—demonstrates.[2]

The analysis of music drama in the first half of the nineteenth century has taken as many different approaches as there have been authors ready to write about it. Grand opéra, the genre cultivated at the Académie royale de musique, has perhaps received most attention, and its history has been written as a statement of political power, a response to the urbanization and industrialization of early-nineteenth-century Europe, a collision with the practices of the so-called boulevard theaters or with romantic ballet, or as a revisiting of the traditions of Gluck and Spontini.[3] The Académie royale de musique as an institution has received much less attention,[4] and other theaters in Paris have fared much worse. The Théâtre italien and the Opéra-Comique have received nothing like the same scrutiny as the Opéra either in terms of their repertory or their institutional structures.[5] Paradoxically, it is the Théâtre-Lyrique (much more like the Odéon than the other two) that has received the treatment these theaters deserve and this book attempts.[6]

Music Drama at the Paris Odéon describes and analyzes the repertory, institution, personnel, audiences, critical responses to, and the social impact of the theater's activities. Almost nothing is currently known of the theater's

2. When Gérard de Nerval linked Rossini, Mozart, and Weber in the stanza that forms this book's epigraph, the only institution that hosted works by all three composers was the Odéon (see Jean Guillaume, Claude Pichois et al., eds., *Gérard de Nerval: oeuvres complètes* [Paris: Gallimard, 1989–93], 1:339). The orthography "Wèbre," found in the original 1832 edition, was adjusted to the correct form in its third printing—in the *Journal des gens du monde* (1834)—although a later publication in *L'Artiste*, 1 August 1849, returned to the original spelling.

3. Jane F. Fulcher, *The Nation's Image: French Grand Opera as Politics and Politicized Art* (Cambridge: Cambridge University Press, 1987); Anselm Gerhard, *The Urbanization of Opera: Music Theater in Paris in the Nineteenth Century*, trans. Mary Whittall (Chicago: University of Chicago Press, 1998 [originally published in 1992 as *Die Verstädterung der Oper: Paris und das Musiktheater des 19. Jahrhundert*]); Karin Pendle, "The Boulevard Theaters and Continuity in French Opera of the 19th Century," in *Music in Paris in the Eighteen-Thirties*, ed. Peter Bloom (Stuyvesant, N.Y.: Pendragon, 1987), 509–35; Marian Smith, "Music for the Ballet-Pantomime at the Paris Opéra, 1825–1850" (Ph.D. diss., Yale University, 1988); and Gilles de Van, "Le grand opéra entre tragédie lyrique et drame romantique," *Il saggiatore musicale: rivista semestrale di musicologia* 3 (1996): 325–60.

4. Yves Ozanam, "Recherches sur l'Académie royale de musique sous la seconde restauration" (Ph.D. diss., École nationale des Chartes, 1981).

5. Two valuable exceptions are Janet Johnson, "The Théâtre Italien and Opera and Theatrical Life in Restoration Paris," 3 vols. (Ph.D. diss., University of Chicago, 1988); and Olivier Bara, "Le Théâtre de l'Opéra-Comique entre 1822 et 1827: la difficile recherche d'un genre moyen" (Ph.D. diss., Université de Paris III, 1998).

6. Thomas Joseph Walsh, *Second Empire Opera: The Théâtre Lyrique, Paris, 1851–1870* (London: Calder, 1981).

work beyond the names of a couple of arrangements that were mounted there (*Robin des bois,* the arrangement of Weber's *Freischütz,* is perhaps the best known) and the impact of the so-called English season of 1827, which brought the works of Shakespeare to Paris. Since the secondary literature on the subject is almost nonexistent, previously untouched sources have a place in this history: the administrative documents in the Archives nationales, private papers of the directors and staff of the theater, material deposited with the censor, manuscript and printed libretti, printed musical material, the contemporary press, and published memoirs.[7]

The book falls into two parts: institution and repertory. The first chapter examines the operatic activities at the Odéon through three different lenses: the physical and material environment in which operatic work took place in the city, *la maison du Roi* and the licensing system that controlled operatic and theatrical operations in the capital, and the general characteristics of music drama in Paris during the Bourbon Restoration (illustrated by reference to a single week's programming). Chapter 2 has two aims: the first is to outline a chronicle of events at the Odéon in order to give a degree of diachronic purchase on the four years during which the theater functioned as an opera house and to introduce the three managers, Claude Bernard, Frédéric du Petit-Méré, and Thomas Sauvage. The second task is to examine the financial background to the workings of the theater, and to give a context for the many negotiations that lay behind music drama at the Odéon. Chapters 3 and 4 attempt to paint a picture of the individuals who had significant roles in the culture that supported the Odéon and in the theater itself. The soloists and orchestra appear in chapter 3 alongside composers and their literary colleagues who wrote or arranged works for the theater. The chapter looks at the types of careers these individuals followed (only a small number were professional composers or librettists), how they found their way to the Odéon, and what happened when their skills were no longer required. Chapter 4 investigates the people responsible for setting the boundaries of activities at the theater, some formal, others vague or arbitrary. It considers the audience in general terms and looks at some of its better-known members—Hector Berlioz and Victor Hugo

---

7. Three texts, each very different, that describe the Odéon constitute its bibliography: Paul Porel and Georges Monval, *L'Odéon: histoire administrative, anecdotique et littéraire du second théâtre français,* 2 vols. (Paris: Lemerre, 1876–82); Christian Genty, *Histoire du théâtre national de l'Odéon: journal de bord, 1782–1982* (Paris: Fischbacher, 1982); *Théâtre de l'Odéon, 1782–1982* (catalog of exhibition held at the Théâtre de l'Odéon, October 1982–May 1983, and at the Mairie annexe du VIe arrondissement, 20 January–20 February 1983) (Paris, 1982). There is also an entry for the theater in Nicole Wild, *Dictionnaire des théâtres parisiens au XIXe siècle: les théâtres et la musique* (Paris: Amateurs des Livres, 1989), 291–96.

among others. It takes up the *jury de lecture* (the theater's reading committee) and the ways in which censorship operated before looking at the con-
trols exercised by the audience and the claque.

The second part of the book engages with questions of repertory. Chapter 5 examines the context for the considerable number of occasional works
that appeared at the Odéon during the 1820s. The lion's share of this stage
music was associated with the royal family—the monarch's name day and
especially the coronation of Charles X in 1825—but the chapter also gives
space to a curious work, *Les trois genres,* that was used to open the opera seasons in 1824. Chapter 6 explores the pasticcio and attempts to give a sense
of the eighteenth-century tradition of pasticci, on which the Odéon's practice was based, in order to dissect, critique, and draw up a typology of music drama that was built out of parts of several different works, often by different composers. Chapter 7's subject is the French tradition, taken first of
all in its most literal sense: the history of French opéra comique that the
Odéon mounted alongside foreign works, and the attempts that the theater
and composers in the capital made to have the theater's license changed so
that it could produce new opéras comiques. The second half of this chapter treats the sense of the French tradition in a more far-reaching fashion,
looking at German and especially Italian music drama with libretti derived
from French literary originals (by Beaumarchais and Molière, for example)
that the Odéon sought to reinstate as it reworked foreign works for its own
stage. The last two chapters in the book consider the reception of Italian and German music drama at the Odéon. Chapter 8 examines works by
Rossini, Meyerbeer, and Mozart and considers the ways in which Italian music drama was adapted to the conventional boundaries of French music
drama with spoken dialogue. The final chapter in the book looks at the tradition of German music drama in Paris, considers works by Weber and an
abortive production of Beethoven's *Fidelio* and concludes with an investiga-
tion of the relationship between the Kärntnertortheater in Vienna and the
Paris Odéon.

Music Drama at the Paris Odéon takes as its subject a musical and theatrical
culture in which revered works by well-known composers (*Don Giovanni,
Fidelio,* or *Le nozze di Figaro*) had a smaller part than modern assessments of
their significance might suggest. Music drama plays a much more complex
role in the culture of which the Odéon was the center than in more traditional accounts of composers' lives and works. For example, a discussion of
such a canonic work as Mozart's *Entführung aus dem Serail* appears only because a couple of its numbers were appropriated for an occasional work,
and the inquiry focuses on the ways in which such borrowings function.
Hence works that are no longer in the operatic repertory (Meyerbeer's
Margherita d'Anjou for example) receive more attention than those that are

(Mozart's *Don Giovanni*).[8] In the same way, the administrative culture that supported the Odéon, the maison du Roi, and the officials who ran it occupies at least as much space as the more traditional concerns of works and their composers.

The subject of this book, then, is an institution: its masters, servants, producers, and consumers; translated into the vocabulary of music drama, this means its staff (ranging from the most humble *ouvreuse* to the best-paid soloist and including the musical and administrative staff), the civil servants who supervised it, the composers and librettists who worked there, and the audience who derived pleasure from its productions. Some might dub such a study as this "microhistory"; the term is not a bad analogy for the study of a lyric theater such as the Odéon whose population was at least as large as an average-size village, by and large local, and subject to the same sorts of tussles (usually, but not always, of an artistic nature).[9] Classic models of microhistory Emmanuel le Roy Ladurie's *Montaillou* and Carlo Ginzburg's *Formaggio e i vermi* (1975 and 1976 respectively) are useful points of reference in this regard.[10] Certain claims of microhistory are worth rehearsing here, in some ways to distance *Music Drama at the Paris Odéon* from them, and in others to align it with some of their implications. Critics of microhistory claim that authors of such studies attempt to read macrohistories out of their microhistories, and that such a procedure is suspect.[11] It is difficult not to sympathize with this position, and it should be stated very bluntly that practices at the Odéon cannot be amplified into a general understanding of Parisian music drama. They form a network of activities that may overlap those of other lyric theaters but in other regards are sui generis. Attempting to separate out the specific from the general is one of the tasks of this book. Invoking the idea of a network of activities opens up an important methodological aspect of microhistory shared with *Music Drama at the Paris Odéon*, and that is the idea of anthropological history centered on the "web of culture" and its methodological underpinning, "thick description." The concept of the web of culture is one that has been adumbrated in musicological writing of a theoretical cast but marginalized in favor of more traditional tales of composers and works in the products of mu-

8. As an aid to the negotiation of (occasionally) unfamiliar music drama, appendix 1 gives the entire lyric repertory of the Odéon during the 1820s in chronological order.

9. Peter Burke, "The Microhistory Debate," in *New Perspectives on Historical Writing*, ed. Peter Burke, 2d ed. (Cambridge: Polity, 2001), 115.

10. Carlo Ginzburg, *Il formaggio e i vermi: il cosmo di un mugnaio del '500* (Florence: Einaudi, 1976); Emmanuel Le Roy Ladurie, *Montaillou, village occitain de 1294 à 1324* (Paris: Gallimard, 1975).

11. For a critique of this view, see Giovanni Levi, "On Microhistory," in *New Perspectives on Historical Writing*, ed. Peter Burke, 2d ed. (Cambridge: Polity, 2001), 100–101.

sicological research.[12] Culture here is not taken to mean the study of art, literature, and ideas—what has brilliantly (but perhaps confusingly for this study) been described as the "opera house" conception of culture—but rather to encompass a network of social practices, among them producing and consuming music drama.[13] The concept (its principal exponent Clifford Geertz places "theory" a long way down his list of priorities) observes that cultures spin webs of meaning out of interlocking threads.[14] Such an idea lies at the heart of this book. The institution is placed in a number of contexts, some close to traditions of music drama, some less so; the Odéon is considered in terms of royal institutions, of producers and consumers, of pasticcio, and so on. Each chapter traces a different thread of the web that has the Odéon at its center. Depending on the subject of individual chapters, different threads interact, and such interaction forms one of the book's subjects.

Music Drama at the Paris Odéon takes as axiomatic a history of cultural artifacts that does not end with their creation but views musical cultures as an amalgam of the old and the new. Revivals—however different they may be from any putative "original"—take their place in an operatic season alongside works that may be enjoying their first run or works that have never gone out of the repertory; a thick description of a musical culture must fully integrate the reception of older works alongside the creation of newer ones. In the case of the Théâtre-Royal de l'Odéon, such a view is difficult to resist since its entire repertory consists of revivals—whether they were productions of works unknown to Paris or of music drama from the *ancien régime* and Revolution. The synchronic segment of operatic history represented in this book examines some works toward the beginning of their careers (*Der Freischütz*), some toward the end of their existence as performed works (Dalayrac's music drama), and others somewhere in the middle of their histories; Mozart is a good example of the last type. In this respect, the book constitutes a case study in the reception of music drama, one that the theater's license renders almost unique in the history of music. The theater was forbidden to produce new compositions, and the occasions where new

12. See Clifford Geertz, "Thick Description: Toward an Interpretative Theory of Culture," in *The Interpretation of Cultures* (New York: Basic Books, 1973), 3–30; and for musicological responses Gary Tomlinson, "The Web of Culture: A Context for Musicology," *19th-Century Music* 7 (1984): 350–62. For a rather rueful commentary on the position of such approaches in music ten years later see Philip V. Bohlman, "On the Unremarkable in Music," *19th-Century Music* 16 (1992): 207.

13. Roy Wagner, *The Invention of Culture* (1981), cited in Peter Burke, "Unity and Variety in Cultural History," in *Varieties of Cultural History* (Cambridge: Polity, 1997), 185.

14. For an account of the relationship between Geertzian thick description, microhistory, and theory, see Levi, "On Microhistory," 102–3 and 104–9.

works (or more often simply new numbers) slipped into the repertory are highlighted as the rarities they are.

The use of the term "premiere" in this book is not unrelated to the question of the large number of works "received" by the Odéon. Strictly speaking, and in common parlance, the first performance of *Der Freischütz* as *Robin des bois* in December 1824 was not a premiere. Yet even a production of a work that was well known in the capital—*Il barbiere di Siviglia*, perhaps—was considered a premiere when it was first staged as *Le barbier de Séville* at the Odéon. This book retains the early-nineteenth-century usage of the term. Large parts of the book attempt to negotiate between original versions of stage works and French translations and arrangements. Original titles remain in reference to works in general terms or in the original language. Correspondingly, French titles denote their Parisian versions.

Prosopographical difficulties abound in the study of early nineteenth-century French theater and opera. In general, all individuals are identified by their full names at first occurrence, and subsequently by their surnames only. However, for actors and actresses, their first names are frequently not given and today unknown, hence the inclusion of simply "Campenaut" or "Lecomte." Normal nineteenth-century practice simply gives a title to women only (Mme or Mlle) and the text of this book replicates this practice (using surnames for women after their first occurrence). However, because this is basically an epistemological problem, the first names of some of women—Stéphanie Montano and Amalia Schütz for example—have emerged from the documentary record, and ignoring them for the sake of consistency seems perverse.

PART ONE

The Institution

Chapter 1

Un délassement honnête et instructif— Music Drama in Restoration Paris

The City

The context for Parisian music drama in the nineteenth century was the city of Paris itself. The dimensions of the city had changed little between the end of the *ancien régime* and the beginning of the Restoration in April 1814.[1] The city was still walled, and the distinction between land *intra muros* and *extra muros* was acute; all parts of the city's populace, except the municipal administrators (who dealt with the city's more modern twelve arrondissements), still thought of its topography in terms of *quartiers* (neighborhoods) and faubourgs.[2] Although differences in fortune were immense, the neighborhood in which sections of the Parisian population lived distinguished its residents as much as any levels of income. Some neighborhoods were more discrete than others: the chaussée d'Antin, for example, had a very narrow mix of population while the area around the Odéon, the faubourg St-Germain, blended a wide range of human conditions and aspirations.[3]

Although the city of the 1820s was not dissimilar from that of the 1780s, its landscape and the fortunes of its population underwent rapid developments after 1815. Yet for much of the rest of France, little changed at all; one commentator has noted that "from Waterloo to the Liberation,

---

1. Bernard Marchand, *Paris: histoire d'une ville (XIXe–XXe siècles)* (Paris: Seuil, 1993), 22–24.

2. Fundamental to any study of Parisian topography is Jeanne Pronteau, *Les Numérotages des maisons de Paris du XVe siècle à nos jours* (Paris: Préfecture de la Seine—Service des travaux historiques, 1966), which notes nineteenth-century changes in numbering of houses and arrondissements: house numbers tended to change only by a few digits, whereas after 1860 the area of the eleventh arrondissement shifted from the Seine's left bank to the right.

3. Anne Martin-Fugier, *La Vie élégante, ou la formation du tout-Paris (1815–1848)* (Paris: Fayard, 1993), 100–103.

everything happened as if only the capital grew."[4] The population of Paris doubled in size between 1800 and 1850, moving from half a million to a million inhabitants.[5] Much of this increase was the result of immigration, especially from the provinces that had suffered greatly during the Revolution and Napoleonic campaigns.[6] Such immigration gained strength during the Empire and increased substantially during the Restoration.[7] During the first five years of the July Monarchy (1830–35), despite the devastating 1832 cholera outbreak, the population of the capital was increasing at a rate of 22,000 inhabitants (net) per annum.[8]

The infrastructure of the city of Paris was lamentably ill equipped to withstand such demographic change. In this respect, Paris in 1815 was little changed from the medieval city, and the famous description of the capital by Louis-Sébastien Mercier—which dates from the 1780s—still represents the situation forty years later.[9] Although projects for improvement in the city during the Revolution had been drawn up, they resulted in no action, and Napoleonic developments were driven by a need to project the city's prestige rather than to enhance its housing stock: no citizen directly benefited from the Arc de Triomphe, for example, or from the statue of the elephant at the Barrière du Trône. Domestic construction was driven by property speculation. The largest growth in Paris was on previously undeveloped sites; developments in the St-Georges quarter, the "Nouvelle Athènes," and the Europe and Poissonnière quarters all gave an opportunity for capitalists to invest or—when the supply of building exceeded demand—to fail.[10] It was said that, in 1843, Paris had enough spare accommodation to receive a visit from the entire population of Lyon.[11] Alongside these developments came new ecclesiastical buildings:[12] the foundation stones of the churches of Notre-Dame-de-Lorette and St-Vincent-de-Paul were laid within days of each other (23 and 25 August 1824), and work continued more purposefully on the church of the Madeleine.[13] However, in the most densely crowded parts of the city, around the Hôtel de Ville and les Halles, investors

4. Marchand, *Paris*, 8.

5. Louis Chevalier, *Classes laborieuses et classes dangereuses à Paris pendant la première moitié du XIXe siècle* (Paris: Librairie générale française, 1978), 313.

6. Marchand, *Paris*, 20.

7. Chevalier, *Classes laborieuses*, 391.

8. Marchand, *Paris*, 12.

9. "Paris en 1815 était encore en majeure partie une ville médiévale" (ibid., 22); Louis-Sébastien Mercier, *Tableau de Paris* (Neufchâtel: Fauch, 1781) is used as a primary source for many twentieth-century accounts of the early-nineteenth-century city.

10. François Loyer, *Paris au XIXe siècle: l'immeuble et la rue* (Paris: Hazan, 1987), passim.

11. Victor Hugo, *Choses vues, 1830–1846* (Paris: Gallimard, 1972), 250.

12. Marchand, *Paris*, 37.

13. Guillaume de Berthier de Sauvigny, *La Restauration, 1815–1830* (Paris: Hachette, 1977), 50 and 65.

had no interest, and the levels of overcrowding and squalor remained constant or increased.

Although certain neighborhoods in the city were more sought-after—and perhaps safer—than others, certain aspects of Parisian life affected every inhabitant from the king to the *ouvreuse* at the Odéon. At the center of environmental difficulties in early-nineteenth-century Paris was the absence of running water and the totally inadequate sanitation. In 1835, when Fanny Trollope visited the city, she remarked how in London running water was piped to second- and even third-story dwellings; in Paris, water was still being transported manually.[14] It is certainly true that the volumes of water delivered in Paris during the 1820s increased, but this could only slightly improve the general level of sanitation in the city. The inadequate water supply was coupled with a system of waste disposal that elicited many demands for improvement. Alphonse Lescot—a *piéton parisien*—gave a vivid account of the Parisian treatment of waste in 1826 in a little pamphlet called *On the Cleanliness of the City of Paris,* criticizing every part of the Parisian sewerage system.[15] An improvement in this position was a central question for the municipality of Paris in the 1820s; it was one that was never resolved. Waste was directed straight into the Seine via the Canal St-Martin.[16] When the wind was in the wrong direction, the stench was perceptible all over the city—even as far away as the Tuileries.[17]

Although by the end of the Restoration Paris had seen a great change in the public provision of transport (the earliest omnibus company opened its first route on 30 January 1828),[18] developments in urban travel in Paris during the 1820s were more or less static. Despite a slight growth in overall number of vehicles from 22,000 in 1819 to between 26,000 and 27,000 in 1825, the ways of getting around the city had changed little. For those wealthy enough to own a vehicle, common provision was irrelevant. For the majority of the population, however, transport was difficult and not particularly cheap. A fiacre, a four-wheeled carriage that could be hired by the journey or by the hour, cost Fr 1.50 during the day (equivalent to the cost of 2 liters of wine or half the daily wage of a manual worker) and Fr 2 at night (rates for the hour were slightly higher). Cabriolets (two-wheeled carriages) were cheaper, available for hire by the day or the month, and covered carriages (*carrosses*) were also available. But of the more than 20,000 vehicles in Paris, those for hire accounted for only about a tenth of the

14. Fanny Trollope, *Paris et les Parisiens en 1825* (1836), cited in Marchand, *Paris,* 38.
15. Alphonse Lescot, *De la salubrité de la ville de Paris* (1826) cited in Sauvigny, *Restauration,* 83–85.
16. Ibid., 87.
17. Ibid., 89.
18. Lucien Dubech and Pierre d'Espeziel, *Histoire de Paris* (Paris: Payot, 1926), 134.

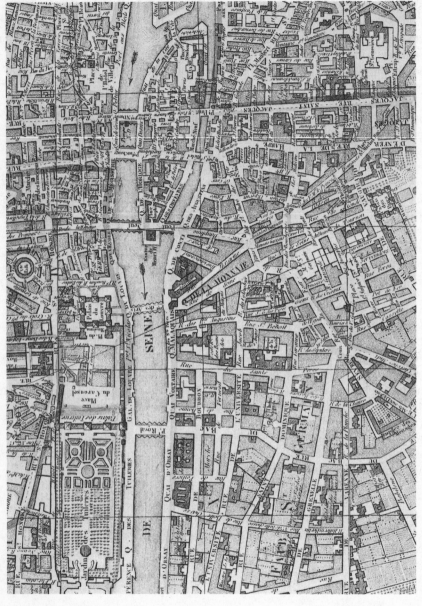

Figure 1. The eleventh arrondissement of Paris in 1826. Portion of *Plan routier de la ville et faubourgs de Paris divisé en 12 mairies, revu et corrigé en 1826* (Paris: Jean, [1826]).

total.[19] The obvious alternative was a horse, but again that option was limited to those with sufficient means. Some soloists at an institution such as the Odéon could afford one; during the run of Giacomo Meyerbeer's *Marguerite d'Anjou* in April 1826 the Odéon's principal tenor, Lecomte, fell from his horse and his role (as Lavarenne) had to be taken by his understudy. Lecomte owned a horse because he had a private income (which explains the interest on the part of the press); there is no record of his male colleagues at the Odéon owning their own transport.[20]

For most of those who worked at the Odéon and for most of its audiences, all journeys had to be made on foot, and—as was the case with most industries in Paris—most of the theater's employees lived locally. Of the fifteen soloists listed in the *Nouvelle biographie théâtrale* of 1826, fourteen lived in the streets around the Odéon (figure 1).[21]

Lecomte's private fortune might have allowed him to live north of the river, yet he stayed in the rue Ste-Hyacinthe; certainly a little further away from the theater than most of his colleagues, but still within walking distance. The only exception to this general rule was Saint-Preux; his work at the Odéon seems to have been little more than a diversion, since his principal activity was as proprietor of a haberdasher's shop in the rue Mandar, north of les Halles. Saint-Preux too might have owned a horse.

More wealthy audiences from the Right Bank (defectors from the Théâtre italien, the Académie royale de musique, and the Opéra-Comique) could get to the Odéon, but Odéon audiences could not reach the chaussée d'Antin, since the former group had access to wheeled transport while the latter group did not. One of the ways in which the extraordinary success of the Odéon was judged was by the large numbers of carriages on the place de l'Odéon; at other times there were usually none.[22] Audiences at the theaters and entertainments on the boulevard du Temple were mostly domiciled within easy walking distance in the area between the faubourg du Temple and the river. For students in the Schools of Medicine and Law, the

19. Henri d'Almarès, *La Vie parisienne sous la restauration* (Paris: Michel, [1910]), 94–96.

20. Lecomte's accident is related by both *Le Courrier des Théâtres* and the *Journal de Paris,* 14 April 1826.

21. The distribution of domiciles by street is as follows: rue de l'Odéon, Adolphe, Mlle Lemoule; rue des Maçons-Sorbonne, Mlle Belmont; rue M.-le-Prince, Coeuriot; rue de l'École de médecine, Mlle Dorgebray, Dupré, Mme Meyssin, Peyronnet, Mlle Pouilley; rue de Vaugirard, Mme Durand, Mme Montano; rue Meslée, Leclerc; rue des Fossés-M.-le-Prince, Léon Bizot; rue Ste-Hyacinthe, Lecomte; rue des Boucheries-St-Germain, Mondonville; rue Mandar, St-Preux.

22. "The inhabitants of the neighborhood see with astonishment what they have never seen before: carriages lined up every night on the place [de l'Odéon]" (Les habitants d'alentour voient avec étonnement ce qu'ils n'avaient pas encore vu, des voitures rangées tous les soirs sur la place [*Le Diable Boiteux,* 18 May 1824]).

Odéon—easily accessible on foot—was their main source of diversion; mélodrame and other entertainment on the boulevard du Temple was twice as far away.

Life for the pedestrian in Paris was wretched. The combination of the streets—mostly unchanged since the Middle Ages, with hopeless conditions underfoot—and the behavior of manic drivers of cabriolets and fiacres made getting from one place to another difficult and sometimes dangerous. The emergence of covered *passages* during the Restoration certainly made pedestrian travel on the Right Bank more comfortable, and the establishment of retail trade within the *passages* had the effect of shifting the focus of commercial activity away from the Palais-Royal toward the boulevards.[23] Such luxury was not extended to the Left Bank, however. A passage was opened in September 1824 between the rue de Seine and the rue Mazarine but had no serious effect on the ease of transport from the faubourg St-Germain to the Right Bank.[24] Although projects to establish pavements were begun in 1823, conditions for most pedestrians remained unchanged until the 1840s.[25] Street lighting was similarly poor: gas lighting was introduced in 1822, but only certain streets were lit by 1829, and in most neighborhoods as late as the July Monarchy the only lighting came from shops that were themselves lit by gas.[26]

The Industry of the East: Faubourgs St-Jacques, St-Antoine, and St-Marceau

While the wealthy members of the Parisian population had the means to go to the opera, it is less obvious exactly how and where the lower echelons of society found amusement. It is also difficult to judge how many had the

---

23. Marchand, *Paris,* 43 and n. 2.

24. The so-called passage de Commerce (Sauvigny, *Restauration,* 58); its opening was reported in *La Pandore,* 3 September 1824.

25. Marchand, *Paris,* 47. The fact that the only pavements in Paris at the beginning of the Restoration were on the rue de l'Odéon and the rue Le Peletier, next to opera houses, is purely coincidental, since both streets were thus furnished at the end of the eighteenth century (Sauvigny, *Restauration,* 56–57). A humorous account of transport explained how "an inhabitant of the Odéon quarter can reach the boulevard du Panorama by crossing nine *passages,* a bridge not open to carriages, several closed courtyards, a garden, and only using a small number of streets among which there are some furnished with pavements" (un habitant du quartier de l'Odéon peut se rendre sur le boulevard du Panorama en traversant neuf passages, un pont non ouvert aux voitures, plusieurs cours fermées, un jardin, et n'à [*sic*] franchir qu'un petit nombre de rues parmi lesquelles il y en a de garnies de trottoirs [*L'Opinion,* 24 September 1826]).

26. Marchand, *Paris,* 37. Not all were in favor of this new technology. Charles Nodier, in his *Essai critique sur le gaz d'éclairage* claimed that it was an English plot to put French producers of oil out of business (Sauvigny, *Restauration,* 97).

means to entertain themselves. A glance at the population of the industrial east of the city throws the Odéon's natural constituency into focus.

The social context of any artistic production in the first quarter of the nineteenth century cannot be described without some invocation of the Industrial Revolution.[27] It is easy however to overestimate the importance of industrial innovation in France during the Restoration and the July Monarchy. During this period, large-scale industrial production made only a slight impact.[28] Of the quarter of a million workers in the city, some worked in the large enterprises in the west of the city: the Manufacture royale des tabacs, the converted Savonnierie works—now dedicated to fine wools— and the carriage works in the Champs-Élysées, although these organizations could hardly be described as exploiting manual labor on a large scale. The more high-density industry was to be found in the east. The quartier St-Marcel exhibited some of the worst industrial conditions in the city. On the premises of tanners, dyers, hatmakers, and textile manufacturers, workers were exploited for miserable return, and the use of machinery meant that some of the worst remunerated workers were women and children. The levels of squalor and danger found in the quartier St-Marcel were sufficiently high for most bourgeois to avoid the area at all costs.[29]

New industries that could benefit from the technological advances of the early nineteenth century were still some way off because of the undercapitalization of French industry.[30] Twenty years of more or less incessant warfare had taken a toll on the country's ability to identify a technological innovation and turn it into industrial production in the same way as England had been able to do. The first French railway was constructed in 1823 but the first passenger service was not put in place until 1832, and the first Parisian railway was not opened until 1837; the system as a whole played little part in the development of French communications before 1840.[31]

However frightful the circumstances of the workers in the larger-scale businesses, they accounted for a smaller part of the overall production of the city than was the case in some parts of early nineteenth-century England. Most output was the result of much smaller operations, and ones that gave a higher quality of life to their practitioners. To move across the river from the quartier St-Marcel was to witness a change from factory pro-

27. Marchand, *Paris*, 7.

28. Many of the key technological innovations that powered the industrial revolution were either developed during, or known in, the 1820s but not used in Paris until after 1830 (ibid., 19).

29. Sauvigny, *Restauration*, 239.

30. Such undercapitalization was largely the result of revolutionary and imperial military campaigns (Marchand, *Paris*, 19).

31. Yves Leclercq, *Le Réseau impossible: la résistance au système des grandes compagnies ferroviaires et la politique économique en France, 1820–1852* (Geneva: Droz, 1987), 14.

duction to the specialized ateliers of the furniture makers in the faubourg St-Antoine. In 1825 the most typical configuration for an atelier was still one worker and an apprentice. But many ateliers employed between 10 and 30 workers, and the owner of the business was not only present but often worked alongside his employees. Two of the furniture makers were exceptional: Vernay and Volge maintained establishments of 110 and 90 workers respectively. The largest, and the most visible, group in the city was—not surprisingly given the rate of new building during the Restoration—construction workers: they were masons, carpenters, slaters, plumbers, painters, glaziers, cabinetmakers, and locksmiths. Just to give some idea of how extensive this group was during the Restoration, there were no fewer than 350 master masons at work in 1828, each of whom might have several deputies at work on different sites.[32]

Since public transport was absent and workers' salaries were not sufficiently high to enable them to purchase private transport, employees lived as close to their work as possible. Families of workers and owners alike would therefore live in the same neighborhood and remain there in retirement.[33] Such structures gave successful neighborhoods a degree of stability, with their own internal hierarchies and suprafamilial organization, and contributed to the rise of an urban bourgeoisie.

Explaining the makeup of the audience of such a theater as the Odéon entails judging salaries, purchasing power, and disposable income. Salaries and the cost of living were traveling in opposite directions during the Restoration. During the previous two decades, average wages had fallen by 6 percent while the price of food had risen by 12 percent (though the cost of clothing had fallen slightly).[34] Between the time that the Odéon opened its doors to music drama and the time that they closed, the price of a 2-kilogram loaf of bread had risen from 51 to 60 centimes and meat had risen from 86 to 106 centimes per kg; the cost of a liter of wine conversely slid from 70 centimes to 68 centimes.

Unemployment was a serious threat to the survival of the poorest paid. At the lowest end of the salary scale, apprentices in factories earned between 40 and 70 centimes per day, whereas the average factory worker took home between Fr 2.50 and Fr 3. Skilled construction workers could earn between Fr. 4 and Fr. 5.[35] These incomes should be judged against a poverty line in mid-Restoration Paris of between Fr 500 and Fr 600 a year. An average

32. *Almanach des bâtiments pour l'an 1828* (Paris, 1828).

33. Sauvigny, *Restauration,* 233.

34. Armand-René Duchatellier, *Essai sur les salaires et les prix de consommation de 1202 à 1830: demande d'une enquête à la Chambre des Députés* (Paris: Libraire du Commerce, 1830), 19. See also Adeline Daumard, *La Bourgeoisie parisienne de 1815 à 1848* (Paris: S.E.V.P.E.N., 1963), 261.

35. *Recherches statistiques de la ville de Paris* (Paris: Rignoux, 1821–60), 4:114–16.

worker, employed for 300 days a year at Fr 2 per day, could survive. A more skilled worker could earn in excess of twice the level of subsistence and would therefore have disposable income.[36] Workers in ateliers were paid by the piece rather than by the day, with the result that individual incomes can be hard to calculate; nevertheless, figures from a variety of sources suggest that a watchmaker could earn Fr 5–15 a day, a slater Fr 5—and good slaters Fr 10–12—compositors Fr 5–15. Office workers could count on a minimum salary of Fr 1,500 per year. Thus some workers—both in factories and in ateliers—were able to save parts of their income to the extent that a minority of them were able to establish themselves in their own businesses; postmortem inventories show that some workers bequeathed property, an income from rent, substantial amounts of furniture, or land outside the capital.[37] The economies that these endeavors required may well have been incompatible with such luxuries as the theater; conversely, these ambitions may well have been coupled with the acquisition of the sorts of cultural capital that the Odéon could offer. In any case, such considerations were of little concern to the moneyed inhabitants of what by the 1820s was beginning to be known as *le tout-Paris*.[38]

Tout-Paris and the Faubourg St-Germain

Paris society, or *tout-Paris,* was composed of four neighborhoods: the chaussée d'Antin, the Marais, the faubourg St-Honoré, and the faubourg St-Germain. The chaussée d'Antin was the home of bankers: Jacques Laffitte, James Rothschild, and Joseph Perier among others.[39] Well connected establishment artists were installed there as well: during the 1820s, Horace Vernet, Jean-Louis-André-Théodore Géricault, and the actress Mlle Mars all lived in the area, although its real artistic heyday was during the following decades when Pauline Viardot, George Sand, Frédéric Chopin, and Friedrich Kalkbrenner would all move to the neighborhood. If the chaussée d'Antin was the home of the new, the Marais was where the oldest families lived and where eighteenth-century customs and values had not lost their cachet. Honoré de Balzac's novel *Une double famille* brilliantly demonstrates the differences between the two groups.[40]

36. Pierre-Marie-Sébastien Bigot de Morogues, *De la misère des ouvriers et de la marche à suivre pour y remédier* (Paris: Huzard, 1832), 52.

37. Sauvigny, *Restauration,* 240.

38. The term *tout-Paris,* which emerges around 1820, constitutes what Martin-Fugier calls a *mondanité ouverte,* a social structure open to nobles and nonnobles alike and influencing, even directing, cultural, as well as economic and political opinion (*Vie élégante,* 25).

39. Bertrand Gille, *Histoire de la maison Rothschild* (Geneva: Droz, 1965–67), 1:471.

40. Honoré de Balzac, *Une double famille* (Paris: Conard, 1912), 273–74.

The faubourgs St-Honoré and St-Germain were separated by water and by politics: by the Seine and by the divide between liberal aristocrats and legitimists. The faubourg St-Honoré was dominated by the households of two figures: Charles-Maurice de Talleyrand and Marie-Jean-Paul-Yves-Roch-Gilbert du Motier, marquis de La Fayette. In the eighteenth-century, the faubourg St-Germain—strictly defined—was the home of aristocratic families when they were not at Versailles. With the center of royal power now at the Louvre, just over the Pont-Royal, the faubourg St-Germain was a home for "that higher level of French nobility who could live in Paris within the orbit of the royal court."[41]

Of the many points of intersection between the four parts of *tout-Paris,* the opera quarter and the boulevards were two of the most significant. The Théâtre-Royal italien was situated on the boulevard to which it gave its name; the Académie royale de musique, in the rue Peletier, was at the junction of the boulevard des Italiens and the boulevard Montmartre, and the Opéra-Comique was a little further south. The Théâtre-Français was about the same distance again further south, at the bottom of the rue Richelieu. Around the junction of the boulevard des Italiens and the boulevard Montmartre were the most fashionable cafés and restaurants—the Café de Paris, Tortoni, la maison Dorée, the Café Anglais, le Grand Balcon, Frascati, and Café Riche[42]—which, along with the three opera houses, occupied a space whose boundaries were little more than 100 m long.[43] Further east along the boulevard Montmartre were the Théâtre des Variétés and (after it turned into the boulevard de Bonne-Nouvelle) the Gymnase dramatique, and then (a few blocks later, into the boulevard St-Martin) the Théâtre de la Porte-St-Martin; finally (after another block or so) the theaters on the boulevard du Temple. However great the traffic between the population of the four quarters that constituted *tout-Paris,* the royal theaters were comfortably set at a distance from the secondary ones.

The faubourg St-Germain was bounded by the Invalides in the west, the Seine (quai d'Orsay and quai Voltaire) in the north, the rue des Sts-Pères in the east and territory associated with foreign missions in the south. It therefore consisted of five roads running west to east: the rue de Bourbon (after the July Revolution of 1830, renamed the rue de Lille), the rue de l'Université, the rue St-Dominique, the rue de Grenelle, and the rue de Varenne. But in the 1820s, the term St-Germain took in this narrowly defined geographical space and those parts of the eleventh arrondissement that ex-

41. Martin-Fugier, *Vie élégante,* 109. During the Empire, the faubourg St-Germain had been the center of aristocratic opposition (Philip Mansel, *The Court of France 1789–1830* [Cambridge: Cambridge University Press, 1988], 81).

42. Martin-Fugier, *Vie élégante,* 133.

43. See the map in Marchand, *Paris,* 46.

Figure 2. Montano in the role of Rosine
(*Le barbier de Séville*). From Alexandre-Marie
Colin, *Collection de portraits des artistes des
théâtres de Paris, dessinés et lithographiés d'après
nature* (Paris: Noël, n.d.), 44.

tended as far as its boundary with the twelfth on the rue St-Jacques, including the Jardin du Luxembourg, the Chambre des Pairs, and the Schools of
Law and Medicine as well as the theater that served them all, the Odéon.

Not only was the Odéon considered to be within the faubourg St-
Germain, it was its artistic and social center. When a translation of Gioachino
Rossini's *Barbiere di Siviglia* by Castil-Blaze (François-Henri-Joseph Blaze),
first staged in Lyon, was mounted at the Odéon, *Le Diable Boiteux* predicted
that it would have a great success "in the faubourg St-Germain."[44] During
the first run of the music drama at the Odéon, Stéphanie Montano was described as "the [Giuditta] Pasta of the faubourg St-Germain" (figure 2);[45]
and again, when Rossini's *Gazza ladra*—once more in Castil-Blaze's transla-

44. *Le Diable Boiteux*, 7 May 1824.
45. *Le Courrier des Théâtres*, 9 May 1824.

tion—was mounted at the Odéon, *La Pandore*'s critic labeled it "la pie du faubourg St-Germain."[46]

The narrowly delimited faubourg St-Germain therefore stood at the west end of a catchment area for the Odéon. At the east end were the Schools of Medicine and Law and the printers, booksellers, lodgings, restaurants, and cafés that supported them. The university environment was central to the culture of the Odéon and to its immediate surroundings. Law and medicine dominated the early nineteenth-century University of Paris. Although eight other universities in France had faculties of law, the most prestigious one was in Paris; it taught not only Parisians but a not inconsiderable number of visitors from the provinces.[47] Apart from Montpellier, Paris was the only faculty of medicine in the country and enjoyed a reputation second to none. The center of national medical education, it attracted students from other European countries and from North America. At the center of medical education was René-Théophile-Hyacinthe Laennec and his colleagues; so prominent was the teaching of medicine that unwarranted royal involvement in his replacement in May 1827 prompted severe student unrest. It was the advance in the study of dissection that particularly distinguished Parisian medical education to the extent that Paris—among other *cognomina*—was known as "the international corpse capital."[48]

The effect on the neighborhoods around the Odéon was what might be expected: they had the largest number of *hôtels garnis* in the capital to house the seven thousand students studying at the two faculties in more or less equal proportions, the lowest number of births and marriages in the city, and occasional civil disturbances, some of which spilled over into the parterre of the Odéon. In such a context, the theater figured in the existence of three entire arrondissements, the tenth to the twelfth. The theater often recruited their mayors (especially of the eleventh and twelfth) to make representations on its behalf to higher authorities; the Odéon—they argued—was the largest employer in the neighborhood with around 500 workers dependent on its existence, and it generated annual turnover in excess of Fr 700,000. And it guaranteed its audience *un délassement honnête et instructif.*[49]

Mayoral support was garnered in three successive years when the Odéon was under threat. The three representations, the first two to the *directeur des beaux-arts,* Louis-François Sosthène de La Rochefoucauld, and the third

46. *La Pandore,* 4 August 1824.

47. Sauvigny, *Restauration,* 335.

48. La capitale internationale du cadavre (ibid., 336).

49. Unsigned letter (headed ministère de l'Intérieur, direction des Belles-Lettres, Sciences et Beaux-Arts, 2e bureau) to baron de La Bouillerie, intendant général de la maison du Roi, 20 March 1828 (F-Pan O^3 1792/V).

to the minister of the interior, Jean-Baptiste-Silvère Gaye, vicomte de Martignac, pressed their point with progressively more vigor. In 1826 the student body was not mentioned at all; in 1827, it was claimed that closure of the theater would threaten the tranquillity of the quarter, because the Odéon was the meeting point for all the students in the neighborhood.[50] A year later, the mayor of the eleventh arrondissement, Antoine-Marie Fieffé, spelled out the problem in the clearest possible terms for the minister of the interior and made clear that removing a safe place of entertainment for the students of the area would result in a danger to public order.[51] Centered on the École de médecine, the Odéon stood between the aristocracy of the (narrowly defined) faubourg St-Germain and the poorest quarters of Paris in the twelfth arrondissement and was right at the center of the lives of students in law in medicine. As the mayors of these arrondissements stressed, the Odéon was the only theater on the Left Bank during the 1820s, and its health was an important component of the prosperity and safety of this populous part of the capital.

The Maison du Roi

The English-speaking world owes the word bureaucracy to the French language. Nowhere is bureaucratic flamboyance more clearly expressed than in the control of royal institutions during the Bourbon Restoration. Given the complex, ambiguous, and highly charged relations between the monarch and his government in the 1820s, it is no surprise that the official responsible for the Intendance générale de la maison du Roi was on the same hierarchical footing as the minister for foreign affairs, or the minister for war. Like the rest of the king's eight to ten ministers, he was responsible for a section, each with its genealogy of subsections, departments, *divisions*, and *intendances*.[52] The sprawling network of subdivisions that depended on the maison du Roi controlled most artistic concerns in the city. This meant that every theater in the capital was ultimately under the control of the king, and exposed to any pressures he might experience. Those theaters that had the name "Royal" as part of their title—and the Théâtre-Royal de l'Odéon was one—could claim a slightly different status from the Théâtre de la Porte-

---

50. Letter from six senior residents of faubourg St-Germain to La Rochefoucauld, 11 November 1826 (F-Pan O³ 1793/III); letters from two mayors (Fieffé of 11th arrondissement, Cochin of 12th) to La Rochefoucauld, 25 May 1827 (F-Pan O³ 1793/II).

51. Letter from Fieffé to ministre, secrétaire d'état au département de l'Intérieur, 1 March 1828 (F-Pan O³ 1792/V).

52. Strictly speaking, when La Bouillerie replaced the duc de Doudeauville in 1827, he did not have ministerial status but the title of intendant général chargé des affaires de la maison du Roi. See Benoît Yvert, ed., *Dictionnaire des ministres de 1789 à 1989* (Paris: Perrin, 1990), 128.

St-Martin, for example, but the secondary theaters were equally under royal control.

The maison du Roi was divided into six *services* and four *intendances*.[53] The *services* comprised (1) secretariat, (2) civil household of the king, (3) buildings, forests, estates, and legal department, (4) pensions and favors, (5) military affairs, and (6) general accountancy. In addition, the four *intendances* were (1) the crown jewels, (2) buildings, parks, and gardens, (3) crown furniture, and (4) beaux arts. Although the last of these four *intendances* was responsible for the capital's theaters, each of the *divisions* and the other three *intendances* depended on an organization at least as complex. The name of the Intendance des beaux-arts had changed twice by the time the Théâtre-Royal de l'Odéon was allowed to perform music drama. From the Restoration until 1 November 1820, it had been called the Intendance des menus plaisirs du Roi: this seventeenth-century term—one among many attempts to reconstruct the *ancien régime*—was then replaced by the title Département des fêtes et spectacles.[54] During the negotiations for the opening of the Odéon to music drama, this organization prevailed and in August 1824 became the Département des beaux-arts.

The organization of the Département des beaux-arts mirrored in its complexity that of the maison du Roi itself; it comprised a secretariat, an inspectorate, and three bureaux. Reporting to the *directeur des beaux-arts* (La Rochefoucauld, for the period after August 1824) were the Direction des fêtes et cérémonies de la cour (headed by La Rochefoucauld's predecessor Louis-Victor-Xavier Papillon, baron de La Ferté), the royal theaters, and the *musées royaux* (responsible to La Rochefoucauld). The administration of the royal theaters was in the hands of La Rochefoucauld himself, who was in turn directly responsible to the minister or *intendant général* of the maison du Roi. Each theater had its own internal hierarchy so that the most humble usher at the Odéon could follow a line of responsibility that ultimately led to the monarch.[55]

The three men who held the position of minister or intendant général of the maison du Roi during the 1820s were very different individuals. The previous career of Jacques-Alexandre-Bernard Law, marquis de Lauriston, had been exclusively military (figure 3). He had been an aide-de-camp to Napoléon Bonaparte and had seen service at the battle of Marengo in 1784 and at the defense of Copenhagen in 1801. Involved in the Antilles, and in

53. Martin-Fugier, *Vie élégante*, 33.

54. This was as part of the wholesale reorganization of the maison du Roi promulgated by royal ordinance, 1 November 1820 (Mansel, *Court of France*, 122).

55. The fact that the minister of the maison du Roi was a minister at all meant that he had the privilege of working alone with the king (ibid., 131).

Figure 3. Jacques-Alexandre-Bernard
Law, marquis de Lauriston. Lithograph
by François-Séraphin Delpech.

the Austrian and Russian campaigns, he had been taken prisoner at the battle of Leipzig. He was promoted steadily from général de brigade in 1802 to général de division in 1805 and on his return to France was appointed captain of the Mousquetaires gris.[56] He became pair de France in 1815 and marquis two years later; he was made minister of the maison du Roi in 1820, a position that he held until 1824, despite taking time off to lead the expeditionary force to the Ebro during the duc d'Angoulême's campaign on the Iberian Peninsula in 1823. He was made maréchal de France upon his return from Spain and *grand veneur* when he moved from the maison du Roi in 1824. He died of an *apoplexie foudroyante* in 1828, apparently in the arms of a dancer from the Opéra.[57]

Lauriston's successor, Ambroise-Polycarpe de La Rochefoucauld, duc de Doudeauville, was a career philanthropist. He had emigrated during the Revolution and on his return was made pair de France in the same year as Lauriston. During the next seven years, he was president of the administration of the École polytechnique and of the Société de l'Instruction élémentaire in addition to other philanthropic activities. He was made *directeur général des postes* in 1822 and succeeded Lauriston at the maison du Roi in 1824. He resigned from this post in 1827 in protest against the disbanding

56. Mansel views Lauriston's appointment as minister of the maison du Roi as one of the critical points in its reorganization (ibid., 129).

57. *LDD-NS* 10:259.

of the Garde nationale. In 1830, he became president of the Société des Établissements charitables.[58]

By contrast to both Lauriston and Doudeauville, François-Marie-Pierre Roullet, baron de La Bouillerie, was a bureaucrat. Throughout the Empire he had been *trésorier général de la couronne* and *domaine extraordinaire,* and became *intendant du trésor de la couronne* in 1814. He was promoted to the Intendance générale of the maison du Roi at Doudeauville's resignation in 1827, and at a time when his financial abilities—stronger than both his predecessors'—were much in demand.[59]

The careers of Lauriston, Doudeauville, and La Bouillerie demonstrate how Bonapartists could happily take over ministerial positions after the Restoration alongside royalists and serve in various capacities during the 1820s. Their careers also demonstrate how the monarch was able to maintain continuity in his household, despite changes of government. When Armand-Emmanuel du Plessis, duc de Richelieu, fell in 1821 and was replaced by Jean-Baptiste-Séraphin-Joseph, comte de Villèle, Lauriston was able to retain his position in the succeeding government; likewise, when Villèle was ousted by Martignac in 1828, La Bouillerie was also able to give continuity to the maison du Roi.[60]

Responsible to the ministers or intendant général of the maison du Roi during the Restoration were La Ferté and La Rochefoucauld. La Ferté had been made *intendant général des menus plaisirs du Roi* in January 1816, and *intendant des théâtres-royaux* in December 1820. He was replaced by La Rochefoucauld when that part of the maison du Roi was reorganized in August 1824. La Rochefoucauld was an ultraroyalist and had been aide-de-camp to Charles-Philippe, comte d'Artois, the future Charles X;[61] he had been a colonel in the Garde nationale before being appointed as *directeur des beaux-arts,* a post he held into the July Monarchy.

La Rochefoucauld has had a very poor press. The origins of his notoriety lay in the memoirs of Louis-Désiré Véron,[62] picked up in the entry in Larousse's *Grand dictionnaire universel du dix-neuvième siècle;* he was ridiculed for insisting on the lengthening of tutus at the Opéra and for the addition of leaves to the sculptures of classical heroes in the Louvre.[63] La Rochefoucauld presided, however, over an immensely successful period in the arts

58. Sauvigny, *Restauration,* 147. See also Martin-Fugier, *Vie élégante,* 39–40; and *LDD-NS* 6: 1154.

59. See Mansel, *Court of France,* 183–84 for a summary of La Bouillerie's economies at the maison du Roi.

60. Ibid., 130.

61. For the significance of the position of aide-de-camp during royalist emigration, see ibid., 98.

62. Louis Véron, *Mémoires d'un bourgeois de Paris* (Paris: Gouet, 1853–56), 3:158.

63. *LDD-NS* 6:1154.

in Paris, not least in music drama. To compare the status of the Académie royale de musique in 1824 with its position in 1831 is to witness a change from an organization in crisis and subject to unending ridicule to an institution that was the envy of Europe. Beyond the opera house, La Rochefoucauld was able to support Louis-Nicolas-Philippe-Auguste, comte de Forbin-Janson, in the formation of the Musée Charles X at the Louvre. The collection of antiquities belonging to Edme-Auguste Durand, seven thousand Egyptian, Greek, and Etruscan objects, and Renaissance artworks, formed the basis for the museum, but it was also the occasion for the creation of a large number of frescoes by Vernet, Antoine-Jean Gros, and Eugène Delacroix.[64]

Much of La Rochefoucauld's success came from the very particular circumstances that surrounded his tenure at the Département des beaux-arts. The same year that he became director, the comte d'Artois (his previous master) became Charles X, and his own father became his superior at the maison du Roi; he had been very close to the previous king's favorite, Madame du Cayla.[65] Unlike La Ferté, or many of his equals in the maison du Roi, La Rochefoucauld had direct access to the monarch and could implicitly claim that authority when dealing with other members of the maison du Roi.

Music Drama in Paris

Operatic and other theatrical institutions in Paris during the first half of the nineteenth century were governed by a series of laws passed in 1806 and 1807 that the maison du Roi was responsible for policing. By the 1820s, there were five royal theaters and four secondary theaters, nine theaters in total permitted by law. The five royal theaters were the Théâtre-Français, the Académie royale de musique (the Opéra), the Théâtre-Royal italien (managed jointly with the Opéra between 1819 and 1827), the Théâtre-Royal de l'Opéra-Comique, and the Théâtre-Royal de l'Odéon, also known as the Second Théâtre-Français. The secondary ones were the Théâtres du Vaudeville, des Variétés, de la Gaîté, and de l'Ambigu comique.[66] By the middle of the 1820s, these four had been joined by the Théâtre de la Porte-

---

64. For a sympathetic and much more even-handed view of La Rochefoucauld than that found in Véron, *Mémoires,* and derivative texts, see Sauvigny, *Restauration,* 356 and 365.

65. His aunt was the comtesse de Montesquieu, a member of one of the most staunchly royalist families in the faubourg St-Germain; La Rochefoucauld himself had refused office under the Empire and led a royalist demonstration in Paris on 31 March 1814 (Mansel, *Court of France,* 81–82, 99, 147).

66. Nicole Wild, *Dictionnaire des théâtres parisiens au XIXe siècle: les théâtres et la musique* (Paris: Amateurs des Livres, 1989), 13–14.

St-Martin and by the Gymnase dramatique. The latter had been known since September 1824 as the Théâtre de Madame because of the patronage of Marie-Caroline-Ferdinande-Louise, duchesse de Berry; it would return to the use of its original name in 1830.[67] Each theater was managed under the terms of a license that controlled the day-to-day running of the institution as well as its repertory.

One of the difficulties in telling the story of nineteenth-century French music drama is the speed with which institutions changed buildings, and the 1820s are no exception. The Académie royale de musique was the most stable: after moving from its position on the rue de Richelieu (the building was demolished after the assassination of Charles-Ferdinand de Bourbon, duc de Berry, in 1820), it continuously occupied the site on the rue Le Peletier until it was destroyed by fire during the night of 28–29 October 1873. Remaining on the same site for over fifty years was a luxury of which most Parisian theaters could only dream. The Théâtre-Royal italien, for example, undertook a significant move in November 1825 from the Théâtre Louvois (where it had been since only 1819) to the Salle Favart (where it would remain until the fire of 1838). Similarly, the Théâtre-Royal de l'Opéra-Comique moved from the Théâtre Feydeau (where it had been since 1805) in April 1829 to the Salle Ventadour; it remained there only until 1832, when it moved to the Salle de la bourse, and in 1840 moved on to its more permanent home at the Salle Favart. The Théâtre-Royal de l'Odéon, having risen from the ashes of the fire of 20 March 1818, remains on the same site to this day.[68]

Each of the five royal theaters in the capital possessed a license that sharply defined its repertory as part of a system designed to avoid any overlap between the royal theaters themselves or between royal institutions and secondary theaters. The Académie royale de musique was the only theater allowed to mount through-composed opera in French; this, and ballets, constituted its sole repertory. The Théâtre-Royal italien was permitted the performance of music drama in Italian only, and the Opéra-Comique was restricted to music drama in French with spoken dialogue: opéra comique. Two of the royal theaters were conceived as homes for spoken drama only, the Théâtre-Français and, in the period up to 1824, the theater that was designed to train its actors, the Théâtre-Royal de l'Odéon.

Changing the license of the Odéon to allow it to produce music drama—the key to the emergence of the opera troupe—meant treading a fine line between enabling the theater to achieve its goals and trespassing on the repertories of the other royal theaters. The Odéon's license was a constant

67. Ibid., 178 and 365.
68. This paragraph is based on the entries in ibid.

and contentious issue for both the theater and the maison du Roi throughout the period 1824–28, but in the form in which it was agreed (rather than in the form that the directors of the Odéon would have preferred), the theater was allowed to perform the repertory of the Théâtre-Français (comedy and tragedy) and opéra comique. For the latter genre there were two restrictions: the Odéon could mount productions of foreign music drama (which meant works with German or Italian libretti) translated into French and opéras comiques provided that they had fallen into the public domain (i.e., ten years had passed since the death of both composer and librettist). Technically, the repertories of the Odéon and the Théâtre-Royal de l'Opéra-Comique overlapped, although the Odéon exploited public domain opéra comique only until it had established enough foreign music drama in its repertory to satisfy its audience's demand.

As in the case of the royal theaters, the licensing of the secondary theaters was largely concerned with the amount of music and dance that could be included in each theater's repertory. The Théâtre du Vaudeville was permitted to perform short plays with interpolated songs (*petites pièces mêlées de couplets*), as long as the songs were based on preexisting tunes, while the Théâtre des Variétés's license allowed it to perform plays *sometimes* with interpolated songs. The Théâtre de la Gaîté was permitted to mount pantomimes as long as they did not include ballets, harlequinades, and other farces, and the Théâtre de l'Ambigu comique possessed a license that permitted a repertory similar to that of the Gaîté except that it was also allowed to play mélodrames as long as they were in one act and in prose; it was forbidden to play vaudevilles.

The two theaters that were permitted to join the four secondary theaters after 1807 were allowed rather freer licenses. Although never technically a secondary theater, the Théâtre de la Porte-St-Martin was permitted to include in its repertory mélodrames, pantomimes with dance, short plays, and prologues in one act with interpolated song. The only stipulation was that these works should have been created especially for the theater and should not be borrowed from other institutions. The Gymnase dramatique had the most complex, and—from the point of view of the royal theaters—the most threatening, license. It was allowed to play works that had fallen into the public domain but in fragments only: one act of a three-act work or a single scene of a one-act work was permitted. Although this license restricted the performance of individual works, it did however open up the possibility of mounting opéra comique and therefore of legally establishing a chorus and orchestra substantially larger than those of most of the other secondary theaters. The director of the Gymnase dramatique, Charles-Gaspard Delestre-Poirson, brought off a brilliant coup by contracting with Eugène Scribe to write for no other secondary theater (he was allowed the liberty of writing for the Opéra-Comique—where he negotiated a similar contract—and

TABLE 1. Repertory at royal theaters, 1 October to 7 October 1825

Date	Théâtre-Français	Académie royale de musique	Théâtre-Royal italien	Théâtre-Royal de l'Opéra-Comique	Théâtre-Royal de l'Odéon
1 October 1825, Sat	Le misanthrope; Le legs	—	Il crociato in Egitto	Joseph; Le maçon	Tartuffe; Les noces de Gamache
2 October 1825, Sun	Rhadamiste; Nanine	—		Françoise de Foix; Les deux mousquetaires	Les trois cousins; Cléopâtre; Robin des bois
3 October 1825, Mon	Le mari à bonnes fortunes; Le médisant	Fernand Cortez; Cendrillon	—	Philippe et Georgette; Marianne; Le trésor supposé	Les vêpres siciliennes; Robin des bois
4 October 1825, Tue	Britannicus; L'école des maris	—	Otello (Domenico Donzelli benefit)	Le valet de chambre; Montano et Stéphanie; Les deux mousquetaires	L'enfant trouvé; Le voyage à Dieppe; Les folies amoureuses
5 October 1825, Wed	L'abbé de l'épée; L'avocat	Pharamond; Le jugement de Paris	—	Jadis et aujourd'hui; Le concert à la cour; La mélomanie	Frédégonde et Brunehaut; Robin des bois
6 October 1825, Thu	Le mari à bonnes fortunes; Le jeu de l'amour et du hasard	—	Cenerentola (Giovanni Battista Rubini debut)	Félicie; Le maçon	Les deux ménages; Le roman d'une heure; Le sacrifice interrompu
7 October 1825, Fri	Iphigénie en Aulide; Le barbier de Séville	La vestale; Le page inconstant	—	Edmond et Caroline; Marianne; Les deux mousquetaires	Luxe et indigence; Robin des bois

SOURCES: Draft listings of repertory, available in all the *grands quotidiens* of the era, were assembled from the *Journal de Paris* and subsequently checked against references in the theatrical press, in particular *La Pandore, Le Courrier des Théâtres, Le Frondeur,* and *Le Diable Boiteux.*

other royal theaters); the result of this was Scribe's and the Gymnase's almost complete monopoly within the genre of the comédie-vaudeville. From 1826 onward, these were adorned with songs composed by the theater's youthful chorus master, Adolphe Adam.

Most theaters in Paris mounted productions every night of the week. The only exceptions were the Académie royale de musique and the Théâtre-Royal italien. The former mounted performances on Monday, Wednesday, and Friday, and the latter on Saturday, Tuesday, and Thursday.[69] On Sunday, therefore, the two most prestigious theaters in the capital were closed. Apart from the Théâtre-Royal italien, all the theaters put on more than one production each evening. At the Académie royale de musique, this was almost invariably an opera in three or five acts followed by a ballet; similarly, at the Théâtre-Français, a tragedy would be paired with a comedy. The Opéra-Comique would put on two or three (depending on their length) of the works that gave the theater its name, and the Odéon would put on music drama together with spoken works—either comedy or tragedy or both.

Works performed in Paris during the first week of October 1825 exemplify the structure of the capital's theatrical repertory (table 1). Many of the royal theaters depended on works that were several generations old. On two nights in the first week of October 1825, the Théâtre-Français paired Jean Racine's *Britannicus* (1669) with Molière's *École des maris* (1661), and Racine's *Iphigénie* (1674) with Pierre-Augustin Caron de Beaumarchais's *Barbier de Séville* (1775). Prosper Jolyot de Crébillon and Pierre Carlet de Chamblain de Marivaux also joined these seventeenth- and eighteenth-century authors as part of the classicizing impulse behind the Théâtre-Français. The repertory of the Académie royale de musique in October 1825, like that of the Théâtre-Français, showed a concern for the past but looked back only to the beginning of the century. Two works by Gaspare Spontini, *Fernand Cortez* (1809) and *La vestale* (1807), were glories of the Empire; although Fernando Sor's ballet *Cendrillon* had been premiered only two years before, *Le jugement de Paris* by Étienne-Nicolas Méhul and others dated from 1793. The picture is complicated by the presence of *Pharamond*. This composite work, by François-Adrien Boieldieu, Henri-Montan Berton, and Rodolphe Kreutzer was only a few months old, but it was one of the compositions produced in celebration of the coronation of Charles X and was limping toward the end of a run that was never destined to be particu-

---

69. Patrick Barbier, *Opera in Paris 1800–1850: A Lively History,* trans. Robert Luoma (Portland, Or.: Amadeus, 1995), 57 (originally published in 1987 as *La Vie quotidienne à l'opéra au temps de Rossini et de Balzac [Paris 1800–1850]*). The change from Tuesday, Friday, and Saturday at the Académie royale de musique took place in 1817; this still left Friday as the most fashionable night at the Opéra.

larly long.[70] Premieres at the Académie royale de musique were infrequent and rarely successful. In the decade before the sudden—and perhaps unexpected—success of Daniel-François-Esprit Auber's *Muette de Portici* in 1828, Spontini's *Olympie* (1819), Anton Reicha's *Sapho* (1822), Franz Liszt's *Dom Sanche* (1825), and Hippolyte-André-Jean-Baptiste Chelard's *Macbeth* (1827) made little impact on Parisian operatic culture. Only Nicolas Isouard's *Aladin ou La lampe merveilleuse* (1822) and Berton's *Virginie* (1823) had any sustained exposure at the Académie royale de musique, and Rossini's *Moïse et Pharaon ou Le passage de la mer Rouge* and *Le siège de Corinthe* marked key moments at the theater on which *La muette de Portici* and its followers would build. The bulk of the repertory consisted of Spontini, with Antonio Sacchini, Christoph Willibald Gluck, and André-Ernest-Modeste Grétry. Of the roughly 110 performances of opera during 1825 (omitting ballet), *La vestale* and *Fernand Cortez* alone accounted for one fifth and Gluck's *Armide* and *Orphée* for only a little less. There were only three performances during the year of Berton's *Virginie* (which rated as a success during the 1820s), and five performances of the young Liszt's *Dom Sanche*.[71]

During the same sample week in October 1825, the Opéra-Comique successfully mixed a number of new works with classics from the previous century. Auber's *Maçon* had received its premiere in May 1825; his *Concert à la cour* was only a year old, as was Berton's *Deux mousquetaires;* Michele Carafa's *Valet de chambre* had appeared in 1823. Alongside these, the Opéra-Comique placed works by Méhul (*Joseph* of 1807, *Le trésor supposé* of 1802) and by Nicolas-Marie Dalayrac (*Philippe et Georgette* of 1791). When Berton's *Deux mousquetaires* was given on 4 October 1825, it was performed alongside his *Montano et Stéphanie*, which had been given no less than a quarter of a century earlier. In the same week, the Théâtre italien and the Odéon were promoting new music drama. Meyerbeer's *Crociato in Egitto* had been premiered at La Fenice the previous year, and Rossini's *Otello* and *Cenerentola* were both less than ten years old. *Semiramide* was premiered at the very end of 1825, *La gazza ladra* was performed seventeen times during the year, *L'italiana in Algeri* nine, *Otello* twenty, and *Cenerentola* fifteen. Not all was new however: *Don Giovanni* was performed by the Théâtre italien ten times during the same year.

Unique among the royal theaters, the Théâtre-Royal de l'Odéon mixed music drama and plays. In general, the latter were either modern works

70. For the context for *Pharamond,* see below, pages 156–58.

71. The figures for performances during 1820–32 are taken from a database prepared by Donald Gíslason to support work on his doctoral dissertation (Donald Garth Gíslason, "Castil-Blaze, *De l'opéra in France* and the Feuilletons of the *Journal des Débats* [1820–1832]" [Ph.D. diss., University of British Columbia, 1992]). I am grateful to Dr. Gíslason for making this information available for this study.

specifically written for the Odéon or classics. All the spoken drama performed in the first week of October 1825 had been premiered between 1819 (Casimir Delavigne's *Vêpres siciliennes*) and 1825 (de Rancé's *Trois cousins*) with the exception of François-Benoît Hoffman's *Roman d'une heure* (1803) and Molière's *Tartuffe* (1669). The fact that *Robin des bois*, the French version of Carl Maria von Weber's *Freischütz*, occurs four times in the same week is testimony to its astounding success ten months after its premiere.[72] On the other three nights were the predecessor to *Robin des bois*—Peter von Winter's *Das unterbrochene Opferfest* of 1796 translated as *Le sacrifice interrompu* and given at the Odéon for the first time a year previously—and two pasticci. *Les folies amoureuses* was one of Castil-Blaze's multi-author pasticci, largely based on works by Weber, and *Les noces de Gamache* was a pasticcio based on the works of Saverio Mercadante that had been premiered at the Odéon in May 1825.

Besides the genres represented there, the distinguishing characteristic of the secondary theaters were the very high levels of repetition. At the Gaîté, *Gustave ou Le napolitain* (by Philippe-Jacques Laroche [pseud., Létoile Hubert], Anicet Bourgeois, and Benjamin Antier) was premiered on 4 October 1825 and was repeated on the next three nights. In the same week, the phenomenally successful *Jocko ou Le singe de Brésil* by Jules-Joseph-Gabriel de Lurieu (pseud., Gabriel) and Claude-Louis-Marie de Rochefort-Luçay was given six nights out of seven at the Théâtre de la Porte-St-Martin, and a parody entitled *Les deux Jockos*, by Lurieu, François-Victor-Armand d'Artois de Bournonville, and Francis Leroi, baron d'Allarde, could be heard twice in the same week at the Théâtre des Variétés. Even in theaters where there was neither a premiere nor the beginning of a very successful run, performances were frequently repeated: of the twenty-seven performances at the Gymnase dramatique, twelve works appeared at least twice, and one (*Le landau*, a play by Édouard-Joseph-Ennemond Mazères and Louis-François Picard) appeared no fewer than six times. By contrast, the Théâtre-Français repeated only one work during the same period, and the Académie royale de musique and the Théâtre italien—hardly surprisingly given their much more restricted performances—repeated nothing.

Falling outside the definition of theaters—royal or secondary—were further places of entertainment that competed for audiences. The Théâtre Comte, for example, was managed by Louis-Christian Comte without license but with the authorization of the prefet de police and was housed in the passage des Panoramas. Originally permitted to put on shows of ven-

72. Here, the single week's repertory is a little misleading. A sample from a year earlier shows that *La pie voleuse* (three performances) appeared alongside a substantial body of opéra comique from the public domain: Grétry's *Richard Coeur-de-Lion*, Dalayrac's *Ambroise*, Grétry's *Zémire et Azor*, and his *Tableau parlant*.

triloquism and magic, by 1822 the Théâtre Comte had been permitted to include dialogue in the scenes that it showed.[73] During the first week of October 1825, there were no fewer than three purely visual entertainments in Paris: the Géorama, Panorama, and Europorama offered their respective views of the entire world, panoramas of Constantinople, and European scenes of the cathedral of Reims during the coronation of Charles X, Hamburg, the Rhine, and the town of Linz on the Danube.[74] Such more or less permanent entertainments were supplemented by temporary curiosities. A well-known example was the arrival of a giraffe in the Jardin des Plantes in May 1827.[75] Less well known, but equally popular was the arrival of elephants at the Théâtre de la Porte-St-Martin in 1825, and on the boulevard de Bonne-Nouvelle in 1825 and 1826.[76] Public enthusiasm for, and expenditure to see, the animals was significant and sustained. Such curiosities were elements in the complex of entertainment of which music drama formed an integral part.

The separation of theaters extended not only to their repertory but also to their staffing and modes of management. The Académie royale de musique and Théâtre-Royal italien were managed directly by the maison du Roi, as was the Odéon before 1824. The Théâtre-Français and the Opéra-Comique were governed by *sociétaires,* senior artists in the theaters, who collectively managed repertory, artistic policy, and financial matters in collaboration with a representative of the Crown. While the Théâtre-Français retained this system of governance, the Opéra-Comique ran into hopeless difficulties just as the Odéon was starting to mount operatic productions, and the sociétaires of the Opéra-Comique retired from the administration of the theater.[77] All other theaters were managed at the risk of a *directeur privilégié*—a licensed manager—responsible to the maison du Roi, and this was the pattern followed by the Odéon beginning with Bernard's management in 1824.

73. Wild, *Dictionnaire,* 103–7.

74. Like the attractions at the royal and secondary theaters, these events were listed in the theatrical press.

75. Described in great detail in Michael Allin, *Zarafa: A Giraffe's True Story, from Deep in Africa to the Heart of Paris* (New York: Walker, 1998).

76. The animal was a gift from the pasha of Egypt to the king of France; *Le Diable Boiteux* (6 May 1825) reported its arrival at Le Havre and published a letter—purportedly from the animal itself—complaining about conditions in the Jardin des Plantes (30 May 1825); a second elephant appeared on the boulevard de Bonne-Nouvelle in November 1825 (*La Pandore,* 28 November 1825). This animal was a third larger than the first, and its strength was exploited for profit (*La Lorgnette,* 2 January 1826). An elephant (unidentified) was to star at the Théâtre de la Porte-St-Martin in *Le véritable artiste ou La grosse bête* (see *La Pandore,* 8 August 1825).

77. Wild, *Dictionnaire,* 329.

Figure 4. Jean-Henri Dupin. Anonymous
lithograph.

Artists and singers at all the theaters in the city were contracted, often for
as much as three years, and their contracts forbade them to act or sing at
any other theater without permission. The Odéon was an unfortunate exception to this rule; a promising artist could be called to one of the other
royal theaters where he or she might develop a career, and there was relatively little that the Odéon could do to resist such interference. Once it
began to employ opera singers, the Odéon was at the mercy not just of
the Théâtre-Français, but also of the Académie royale de musique and the
Opéra-Comique. The Gymnase dramatique, among the secondary theaters,
had a similar role and suffered similar difficulties.[78]

Despite the strict segregation of genres between theaters, literary or dramatic themes passed from one stage to another with great rapidity. The
most common way for this to take place was by parody. Three months after
the premiere of Boieldieu's *Dame blanche* at the Opéra-Comique in 1825,
there appeared *La dame jaune* at the Théâtre du Vaudeville by Mazères,
Pierre-François-Adolphe Carmouche, and Jean-Henri Dupin (figure 4).

---

78. Bernard Léon, from the Gymnase dramatique, tried very hard to avoid being poached
by the Opéra-Comique at the end of 1824 (*La Pandore,* 5 December 1824).

Figure 5. Daniel-François-Esprit Auber.
Lithograph by Alfred-Léon Lemercier.

The responses to Delavigne's *Vêpres siciliennes*, premiered at the Odéon on 23 October 1819, were even more rapid; a parodie-vaudeville of the same name by Eugène Scribe and Anne-Honoré-Joseph Duveyrier (pseud., Mélesville) appeared on 17 November at the Théâtre du Vaudeville, followed at an interval of five days by *Les vêpres odéoniennes* (by Antonin-Jean-Baptiste Simonin and d'Artois de Bournonville) at the Théâtre des Variétés. Music drama at the Odéon was not exempt from this type of parody: four months after the premiere of *Robin des bois* (known informally as *Le chasseur noir*), there appeared *Le chasseur rouge* at the Théâtres des Variétés (by Marie-Emmanuel-Guillaume-Marguerite Théaulon de Lambert and Clotilde-Marie Collin de Plancy). A prose parody also accompanied *Robin des bois*'s early days.[79]

Parody was but a single aspect of the more widespread practice of sharing across genres—and therefore across theaters—of a single literary theme. A good example of this is the treatment of speechlessness in a variety of genres during 1828. Auber's *Muette de Portici* of 1828 shared its subject matter with Carafa's *Masaniello* of the previous year; the former was written for the Académie royale de musique, the latter for the Opéra-Comique (figures 5 and 6).

79. *Jérôme Gâcheux à la représentation de Robin des bois: pot-pourri en trois actes* (Paris: Vergne, 1825). Barbier (*Opera in Paris*, 87–92) notes parodies from other periods.

Figure 6. Michele Carafa. Anonymous
lithograph.

While both took the history of the Neapolitan uprising of 1647 as their
subject, it was the presence of a mute character in Auber's work that really
caught the Parisian theatrical imagination. During the four months following the premiere of *La muette de Portici,* works in which mutes figured
appeared all over the capital and in all genres: a mélodrame at the Théâtre
des Variétés, a *pièce mêlée de vaudevilles* at the Théâtre Comte, a *pantomime
dialoguée* at the Théâtre du Luxembourg, a *folie-revue* at the Théâtre des
Variétés, a parodie-vaudeville at the Théâtre de la Porte-St-Martin, and a
comédie-vaudeville at the Théâtre du Vaudeville. The Odéon contributed
by reviving Dalayrac's *Deux mots ou Une nuit dans la forêt,* as did the Opéra-
Comique. Up to three or four works featuring mutes could be found every
night on Parisian stages during April and May 1828.[80]

Although managers and artists were shackled to the institutions in which
they worked, this was by no means true for composers and librettists. They
could write for whichever institution they thought would be likely to mount
their works, provided that what they wrote conformed to the generic constraints of the individual theater. There is no better example of the ease
with which a composer could move from one theater to another than Gia-

80. See Sarah Hibberd, "Magnetism, Muteness, Magic: *Spectacle* and the Parisian Lyric
Stage *c*1830" (Ph.D. diss., University of Southampton, 1998), bibliography on 113 and passim
on this and other examples.

Figure 7. Giacomo Meyerbeer. Lithograph by
Ligny frères after Antoine Maurin.

como Meyerbeer's Parisian career in the 1820s (figure 7); he started in
1825 with a revised version of his *Crociato in Egitto* at the Théâtre italien,
moved to the Odéon with a version in French of his *Margherita d'Anjou*
(coupled with his *Emma di Resburgo*), and then attempted the following year
to mount a new opéra comique at the theater of the same name.

This was *Robert le diable;* it never appeared at the Opéra-Comique but was
one of the most prominent events in Parisian nineteenth-century theatrical
history when it was premiered in a revised form at the Académie royale de
musique in 1831. Each of these works was carefully crafted or reworked to
adhere to the generic constraints of the theater in question: *Il crociato*
needed to have new arias written for the singers at the Théâtre italien,
Margherita d'Anjou and *Emma di Resburgo* had to be completely reworked to
a French libretto based on the model for the Italian original, and *Robert le
diable* had to lose its spoken dialogue, which was replaced with accompanied
recitative, when it was recast for the Académie royale de musique.[81]

Parisian theaters shared the products of the atelier of Pierre-Luc-Charles
Ciceri. He was responsible for the decorations of many theaters throughout
the 1820s and 1830s; the Feydeau and Louvois are examples. More important, his workshop was responsible for set design all over the capital; there

81. See Mark Everist, "Giacomo Meyerbeer and Music Drama at the Paris Odéon during
the Bourbon Restoration," *19th-Century Music* 16 (1993): 124–48; and idem, "The Name of
the Rose: Meyerbeer's *opéra comique, Robert le Diable,*" *Revue de musicologie* 80 (1994): 211–50.

is evidence that he worked at theaters as prestigious as the Académie royale de musique and as mundane as the Cirque Olympique. He is also known to have worked at the Théâtre de la Gaîté, the Panorama dramatique, the Théâtre de la Porte-St-Martin, and the Théâtres des Nouveautés after its opening in 1827.[82] Ciceri's sets were also used at the Odéon throughout its life as an opera house: his name was associated with sets for *Robin des bois, La dame du lac, Marguerite d'Anjou,* and *La folle de Glaris.*[83] It is possible that more sets were the product of the Ciceri workshop, but no record of them has survived.[84]

The Odéon followed the theatrical year that governed every theater in the capital. The year began after Easter and ran without any substantial break until Holy Week the following year, when the royal theaters were closed. Carnival season and Lent were registered in the theatrical year but the observation of these dates—although they affected masked balls—made little impact on performances of music drama.[85] The summer, when high temperatures tended to keep audiences away from the theaters, was a time when theater directors avoided launching new works, and the winter period from October to March usually saw the greatest levels of innovation and experiment.

The timing of performances at the Odéon was erratic and subject to various pressures. The requirement that the theater mount three works—comedy, tragedy, and music drama—every night meant that evenings could be long. When the Odéon had been promoting music drama for two years, things started to get out of hand: "[long performances] tend to enfeeble the artists without any satisfactory result for the public. A performance that starts at 6:15 P.M., not to finish until 11:00 P.M. is more of a trial than an amusement." The journalist responsible for this report suggested that the Odéon was ducking its responsibilities for playing all three genres: "To offer a tragedy or a long comedy to a few diligent members of the audience who are able to arrive at the Odéon before 7:00 P.M. is not to satisfy their obligation of playing first-rank repertory; it is to act like schoolboys, to get rid of onerous homework."[86] Furthermore, there were repeated complaints

82. See Wild, *Dictionnaire,* passim.

83. See *Gazette de France,* 8 December 1824 (*Robin des bois*); *Journal de Paris,* 2 November 1825 (*La dame du lac*); *La Pandore,* 12 March 1826 (*Marguerite d'Anjou*); and *Journal de Paris,* 22 April 1827 (*La folle de Glaris*).

84. Nicole Wild, "Fashioning Romanticism: Ciceri, a Stage Designer" (typescript).

85. See the reminder in *Le Diable Boiteux* (25 January 1825) that the carnival season lasted only thirteen days that year.

86. Offrir une tragédie ou une grande comédie à quelques spectateurs diligents qui peuvent arriver à l'Odéon avant sept heures, ce n'est pas satisfaire à l'obligation qu'on a de jouer le répertoire du premier ordre, c'est faire comme les écoliers, se débarrasser d'un devoir qui pèse (*La Pandore,* 3 May 1826).

in the press that the theater never started its performances at the times that were advertised.[87]

Unlike many of the royal theaters, the Odéon could not afford a comprehensive system of understudies; its program of activities was regularly disrupted by indisposition. Illness could delay rehearsals for a premiere, for example when Mlle Pouilley was ill, and the rehearsals for *Le sacrifice interrompu* had to be broken off in October 1824, or again a month later when Montano was indisposed.[88] Earlier, another of Montano's illnesses meant that performances of *Le barbier de Séville* also had to be stopped.[89] Occasionally, stand-ins could be found, but this was purely fortuitous, as when Pouilley was able to replace Mlle Florigny in the role of Ninette in *La pie voleuse*.[90] Sometimes there was no answer other than quick thinking for things that went wrong on stage. Complications during a performance of *Robin des bois* in December 1826 demonstrated what could happen without the support of an understudy. The soprano Amélie Dorgebray was taken ill on stage, and Amalia Schütz improvised her way out of the situation by leading the conductor and the orchestra through the second act and cutting all the music in which Dorgebray had a part.[91]

Rehearsal, dress rehearsal, and premiere were often confused, and nowhere more so than at the Odéon. A typical and recurrent thread that ran through popular and press responses to the theater's work was that the first night was often more like a dress rehearsal than what might be understood as a fully prepared premiere. Furthermore, this type of performance might present a musical or literary text that was still not finally settled, one that could well be—and frequently was—modified as a result of commentary in the theatrical press. The text of *Robin des bois,* for example, changed a great deal during its early performances. At the first night of *Othello,* the critic of the *Journal des Débats* said that premieres at the Odéon were regularly like dress rehearsals elsewhere.[92]

Issues of topography and demography underpin many of the controlling forces of Parisian music drama. The right-bank theater district, which included the Académie royale de musique, the Théâtre italien, and the Opéra-Comique, acted as a fulcrum for the activities of Parisian society. Similarly, the Odéon, the only left-bank theater, acted as a focus for students in the arrondissement and for the aspirant middle classes among whom they lived

87. Ibid., 31 May 1826.
88. Ibid., 10 October and 5 November 1824.
89. Ibid., 27 May 1824.
90. *Le Diable Boiteux,* 7 October 1824.
91. *L'Opinion,* 10 December 1826.
92. *Journal des Débats,* 27 July 1825.

and worked. The distance of the Odéon from the right-bank theaters, the essentially local nature of its clientele, and the difficulties and cost of urban transport all contributed to the autonomy of an institution that—even before the emergence of music drama there in 1824—followed a very different path to other theaters in the capital.

Parisian music drama was caught up in a network of relationships between audiences of differing motivations and a bureaucracy that controlled almost all its functions. The repertory of an institution was controlled by license, at the Académie royale de musique as well as the Odéon or any of the secondary theaters. In the case of the Odéon, it allowed the management to countenance the production of music drama whereas its immediate history had been one in which the theater had been dedicated to spoken drama. The day-to-day running of Parisian lyric theaters was very different from what is expected from an opera house today. Whereas the Académie royale de musique and the Théâtre italien were open for three nights a week each, and the latter was closed during the summer, the Opéra-Comique and the Odéon were not only open every night of the year except for Holy Week and a couple of other holidays but usually put on two or three productions a night.

With two opera houses dedicated to indigenous works and a third to Italian music drama, Paris was already an international center for stage music. Although the lion's share of opéra comique was composed by French men and women, foreign composers gave it an international profile that was hard to match elsewhere in Europe. Around 1800 Spontini and Cherubini were the most prominent examples, but by the 1820s opéras comiques by Carafa, Catrufo, Garcia, and Paër could be heard.[93] The Académie royale de musique was forging a truly international genre. Gluck was the model, and Spontini his most obvious successor. In the 1820s Spontini, Reicha, and Liszt, however unsuccessful productions of their works might have been, laid the ground for the successes of first Rossini and then Meyerbeer. Italian opera had a fine home in Paris, and French music drama was strongly influenced by international practices. A gap in this otherwise pan-European operatic environment was stage music from German-speaking lands. In a decade that saw, in consecutive years, the end of the careers of Weber, Beethoven, and Schubert, this was a gap in the operatic market just waiting to be filled. The Odéon was exactly the institution to fill it.

93. During the 1820s the audience heard Michele Carafa's *Jeanne d'Arc à Orléans* (1821), *Le solitaire* (1822), *Le valet de chambre* (1823), *L'auberge supposé* (1824), *Sangarido* (1827), *Masaniello* (1827), *La Violette* (1828), and *Jenny* (1829); Gioseffe Catrufo's *Intrigue au château* (1823), *Le voyage à la cour* (1825), and *Les rencontres* (1828); Manuel Garcia's *Deux contrats de mariage* (1824); and Ferdinando Paër's *Maître de chapelle ou Le souper imprévu* (1821).

Chapter 2

L'obligation de jouer le répertoire du premier ordre—Repertory and Management at the Odéon

Regulating the Odéon

The *directeur privilégié*—the manager—of the Théâtre-Royal de l'Odéon guided the work of its *régisseurs* (directors). During the 1820s, when the theater was mounting productions of music drama, comedy, and tragedy, the theater boasted up to three directors. In 1825, two were responsible for the two branches of spoken theater and one for music drama. By the following year, this had been changed to one director for music drama and one for plays, while a third held the position of assistant director. In 1827 there were two directors for music drama and only one for plays. As the Odéon's financial crisis rolled out of control in 1828, the number of directors was cut to two: one each for music and spoken drama. In addition to the directors, the administrative staff of the theater consisted of secretaries to the directors and to the administration, and a secretary responsible for the library who was also the prompt.[1] Although the administrative structure changed from year to year as directors came and went, individuals remained associated with the institution. Douesnel, for example, was *second régisseur* in 1824, one of two directors of spoken drama in 1825, *sous-régisseur* again in 1826, director in 1827, and had left the theater by 1828. By contrast Édouard was *régisseur de la comédie* throughout the period 1824–28. In general, all the officials at the theater were full-time administrators. The exceptions were Édouard, who occasionally took nonsinging roles in music drama,[2] and Bernard, the Odéon's first opera manager. Not only a success-

---

1. The annual *Almanach royal, pour l'année bissextile M. DCCC. XXIV* (Paris: Guyot et Scribe, 1824) and its successors give an annual overview of the changes in the Odéon's administrative personnel that were effected by, or forced on, the theater at different times during the year.

2. Édouard was most famous in the nonsinging title role of *Robin des bois*.

ful theatrical entrepreneur, Bernard had been the *premier basse-taille* in Lille and was able to deputize for his colleagues Lemaire in the role of Reynold in *Robin des bois* and for Valère in the role of Basile in *Le barbier de Séville*.[3]

The manager's line of responsibility led upward to the maison du Roi, and the relationships between the theater and the royal household were regulated by two series of documents. The first was the *règlement* for the theater, which had been promulgated in two parts, in 1819 and 1822. The second was Bernard's license, governed by a contract drawn up between Bernard and the maison du Roi. The *règlement*'s first part governed the actions of all who worked in the theater, from the manager to the cleaner.[4] It explained how the theater's reading committee was to judge new works and when the cleaners had to be out of the building (by 9 P.M. or, in winter, 10 P.M.).[5] The fuller 1819 document was designed to review the operations of the theater at its reopening after the fire of 20 March 1818. The 1822 text tidied up a number of significant details. One of the key changes was that the oversight of the performances had been left in 1819 to a *semainier*— a member of the acting troupe acting for a week at a time[6]—in 1822 this responsibility was transferred to a dedicated *régisseur,* a post that proliferated as the opera troupe began work.[7] The system of fines for misdemeanors by members of the Odéon staff was also changed; these were aimed at actors who did not attend or were late for rehearsals. The scale in 1819 was simple: missing one's first entry entailed a fine of Fr 1.50, missing one's second entry cost Fr 3, and missing the entire rehearsal cost Fr 10. If the absences were from a dress rehearsal, the fines were doubled.[8] In 1822 the nature of the scale remained the same, but the exact sums were calculated as a portion of one's salary; thus, to miss the first entry in a rehearsal cost a month's salary; if the second entry was missed, an additional 50 percent of the month's salary; if the entire rehearsal was missed, an additional 25 per-

---

3. *Le Courrier des Théâtres,* 27 August 1827 and 17 December 1824. For some critics, Bernard was almost too successful: "Bernard played Basile. It was probably to allow Valère some rest. Whatever the reason, the audience had no cause to complain. Bernard sang and acted in such a way as to make one fear that a right-bank director might call him, by order to [début at] his theater. Happily, this remnant of theatrical feudalism no longer exists!" (M. Bernard jouait Basile. C'était probablement pour laisser quelque repos à Valère. Quoi qu'il en soit, le public n'a eu aucun motif de s'en plaindre. M. Bernard a joué et chanté de manière à faire craindre qu'un directeur de la rive droite ne l'appelât par ordre à son théâtre. Heureusement ce reste de féodalité dramatique n'existe plus! [*La Pandore,* 12 January 1825]).

4. *Règlement pour le second théâtre français* (Paris: Ballard, [1819]); Paris, Bibliothèque de l'Arsenal, R^t.2539; *Second Théâtre-Français: Règlement* (Paris: Ballard, [1822]); F-Po Arch. Th. Paris: Odéon.28.

5. *Règlement* (1819), 15–16; *Règlement* (1822), 14–17; *Règlement* (1819), 47.

6. Ibid., 9–12.

7. *Règlement* (1822), 3.

8. *Règlement* (1819), 13–14.

cent. If it was a dress rehearsal that was missed, the fine was increased by a further 10 percent.[9]

The arrival of Bernard at the Odéon marked a radical change in the contractual relationship between the manager and the maison du Roi. It was the first royal theater to engage a manager who would administer the theater at his own risk.[10] Previously, under the direction of Michel-Ambroise de Gimel and before him Adolphe-Gentil de Chabagnac, the Odéon was run at the expense of the maison du Roi and incurred massive losses. Passing the theater to a *directeur privilégié* meant that there would be no charge to the maison du Roi beyond any subvention that it and the manager would determine in advance. The subvention proved a key factor in the success or failure of the theater right up until the collapse of the opera troupe in 1828.

Claude Bernard

Bernard was manager of the theater in Antwerp when he entered into negotiations with the *intendant des théâtres-royaux,* the baron de La Ferté, in early August 1823 to take over the management of the Odéon (his contract ran from April 1824 to January 1826). La Ferté was at something of a disadvantage since his superior, the minister at the maison du Roi—Lauriston—was commanding the expeditionary force to the Ebro and therefore unable to attend to the matter himself.[11] Thus La Ferté lacked the support of a minister to advise him as he discussed the contract with Bernard. This circum-

---

9. *Règlement* (1822), 12. There were additional fines for being ill without appropriate documentation, or for refusing to allow the manager or the director to verify that the illness was genuine. No further *règlement* modifies either the 1819 or 1822 documents, although there does exist a manuscript "Ordonnance portant règlement sur la surveillance, l'organization sociale et l'administration du Théâtre-Royal de l'Odéon," dated 2 November 1815 signed by Louis XVIII and La Ferté in F-Pn n.a.f. 3042, fols. 109^r–20^v.

10. This was the case at most of the secondary theaters, e.g., the Théâtre de la Porte-St-Martin (Nicole Wild, *Dictionnaire des théâtres parisiens au XIXe siècle: les théâtres et la musique* [Paris: Amateurs des Livres, 1989], 368).

11. A sense of Lauriston's divided loyalties is evident in a letter he wrote to Alexandre de La Motte-Baracé, vicomte de Senonnes, on 8 July 1823: "Things are . . . moving along quite quickly; I believe San Sebastián will surrender in two or three days; we will see what happens in Pamplona. But the most important thing is Cádiz and the fate of the King. . . . If you can finish the business with the Odéon, suitably, I shall think of you as the greatest genius of all. Pursue this matter vigorously which would give me much pleasure" (Les affaires . . . marchent assez vite, je dois croire que St-Sébastien se rendra sous 2 ou 3 jours, nous verrons pour Pampelune. Mais ce qui est important c'est Cadiz, et le sort du Roi. . . . Si vous pouvez finir convenablement l'affaire de l'Odéon, je vous tiens pour le docteur des docteurs. Poussez cette affaire vivement, cela me fera beaucoup de plaisir [*Catalogue: Salon prestige du livre ancien, septembre 2000* (http://www.franceantiq.fr/general/books/autographes/toutf4.htm; consulted on 5 October 2000)]).

stance affected the negotiations in three key areas: repertory, artists' contracts, and the ownership of the theater building itself.

The first draft of Bernard's contract was prepared some time before
6 August 1823. The subvention was fixed at Fr 60,000 per annum and at the
time proved unproblematic. The definition of the repertory was more in-
tricate. The first draft of the contract gave the repertory as follows: "tragedy,
comedy, and if he [the manager] wishes, opéra comique, insofar that it concerns works fallen into the public domain, and works taken from the Italian
and German repertories."[12] A slight change made in the margin of the document imparts precision to the language but leaves the substance unal-
tered: opéra comique is qualified by the clause "but for this last genre, works
that have fallen into the public domain."[13] The second draft contained a
lengthy change that exhibits signs of Bernard's authorship combined with
some hard bargaining with La Ferté. It adds to the list of genres "*comédie
mêlée des chants,* that is to say all those works depending on the old repertory
of the Théâtre-Français in which are found one or more arias, but absolutely not, under any circumstances, works coming from the repertory of
the [Théâtre du] Vaudeville, nor any works having such a character."[14] This
was the text that defined the Odéon's repertory, and to which Bernard
signed his name on 16 August 1823.

As soon as Bernard found out what this clause really meant, he regretted
signing a contract that included it. A week later, he approached the question of changing the name of the theater from Second Théâtre-Français
to Second Théâtre-Royal; this was uncontentious, and La Ferté was happy
to oblige. In the same letter, Bernard drew attention to the fact that that he
could not promote new opéra comique and that he was therefore restricted
to works by François-André Philidor (by which he meant eighteenth-
century repertory in which no audience had any interest; he was, needless
to say, exaggerating) and translations.[15] Bernard's understanding of the
public domain had been that it excluded works whose composers and librettists were either still alive or who had died within the previous ten years.
This meant that the works of Auber, Boieldieu, and their contemporaries
who composed for the Opéra-Comique were out of the Odéon's reach, and

12. La tragédie, la comédie et s'il le désire l'opéra comique, en ce qui concerne les pièces
échues au domaine public, seulement, et les pièces prises dans le répertoire italien et allemand
(F-Pan O³ 1790/I).

13. L'opéra comique, mais pour ce dernier genre, les pièces échues au domaine public
(ibid.).

14. Et la comédie mêlée de chants, c'est à dire toutes celles des pièces dépendantes de
l'ancien répertoire du Théâtre Français dans lesquelles il se trouve un ou plusieurs airs mais
nullement, ni sous aucun prétexte les pièces provenantes du répertoire du Vaudeville ni au-
cunes pièces qui en aient le caractère (ibid.).

15. Letter from Bernard to La Ferté, 23 August 1823 (F-Pan O³ 1790/I).

Bernard clearly knew this. He did not understand that the term also excluded new opéras comiques. He had been aiming to address a particular constituency of composers and librettists: those Prix de Rome laureates who, on their return from their European tours, could not get their works performed at the Opéra-Comique. It is easy to imagine Bernard's dismay when he realized that he had just signed a contract—effectively with the monarch—agreeing to exclude the very types of work he was trying to encourage, and from which he was hoping to profit.

Lauriston had been back in the capital, after his return from Spain, for only a month when Bernard wrote to him for a third time (the first two letters are lost) about the question of new opéra comique. He began to develop the argument along lines that were present in embryo in the 23 August letter to La Ferté; he argued that the Opéra-Comique had no need of a monopoly on new works since it had no shortage of new compositions, and it would take ten years to exhaust its current backlog of new opéras comiques.[16] Lauriston's reply to Bernard has not been preserved, but the large number of subsequent attempts at reopening this issue suggest that he refused the request to play new opéras comiques. Bernard's claim to be acting altruistically, on behalf of Prix de Rome laureates, was less than half true; he was at least as much concerned by the clear equation between novelty and high box-office receipts as he was with the artistic fortunes of the next generation of composers.

The issue of new opéra comique was not the only item on the agenda, and Lauriston might well have wished that La Ferté had taken enough time over the original contract to make entirely clear to Bernard what repertory he was entitled to play. There were other significant problems that La Ferté had not foreseen. Astonishingly, one of these was the ownership of the theater building itself. La Ferté had acted as if the physical building called the Théâtre-Royal de l'Odéon, as well as the right to exploit its license, was in the gift of the maison du Roi.[17] In fact, as Lauriston rather tartly remarked to La Ferté in March 1824, the building was owned by the Chambre des Pairs—of which Lauriston himself had been a member since the beginning of the Restoration.[18] Crass as this mistake was, there was an easy remedy, and the matter was settled amicably between Bernard and the *grand référendaire* of the Chambre des Pairs, Charles-Louis Huguet, marquis de Sémonville (figure 8).[19]

16. Letter from Bernard to Lauriston, 2 January 1824 (F-Pan O³ 1790/VI).
17. The ownership of the building was never in question during the negotiations and drafting of the contract in August 1823 (see F-Pan O³ 1790/I).
18. Letter from Lauriston to La Ferté, 23 March 1824 (F-Pan O³ 1791/I).
19. The settlement is recorded in ibid.

Figure 8. Charles-Louis Huguet, marquis de
Sémonville. Lithograph by Bove after Lebec.

The relationship between Sémonville and the managers of the Odéon
was to remain cordial throughout the 1820s, and the Chambre des Pairs was
one of the institutions that came to the theater's rescue when it encountered difficulties.[20]

La Ferté had given Bernard legally binding permission in the August 1823 contract to deal with the personnel of the theater according to
his own preferences. Most of the artists at the Odéon already held contracts with the theater that had also been agreed with the maison du Roi.
Bernard's subsequent action resulted in a proposed reduction in salary for
a number of the biggest names at the Odéon who had thought their salaries
were secure. Lauriston's attempts to settle this matter were frustrated by
the reluctance of members of the theater's administration to agree over the
cuts, and the existence of radically different written accounts of the same
meetings. The sums of money were not small: the largest amount mentioned was in excess of Fr 22,000. Lauriston eventually gave up and agreed
to fund the difference directly from the maison du Roi—although he forced
the agreed sum down—with military precision—to Fr 12,966.64.[21] As

20. After 1820, the *grand référendaire de la Chambre des Pairs* was granted access to the *grand
cabinet* (Philip Mansel, *The Court of France 1789–1830* [Cambridge: Cambridge University
Press, 1988], 127). In 1828 he was allowed the same right as the king's ministers: to see him
alone between eight and nine o'clock in the evening without appointment (163).

21. This paragraph is a summary of an extensive correspondence between the Odéon
artists and the maison du Roi, reports, and minutes of meetings (see F-Pan O[3] 1791/VII).

Lauriston put most of these matters in order, he ignored his intendant. The archives from this period are full of letters from Lauriston to La Ferté—some dealing with relatively trivial matters—outlining Lauriston's decision and notifying his intendant merely as a matter of courtesy; La Ferté was replaced by La Rochefoucauld in August 1824.[22]

If Lauriston, and not La Ferté, had negotiated Bernard's contract in August 1823 there would have been no loose ends, and the latter would not have been left in any doubt about the nature of the article in the contract that concerned the repertory he was allowed to promote. If Bernard had got his own way, the Odéon would have rapidly emerged as a second theater dedicated to opéra comique and in a more or less permanent standoff with the Opéra-Comique throughout the 1820s. In such circumstances, translated Italian and French music drama might not have emerged in the capital. Efforts to continue the long run of *Robin des bois,* for example, might not have seemed quite so essential if an opéra comique by Louis-Joseph-Ferdinand Hérold, Adolphe Adam, or even Berlioz had been ready for staging. Or Lauriston could have refused to allow *any* opéra comique—even works in the public domain—to be played at the Odéon. The likely result would have been Bernard's refusal to take on the management of the Odéon, or the theater's more or less immediate financial collapse. As events were to show, only very successful music drama could support the entire range of activities at the theater.

Bernard's original contract stipulated a subvention from the maison du Roi of Fr 60,000. Within months of starting operations, Bernard realized that this sum was not going to be sufficient. He had concentrated so hard on trying to establish the repertory he needed for the theater that he had ignored perhaps the single most important financial element in its survival. Furthermore, while the theater was closed during mourning for the king, box-office income had been reduced to nothing (Louis XVIII had died on 16 September 1824, and the theater did not reopen until 25 September). Bernard had three strategies to remedy this situation: to appeal for an indemnity against the lack of box-office receipts, to request an advance of the next quarter's subvention, and to renegotiate the subvention itself. He pursued all three and was completely successful.

In requesting an indemnity against lack of box-office income, Bernard was on strong ground. He observed that the king's death not only resulted in closure of the theater, suspending performances, but stopped rehearsals as well. He also noted that the two main constituencies of the Odéon's audience—the aristocracy of the faubourg St-Germain and the students at the university—were prevented from going to the theater, the former by *la*

22. Ibid.

décence et l'étiquette and the latter because they were forbidden from attending during the period of mourning.[23] Bernard calculated the loss at Fr 2,000 per day for eleven days. La Rochefoucauld agreed to settle and went so far as to arrange a payment that would avoid the attention of other theaters in similar (but unrelieved) circumstances.[24]

Just before Lauriston left the maison du Roi, Bernard described the most critical position in which he found himself: he was not able to pay salaries for August 1824 without the aid of a loan. Bernard—not a longtime Parisian resident, and therefore without the sorts of contacts who could advance the sorts of sums likely to improve the situation—successfully appealed to the maison du Roi for an advance of the subvention for the last three calendar months of 1824 (a quarter of the annual sum, Fr 15,000); he hoped that this would keep the Odéon financially stable until the winter, when box-office receipts could normally be expected to rise.[25]

Loans and indemnities could not solve the theater's real financial problems; these were the result of an inadequate subvention. Bernard outlined the problem to La Rochefoucauld in early September 1824; at this stage, he was able to report on box-office receipts and expenditure for a period of five months. Bernard's figures were clear: box-office takings ran to Fr 166,006.15, to which could be added five months of subvention (Fr 25,000), which made a credit total of Fr 191,006.15. Against this had to be set a debit total of Fr 252,987.88, leaving Bernard with a shortfall of Fr 61,981.73. In support of his claim for an additional subvention, Bernard could point in three directions: toward the massive savings that the maison du Roi was making on the Odéon, to the benefit that accrued to the neighborhood in which the Odéon was situated, and to his own particular position vis-à-vis other theaters in Paris. The savings to the maison du Roi had been considerable when Bernard was appointed. Previously, the theater had cost the maison du Roi Fr 300,000 per annum. Even after his subvention had been subtracted and account been taken of various other start-up costs, Bernard reckoned that the current savings to the maison du Roi were Fr 210,000. Bernard observed that the Odéon was benefiting local shops, cafés, grocers, and landlords; each of the 230 workers at the Odéon had spouses and families. "Everyone gains," said Bernard, "except the manager."[26] He pointed out the weakness of his own position: on the one hand he had no shareholders as he would if he were managing a secondary theater, and on the other he did not benefit from the system in place at the

23. Letter from Bernard to La Rochefoucauld, 28 September 1824 (ibid.).
24. Letter from Bernard to La Rochefoucauld, 6 November 1824. The Fr 22,000 were paid in full (ibid.).
25. Letter from Bernard to Lauriston, undated but before 4 August 1824 (ibid.).
26. Letter from Bernard to La Rochefoucauld, 8 September 1824 (ibid.).

Opéra-Comique or Comédie-Française where losses were carried by the institution. While Bernard knew what he was getting into by taking on the Odéon at his own risk, equally the maison du Roi knew that financial collapse would simply mean taking the theater back into its own control. Lauriston—according to Bernard, at least—had not brought the latter to the Odéon to ruin him.

Bernard had pointed to a deficit in the region of Fr 60,000, and the maison du Roi, after two reports to the king, agreed to a new contract in which the subvention was raised by Fr 40,000 to Fr 100,000.[27] It is unlikely that Bernard was content with this contract but probably thought that it was the best he could do at the time. He had written to La Rochefoucauld asking— even after he had been expressly forbidden to ask further—for the sum to be increased to Fr 110,000; he was certainly putting down a marker for future negotiations.[28] There is a certain irony in the fact that the day before Bernard signed his revised contract on 8 December 1824, *Robin des bois* received its premiere and guaranteed the theater's financial stability for the foreseeable future.

When Bernard compared himself unfavorably to the managers of the secondary theaters who were supported by shareholders, he must have thought of opening up the Odéon in a similar way. In November 1823, he had written to Lauriston to ask permission to raise money by issuing shares in the theater. He proposed raising Fr 100,000 by this means. Lauriston's reply was surprising: he effectively said that it was none of his business, and that Bernard could proceed comfortably with issuing shares in the theater in the knowledge that this would not conflict with the conditions of his license.[29] Bernard took Lauriston at his word. On 8 July 1825, a society was formed, and shares issued. Since Lauriston seemed to have little interest in the process, Bernard valued the business at Fr 200,000 rather than the Fr 100,000 he had mentioned earlier. The *fonds de société* was divided into 40 shares of Fr 5,000 each. The shareholders were guaranteed interest of 6 percent per annum, and a further 4 percent dividend if a surplus remained in the *fonds* after payment of interest.[30] As a result of this action, and of increased box-office receipts, the question of the subvention for the Odéon went into abeyance for nearly two years. When the license was transferred from Bernard to Frédéric du Petit-Méré on 1 April 1826, the subvention remained at the level it had been in Bernard's revised contract of

27. Bernard's revised contract of 8 December 1824 is in ibid.

28. Letter from Bernard to La Rochefoucauld, 6 November 1824 (F-Pan O^3 1791/III).

29. Letter from Bernard to Lauriston, 28 November 1823 and Lauriston's reply, 17 December 1823 (F-Pan O^3 1791/VII).

30. Though the 8 July 1825 share issue's *acte de société* has not survived, this comment assumes that its conditions were the same as those of the 29 July 1826 *acte* (F-Pan O^3 1792/II).

Fr 100,000.[31] Issuing shares in the theater now meant that its governance was more complex. For example, when Bernard wished to divest himself of the direction of the theater, he had to obtain the agreement of the shareholders to resign and pass the direction on to Frédéric. This he secured only with difficulty, and the result was a revision to the *acte de société* dated 15 January 1826.[32]

When the Odéon's opera troupe started work in April 1824, it was limited to translations and opéra comique in the public domain. Music drama in translation encompassed two types: a single work translated from Italian or German into French (which might well involve some arrangement) and pasticci, in which numbers from different works—either by one or several composers—were assembled in order to set a new libretto in French. Even before the Odéon had opened, public discussions of the merits of translation had been reopened in the press; they centered on a planned performance of Rossini's *Donna del lago* as *La dame du lac* at the Opéra-Comique. The verdict had been almost universally hostile, the most generous view at best ambivalent. After reporting the plans to mount the work, and explaining that they had been dropped, a critic wrote that "Italian music is however the only good thing to come to us from old Rome or antique Naples (Parthenope)."[33] Other critics alluded to the "stupid libretto of *La dame du lac* clanging to the sound of Rossini's music."[34] Further accounts were equally negative, but one at least attempted a more analytic view of the translation of Italian music drama into French. The three reasons against mounting *La donna del lago* in French at the Opéra-Comique were that the idolatry for the music of Rossini should not be allowed to spread from the Théâtre italien to the Opéra-Comique, that the French singers at the Opéra-Comique would not be able to handle Italian vocal styles, and that more arrangements would follow.[35]

Such was the environment in which Bernard put together his team of artists for the first productions of music drama under his management. He opened on 27 April 1824 with *Les trois genres,* an occasional work that itself staged the three genres that fell within the license of the theater: comedy, tragedy, and music drama. For over a week, he allowed *Les trois genres* to be performed alongside the Odéon's traditional repertory of spoken drama:

31. Frédéric du Petit-Méré's contract is in F-Pan O³ 1792/II.

32. Two letters survive from Bernard to La Rochefoucauld, 22 December 1825 and 17 January 1826, which recapitulate the dealings with the shareholders' views of the transfer of the license to Petit-Méré (F-Pan O³ 1792/V).

33. La musique italienne est pourtant aujourd'hui la seule bonne chose qui puisse nous venir de la vieille Rome et de l'antique Parthenope (*Le Diable Boiteux,* 9 February 1824).

34. *Le Courrier des Théâtres,* 27 January 1824.

35. Ibid., 19 February 1824.

Jane Shore, Luxe et indigence, Les vêpres siciliennes, and such classics as Racine's *Iphigénie.*[36] On the 6 May, however, Bernard premiered Rossini's *Barbier de Séville* in Castil-Blaze's translation, a version of the work that had been in circulation in provincial opera houses since 1821, and also an obvious and unobjectionable choice.[37] Its success prompted an astonishing series of premieres, during May and June 1824, of public domain works. The activity in this period (summarized on table 2) may be read as a curtain-call of late-eighteenth-century French music drama that included some of the best known works of Grétry and Dalayrac.[38]

Interspersed among these works was the first of Castil-Blaze's pasticci to appear at the Odéon. Like *Le barbier de Séville, Les folies amoureuses* had already been in circulation in provincial theaters and was well received in Paris. With these two works and nearly a dozen public-domain opéras comiques, Bernard changed the face of the Odéon almost overnight and won over those critics who had been most hostile to the idea of music drama at the Odéon.[39] Translations and public-domain opéras comiques would henceforth be judged on their merits, and on those of their performers, and not on ideological objections to translated music drama or a residual fear of a second theater for opéra comique.[40]

The only thing that might have been able to stop the triumphant career of music drama at the Odéon was the hot summer weather that turned most opera houses into infernos and deterred most audiences. At the end of June 1824, all the Odéon audiences were said to be not in the theater but in the Jardin du Luxembourg, and it was also said that theater managers in the capital had all been praying for a change in the weather, a plea that had resulted in several days of rain.[41] High summer nevertheless saw the

36. Pierre-Chaumont Liadières's tragedy *Jane Shore* had been premiered earlier that month at the Odéon, on the same night that a mélodrame of the same title was given at the Théâtre de la Pte-St-Martin; J.-B. Rose Bonaventure Violet d'Épagny's *Luxe et indigence ou Le ménage parisien* had also been premiered at the Odéon in January 1824; Casimir Delavigne's *Vêpres siciliennes* had been premiered at the Odéon on 22 November 1819.

37. This was known to the Parisian press; see *Le Diable Boiteux,* 7 May and 3 June 1824.

38. Further detail on the works listed in tables 2 to 4 is given in appendix 1.

39. *Le Courrier des Théâtres,* 25 June 1824.

40. This would not stop some commentators from regretfully noting the lowly place that spoken drama held at the Odéon as a result. See *La Pandore,* 9 April 1825, which perhaps correctly blamed music drama at the Odéon for the ruin of *l'art dramatique* there. Yet aesthetic questions centering on Italian or German music drama did not disappear; they simply became separated from judgments concerning the success or value of productions at the Odéon.

41. *La Pandore,* 29 June 1824. "The public that, snail-like, appears at performances only after rain, has returned as in previous days to fill the theatrical reservoirs that are so often dry during the summer" (le public qui, semblable aux limaçons, ne se montre au spectacle qu'après la pluie, est revenu, comme les jours précédents, remplir les citernes dramatiques, trop souvent à sec pendant l'été [30 June 1824]).

TABLE 2. Operatic repertory during Claude Bernard's management

Date of Premiere	Translations and Pasticci	Ancien Répertoire	Occasional Works
27 April 1824			Les trois genres
6 May 1824	Le barbier de Séville		
13 May 1824		Le tableau parlant	
16 May 1824		La fausse magie	
18 May 1824		L'épreuve villageoise	
26 May 1824		Le tonnelier	
27 May 1824		Richard Coeur-de-Lion	
1 June 1824		Ambroise	
5 June 1824	Les folies amoureuses		
18 June 1824		Zémire et Azor	
22 June 1824		Sylvain	
29 June 1824		Raoul, sire de Créqui	
12 July 1824		Blaise et Babet	
23 July 1824		Philippe et Georgette	
2 August 1824	La pie voleuse		
1 September 1824		Les fausses apparences	
19 October 1824		La rosière de Salenci	
21 October 1824	Le sacrifice interrompu		
7 December 1824	Robin des bois		
6 February 1825		Les rêveries renouvelées des Grecs	
9 May 1825	Les noces de Gamache		
1 June 1825		Raoul Barbe-Bleu	
7 June 1825			Louis XII
30 June 1825		Les Français au sérail	
25 July 1825	Othello		
16 August 1825	La comédie à la campagne		
31 October 1825	La dame du lac		
17 November 1825	Preciosa		
14 January 1826	La forêt de Sénart		

SOURCES: Draft listings of repertory, available in all the *grands quotidiens* of the era, were assembled from the *Journal de Paris* and subsequently checked against references in the theatrical press, in particular *La Pandore, Le Courrier des Théâtres, Le Frondeur,* and *Le Diable Boiteux.*

premiere of Rossini's *Gazza ladra* in Castil-Blaze's translation as *La pie voleuse,* and two more works by Grétry.

The winter of 1824 and the first half of 1825 were dominated by German music drama and one work in particular: Weber's *Freischütz* in Castil-Blaze's arrangement as *Robin des bois.* The winter began well with Winter's singspiel *Das unterbrochene Opferfest (Le sacrifice interrompu)* on 21 October. This work generated an excitement in the capital that would be capped only by that of *Robin des bois* two months later. Paris was ablaze with discussions of the relative merits of Italian and German music drama in French, whether such a work as *Le sacrifice interrompu* could survive its terrible libretto, and how difficult German music was to listen to. Six weeks after *Le sacrifice interrompu, Robin des bois* was premiered. The opening nights were not without their difficulties, but by its third or fourth performance, there was not a critic in the city who would argue against the qualities of the work. The levels of critical enthusiasm for the work had not been seen since the first Rossini performances in Paris, and the impact of Weber's music on Parisian artistic culture looked set to match that of his Italian contemporary.

The success of *Robin des bois* was almost unparalleled. It kept back premieres of other foreign music drama until the early summer of the following year (see table 2). The management of the Odéon milked the piece for all it was worth. In February 1825, for example, *Robin des bois* played for ten nights out of twenty-eight. In comparison, *Le barbier de Séville* played twice, and *La pie voleuse* and *Les folies amoureuses* once each. Of the old repertory, *Zémire et Azor, Raoul, sire de Créqui,* and *Blaise et Babet ou La suite des "Trois fermiers"* appeared once each, and *Les rêveries renouvelées des Grecs* (itself a parody of Gluck dating originally from 1779 but new to the Odéon) was given four times during the month. The success of *Robin des bois* would continue,[42] was without precedent, but would not be replicated.

Summer 1825 began with the premiere of the Mercadante pasticcio, *Les noces de Gamache,* and ended with those of Rossini's *Othello* and Domenico Cimarosa's *Impresario in angustie,* translated as *La comédie à la campagne.* From the public domain, Grétry's *Raoul Barbe-Bleu* was premiered in June, and *Louis XII ou La route de Reims* was written especially for the coronation of Charles X. *Les Français au sérail* was premiered in June 1825. This was a rare case of a work from the *ancien répertoire*—François Devienne's *Visitandines* of 1792—subjected to a systematic reworking, and for which a new libretto was published. This premiere threw the theater into

42. Repertory in March or April would be similar but complicated by the closure of the theaters during Holy Week, from the end of March to the beginning of April (Easter Sunday was 3 April 1825).

direct competition with the Opéra-Comique, which was also reworking *Les visitandines*.

La dame du lac, the translation of Rossini's *Donna del lago*, received its premiere on the last day of October 1825. There may have been a degree of bravado in this choice of a traditionally poor day in the theatrical year (theaters were closed on 1 November); it does not seem to have prevented a successful premiere.[43] The months before the premiere of *La dame du lac* were exciting ones for Paris: two music dramas based on works by Sir Walter Scott were planned to appear at competing theaters during the winter of 1825: *La dame du lac* at the Odéon and Boieldieu's *Dame blanche* at the Opéra-Comique (figure 9).[44]

The Odéon had a head start and won the race, although *La dame blanche* was the work that made a permanent mark on Parisian operatic culture (in its ability to pull in crowds for longer than any other work, it held the same status at the Opéra-Comique as did *Robin des bois* at the Odéon).

La dame du lac was followed by the Odéon's first thoroughgoing failure. Weber's *Preciosa* appeared for the first time on 17 November 1825, almost exactly a year after *Robin des bois*. This was no coincidence, since it was hoped (in vain) that Weber's name would again enhance the Odéon's reputation. *Preciosa* disappeared but not entirely without trace, since it was to reappear a year later as a source for the pasticcio *Les bohémiens*. Enthusiasts for Weber's music did not have long to wait, however. At the beginning of January they heard more of the composer's music in Castil-Blaze's pasticcio, *La forêt de Sénart ou La partie de chasse de Henri IV*. This was the last new production under Bernard's management.

One of the mysteries of the history of the Odéon was why—when the theater was running as well as it ever would—Bernard chose to leave the theater to take up the management of the relatively insignificant theater in Liège. Certainly, the financial situation of the Odéon was finely balanced. And

43. *La Pandore*, 4 November 1825.

44. "While M. Auber [*sic;* recte M. Boieldieu] strains to finish the score of *La dame blanche,* the Odéon announces its next production, of *La dame du lac* by Rossini. The subject of these two operas being the same, it will be interesting to compare the work of the two masters, which will necessarily have Sir Walter Scott as judge, during his stay in Paris" (Pendant que M. Auber [*sic*] s'exténue à terminer la partition de la *Dame blanche,* l'Odéon annonce la prochaine représentation de la *Dame du lac,* musique de Rossini. Le sujet de ces deux opéras étant la même, il sera curieux de comparer le travail des deux maîtres qui auront nécessairement Sir Walter-Scott pour juge, pendant son séjour à Paris [*Le Frondeur,* 29 August 1825]). Rumors of Scott's visit to Paris during the winter of 1825 were widespread (but he came in September 1826). The operas do not have a common subject: *La donna del lago* is based indirectly on Scott's poem *The Lady of the Lake* and *La dame blanche* on an amalgam of Scott's novels, esp. *Guy Mannering* and *The Monastery*.

Figure 9. Sir Walter Scott. Lithograph by François-Auguste
Garnier.

Bernard's successor would find it difficult to make ends meet during his tenure. Yet the Odéon's position was as good as it was ever going to be: more or
less financially viable and artistically successful. The reasons for Bernard's
departure from the Odéon must be sought elsewhere.

Before Bernard came to the Odéon, he had been manager of the theater
in Brussels, where he had taken over in 1819. He met a member of the
chorus, Charlotte Kerckhoven, with whom he began a liaison, and when—
after his time in Antwerp—he moved to the Odéon Kerckhoven took a
position in Rouen so that they could continue their affair. According to
Bernard's deposition to a Parisian lawyer in 1832, she behaved scandalously
while Bernard was still manager of the Odéon and threatened to expose
him. Bernard's reaction was to leave the management of the high-profile

Odéon in favor of the theater in Liège,[45] which had the advantage of being much further away from Rouen. All the signs pointed to a hasty retreat from Paris. The press got wind of Bernard's impending departure only in January 1826, when it was reported that he would leave on 1 April. Other reports suggested that he would co-manage with his successor for a year.[46] None of this was true; Bernard fled, and his successor, Frédéric du Petit-Méré, took over the management of the Odéon within a few days on 1 February 1826. Bernard not only left Paris with his reputation intact, but he left behind a theater and a neighborhood that were quick to recognize what he had done for them during his twenty-two months as manager. Within days of Bernard's taking over the theater, Le Courrier des Théâtres could write that "the public of this neighborhood (the faubourg St-Germain), enchanted to see the Odéon improve, and to see its entertainments varied with so much energy, is beginning to take M. Bernard under its protection; there is a tacit understanding established between the protector and the protected from which one can only expect excellent results."[47] No one had ever had any doubts about the artistic pace of Bernard's management; in June 1824 the press exclaimed that the Odéon gave no one time to breathe because of the relentless pace of premieres and revivals.[48] In its roundup of the previous theatrical year at the beginning of 1825, the Journal de Paris singled out the Odéon as the most successful theater in the capital, and by March the theater was ironically placed at the "center of the chaussée d'Antin"— the right-bank theater district.[49] In September 1826, after Bernard had been gone six months, the press still looked back to him as the manager who had revivified the Odéon's fortunes.[50]

Frédéric du Petit-Méré

Frédéric, as he was known to the Parisian theatrical world, knew the Odéon well. He had been able to observe its climb to operatic power during 1824 and 1825 from his position as director at the Théâtre de la Gaîté, and there had been rumors of his making a sideways move to a similar position at the

45. Bernard's deposition, dated 31 December 1832 (F-Pn n.a.f. 3042, fol. 197^r).

46. Le Courrier des Théâtres, 31 January 1826.

47. Le public de ce quartier (faubourg St-Germain), enchanté de voir ainsi se monter l'Odéon, et ses plaisirs variés avec tant de zèle, commence à prendre M. Bernard sous sa protection; il s'établit, entre le protecteur et le protégé, une tacite intelligence dont on ne peut attendre que d'excellents résultats (Le Courrier des Théâtres, 28 May 1824).

48. Le Diable Boiteux, 22 June 1824.

49. Journal de Paris, 2 January 1825; Le Courrier des Théâtres, 19 March 1825.

50. Le Courrier des Théâtres, 7 September 1826.

TABLE 3. Operatic repertory
during Frédéric du Petit-Méré's management

Date of Premiere	Translations and Pasticci	Ancien Répertoire	Occasional Works
2 March 1826	La jeune aveugle		
11 March 1826	Marguerite d'Anjou		
13 June 1826	La fausse Agnès		
16 July 1826		Maison à vendre	
22 July 1826	Les noces de Figaro		
7 August 1826	Le neveu de Monseigneur		
15 September 1826	Ivanhoé		
4 November 1826			L'école de Rome
23 November 1826	Les bohémiens		
22 January 1827	Le testament		
6 February 1827	Emmeline		
24 February 1827	Monsieur de Pourceaugnac		
21 April 1827	La folle de Glaris		
14 May 1827		Adolphe et Clara	

SOURCES: Draft listings of repertory, available in all the *grands quotidiens* of the era, were assembled from the *Journal de Paris* and subsequently checked against references in the theatrical press, in particular *La Pandore, Le Courrier des Théâtres, Le Frondeur,* and *Le Diable Boiteux.*

Odéon in December 1825.[51] He was able to continue Bernard's regime with little difficulty, both because many of the plans from which he was able to benefit had been laid while Bernard had been manager, and because he had seen how Bernard had planned his repertory. Both of them recognized *l'obligation de jouer le répertoire du premier ordre.*[52]

Music drama at the Odéon during Frédéric's tenure as manager (from February 1826 to May 1827) was governed by the same license as the one that controlled Bernard's management of the theater. Despite frequent attempts to enlarge the repertory of opéra comique to include new works, the operatic repertory remained translations of foreign music drama (complete works and pasticci) and opéras comiques in the public domain. The overall repertory during Frédéric's management is given in table 3. Where it differs from that of Bernard's regime is in the balance between foreign works and public-domain opéra comique. Of the fourteen premieres mounted during

51. *La Pandore,* 20 January 1826. Perhaps Frédéric became an obvious contender because he was being considered for a post as director of the theater when the position as manager fell vacant.

52. "The obligation of playing the very best works" (*La Pandore,* 3 May 1826).

Frédéric's period as manager, only two (14 percent) were of opéra comique from the *ancien répertoire,* as opposed to a proportion of 57 percent under Bernard. This is naturally testimony to Bernard's ability to replace the *ancien répertoire* with foreign works, an ability that Frédéric tried to emulate, for it was without doubt foreign works—not those of the public domain—that continued to bring in audiences and ensure the financial viability of the theater.

One of Frédéric's most valuable inheritances from the previous regime was what could be termed "the 1826 plan." This was a coordinated attempt to bring three composers, Rossini, Meyerbeer, and Weber, to the Odéon to mount pasticci based on their preexistent works. It was the closest the Odéon could come, under the terms of its license, to putting on new works by living composers. Although the plan must have been developed with Bernard's approval, the conductor Pierre Crémont, along with Thomas Sauvage, drove the project forward and negotiated with the composers. The idea came to fruition under Frédéric's management and by March 1826 the plan looked set firm, with each work planned for performance at two-monthly intervals: Meyerbeer's *Nymphe du Danube* in July 1826, Rossini's *Ivanhoé* in September, and Weber's *Bohémiens* in November. *La nymphe du Danube* collapsed, but *Ivanhoé* went ahead as planned, and even *Les bohémiens* was staged, although Weber's death in June 1826 robbed the Odéon of the cachet of the composer's collaboration.

The idea of bringing Meyerbeer into the 1826 plan had been generated, at least in part, by the work toward the successful premiere of *Marguerite d'Anjou* in March 1826. Being an amalgam of two works masquerading as one, this was one of the stranger, as well as one of the greater, successes of the early part of 1826. Frédéric also put on two pasticci by Castil-Blaze, *La fausse Agnès* and *Monsieur de Pourceaugnac;* the latter was the only one of Castil-Blaze's four pasticci to have been written expressly for the Odéon. German composers continued to be well represented during Frédéric's tenure: Adalbert Gyrowetz, *La jeune aveugle* (*Der Augenarzt*); Johann Baptist Weigl, *Emmeline ou La famille Suisse* (*Die Schweizerfamilie*); and Conradin Kreutzer, *La folle de Glaris* (*Adele von Budoy; Cordelia*). Tucked in among what today might be considered by some "forgotten" composers, was a work by Mozart, *Les noces de Figaro* (*Le nozze di Figaro*). The audiences went as much, perhaps more, to hear Beaumarchais's lines than Mozart's music.[53] Frédéric's repertory concluded with two opéras comiques from the public domain, both by Dalayrac, *Maison à vendre* and *Adolphe et Clara,* and by a work for the feast of Saint Charles. Despite the fact that the last work, *L'école de Rome,* was by two living composers and technically broke the terms of the

53. *Le Courrier des Théâtres,* 23 July 1826.

Odéon's license, Frédéric escaped censure and continued to mount and promote music drama in translation during the winter of 1826–27.

A much more serious threat to the Odéon's well-being was the possibility of another theater following suit in mounting productions of music drama in French translation. The threat came from what might be thought to be an unlikely quarter: the Académie royale de musique, with Rossini's adaptation of *Maometto II* and *Mosè in Egitto* as *Le siège de Corinthe* and *Moïse et Pharaon*. Both works were premiered during Frédéric's management of the Odéon: *Le siège de Corinthe* on 9 October 1826 and *Moïse et Pharaon* on 26 March 1827. Rossini decided to make his debut at the Académie royale de musique with French versions of Italian works not only after the Odéon had been doing the same for two years, but also at exactly the moment when he himself was involved in assembling a pasticcio, *Ivanhoé,* for the same theater. Both Rossini and Castil-Blaze aimed to adjust his Italian works as precisely as possible to the French stage. Castil-Blaze, working for provincial opera companies and eventually for the Odéon, changed the *recitativo semplice* into spoken dialogue, whereas Rossini—whose products had to adhere to the conventions of the Académie royale de musique—needed to supply accompanied recitative in French. Furthermore, although Castil-Blaze had undertaken the literary and musical work himself, the libretti for *Le siège de Corinthe* and *Moïse et Pharaon* were translated and new lines written by, respectively, Luigi Balocchi and Alexandre Soumet, and Balocchi together with Victor-Joseph-Étienne de Jouy, while Rossini undertook the musical adaptations.[54]

Many of the changes made to *Maometto II* and *Mosè in Egitto* will become familiar as the details of works arranged for the Odéon emerge during the course of later chapters. Large-scale resequencing of numbers is common: the *introduzione* to *Mosè in Egitto* reappears in act II of *Moïse et Pharaon,* for example, and part of the *terzettone* from act I of *Maometto II* is placed in act III of *Le siège de Corinthe.* In the latter work, Rossini recast the role of Calbo (originally written as a *travesti* role for Adelaide Comelli in *Maometto II*) as a tenor for the rising star of the Académie royale de musique, Adolphe

54. The reworking of *Mosè in Egitto* and *Maometto II* has received a great deal of attention. See Paolo Isotta, "Da *Mosè* a *Moïse,*" *Bollettino del Centro Rossiniano di studi* 1–3 (1971): 87–117; idem, ed., *Gioacchino Rossini: Mosè in Egitto, Azione tragico-sacra; Moïse et Pharaon, Opéra en quatre actes; Mosè, Melodramma sacro in quattro atti* (Turin: Unione tipografico-editrice torinese, 1974); Marcello Conati, "Between Past and Future: The Dramatic World of Rossini in *Mosè in Egitto* and *Moïse et Pharaon,*" *19th-Century Music* 4 (1980–81): 32–47; Richard Osborne, *Rossini* (London: Macmillan, 1986), 208–13 and 237–42; Giuseppe Ierolli, "*Mosè e Maometto:* da Napoli a Parigi" (Tesi di laurea, Università degli studi di Bologna, 1989–90). For *Le siège de Corinthe,* see Anselm Gerhard, *The Urbanisation of Opera: Music Theater in Paris in the Nineteenth Century,* trans. Mary Whittall (Chicago: University of Chicago Press, 1998), 68–84.

Nourrit.[55] All these changes are familiar from arrangements at the Odéon (by Castil-Blaze and by others), and from the creation of *Ivanhoé*. The composer would replicate this successful technique when he reworked *Il viaggio a Reims* as *Le comte Ory* in 1828, and the Académie royale de musique would go beyond Italian music drama and mount a translation and arrangement of Weber's *Euryanthe* in 1831.[56]

Le siège de Corinthe and *Moïse et Pharaon* did little to lure audiences from the Odéon to the Académie royale de musique. They did however break the monopoly on French translations from Italian that the Odéon had enjoyed for nearly two years. The effect was felt not so much on the box office as in the sense that the Odéon was no longer offering generically unique works. Although of the two works that Rossini chose for translation for the Académie royale de musique, *Maometto II* had not been staged by the Théâtre-Royal italien, *Mosè in Egitto* was well known there. Even the entertainment of running a French version of Rossini while the Théâtre italien put on something close to the original was now no longer something on which the Odéon had a monopoly.

Frédéric succeeded in continuing the patterns of repertory established by his predecessor; he was also subject to the same sorts of financial difficulties. The *fonds de société* that Bernard had built up of Fr 200,000 had not lasted long, and by June 1826 Frédéric was writing to La Rochefoucauld setting out the perilous financial position of the Odéon. He explained—while subjecting Bernard's management to unbridled criticism—that he had lost Fr 20,000 during the months of May and June 1826 because of poor receipts; in addition, he claimed that Bernard had left debts of Fr 40,000, had also spent Fr 80,000 on costumes, instruments, and other equipment for the theater, and had received Fr 30,000 clandestinely (Frédéric's word is *pot-de-vin*, which has the sense of a bribe). The *fonds de société* thus held only Fr 30,000, which Frédéric thought would barely cover the losses during July and August.[57]

Frédéric's specific request to La Rochefoucauld was that he should be allowed to set up a pension fund, along the lines of those at the other royal theaters. He stressed how much more stability this would give to his artists,

55. See, for a full account of the textual history of *Maometto II* and *Mosè in Egitto* as *Le siège de Corinthe* and *Moïse en Égypte*, Philip Edward Gossett, "The Operas of Rossini: Problems of Textual Criticism in Nineteenth-Century Opera" (Ph.D. diss., Princeton University, 1970), 394–429 and 455–87.

56. The materials for the production of *Euryanthe* at the Académie royale de musique all survive in F-Po A.497.a. See Mark Everist, "Translating Weber's *Euryanthe:* German Romanticism at the Dawn of French *Grand Opéra,*" *Revue de musicologie* 87 (2001): 67–104.

57. Letter from Petit-Méré to La Rochefoucauld, 27 June 1826 (F-Pan O³ 1792/I).

but—more to the point—it would enable him to reduce salaries by 5 percent a year. The overall expenditure per annum for the theater was Fr 679, 683.12, of which Fr 480,000 were salaries; the theater had a shortfall of Fr 63,378. Reducing the salary bill by 5 percent would have reduced the debt by Fr 24,000—a reduction of 38 percent in the deficit—and thus represented a risk-free means of improving the theater's financial state.[58]

At the same time he approached the maison du Roi for indirect support, Frédéric and his shareholders agreed to revalue the business. The *fonds de société* was raised to Fr 500,000, divided into 200 shares of Fr 2,500 each. The 40 original shareholders exchanged one old share of Fr 5,000 for two new ones of Fr 2,500, and the remaining 120 shares were offered for sale. Frédéric cleverly waited until the winter, when box-office receipts were at their highest, before advertising the new shares and sent out printed invitations in early December 1826.[59] This December 1826 share issue was not successful, and by April 1827, only about a third of the supplementary shares had been sold.[60] Furthermore, by May 1828 Thomas Sauvage (Frédéric's successor) had dissolved the society, because he was trying to dismiss its *vérificateur général.* Sauvage did not take over the direction of the theater until 1 June 1827, and the *société* probably continued to exist until that time It is however quite possible that the poor response to the December 1826 invitation to purchase shares triggered a move to disband the *société* six months later.[61]

Just as it was becoming clear that the December 1826 share issue was not going to have its desired effect, the theater switched direction and began negotiations with the maison du Roi to double the subvention from Fr 100,000 per annum to Fr 200,000. At the beginning of 1827, the mayors of the 11th and 12th arrondissements wrote directly to the duc de Doudeauville, over the head of La Rochefoucauld, reinforcing this request. Frédéric needed just this support, and if his own account of the affair is to be believed (and this is in the context of a letter to the *premier ministre,* Villèle), Doudeauville was much inclined to accept the claim and had the authority to act. He had already granted Frédéric an advance of no less than Fr 50,000 against the Fr 100,000 increase some time in early 1827.[62] This plan fell apart because of outside circumstances. On 29 April 1827, Villèle abolished the Parisian Garde national, and Doudeauville resigned in pro-

---

58. Ibid.
59. A single copy of the advertisement survives in F-Po Arch. Th. Paris: Odéon.43.
60. F-Pan O³ 1792/I: letter from Petit-Méré and Sauvage to La Rochefoucauld, 26 April 1827.
61. Letter from Sauvage to La Rochefoucauld, 8 May 1828 (F-Pan O³ 1793/III).
62. Letter from Petit-Méré to Villèle, 25 May 1827 (F-Pan O³ 1792/V).

test.[63] This meant that all the careful work Frédéric had done in the previous four months to ensure the doubling of the subvention had been wasted. The baron de la Bouillerie, the new minister at the maison du Roi, was unlikely to acquiesce to a request of this sort in the first few months of his appointment; a professional civil servant, he was interested in streamlining the maison du Roi, not increasing its budget.

Frédéric's attempts to remedy the situation smack of desperation. A month after Doudeauville's departure, he wrote to the marquis de Lauriston explaining the situation and asking for support. Although Lauriston had moved from the ministry of the maison du Roi to become *grand veneur* in 1824, before Frédéric had become involved with the Odéon, he now held a position of some importance, not because of its intrinsic significance but because the hunt was a part of the household that the king valued highly; Charles X was famed for his love of hunting to the point that he was known as—amusingly, in the context of this study—"Robin des bois."[64] The king might pay attention to Lauriston. Frédéric's correspondence with Lauriston shows however that the latter was not inclined to listen favorably to the Odéon's manager;[65] the next day Frédéric wrote directly—but with little chance of success—to the premier ministre Villèle. The plan to double the Odéon's subvention had disappeared with Doudeauville. Frédéric's lack of persistence could be attributed either to the fact that he had already agreed to stand down from the direction of the Odéon or to the symptoms of the coronary aneurysm that would kill him nine weeks later.[66]

Thomas Sauvage

Thomas-Marie-François Sauvage's tenure of the Odéon (from June 1827 to October 1828) was never stable. Although he had taken a major part in the teams that produced *Robin des bois* and other successes in the previous three years, the first thing he did when appointed as manager was to close the theater, ostensibly for refurbishment, for ten weeks from the beginning of July to the middle of August 1827. This was a way of avoiding the low box-office receipts that he anticipated throughout the summer months and, by not paying his staff, he achieved a degree of saving. Exactly how the manual and

63. André Jardin and André-Jean Tudesq, *Restoration and Reaction: 1815–1848,* trans. Elborg Forster (Cambridge: Cambridge University Press, 1983), 65 (originally published in 1973 as *La France des notables*).

64. Mansel, *Court of France,* 140.

65. Two letters from Petit-Méré to Lauriston survive, 23 and 24 May 1827 (F-Pan O³ 1792/V).

66. Frédéric had been described as seriously ill in the late summer of 1826 (*Le Courrier des Théâtres,* 21 August 1826) and probably never properly recovered. He died on 5 July 1827.

TABLE 4. Operatic repertory
during Thomas Sauvage's management

Date of Premiere	Translations and Pasticci	Ancien Répertoire	Occasional Works
20 August 1827		*La maison isolée*	
22 August 1827	*Les deux Figaro*		
7 September 1827	*Tancrède*		
13 October 1827	*L'eau de jouvence*		
23 October 1827		*Camille*	
3 November 1827			*Charles V*
24 December 1827	*Don Juan*		
1 February 1828		*Les deux aveugles*	
18 February 1828	*Les brigands de Schiller*		
4 May 1828		*Les deux mots*	
18 May 1828		*Gulnare*	
10 April 1828	*Le dernier jour de Missolunghi*		
28 May 1828		*Le déserteur*	

SOURCES: Draft listings of repertory, available in all the *grands quotidiens* of the era, were assembled from the *Journal de Paris* and subsequently checked against references in the theatrical press, in particular *La Pandore, Le Courrier des Théâtres, Le Frondeur,* and *Le Diable Boiteux.*

clerical staff got by during this period is far from clear, but the action was to rebound badly on him during the following year.

When the Odéon reopened on 18 August 1827, the repertory looked familiar (table 4). The opening work was *Le barbier de Séville,* and a new public domain opéra comique, Dalayrac's *Maison isolée ou Le vieillard des Vosges,* appeared two days later. In three consecutive months there were as many premieres: a translation of Carafa's *Due Figaro* as *Les deux Figaro,* Rossini's *Tancredi* (*Tancrède*), and what was effectively a new opéra comique but tolerated because it was written by a foreigner, Conradin Kreutzer's *Eau de jouvence.* Another Dalayrac work followed, *Camille ou Le souterrain,* and the name day of Charles X was celebrated with *Charles V et Duguesclin* on 3 November. Of these, *Les deux Figaro* and *Tancrède* were the result of Frédéric's energies.[67] Given that Kreutzer's *Folle de Glaris* was associated with Amalia Schütz, it seems highly likely that she was the agency by which *L'eau de jouvence* was promoted at the Odéon, not negotiation on Sauvage's part.

67. *Les deux Figaro* was announced in the press before Sauvage took over (*Journal de Paris,* 22 May 1827), as was *Tancrède* (*La Pandore,* 13 February 1827).

The first major initiative for which Sauvage could claim credit—apart from closing the theater for the summer—was to rent the Odéon during September 1827 to a visiting troupe, the Théâtre anglais led by Abbott.[68] Although this is perhaps one of the most famous episodes during the Restoration history of the theater, its significance has been exaggerated. The reasons for the English troupe's taking space at the Odéon were entirely accidental, although fortunate from Sauvage's point of view. A Parisian impresario, Émile Laurent, had been trying to bring an English troupe to Paris since the mid-1820s; he wanted to capitalize on the eventual success of Penley's performances of English classics in 1822. Laurent had contracted with Frederick Yates to establish an English theater in Paris, to run in alternation with the Théâtre-Royal italien, but had been rebuffed by La Rochefoucauld. Laurent had then proposed building his own theater for English drama and a theater built by subscription; both proposals were also rejected. In July 1827 however, his original plan to alternate performances with the Théâtre italien was accepted (and he was to take over the management of the Théâtre italien on 2 October 1827). At the last minute, this proposal was again rejected by the Commission des théâtres royaux, and Laurent was lucky to find Sauvage, who was prepared to allow the Théâtre anglais space at the Odéon.[69]

It is difficult to see what advantage lay in this for Sauvage, given that Laurent paid him only Fr 1,400 per night for the use of the theater. As will be seen, music drama at the Odéon continued, and there was no question of Sauvage not paying his staff, and in any case the manual workers at the Odéon—the *ouvreuses* and the *machinistes*—still had to work. The plan went off rather badly, since after twelve performances at the Odéon, Laurent became the manager of the Théâtre italien, and the English troupe left the Odéon for the Salle Favart.[70]

The performances of the Théâtre anglais dovetailed very neatly with those of the Odéon's troupe, as can be seen from the first week's program (table 5) although, in contrast to the usual careful planning of the Odéon's programs, this schedule seems curious in some respects. The Théâtre anglais performed three times a week, and their first week was typical. The Odéon responded with an old work that had an immediate currency in the

---

68. Much has been written on the Théâtre anglais during 1827 and 1828, and in general the role of the Odéon as a venue has been overestimated. Still the best account (unmatched by modern versions) is Joseph-Léopold Borgerhoff, *Le Théâtre anglais à Paris sous la restauration* (Paris: Hachette, 1912).

69. Ibid., 35–41.

70. For a full calendar of performances by the Théâtre anglais, see ibid., 229–333, complete and correct with the exception that the performance on 8 January 1828 was given at the Théâtre italien and not, as Borgerhoff suggests, at the Odéon.

TABLE 5. Repertory during first week of Théâtre anglais

Date	Théâtre anglais	Odéon, Drama and Comedy	Odéon, Opera
6 September 1827	The Rivals; Fortune's Frolic		
7 September 1827		Les deux Anglais	Tancrède (prem.)
8 September 1827	She Stoops to Conquer; Love, Law and Physic		
9 September 1827		Tartuffe	
10 September 1827		La première affaire	Tancrède
11 September 1827	Hamlet; The Irish Tutor		
12 September 1827		La première affaire	Tancrède

SOURCES: Draft listings of repertory, available in all the *grands quotidiens* of the era, were assembled from the *Journal de Paris* and subsequently checked against references in the theatrical press, in particular *La Pandore, Le Courrier des Théâtres, Le Frondeur,* and *Le Diable Boiteux.*

first week of September 1827, Pierre-François Camus's *Deux Anglais,* and—no doubt to satisfy their traditional audience's amour-propre, Molière's *Tartuffe. La première affaire* was another play by Camus that had opened at the Odéon at the end of August and was in the middle of a successful first run. The strangest part of the opening days of the Théâtre anglais at the Odéon was that Sauvage put on the premiere of the translation of Rossini's *Tancredi* the day immediately after the English troupe's first night. To try and compete with the English troupe would have been to invite confrontation with Laurent, and to mount a major new premiere also meant exhausting his audiences. The Théâtre anglais continued at the Odéon, putting on twelve performances in four weeks (*Romeo and Juliet* on 15 and 20 September—witnessed by Berlioz—and *Othello* on 25 September), and moved on 4 October to the Théâtre-Royal italien, where the audience could hear an English play and Italian music drama (Rossini's *Torvaldo e Dorliska* and *Il barbiere di Siviglia,* Francesco Morlacchi's *Tebaldo e Isolina;* Nicola Antonio Zingarelli's *Giulietta e Romeo,* and Cimarosa's *Matrimonio segreto*) on the same evening. Sauvage was quite clear in a letter to La Rochefoucauld that the departure of the Théâtre anglais was unforeseen and damaging to the theater's interests.[71]

The Odéon managed to bring the English troupe back at the very end of the year but, in doing so, damaged the fortunes of the last translation to ap-

71. F-Pan O³ 1792/V.

TABLE 6. Repertory during Christmas period 1827–28

Date	Théâtre anglais	Odéon: Drama and Comedy	Odéon: Opera
22 December	Jane Shore; The Blue Devils		
23 December		Mérope; L'important; Héritage et mariage	
24 December			Don Juan (prem.)
25 December	CLOSED		
26 December	CLOSED		
27 December	Hamlet; Three Weeks after Marriage		
28 December			Don Juan
29 December	Venice Preserved: The Sleepwalker		
30 December		L'homme du monde	Le barbier de Séville
31 December			Don Juan
1 January		L'important; Anglais et français	Les noces de Gamache; Adolphe et Clara
2 January			Don Juan

SOURCES: Draft listings of repertory, available in all the *grands quotidiens* of the era, were assembled from the *Journal de Paris* and subsequently checked against references in the theatrical press, in particular *La Pandore, Le Courrier des Théâtres, Le Frondeur,* and *Le Diable Boiteux.*

pear at the Odéon: Mozart's *Don Giovanni*. Christmas Eve was never a good night on which to mount a premiere of a work that critics hoped might replicate the success of *Robin des bois;* but the immediate context of *Don Juan* was particularly odd (table 6).

Normal practice was to highlight a premiere by surrounding it with well-known and unobjectionable works and then carefully to repeat the performances, often modified in the light of the response to the premiere. The position in which *Don Juan* was placed at the end of 1827 seemed specifically designed to neutralize any impact that it might make. Sauvage might have thought that the romantics who would travel across Paris to hear the English players would also respond well to Mozart's *Don Giovanni*, but it was a much more valuable commodity than Sauvage seemed to think. It had not been heard very much in Paris in recent years. At the Théâtre-Royal italien, it had been heard only six times in 1826, and not at all in 1827; there would be one performance there on 6 March 1828. This would have been an ideal moment to give as high a profile as possible to *Don Juan* at the Odéon, instead of which Sauvage buried its premiere just before the theater closed for Christmas, and in competition with the return of the English troupe. The latter came to the Odéon only five times, but during that time they managed not only to run through most of their repertory but also to premiere *King Lear* with Terry, before they returned again to the Théâtre-Royal italien and other venues.[72]

The fundamental administrative arrangements that had underpinned Bernard's and Frédéric's regimes collapsed in the face of Sauvage's attempts to change the structure and function of the theater. La Rochefoucauld's attempts to merge the theater with the Théâtre de la Porte-St-Martin, and to cut Sauvage's subvention, started as soon as the Odéon reopened for business after the summer of 1827.[73] Sauvage's propensity for legal feuding with his staff and employees hardly helped the matter, but the theater encountered rising debt, and—despite repeated successful requests for advances against subvention in later 1827 and early 1828—he was incapable of keeping the business afloat.[74] His reaction was to close the opera troupe at the Odéon. He proposed this in December 1827, and the resulting fracas was very difficult to hide from the theatrical press.[75] Despite protests from the opera troupe, Sauvage announced in January that contracts for a large number of the artists—MM. Auguste, Sirand, Leclerc, Saint-Preux, and Déricourt; Mesd. Milen, Derfeuille, Durand, and Mondonville—would not be renewed after Easter 1828.[76]

By May 1828, it was clear that Sauvage was unable to pay his staff, and the mayors of the 11th and 12th arrondissements had to write to La Rochefoucauld in defense of the theater if not in support of its manager.[77] By the end of the next month his creditors were prepared to wait no longer.[78] The resulting disturbances of July 1828 were a result of meetings with the creditors that did not reach conclusions that would result in the payment of the actors at the theater. Debts were estimated at Fr 500,000.[79] The actors effectively withdrew their labor in the middle of July and, in response to Sauvage's attempts to put on a performance on 13 July with other actors, the

72. Borgerhoff, *Théâtre anglais*, 111.

73. F-Pan O³ 1792/V; *Journal de Paris*, 5 August 1827.

74. E.g., the mismanaged affairs of Lecomte in April 1828, described below, page 78; and see F-Pan O³ 1792/II.

75. E.g., *Le Courrier des Théâtres*, 3 December 1827.

76. *La Pandore*, 9 January 1828.

77. 25 May 1828 (F-Pan O³ 1793/II).

78. Meetings between Sauvage and his creditors were being set up from 2 July 1828 onward (ibid.).

79. *Journal de Paris*, 13 July 1828.

prefet de police, Louis-Marie de Belleyme, closed the theater;[80] it remained closed until 5 October. Angry exchanges were published in the press between representatives of the Odéon artists and Sauvage,[81] but no resolution was forthcoming. Sauvage was arrested for debt on 9 August and, despite his apparent shortage of money, managed to post bail in the sum of Fr 10,000.

For the next six weeks, the maison du Roi, the employees of the Odéon, Sauvage, and two potential new managers (Charles-Jean Harel and Frédéric Lemétheyer) haggled over the fate of the theater with its creditors.[82] The stage remained dark for two months and was not to see music drama on a regular basis again.[83]

Central to the functioning of the Odéon were its managers, and the four-year life of its opera troupe can be judged according to their success or failure. After two years running the theater, Claude Bernard was considered to have been almost solely responsible for the revival of its fortunes, and it is difficult to disagree with this view. He had worked hard with a lyric troupe that had been restricted in its early months to a repertory of public domain opéra comique that might—uncharitably—be described as the Opéra-Comique's waste bin. Alongside this repertory, however, he had introduced a number of translations of Italian and German music drama, one of which— *Robin des bois*—had such an impact that it immediately solved emergent financial difficulties. Problems with money would never go away, and Bernard's successor, Frédéric du Petit-Méré, also faced the task of putting the theater on a sound financial footing. Unfortunately, both managers left the theater in the middle of negotiations that might have stabilized the theater once and for all: Frédéric withdrew after fifteen months for reasons of ill health and died shortly afterward, and Bernard left hurriedly as a result of what may very well have been blackmail. In consequence, the theater lurched from one period of instability to another. Thomas Sauvage had neither the inclination nor the ability to hold the Odéon together after two serious setbacks, and the unseemly events during the summer of 1828 served to throw into the background the theater's enormous artistic achievements during the previous four years.

The shift away from public-domain opéra comique started by Bernard in late 1824 was continued throughout 1825 with the introduction of more

80. Ibid., 14 July 1828. The correspondence between Belleyme and La Rochefoucauld, dated 13 and 15 July, is F-Pan O³ 1792/II.

81. See the issues of the *Journal de Paris* for 14–17 July 1828.

82. The details are laid bare in F-Pan O³ 1792/I–VI.

83. Other companies put on music drama at the Odéon; the Théâtre italien's use of the hall between October 1838 and March 1841 was the most extensive (Wild, *Dictionnaire*, 294).

Italian and German works alongside the continued performance of works already premiered. Much of the success of Frédéric's regime was founded on plans laid by Bernard—most especially the 1826 "plan," although it is to Frédéric's credit that these projects were pursued relentlessly. Key here was the figure who remained constant throughout the Odéon's involvement in music drama, its music director, Pierre Crémont; closely involved in many individual projects, he would have had a great deal of responsibility during the transition between Bernard and Frédéric.

The increase in activity during the opera troupe's first six months is mirrored by its decline. Laying off a certain proportion of the opera troupe at Easter 1828 pointed the way for Sauvage's gradual rundown and closure of music drama at the theater during the summer of that year.

Chapter 3

Cet ensemble si harmonieux et si parfait—
The Odéon's Personnel

Soloists

Establishing a team of soloists capable of performing such a demanding and fast-changing repertory as the one in place at the Odéon posed problems for Bernard and his successors. Their solution was to recruit successful artists from provincial theaters—Lyon, Marseille, Nantes, and Bordeaux, for example—and to look hard at artists at the secondary theaters in Paris who might be suitable for work in an opera house. The opening cast was heavily dependent on artists with backgrounds in the provinces. The two tenors, Campenaut and Lecomte, had recently arrived from Bordeaux and Lille respectively (figures 10 and 11). Of the other male principals, Camoin (*premier basse-taille*), came from outside the capital, and Valère (*jeune premier basse-taille*) also came from Lille.[1] The origins of the artist taking the *deuxième et troisième basse-taille* roles, variously known as Auguste Maire or Lemaire, are unknown; he was already being replaced during the first run of *Robin des bois* and did not figure in the 1825 listings for the theater. Léon-Bizot seems to have been a Parisian, and one of the few artists working at the theater both when it opened and when it closed; he switched from second tenor to *baryton* in 1825 when the *baryton* from the opening season, Gignon, left. Among the women, Mme Camoin had come to Paris with her husband, and Mlle Florigny was recruited from the Gymnase dramatique. Mme Letellier reportedly appeared at the Opéra-Comique before she came to the Odéon (figure 12).[2] But Montano was in many respects the artistic leader of the

---

1. *Journal de Paris,* 9 May 1824.
2. *Le Diable Boiteux,* 8 March and 28 April 1824.

73

Figure 10. Campenaut in the role of Almaviva (*Le barbier de Séville*). From *Petite galerie
dramatique, ou Recueil de différents costumes
d'acteurs des théâtres de la capitale* (Paris:
Hautecoeur-Martinet, n.d.), 6:556.

vocal principals. Her long career had included singing in Paris at the Théâtre des Variétés over a decade before the opening of the Odéon to music
drama, and work in Antwerp, Saint Petersburg, and Brussels.[3]

Patterns of recruitment that depended in part on provincial theaters
continued throughout the 1820s but were tempered by an increasing de-
pendence on artists with experience in the capital. Léon-Chapelle joined
the troupe in 1825 from Amiens but lasted only a season.[4] In the same year
Mlle Lemoule was recruited from Brussels via Rouen[5] and remained with
the theater until it stopped performing music drama. Although Gilbert

3. *La Pandore*, 4 January 1824.
4. *Le Courrier des Théâtres*, 19 April 1824.
5. Ibid., 19 July 1824.

Figure 11. Lecomte in the role of Almaviva
(*Le barbier de Séville*). From Alexandre-Marie
Colin, *Collection de portraits des artistes des théâtres
de Paris, dessinés et lithographiés d'après nature*
(Paris: Noël, n.d.), 41.

Duprez had been in Italy immediately before his arrival at the Odéon, he
was a product of the École royale de chant; similarly Monnier came from
the Opéra-Comique, and Peronnet, a key artist until the end of the opera
seasons, had worked previously at the Gymnase dramatique after work in
Marseille and Bordeaux.[6]

Even once the opera troupe had been successfully recruited, maintain-
ing a stable team was a serious challenge to any manager, for whom the possibility of one of the Odéon artists being called to appear at one of the other
royal theaters was a constant threat. The most successful and experienced
of the Odéon's tenors, Lecomte, was at the center of such a bid and serves
as an example of how vigilant the Odéon's management had to be in pro-
tecting its greatest artists but also how, once they had a sense of their own
value, soloists could create easily as many problems if they were retained.

6. *Almanach des spectacles pour l'an 1825* (Paris: Barba, 1825), 382.

Figure 12. Letellier in the role of Nancy
(*Robin des bois*). From *Petite galerie dramatique, ou Recueil de différents costumes d'acteurs
des théâtres de la capitale* (Paris: Hautecoeur-
Martinet, n.d.), 6:558.

His voice was, by all accounts, brilliant with a very wide range and was
coupled to a stage presence that made, for example, his portrayal of the
title role in Rossini's *Othello* the talk of Paris. He not only took the principal roles that might have been expected of him—the title roles in *Don
Juan* and *Ivanhoé*, Almaviva in *Le barbier de Séville*, Lavarenne in *Marguerite
d'Anjou*—but was also successful in roles in such public-domain repertory
as *Richard Coeur-de-Lion* and *Le tableau parlant*. Despite the account given
by Eugène-François Garay de Monglave (known as Maurice Dufresne)—
pointing to a deficient technique and occasional poor tuning—reviews of
Lecomte's performances during the 1820s did not echo such infelicities.[7]
He was respected both as a singer and an actor, although it was said that
he tended to project roles from singspiel with the degree of gravity that was

7. Eugène-François Garay de Monglave, *Nouvelle biographie théâtrale* (Paris, 1826), 110–11.

more appropriate to opera seria. The esteem in which he was held was reflected in a very successful benefit on 18 January 1825;[8] when a further benefit performance was given on 24 February 1827, and the outcome was disappointing (the box grossed only Fr 1,500), Frédéric had promised Lecomte Fr 2,500 and was therefore obliged to made good the difference from the administrative coffers.[9]

Within six months after the opening of the Odéon to music drama, Lecomte was claimed by the Académie royale de musique. As ever, Bernard's astute handling of the affair protected the Odéon's interests and retained Lecomte at the theater. In such negotiations, the artists themselves were powerless to affect their positions and were effectively traded by managers of opera houses with the process overseen by the minister at the maison du Roi. The Académie royale de musique had asked to borrow Lecomte during the latter part of 1824 to cover for Nourrit (*père*), who was entitled to holiday; Bernard acquiesced, but Nourrit—like many of his colleagues— bought out his holiday entitlement and Lecomte was able to continue at the Odéon uninterrupted because he was not needed at the Académie royale de musique. It was exactly this procedure that the administrators of the Académie royale de musique were trying to circumvent when they attempted to recruit Lecomte permanently. The manager of the Académie royale de musique, Raphaël de Frédot Duplantys, explained that the institution had only two tenors, Nourrit *père* and *fils*, and that this position meant that they could negotiate an increase in the cost of buying out their holidays (the family in effect had a monopoly); the presence of a third permanent tenor—Lecomte—would weaken the Nourrit family's position and strengthen that of the theater. Bernard's response was that he could allow the Académie royale de musique to continue to borrow Lecomte only when he was needed; he was supported by La Rochefoucauld, and when the conseil d'adminstration of the Académie royale de musique was unable to come up with an alternative solution to the matter, Bernard's was adopted.[10]

Lecomte pulled the Odéon's administration in two directions; he was one of its finest artists but difficult to control. Managers had to ensure that he was sufficiently happy to remain at the theater but also had to put up with inconsistency and unreliability. The beneficiary of a private income (he was always referred to Sieur Lecomte in official correspondence), he stood apart from the other principals at the theater in terms of salary, status, and the respect in which he was held by the administration. He had enjoyed four

8. *Journal de Paris*, 20 January 1825.

9. *La Pandore*, 24 February 1827.

10. The contents of this paragraph are based on documents contained in F-Pan O³ 1792/VI.

very successful years in Lille before joining the Odéon and in September 1824 was offered the management of the theater there.[11] By the end of October, he had obtained the license to run the theater for five years from 20 April 1825; it was only the promise of the call to the Académie royale de musique that made him give up the opportunity.[12] Even without such distractions as the Académie royale de musique or the theater in Lille, Lecomte could cause the Odéon difficulty. Productions were interrupted because of the death of Lecomte's father,[13] and—as has already been seen—a performance of Meyerbeer's *Marguerite d'Anjou* was nearly abandoned because of Lecomte's equine misadventures. The evening was able to continue only because the manager, possibly sensitive to Lecomte's unreliability, had already asked Coeuriot to understudy the role of Lavarenne (figure 13).[14] Lecomte's illness also disrupted early performances of *Ivanhoé*.[15] But the same journals that were so weary of Lecomte's indispositions were excited about his recovery, and their advice was clear: "Lecomte is fit, and *Ivanhoé* plays tonight; leave home early!"[16]

It would have been unreasonable to expect the state of affairs between the theater and Lecomte to have been sustained, and after Sauvage had taken over from Frédéric, matters began to deteriorate. During the summer of 1827 the artists at the Odéon had lost two months' salary while the theater was being renovated. Lecomte insisted on repayment of this salary, and Sauvage—who had little choice if he was not to lose his star tenor—agreed to pay Fr 600 per month. Because of the financial difficulties of the theater, Sauvage and Lecomte settled on Fr 300 in March 1828 and Fr 900 in April. The same evening that the deal was struck, Lecomte threatened not to perform if he was not paid immediately, because he knew that Sauvage had a Fr 1,000 note in his pocket. The former repeated his threat at the box office, outside the theater, in the place de l'Odéon, and even in the cafés around the square. Sauvage, challenged with a public threat to his authority, refused to pay until after the performance. Because artists were obliged to perform by law, when Lecomte refused to perform the matter was turned over to the commissaire de police and the former was accordingly imprisoned overnight. The prefet de police forbade Lecomte to perform and the latter agreed to resign forthwith.[17] By the beginning of the next month, Lecomte had taken up a new position in Brussels.[18]

11. *Le Courrier des Théâtres,* 10 September 1824.
12. *La Pandore,* 28 October 1824.
13. *Le Frondeur,* 22 November 1825.
14. *Le Courrier des Théâtres,* 14 April 1826.
15. Ibid., 1 October 1826.
16. Ibid., 4 October 1826.
17. This paragraph is based on documents in F-Pan O³ 1792/VI.
18. *La Pandore,* 10 May 1828.

Figure 13. Coeuriot in the role of
MacGregor (*La dame du lac*). From *Petite
galerie dramatique, ou Recueil de différents
costumes d'acteurs des théâtres de la capitale*
(Paris: Hautecoeur-Martinet, n.d.), 6:566.

Soloists at the Odéon included those at the very beginning and very end
of their careers. Montano was one of most experienced members of the
opera troupe when the Odéon opened in April 1824. She was to stay at the
Odéon until, her voice exhausted, she left Paris for Naples. Apart from a
tour in the first half of 1826 during which her greatest triumphs were in
Bordeaux, she took every contralto role available at the Odéon; of these,
her greatest successes were Rosine in *Le barbier de Séville*, Malcolm in *La dame
du lac*, and Isaure in *Marguerite d'Anjou*. Montano was one of the few artists
at the Odéon who had the confidence to insert extraneous arias into the
role she was singing. Contemporary responses to her inclusion of a Rossini
aria in the Odéon's version of Devienne's *Visitandines* as *Les Français au sérail*
were confused. Montano was a popular figure, but many considered that
these interpolations were misconceived. It was thought inappropriate to

have given so many arias to a *comprimaria* (Montano's role was Zélia in *Les Français au sérail*), because they disrupted the action.[19] Montano might well have been encouraged in her inclusion of Rossini, because a year before, when she had substituted an (unidentified) French aria for "Di tanti palpiti" in the lesson scene in *Le barbier de Séville,* the audience and critics had been hostile: they liked Rossini's aria better than any extraneous—but indigenous—interpolation, and the episode prompted a reflection on the respective values of Italian aria (much preferred) and French *romance.*[20]

Despite possibly misjudging her audience from time to time—in the context of consistent surefootedness throughout her time at the Odéon— Montano was one of the most successful Odéon artists in the wider Parisian musical field. The publication of the full score of *La dame du lac* with a portrait of Montano as a frontispiece was a tribute paid rarely to any artist on the Parisian lyric stage, and almost unheard of at the Odéon. Perhaps even more striking was Montano's central role in one of the *concerts spirituels* planned for Holy Week in 1825. Some of the finest singers in Paris were to support her in an event that any principal from the Académie royale de musique or Opéra-Comique would envy (described in chapter 4).

Within weeks of her arrival at the Odéon, Montano had become "the [Giuditta] Pasta of the faubourg St-Germain."[21] Given the affection with which Pasta was then regarded at the Théâtre-Royal italien, this was praise of a high order. Montano's reputation gave her a rare authority at the Odéon that could stand her in good stead even in the face of disaster. Winter's *Sacrifice interrompu* had been in the repertory for over a year when it was decided to reduce it from three acts to two.[22] Six weeks later, Montano was about to deliver Elvire's act-three aria (now in act two) when the curtain came down on her head because the stagehand thought that the old second act had finished. In the normal course of events, and if other singers had been involved, this would have resulted in a near riot but—apart from isolated whistles and jeers directed toward the operator of the curtain—under the spell of Montano's authority, the audience calmly waited for the curtain to be raised so that the act could continue.[23]

By the time of her return from Bordeaux in the summer of 1826, Montano's status at the Odéon meant that she was capable of bringing not only the activities of the theater but the traffic of the entire neighborhood to a halt.

19. Ibid., 1 July 1825.
20. *Le Diable Boiteux,* 6 July 1824; *Le Courrier des Théâtres,* 8 July 1824.
21. *Le Courrier des Théâtres,* 9 May 1824.
22. *La Pandore,* 9 September 1825.
23. Ibid., 24 October 1825.

Last Saturday [1 July 1826], the entire neighborhood of the Chambre des Pairs was on the lookout. Women opened their shutters, children leaned out of their windows, people crowded into the streets, the greengrocers came out of their shops. Suddenly the firemen from the Odéon theater appear on the roofs. Madame Montano, who lives opposite, appears at her window, her eyes bathed in tears, her hands raised to the sky. Everyone is concerned, everyone is curious and no one can explain the great happening that is causing so much confusion. Eventually, everyone hurries into the Jardin du Luxembourg; stones are thrown, trees are climbed. A child soon returns surrounded by the crowd who utter cries of joy. He goes up to Madame Montano who receives him with open arms. Rosine's tears no longer flow; the child returns her fugitive parakeet: Vert-Vert has returned to the parlor.[24]

In 1826, the influential Monglave pointed to Montano's brilliant early career based on a fine voice, but also to the first physical and vocal hints of rapidly approaching age. While she could conceal the damage to the former with sartorial sleight-of-hand, she could disguise the latter only by transposition.[25] Whether this is simply the fact that Montano's voice moved down in range or she was transposing numbers during the course of her time at the Odéon is difficult to say.[26] Nevertheless, Monglave was of the opinion that she was due for retirement from the stage and that she should restrict herself to teaching.

Public reaction to Montano's declining powers did not appear until May the following year. Although she had sung Rosine in a way that had pleased everyone on 6 May 1827,[27] her performance at a concert a fortnight later marked the beginning of the end. The Bohrer brothers gave a concert at the Odéon on 19 May in which Montano and Pouilley sang a duet that was

24. Samedi dernier [1 July 1826] tout le voisinage de la chambre des pairs était sur pied. Les dames ouvraient leurs persiennes, les enfants se penchaient à leurs croisées, le peuple se pressait dans les rues, les épiciers sortaient de leurs boutiques. Tout à coup les pompiers de garde au théâtre de l'Odéon se montrent sur les toits. Madame Montano, qui loge vis-à-vis, paraît à sa fenêtre, les yeux baignés de larmes, les mains levées au ciel. Tout le monde est inquiet, tout le monde s'interroge, et personne ne peut expliquer le grand événement qui cause tant de confusion. Enfin l'on se précipite dans le jardin de Luxembourg; on jette des pierres, on monte aux arbres. Un enfant revient bientôt environné de la foule qui pousse des cris de joie. Il monte chez Mme Montano, qui le reçoit à bras ouverts. Les larmes de Rosine ne coulent plus; l'enfant lui a rendu son perruche fugitive: Vert-Vert est rentré au parloir (*L'Opinion*, 4 July 1826). On 2 November *L'Opinion* gave the correct name of Montano's parakeet as Jacquot.

25. Monglave, *Nouvelle biographie*, 134–35.

26. The published scores would not have recorded ad hoc transpositions, and the manuscript performance material—which might have betrayed such transposition—has not survived.

27. *Journal de Paris*, 6 May 1827.

"heard with displeasure. Mme Montano has completely lost her voice."[28] Montano did not need to be told twice. On 23 June, it was reported that she had broken her engagement with the Odéon, and by 13 September that she had accepted a position in Naples.[29] On her way there, she sang in a production of Meyerbeer's *Marguerite d'Anjou*.[30] Montano's career in Paris had ended.

At the same time that Montano ended a distinguished career at the Odéon, Gilbert Duprez made his debut there. He developed his voice in Italy between 1829 and 1836 and created the role of Edgardo in Gaetano Donizetti's *Lucia di Lammermoor* at the Teatro San Carlo in Naples on 26 September 1835. On the basis of this success, he returned to Paris as the logical successor to Adolphe Nourrit. The list of works in which he created the tenor roles reads like a history of French grand opéra from 1838 (Berlioz's *Benvenuto Cellini*) to 1847 (Verdi's *Jérusalem*). He would become one of the most significant vocal pedagogues of the second half of the nineteenth century.[31] But before he left for Italy in 1829, Duprez served the Odéon for nearly three years.[32] The Odéon had recruited him in November 1825, on his return to Paris from a sojourn in Italy. Léon-Bizot, second tenor at the theater, who had taught Duprez while he was at Alexandre-Étienne Choron's École royale et spéciale de chant, may have facilitated his acquisition. Duprez's debut at the Odéon was in the role of Almaviva in the *Le barbier de Séville*, and was followed closely in the press.[33]

Duprez's debut was marked by his vocal ability and his weakness as an actor. "As an actor, M. Duprez is not very able: from his extraordinary gestures, from the undulating movements of head, it is clear that he has returned from Italy."[34] The press were entirely agreed on his good voice, agility, and sound technique. His voice was sweet and *flûté* and reminded one reviewer of the voice of the castrato Giovanni Battista Velluti; another scolded Duprez for a predilection for *roulades* (although that might well

28. A été écouté avec défaveur. Mme Montano a tout-à-fait perdu sa voix (*La Pandore*, 21 May 1827).

29. *Le Courrier des Théâtres*, 23 June 1827; *Journal de Paris*, 13 September 1827.

30. *Le Courrier des Théâtres*, 3 November 1827.

31. See the summary of Duprez's career by John Warrack and Sandro Corti ("Duprez, Gilbert," *The New Grove Dictionary of Opera*, ed. Stanley Sadie [London: Macmillan, 1992], 1: 1281).

32. This and the following paragraph correct the curious statement by Karl-Josef Kutsch and Leo Riemens ("Duprez, Gilbert," *Großes Sängerlexikon* [Bern: Francke, 1987–94], 1:801) that Duprez's début at the Odéon had come to nothing.

33. Reviews of Duprez's début are in *Le Frondeur*, *La Pandore*, and *Le Courrier des Théâtres*, 2 December 1825; and in *L'Opinion*, 10 December 1825.

34. Comme acteur, M. Dupré n'est pas très habile: à ses gestes outrés, à ses mouvements de tête onduleux, on voit qu'il revient d'Italie (*Le Frondeur*, 2 December 1825).

have been a ritual criticism from a French critic for any singer trained in Italy). Duprez's singing of lines that required a tender or impassioned delivery was also received favorably. In general the reviews were full of praise and anticipated greater things to come. Duprez was under the shadow of Lecomte throughout 1826 and 1827 but took on a number of the latter's roles: the title role in *Ivanhoé* and Tony in *Robin des bois,* as well as Almaviva. He also participated in such new works as *Le neveu de Monseigneur, Le testament,* and *Les bohémiens.* The circumstances of the composition and first performance of Duprez's *Cabane du pêcheur* at Versailles remain mysterious; the libretto was by his brother Édouard, and the work remained unpublished. It seems to have had nothing to do with the Odéon.[35] Duprez's wife joined the Odéon troupe in March 1827, and the two could be heard together in Dalayrac's *Adolphe et Clara* in May that year.[36]

International soloists did not often join the opera troupe. Amalia Schütz was one exception who contributed substantially between the end of 1826 and the middle of 1828. Although better known to posterity than most of her colleagues at the Odéon, her time there has been almost entirely disregarded. Her reputation preceded her arrival in Paris in November 1825, and she made her debut at the Théâtre-Royal italien on 14 November in the role of Malcolm in *La donna del lago;* aged twenty-one, she had already sung this role at the Kärntnertortheater in Vienna earlier that year.[37] Despite signing a year's contract at the Théâtre-Royal italien in February 1826, she sang in only eighteen performances between January and October. When her contract expired in October 1826 and she planned to take up an engagement in Genoa, it emerged that Schütz had signed her contract without telling the theater's administration that she was pregnant, which explains the greatly reduced number of performances that she gave.[38] Schütz's doubtful position at the Théâtre-Royal italien in September and October 1826 had, among other results, the effect of sabotaging a revival of Meyerbeer's immensely successful *Crociato in Egitto.*[39] Despite her cavalier attitude to a contract issued by one of the most prestigious Italian opera houses in Europe, Schütz sang a number of roles: the title role in *La Cenerentola,* Emma in *Zelmira,* Malcolm in *La donna del lago,* Arsace in *Semiramide.* She was greatly overshadowed in the summer of 1826 by Henrietta Sontag, who took over the role in *La Cenerentola* on July 26. Fortunately for Schütz,

35. *La Pandore,* 15 January 1827.

36. *Journal de Paris,* 21 May 1827.

37. Kutsch and Riemens' entry for Amalie Schütz-Oldosi (*Großes Sängerlexikon,* 3:906–7) makes no reference to Schütz's activities at the Théâtre italien or at the Odéon.

38. *Le Courrier des Théâtres,* 4 November 1826; this exchange is in F-Pan O[3] 1742/134.

39. Mark Everist, "Giacomo Meyerbeer and Music Drama at the Paris Odéon during the Bourbon Restoration," *19th-Century Music* 16 (1993): 135–36.

the difference between the two singers' voice types minimized obvious competition and meant that Sontag took the roles of Rosina in *Il barbiere di Siviglia,* Carolina in *Il matrimonio segreto,* and Elena in *La donna del lago.*

The projected engagement in Genoa evaporated, and Frédéric du Petit-Méré contracted with Schütz for a few performances at the Odéon before her departure from the capital. (Despite continued announcements of a revival of *Il crociato in Egitto,* she was not to sing again at the Théâtre-Royal italien for nearly two years.) [40] Schütz's first performance as Anna in *Robin des bois* was an enormous success, and Frédéric was forced to repeat the performance on two consecutive evenings. During the eighteen months that she was at the Odéon, Schütz took on many of the roles that had been key to the theater's success: Anna in *Robin des bois,* Rosine in *Le barbier de Séville,* and Édelmone in *Othello.* She was also destined for one of the principal roles in the Meyerbeer pastiche *La nymphe du Danube,* which was never completed.[41] Comparisons were drawn between Schütz and the English theater company then in Paris: both were highly valued in Paris but apparently scorned in their home countries.[42] Schütz's portrayal of Édelmone in *Othello* was favorably compared to Harriet Smithson's depiction of the same character that Odéon audiences had witnessed the previous month.[43]

Although Schütz was an obvious asset to the Odéon, she was a vulnerable target for predatory critics; during April and May, she was the victim of a savage hostile campaign. On 22 March 1827, *Le Courrier des Théâtres* aligned itself with most other journals in Paris when it celebrated Schütz's success and suggested that she should be given even greater exposure. During the month that followed, there was a serious break between the *Courrier* and Schütz or her husband, and the journal subjected the premiere of *La folle de Glaris,* in which Schütz was taking the title role, to a scathing critique. Although the opening night—as was the tradition at the Odéon little more than an open rehearsal—was less than successful, by the second and third performances *La folle de Glaris* was drawing crowds from all over Paris.[44] Reports in *Le Courrier des Théâtres* came close to being mendacious: the box-office receipts for the third performance of *La folle de Glaris* were Fr 400, it commented, and Schütz's salary was Fr 12,000; in other words, the theater had been more or less empty, and such a return hardly justified her salary. During the previous week, Schütz's husband had remonstrated with the journal's management and published a letter that resulted in yet more hos-

40. E.g., *Le Courrier des Théâtres,* 12 November 1826.

41. Everist, "Meyerbeer," 136–43.

42. *Le Courrier des Théâtres,* 13 October 1827. It is not clear what evidence forms the basis of the claim that the English theater was not appreciated in London.

43. *Journal de Paris,* 26 September 1827.

44. Ibid., 27 April 1827.

tility from the journal. The affair was perplexing because other journals were very supportive of Schütz's endeavors; on 25 April, for example, the *Journal de Paris* had likened Schütz to Pasta, an accolade that Schütz shared with Montano. *Le Courrier des Théâtres* continued its attacks on Schütz until November when it gave up. At the height of its campaign, it changed her name to *Mme Chute* (failure).[45] As 1827 turned into 1828, things began to go less well for Schütz. Her benefit on 11 February 1828 was a disaster, and by the summer, the theater itself was in serious financial trouble. In August 1828 she took the title role in *Tancredi* and the role of Rosina in *Il barbiere di Siviglia* at the Théâtre-Royal italien and finally left the capital for a career in Italy, where her greatest triumph was the premiere of Donizetti's *Campanello di notte* at the Teatro Nuovo in Naples on 1 June 1836.[46]

Husband-and-wife teams who took roles in music drama at the Odéon could be both an advantage and a disadvantage. Valère and Mlle Florigny were part of the original opera troupe at the Odéon and were married in the summer of 1824 (figures 14 and 15). In June that year they were summoned together to the Opéra-Comique.[47] Poaching a married couple might have been efficient for the Opéra-Comique, but it was doubly problematic for the Odéon. Bernard was unable to counter the Opéra-Comique's advances, and the couple were due to make their debut in April 1825. At that point the Opéra-Comique's plan backfired: Mme Florigny-Valère, possibly weakened by serious bronchial difficulty the previous winter, died in childbirth in May that year.[48] Valère was described both as a *jeune premier basse-taille* and as a *basse chantante*.[49] Press reports were indulgent and stressed his youth and ability to develop.[50] His debut was in *Le barbier de Séville* as Basile, and he was especially praised for his performance of the "calumny" aria.[51] When a debutant, Adrien, substituted for him in June 1824, the two singers' performances of the same aria attracted comment. One critic noted the setting of the lines "Et l'on voit le pauvre diable/menacé comme un coupable" and claimed that Adrien sang them as if he were suffering from the effects of calumny rather than planning it (example 1).[52]

Suggesting that Valère projected these lines rather successfully, the reviewer noted that "Basile speaks about calumny in the same way as a lover

45. E.g., *Le Courrier des Théâtres*, 14 May 1827.

46. Kutsch and Riemens, *Sängerlexikon*, 3:907. She took the role of Serafina alongside Giorgio Ronconi and Raffaele Cassaccia.

47. *La Pandore*, 22 June 1824.

48. Ibid., 25 May 1825.

49. *Almanach royal* (1824), 88; *Journal des Débats*, 9 April 1824.

50. *Le Courrier des Théâtres*, 7 May 1825.

51. *La Pandore*, 20 May 1824.

52. *Le Diable Boiteux*, 22 June 1824.

Example 1. Rossini/Castil-Blaze, *Le barbier de Séville*. Aria "C'est d'abord rumeur légère," bars 72–90.

Figure 14. Valère in the role of Richard
(*Robin des bois*). From *Petite galerie dramatique, ou Recueil de différents costumes d'acteurs
des théâtres de la capitale* (Paris: Hautecoeur-
Martinet, n.d.), 6:557.

speaks about his mistress." Valère took the role of Richard (Caspar) in the
premiere of *Robin des bois* and was one of the few to be praised.[53] When the
announcement of his call to the Opéra-Comique was made, Margaillon was
named as his successor, and Valère made his successful debut at the Opéra-
Comique on 22 July 1825.[54]

Mlle Florigny was better known than her husband-to-be when they both
started work with the Odéon troupe in 1824. She was employed as one of
two *premières cantatrices;* the other was Stéphanie Montano.[55] While Montano
took the role of Rosine in early performances of *Le barbier de Séville,* Florigny
was working her way through the old repertory: Grétry's *Tableau parlant, La*

53. Ibid., 8 December 1824.
54. *Le Courrier des Théâtres,* 21 August 1824; *La Pandore,* 24 July 1825.
55. *Journal des Débats,* 9 April 1824.

Figure 15. Florigny in the role of Anna
(*Robin des bois*). From Alexandre-Marie Colin,
*Collection de portraits des artistes des théâtres
de Paris, dessinés et lithographiés d'après nature*
(Paris: Noël, n.d.), 52.

fausse magie, and *Zémire et Azor*.[56] She also sang in *Les trois genres*.[57] Although
she was a successful Anna in *Robin des bois* (she, like her husband, was one
of the very few artists who were praised at the premiere), her greatest success was as Ninette in *La pie voleuse* in August and September 1824. This was
one of the occasions when the Odéon mounted a translation of a Rossini
at the same time that the Théâtre italien put on a version of the original.
Florigny's interpretation was viewed as favorably as had been Ester Mombelli's at the Théâtre italien.[58]

    56. E.g., *Le Courrier des Théâtres*, 22 May 1824 (*Le tableau parlant*); *Le Diable Boiteux* (*La fausse
magie*), 23 May 1824; *La Pandore*, 20 June 1824 (*Zémire et Azor*).
    57. *Le Courrier des Théâtres*, 29 April 1824.
    58. Ibid., 18 August 1824.

Mlle Lemoule replaced Florigny as *première chanteuse* after the latter's ill-fated move to the Opéra-Comique; she was to remain at the Odéon until the beginning of 1828.[59] Mondonville arrived at the Odéon from the Opéra-Comique in 1826 and made his debut in May of that year.[60] By December 1826, the two had married. They continued successful careers at the Odéon until 1828 when, sensing the impending difficulties with Sauvage and his administration, they both left for the Opéra-Comique. Claude Bernard had no small difficulty recruiting Mondonville. Having made his debut with some success at the Opéra-Comique, Mondonville could reasonably have expected to rise there to the rank of *sociétaire*. When he lost his position, the Opéra-Comique seemed unwilling to allow Bernard to give him a home at the Odéon; up to a week before his debut, the press did not know if he had been recruited or not.[61] Mondonville's debut at the Odéon was a spectacular success: he was paired with Peronnet, who was also making his debut at the theater, and they took the roles, respectively, of Figaro and Almaviva in *Le barbier de Séville*. By all accounts, Mondonville was well suited to the role. A contemporary described him as "a little round and fat man, with a chubby, interesting face, expressive eyes, a mocking smile: a consummate actor and a first-class singer."[62] Reviews of his debut gave a detailed account of his abilities, gently chiding him for his provincial ornamentation in dubious taste. He was criticized for attempting to imitate the legendary Nicolas-Jean-Blaise Martin without the benefit of the same voice and for overusing falsetto in such roles as Figaro in *Le barbier de Séville*.[63] Other critics pointed to "the beauty of his low notes, the mellowness of his *fioriture* [that] repeatedly excited approving murmurs."[64] During the short period he was at the Odéon, Mondonville was assigned, in addition to Figaro, the title role in *Les noces de Figaro*, Crispin (*Les folies amoureuses*), the male lead in the aborted *Nymphe du Danube*, and Sgnarelle (*Don Juan*).

Mlle Lemoule joined the Odéon after a career in Brussels and Rouen. She made her debut in May 1825 (shortly before the death of her predecessor, Florigny-Valère), in the role of Rosine in *Le barbier de Séville*. Her voice was praised for its rare brilliance and purity but she was criticized for a lack of taste, and for overornamentation that distorted the existing melody. She was recommended to find a good teacher.[65] By mid-July, she

59. Ibid., 19 July 1824.

60. Ibid., 7 May 1825.

61. *La Pandore*, 1 May 1825.

62. Petit homme gros et rond, figure grassouillette et piquante, yeux expressifs, sourire moqueur, acteur consommé, chanteur du premier mérite (Monglave, *Nouvelle biographie*, 133).

63. *Le Courrier de Théâtres*, 9 May 1826.

64. La beauté de ses notes graves, le moelleux de ses fioriture ont excité à plusieurs reprises des murmures approbateurs (*Le Frondeur*, 11 May 1826).

65. *Le Diable Boiteux*, 7 May 1825.

had taken at least part of this advice and was taking lessons from the veteran artist from the Opéra-Comique, Louis-Antoine-Eléonore Ponchard.[66] She continued to take over the late Florigny-Valère's roles, beginning with Ninette in *La pie voleuse.* In the competition with the Théâtre italien sparked off by Florigny and Mombelli, she did not make the same impression as her predecessor. Comparing the two versions of Rossini's *Otello,* it was said that "she reaches the high notes with enough ease, but she lacks consistency and security in the middle register; this is no doubt the reason why she made so little impact in the fine duet 'Je veux de mon amie.'"[67] Much of the late summer 1825 was clouded by her sickness, and it was only in November, when she took on the role of Hélène in *La dame du lac,* that she began to realize her full potential.[68] Lemoule stayed at the Odéon even when the theater in Rouen was entitled to have her back, and the manager in Rouen had to be paid Fr 12,000 to release her (figures 16 and 17).[69]

The Odéon's institutionalized distinction between "modern" translations and works from the *ancien répertoire* reflected in different styles of singing. The distinction exemplified in the works of Rossini and Grétry, dramatized on the boards of the Odéon almost every night, was one of the largest. Most singers moved from one style to another with reasonable ease or, at least, evolved a mode of delivery that would work in both repertories. Two exceptions, Peronnet representing the new and Mme Meyssin the old, give some idea of the ways in which the two styles of singing differed, and of the tensions that resulted from this coexistence in the mid 1820s.

Peronnet made his debut in a performance of *Le barbier de Séville* on 6 May 1826. He had "a tenor voice of the most pleasant timbre, restrained on low notes and extensive on high ones; he makes use of this falsetto with great artistry and ornaments with an extraordinary facility; however, he lacks power and scarcely makes himself heard in ensembles."[70] He was soon taking principal roles in *Le neveu de Monseigneur, Les folies amoureuses, L'école de Rome,* and *Les bohémiens.* Apart from pointing to his weakness as an actor, Monglave was generous in his praise of Peronnet but was quite clear that the singer's lack of power and his enthusiasm for ornamentation meant that

---

66. *La Pandore,* 14 July 1825.

67. Elle atteint les notes élevées avec assez de facilité, mais elle manque de consistance et de fermeté dans le médium; c'est à cette cause sans doute qu'il faut attribuer le peu d'effet qu'elle a produit dans le beau duo "Je veux de mon amie" (*Le Diable Boiteux,* 26 July 1825).

68. See *Le Frondeur,* 8 November 1825; *La Lorgnette,* 9 November 1825.

69. *Le Courrier des Théâtres,* 20 March 1826.

70. Une voix de ténor du timbre le plus agréable, restreinte dans les sons graves, et très étendue à l'aigu; il se sert de ce fausset avec beaucoup d'art, et brode avec une facilité extraordinaire; toutefois il manque de force, et se fait à peine entendre dans les morceaux d'ensemble (*Journal de Paris,* 8 May 1826).

Figure 16. Lemoule in the role of
Marguerite (*Marguerite d'Anjou*). From
*Petite galerie dramatique, ou Recueil de dif-
férents costumes d'acteurs des théâtres de la
capitale* (Paris: Hautecoeur-Martinet, n.d.),
6:571.

"Peronnet will never sing Grétry; he proved it a few days ago in *Zémire et
Azor.*"[71] Mme Meyssin made her debut at the Odéon on 27 April 1825. Her
first role was Hélène in Grétry's *Sylvain,* and by all accounts she was very
successful.[72] Other works from the *ancien répertoire* in which she sang were
Richard Coeur-de-Lion and *Raoul Barbe-Bleu,* and she seems rarely to have
participated in the modern repertory of Rossini and German composers

71. M. Peronnet ne chantera jamais Grétry: il nous l'a prouvé, il y a peu de jours dans
l'opéra de *Zémire et Azor* (Eugène-François Garay de Monglave, *Petite biographie théâtrale* [Paris,
1826], 75).

72. *La Pandore,* 27 April 1825.

Figure 17. Lemoule in the role of Lélia
(*Ivanhoé*). From *Petite galerie dramatique,
ou Recueil de différents costumes d'acteurs des
théâtres de la capitale* (Paris: Hautecoeur-
Martinet, n.d.), 6:577.

translated into French. The single exception is the translation of Cimarosa's
Impresario in angustie translated as *La comédie à la campagne,* in which she appeared in August 1825.[73] This narrow range of roles is explained by the
rather full account given of her singing in the *Petite biographie des acteurs et
actrices:*

> The Odéon is the representative of the new school of singing. But the old
> method, that method that made the powdered wigs swoon with pleasure in
> the orchestra of the Opéra when [Étienne] Lainé, of deafening memory,
> murdered the music of Gluck, is still represented at the faubourg St-Germain

73. *Le Frondeur,* 17 August 1825. It is difficult, however, to argue that Cimarosa constitutes
anything other than an eighteenth-century tradition and has little to do with the style of
singing associate with Rossini.

[Odéon] by two or three singers. Mme Meyssin's singing seems to us, above all, to fulfill the conditions imposed on those hawkers of the *ancien régime* who used to break their audience's eardrums. It is necessary to have seen Mme Meyssin in *Raoul Barbe-Bleu, Sylvain,* and *Richard Coeur-de-Lion* to get an idea of what that old school of music was like. Go and hear her, adversaries of innovation, and then rejoice, if you have the courage, at the expense of Italian singers.[74]

The same critic observed that Meyssin must have had vigorous lungs to detach notes in the way that she did and vigorous ears to put up with the deafening noise that resulted. He continued, "As for the music of Rossini, do not speak to her of it; it's all Greek to her."[75]

Modern voice-types differed from those of the *ancien régime,* and commentators in the 1820s were quick to identify the difference between the two. Mme Meyssin represented an artist of the old school incapable of dealing with the new, and Peronnet was a "modern" with no appreciation of the old repertory. This distinction was couched in terms of an old style that was high in volume and that exploited severe articulations, and a new style in which a tenor with a subtle falsetto and the ability to ornament was unsuited to the works of Grétry and his contemporaries. The Odéon in the mid 1820s witnessed the conquest of an old French style of singing by a modern Italian one; the same victory would be repeated at the Académie royale de musique at the end of the decade.

In opéra comique, in which spoken dialogue alternated with music, differences in ability between acting and singing were a consistent feature of commentaries on performances of music drama. Examples at the Odéon are legion, and accounts of Mlle Pouilley's abilities are instructive. She took over the role of Léonore in *Les folies amoureuses* previously sung by Mlle Florigny and was very well received. She was reputed to be a singing pupil of Rossini, and the critic from the *Diable Boiteux* took this as an asset. He did, however, ask in an incredulous tone who had given her lessons in acting, from which it may be concluded that her stagecraft was less than adequate.[76]

---

74. L'Odéon est le représentant de la nouvelle école de chant. Mais l'ancienne méthode, cette méthode qui faisait pâmer de plaisir les têtes à perruques de l'orchestre de l'Opéra, lorsque Lainé, d'assourdissante mémoire, écorchait la musique de Gluck, est encore représentée au faubourg St-Germain par deux ou trois chanteurs. Le chant de Mme Meyssin nous semble, surtout, remplir toutes le conditions imposées à ces crieurs de l'ancien régime qui brisaient le tympan de leurs auditeurs. Il faut avoir vu Mme Meyssin dans *Raoul Barbe-Bleu, le Sylvain* et *Richard Coeur-de-Lion,* pour se faire une idée de ce qu'était l'ancienne école de musique. Allez l'entendre, adversaires des innovations, et égayez-vous ensuite, si vous en avez le courage, aux dépens des chanteurs italiens (Monglave, *Petite biographie,* 56).

75. Quant à la musique de Rossini, ne lui en parlez pas; c'est du grec pour elle (Monglave, *Nouvelle biographie,* 128–29).

76. *Le Diable Boiteux,* 10 September 1824.

Good acting and singing, when found together, were cause for much praise. The two artists at the Odéon who demonstrated such skill were Peronnet and Montano, although the latter, as reviews of *La dame du lac* suggest, was not immune to charges of paying insufficient attention to dialogue.[77] Even when an artist could act competently as well as sing, this was not always good enough for the critics. The criticism of Lecomte for playing the role of Tony/Max in *Robin des bois* as if he were a Roman emperor can be read as a commentary on the singer's relative abilities in singing and acting.[78] Dorgebray was similarly criticized—in the context of fulsome praise for her singing—for exhibiting a bitter and hard voice in dialogue.[79] Coeuriot's acting focused attention on this issue, however. Poor dialogue, even when well delivered, could amuse the audience.[80] When combined with a less than capable artist, this could be disastrous. Coeuriot's speaking voice was so problematic that it was said that all the works in which he played turned into *opere buffe* because he made the audiences laugh so much. Specifically, his speaking voice was unattractively nasal.[81] It was suggested, entirely logically, that he would be better placed at the Académie royale de musique, where spoken dialogue was not employed. It was also rumored that Schütz spoke French so badly that the dialogue in *Tancrède* was abbreviated to minimize her inability.[82]

The Orchestra

Before 1824, the Odéon had always had an orchestra to play overtures and incidental music for its stage productions. In comparison with what it was to become, the orchestra in the period up to 1824 was of modest proportions; it consisted, in addition to the *chef d'orchestre,* of two each of first violins, second violins, and violas, one cello, two double basses, two flutes, an oboe, a horn, and two bassoons, totaling fifteen players.[83] Four, perhaps five, of the fifteen players were retained in the Odéon orchestra when it turned to music drama: the violinists Seghers, Rivals, and Delbouille and the flutist Advié. It is possible that the bass player, Tillmann, switched to cello in the

---

77. *Le Frondeur,* 11 May 1826 (Peronnet) and 13 May 1826 (Montano); 8 November 1825 (review).

78. *Le Courrier des Théâtres,* 12 March 1825.

79. *Le Diable Boiteux,* 24 April 1825.

80. A good example was the premiere of Weber's *Preciosa* (*Le Frondeur,* 18 November 1825).

81. See references in *La Pandore,* 12 May and 2 November 1825; *Le Frondeur,* 8 November 1825.

82. *Gazette de France,* 7 September 1827.

83. *Almanach des spectacles pour l'an 1824* (Paris; Barba, 1824), 89.

opera orchestra, since a player of that name is listed.[84] After the demise of the opera troupe, the orchestra returned to the same strength it had in early 1824.[85]

During the period 1824–28, the orchestra at the Odéon quadrupled in size and began to rival those of the major lyric theaters in the capital. The largest ensemble in Paris was the orchestra of the Académie royale de musique; the orchestras of the Opéra-Comique, Théâtre italien and the Odéon were all of a similar size.[86] The dimensions of the Opéra-Comique orchestra fluctuated more than the others and was certainly stronger in lower strings; it also tended to have three of most woodwinds, but since the scorings for most of its repertory were for two flutes, oboes, and so on, it seems unlikely that this represented a larger number of players in the pit at any one time. The Odéon orchestra normally consisted of four or more desks of first and second violins, two desks of violas, three of cellos and basses, and single woodwind and brass including four horns and trombones. It might not have been the largest in Paris but, in European terms, could rival all but the very largest orchestras.[87]

In the first four months of 1824, two-thirds of the existing players were released, and a mostly new orchestra that could handle the demands of the repertory that was being planned for the theater put in place. The instrumentalists who continued to play at the theater were deemed some of the least valuable to the new regime.[88] Seghers was demoted to the second desk of first violins and Rivals to the third, whereas they had shared the first desk before 1824. The newcomers were the young men who were to characterize the style of the orchestra during the course of the next five years. The exceptions were Pierre Crémont and Nathan Bloc, who were brought in over the heads of the resident players to provide leadership; this successful team of conductor and leader stayed together until the opera troupe was disbanded in 1828.[89] Some key woodwind players were also more experienced. Paul-Hippolyte Camus had won the first prize for flute at the Conservatoire ten years before the Odéon orchestra was assembled and had previously served at the Théâtre de la Porte-St-Martin and the Gymnase dramatique; the clarinetist Mocker was recruited from the orchestra of the

---

84. *Almanach des spectacles* (1825), 119.

85. Ibid.

86. This commentary is based on the listings in the *Almanach des spectacles* from 1825–28.

87. For a preliminary account of the sizes of orchestras in such a comparison of this sort, see Adam Carse, *The Orchestra from Beethoven to Berlioz: A History of the Orchestra in the First Half of the 19th Century, and of the Development of Orchestral Baton-Conducting* (Cambridge: Heffer, 1948), 18–66 and 487–94.

88. The list of payments is in F-Pan O³ 1793/I.

89. For Crémont's biography, see *FétisB* 2:387–88.

Grand Théâtre in Lyon, where he had been since 1822.[90] Of the new players, many were prizewinners from the Conservatoire, and the Conservatoire continued to supply new players as others left the orchestra.

At its best, the Odéon orchestra could rival every other orchestra in Paris. In the late summer of 1827, it was reported that for some time the Odéon orchestra had been the best in Paris, therefore (with typical Parisian confidence) the best in Europe. The report continued:

> Indeed, who could not be struck by the vigor, the unanimity of the verve of this team of instrumentalists who seem to bring, in the execution of a symphony or an [operatic] accompaniment, all the soul and intelligence that one could wish from each of them in the execution of a concerto. The public, electrified by this so perfect and harmonious ensemble (*cet ensemble si harmonieux et si parfait*) covered the overture to *Le barbier [de Séville]* with applause.[91]

Comparisons were regularly made with the orchestra of the Opéra-Comique —and always in favor of the Odéon—or with the Théâtre italien, deemed roughly comparable to the Odéon orchestra.[92] Direct comparisons with the orchestra of the Académie royale de musique were rarely made, although such a comparison (again in the Odéon's favor) is implicit in the report just cited.

With an orchestra playing seven nights a week, it must have stumbled occasionally. At the very beginning of the opera seasons, the orchestra was lightly chided for accompanying a little heavily in *Les trois genres*.[93] Sometimes, the orchestra as a whole was singled out for criticism, as it was in a review of *Othello* in September 1827; the conductor, Crémont, was held responsible on this occasion.[94] Crémont, however, was largely identified with the success of the orchestra, and it is understandable that when performances were disappointing he received the blame. When judgments of the orchestra's success are examined, however, Crémont too received most of the credit.

The qualities that were regularly and continually admired in the Odéon orchestra were its size, its uniformity of sound, individual technical expertise, intelligence, vigor and spirit, and ensemble (the youth of the orchestra

90. Ibid., 2:171 (Camus), and 6:155–56 (of the father and son named Mocker, the son is probably the Odéon player).

91. En effet, qui ne serait frappé de la vigueur, de l'accord de la verve de cette union d'instrumentistes qui semblent apporter dans l'exécution d'une symphonie ou d'un accompagnement toute l'âme et l'intelligence qu'on pourrait exiger de chacun d'eux en particulier dans l'exécution d'un concerto. Le Public, électrisé par cet ensemble si harmonieux et si parfait, a couvert d'applaudissements l'ouverture du *Barbier* (*Journal de Paris*, 20 August 1827).

92. *Le Diable Boiteux*, 29 May 1824; *La Pandore*, 8 May 1824.

93. *Le Courrier des Théâtres*, 29 April 1824.

94. Ibid., 26 September 1827.

explains many of the more abstract qualities mentioned). Individual technical expertise was taken for granted, and on one occasion when an unidentified woodwind player missed his cue, it was reported in merciless detail in the press (this is the only surviving account of such a disaster).[95] Ensemble was regularly praised and widely discussed. One account written shortly after the premiere of *Robin des bois* employed an extended military metaphor to praise the quality of the orchestra's tutti sound.

> The new order in which M. Crémont has placed his soldiers seems fortunate to me. He has drawn them up according to the nature of the instrument, so that, supported the one by the other, there results from their union a larger power of harmony. Indeed, the violins, surrounded on all sides by the redoubtable double basses, ought to lose their stridency (*éclat*), and the humble flute could scarcely be heard alongside the formidable trombone. When the military phalanxes advance to the front, the soldiers cannot be separated from the army; and if sometimes the latter march pell-mell, it is when victory has deserted their banners.[96]

The description also shows that Crémont laid out his orchestra according to instrumental type (string, wind, brass) and not according to pitch (with higher-pitched instruments at the front of the orchestra and lower-pitched ones at the back). The orchestra could excel in a production that was otherwise wretched. A revival of Dalayrac's *Camille ou Le souterrain* was damned as being of desperate mediocrity, but the critic went on to stress that the music was played by the youngest and the most vigorous orchestra in Paris.[97]

Composers

Among the composers involved at first hand in productions at the Odéon were well-known ones, those making their debut, even members of Parisian orchestras. Established Parisian composers involved in the activities of the Odéon were Auber, Boieldieu, and Hérold, but given that the Odéon was forbidden to produce new opéras comiques, their participation in productions at the Odéon was destined to be marginal.[98] Other living composers

95. Ibid., 3 June 1826.
96. Le nouvel ordre dans lequel M. Crémont a placé ses soldats, me paraît heureux. Il les a rangés par nature d'instrument, de sort que, soutenus l'un par l'autre, il résulte de leur union une plus grande puissance de l'harmonie. En effet, les violons, cernés sur tous les points par les redoutables contrebasses, devaient perdre leur éclat, et l'humble flûte pouvait à peine être entendue à côté du formidable trombone. Quand les phalanges guerrières s'avancent au combat, on ne sépare pas les soldats d'une même arme; et si quelquefois ceux-ci marchent pêle-mêle, c'est lorsque la victoire a déserté leurs drapeaux (*La Pandore*, 20 December 1824).
97. Ibid., 25 October 1827.
98. Scholarly biographical work on these figures is slender. See Charles Malherbe, *Auber* (Paris: Laurens, 1911); Ray Longyear, "D. F. E. Auber: A Chapter in French Opera Comique" (Ph.D. diss., Cornell, 1957); Herbert Schneider, *Chronologisch-thematisches Verzeichnis sämtlicher*

Figure 18. François-Adrien Boieldieu.
Engraving by Edmé Quenedey.

(Winter, Beethoven, Mercadante, Gyrowetz, and Weigl) were involved only
vicariously because their works served as models for productions adapted
without their intervention; none of these composers ever set foot in the
11th arrondissement.[99]

At the time of his only involvement with the Odéon in 1824, François-
Adrien Boieldieu was close to the end of a long and distinguished career
(figure 18). After his contribution to *Les trois genres,* he wrote only a hand-
ful of works; some were collaborations (*Pharamond* in 1825 for the Académie royale de musique and *La marquise de Brinvilliers* in 1831 for the Opéra-
Comique), but others were such fully fledged opéras comiques as *Les deux
nuits* (1829) and the phenomenally successful *Dame blanche* of 1825. And by
the time Auber contributed to *Les trois genres,* his career was a decade old;
he had just produced a successful series of opéra comiques culminating in
Leicester ou Le château de Kenilworth and *La neige ou Le nouvel Éginard* (both

Werke von Daniel François Esprit Auber, 2 vols. (Hildesheim: Georg Olms Verlag, 1994); Lucien
Augé de Lassus, *Boieldieu* (Paris: Laurens, 1908); Georges Favre, *Boïeldieu: sa vie, son oeuvre,* 2
vols. (Paris: Droz, 1944–45); Arthur Pougin, *Hérold* (Paris: Laurens, 1906).

99. Beethoven and Winter would die before the Odéon opera seasons ended, whereas
Weigl, Gyrowetz, and Mercadante lived (respectively) until 1846, 1850, and 1870.

1823). If both Boieldieu and Auber contributed to the Odéon's music drama at the beginning of the period, Auber's younger contemporary, Louis-Joseph-Ferdinand Hérold, contributed to a single production, *Le dernier jour de Missolunghi,* at the end. Hérold lived until 1833. By 1828, the first of his three best-known works, *Marie* (1826), had been premiered at the Opéra-Comique; the two other works by which he is remembered, *Zampa* and *Le pré aux clercs,* both for the Opéra-Comique (in 1831 and 1832 respectively), postdate his involvement with the Odéon. All three composers were active at different theaters. Although Hérold's compositions were almost all for the Opéra-Comique, he spent the period 1826–31 at the Académie royale de musique as vocal director and composed substantial amounts of ballet music.[100]

If one name has been linked to the Odéon, it is that of Castil-Blaze. Yet his involvement with the administration of the theater was much less than has been suggested.[101] Although his translations and adaptations were used at the theater, the largest part of Castil-Blaze's arrangements and pasticci was prepared for theaters in Lyon, Nîmes, Lille, or elsewhere in Paris. Castil-Blaze worked on only three productions specifically for the Odéon: *Robin des bois, La forêt de Sénart,* and *Monsieur de Pourceaugnac. Robin des bois* had been destined for the Gymnase dramatique but found its way to the Odéon via a series of circuitous routes. As a pasticcio of works by Weber, *La forêt de Sénart* was closely associated with *Robin des bois. Monsieur de Pourceaugnac* was the fourth and last in a series of pasticci that Castil-Blaze produced for various theaters and was the only one that was designed with the Odéon in mind. It was perhaps the most unambitious, in consisting mostly of material from Rossini's music dramas from the second decade of the century but—in its use of the music of a single composer—was more in line with other pasticci specifically composed for the Odéon. During this time, Castil-Blaze's energies were equally directed toward writing *feuilletons* for the *Journal des Débats* and developing his own music-publishing business. Like him— and many other musicians in Paris in the period—Antonio Francesco

100. Nicole Wild, *Dictionnaire des théâtres parisiens au XIXe siècle: les théâtres et la musique* (Paris: Amateurs des Livres, 1989), 313. His two deputies were Jean-Marie Schneitzhoeffer and Fromental Halévy. His best-known ballets are *Astolphe et Joconde* (1827), *La somnambule* (1827), *Lydie,* and *La belle au bois dormant* (both 1828). See *FétisB* 4:310.

101. Once Berlioz assigned Castil-Blaze the role of a musical villain, the levels of invention surrounding Castil-Blaze and the Odéon soared, seemingly without reference to the record. The most inventive is the claim that he *directed* the Odéon (Catherine Nazloglou, "Castil-Blaze [Blaze, François Henri Joseph]," *The New Grove Dictionary of Music and Musicians,* ed. Stanley Sadie [London: Macmillan, 1980], 3:872–73). For a more reasoned and better-informed biography, see Donald Garth Gíslason, "Castil-Blaze, *De l'opéra en France* and the Feuilletons of the *Journal des Débats* (1820–1832)" (Ph.D. diss., University of British Columbia, 1992).

Gaetano Saverio Pacini was a publisher who composed and arranged. A friend of Rossini, he undertook the lion's share of work on *Ivanhoé* and probably most, if not all, of *Le neveu de Monseigneur.* His compositional enterprises were limited to three opéras comiques written during the first decade of the century, and he made his subsequent reputation as a publisher.[102] As a composer of opéras comiques, Jean-Frédéric-Auguste Lemierre de Corvey followed an indifferent career in the 1790s and early 1800s that was disrupted by military service (he saw action at Waterloo in 1815). By the middle of the 1820s, he was reduced to correcting proofs for others to support himself and his two daughters. His work on two Rossini translations—*La dame du lac* and *Tancrède*—and on the Rossini pastiche *Le testament* was probably more successful than the two opéras comiques presented at the theater of the same name during the 1820s.[103]

Foreign composers were at an advantage when it came to working at the Odéon, since their works were specifically allowed to be performed there, as long as their libretti were written in, or translated into, French. Rossini may have made fleeting visits, while others—Meyerbeer, Conradin Kreutzer, and Carafa—worked longer at the theater. Even Weber was planning work at the Odéon, despite the apparent difficulties with Castil-Blaze, *Robin des bois,* and *La forêt de Sénart.* Rossini's position at the Odéon is centered on the production of *Ivanhoé* in 1826. Although the arrangement of this pasticcio was entrusted to Pacini, it is clear that Rossini made some musical contribution. He was also widely reported to have been present at the Odéon to supervise performances (though having had troublesome dealings with the Odéon in 1825 concerning the interpolation of a duet from *Semiramide* into the Odéon's arrangement of *La donna del lago* as *La dame du lac,* he seems to have taken not a great deal of interest in the other French translations of his works at the theater). It is quite likely that he undertook the work because of his involvement with Pacini, and if he did, he may have been indirectly involved in the preparation of the pasticcio *Le neveu de Monseigneur,* since this was also prepared by Pacini around the same time. Both *Ivanhoé* and *Le neveu de Monseigneur* could be read as part of Rossini's assimilation of the skills required to write music drama in French. In three months Rossini certainly contributed to two and perhaps three works for the French stage based on his own Italian originals: *Le neveu de Monseigneur* (Odéon, August 1826), *Ivanhoé* (Odéon, September 1826), and *Le siège de Corinthe* (Académie royale de musique, October 1826). *Moïse et Pharaon*

102. What little is known of Pacini's biography is given by Richard McNutt ("Pacini, Antonio Francesco Gaetano Saverio," *Grove 6* 14:66).

103. *FétisB* 5:265. Fétis lists *Le testament* as a work by Lemierre de Corvey and calls *La dame du lac* and *Tancrède* arrangements. The entry in *Grove 6* (10:653) adds dates to some items in the work list but nothing else to the entry in *FétisB.*

would follow in March 1827. As a series of exploratory projects toward the success of *Guillaume Tell* at the Académie royale de musique in 1829, all played a part in Rossini's assimilation of French music drama.

Of the foreign composers active in Paris in the 1820s, none was more ambitious than Giacomo Meyerbeer. Before the premiere of *Robert le diable* in 1831, he had planned or executed works at all four Parisian lyric theaters. The most influential productions were those of *Il crociato in Egitto* at the Théâtre italien and of *Marguerite d'Anjou* at the Odéon.[104] The composer was also proposing a version of *Il crociato in Egitto* at the Académie royale de musique, and the original version of *Robert le diable* had been planned for the Opéra-Comique in 1826–27.[105] On the basis of the achievement of *Marguerite d'Anjou* at the Odéon, the pasticcio *La nymphe du Danube* was to follow.

In between spells of employment at the Kärntnertortheater in Vienna, Conradin Kreutzer visited Paris. He may have come at the suggestion of Amalia Schütz, who apparently was responsible for obtaining Kreutzer's score of *Cordelia* as the basis for *La folle de Glaris* and who played Adèle at the Odéon. It is not certain whether Kreutzer was present for the premiere of *La folle de Glaris* in April 1827; he must have been in the city by the time *L'eau de jouvence* was premiered, since this was a new composition.[106] Exactly what role Jérôme Payer had in bringing Kreutzer to Paris is unclear; he seems to have added numbers to *La folle de Glaris*—for which the production was chastised—and returned to a position in Vienna at the same time as his Viennese colleague.[107]

Michele Carafa could hardly be called a foreign composer in the mid 1820s. Although he did not take up French citizenship until 1834, he had been writing French music drama since 1821 when his *Jeanne d'Arc* was successfully premiered and published with a strategic dedication to Luigi Cherubini. Although he continued to write works for the Italian stage until 1829 (*Le nozze di Lammermoor* was premiered at the Théâtre italien; his last production for an Italian theater had been *Il paria* for La Fenice in 1826), most of his successes were destined for the Opéra-Comique. His reputation rested in the 1820s on *Le solitaire* (1822), *Le valet de chambre* (1823), *Masa-*

104. Francis Claudon, "Meyerbeer: *Il crociato:* le grand opéra avant le grand opéra," in *L'opera tra Venezia e Parigi,* ed. Maria Teresa Muraro (Florence: Olschki, 1988), 119–31; Jean Mongrédien, "Les débuts de Meyerbeer à Paris: *Il crociato in Egitto* au Théâtre Royal Italien," in *Meyerbeer und das europäische Musiktheater,* ed. Sieghart Döhring and Arnold Jacobshagen (Laaber: Laaber, 1998), 64–72.

105. Mark Everist, "The Name of the Rose: Meyerbeer's *opéra comique, Robert le Diable,*" *Revue de musicologie* 80 (1992): 211–50.

106. For the best piece of evidence that Kreutzer was indeed in Paris for the premiere of *L'eau de jouvence,* see the one-line assertion in *FétisB* 5:112.

107. See *La Pandore,* 6 September 1825; *Le Frondeur,* 28 September 1825.

niello (1827—the immediate predecessor to Auber's *Muette d' Portici*), *La violette* (1828), and *Jenny* (1829).[108] Whether the composer was involved in the arrangement of his *Due Figaro* as *Les deux Figaro* at the Odéon is an open question. He was certainly in Paris for the premiere of his *Sangarido* on 19 May 1827 and had presumably been in the city for some time.[109]

Given Weber's discontent over the Odéon's production of *Robin des bois* (discussed below in chapter 9), he seems an unlikely collaborator in music drama at the Odéon, but in fact the composer had been negotiating with the Odéon from late 1825 to put on a revision of *Preciosa* as *Les bohémiens* (it took place posthumously in November 1826) and a Parisian production of *Oberon*. If he had not died in June 1826, *Oberon* would have made a very straightforward adaptation for the Odéon stage because it already had spoken dialogue and could be easily converted to an opéra comique. The private support the theater gave the composer would then have become public, with rather different consequences for the parties' reported relations.[110]

Luc Guénée and Auguste-Gustave Vogt were two instrumentalists from outside the Odéon orchestra who contributed to its musical arrangements. The former was a violinist, and the latter the principal oboist, at the Académie royale de musique.[111] Guénée was responsible for assembling the Mercadante pasticcio *Les noces de Gamache* and may have been involved in the predominantly Rossini pasticcio *Le neveu de Monseigneur*.[112] Vogt, with Crémont, made the musical arrangement of Winter's *Das unterbrochene Opferfest* as *Le sacrifice interrompu;* his compositions consisted predominantly of works for oboe and included an unpublished "Méthode de hautbois." Guénée wrote a range of chamber and instrumental works but also some opéras comiques. *Les noces de Gamache* and *Le sacrifice interrompu* are the only examples, respectively, of the works of Mercadante and Winter mounted at the Odéon, and they may have been the results of particular interests on the part of the two musicians. Vogt's interest in *Le sacrifice interrompu* may have been stimulated by hearing performances of the work when he was with the

108. Julian Budden, "Carafa (de Colobrano), Michele [Michel] (Enrico-Francesco-Vincenzo-Aloiso-Paolo)," *Grove Opera* 1:726–28.

109. *FétisB* 2:183.

110. Even Fétis was unaware of Weber's negotiations with the Odéon. His account of Weber's visit to Paris (*FétisB* 8:431) is dominated by his footnote outlining Weber's visit to his composition class at the Conservatoire, their subsequent stroll on the boulevard Poissonnière, and Fétis's view of Weber's understanding of modality and tonality.

111. Fétis again provides the fullest account of Vogt's career (ibid., 8:380–81); they shared a composition teacher, Jean-Baptiste Rey. For a complete list of works, see Roger Cotte and Françoise Cossart, "Vogt, Gustave" (13:1906–8).

112. Fétis claims that Guénée inserted compositions of his own into his arrangements of Italian music drama (ibid., 4:131) but does not say if the *"several* Italian operas for the French stage" take in more than these pieces at the Odéon.

Napoleonic army in Vienna in 1805; *Das unterbrochene Opferfest* had been premiered there nine years earlier.

Many members of the Odéon orchestra contributed to the musical arrangement of the repertory played at the theater. Of the two musicians who assembled *Louis XII ou La route de Reims,* the shadowy Leroux has left almost no trace at all. His colleague, Alphonse Vergne, was the principal second violin of the Odéon orchestra and not only arranged Mozart's music but wrote two numbers that are attributed to him in the libretto.[113] By far the most prolific musical arranger at the Odéon was Pierre Crémont, the conductor of the orchestra. He was single-handedly responsible for the musical arrangement of *La comédie à la campagne, Preciosa, Marguerite d'Anjou, Les bohémiens,* and *Emmeline ou La famille Suisse* and, with Vogt, of *Le sacrifice interrompu.* Although he worked with a wide range of literary figures, his most frequent collaborator was Thomas Sauvage, with whom he produced *Marguerite d'Anjou, Preciosa, Les bohémiens,* and the aborted *Nymphe du Danube.* He was often responsible for taking the initiative in setting up relations with musicians outside the Odéon, as his correspondence with Weber suggests. Since he came to the Odéon from the Opéra-Comique, he may also have been responsible for recruiting Auber and Boieldieu to compose the music for *Les trois genres.* By 1824, Crémont's career had encompassed directing the French theater in Saint Petersburg (the opera troupe that existed peripatetically in Moscow after the French army burned the first Bolshoi Theater in 1812) and working as *sous-chef* and then *troisième chef* at the Opéra-Comique. Crémont was credited with much of the Odéon's success, not just the quality of the playing and singing, but also for either arranging works or for brokering deals with others to undertake arrangements for the theater.

Exactly which member of the Tolbecque family was the musician who participated in *Charles V et Duguesclin* is difficult to tell. If the *Journal de Paris* is correct in stating that all three members of the team were at the Odéon, then that rules out the brothers Isidore-Augustin-Joseph and Julien-Joseph, since the former was at the Académie royale de musique and the latter had left the Théâtre italien the previous year to direct the music at the Tivoli Gardens. Hence either Jean-Baptiste-Joseph Tolbecque—the viola player at the Odéon—or Charles-Joseph Tolbecque—first violin at the Opéra-Comique in 1824 and almost certainly at the Odéon (as Tolbecque jeune) from 1826 onward—was the musician in question. In any case, neither member of the Tolbecque family contributed more than once to the musi-

---

113. Vergne is only slightly less shadowy than Leroux; Fétis has no entry. Vergne's death was reported in *L'Opinion,* 11 July 1826. A requiem of his composition had been played for his colleague, the bass player Félix Blanchard, a year earlier (*Le Courrier des Théâtres,* 12 April 1825).

cal arrangements at the Odéon, and only Charles-Joseph composed, and that was after 1830; the latter seems the more likely candidate for having executed the work on *Charles V et Duguesclin*.[114] Louis-Alphonse Gilbert and Jean-Baptiste-Louis Guiraud were the other two members of the Odéon orchestra who produced *Charles V et Duguesclin*. Cellist and violist in the Odéon orchestra in 1827, they had also won prizes in the Prix de Rome in 1827.[115] Gilbert became the organist at Notre-Dame-de-Lorette in Paris.[116] Guiraud left for New Orleans, and his son, Ernest, returned to Paris in 1849 to a career as a composer overshadowed by his composition of the recitatives to Georges Bizet's *Carmen* and work with Hector Berlioz on *L'enfance du Christ*.[117] Like their colleague Tolbecque, they swapped their bows for pens only on this occasion, to assemble a work for the Odéon. It is possible that they were working for financial gain, since they were all on the lowest rate of pay for rank-and-file string players (Fr 800 per year). It is difficult to identify the three musicians' contributions to this work because so little remains, but it seems to have been an original composition, rather than a pasticcio.

During the Bourbon Restoration, younger composers were petitioning Parisian institutions to allow them to mount opéras comiques. The Odéon made every effort to help them and would have helped itself in doing so, had it been successful. Nevertheless, four recent laureates managed to present some work at the Odéon: Toussaint-René Poisson, Aimé-Ambroise-Simon Leborne, Auguste Panseron, and Pierre-Gaspard Rolle. Little is known of Poisson. He arranged Gyrowetz's work *Der Augenarzt* as *La jeune aveugle* in March 1826 and had won second prize in the Prix de Rome in 1819. He does not appear to have been a player in any Parisian orchestra, nor to have published any music.[118] In contrast to Poisson, Leborne was at the beginning of a highly successful career when he arranged Carafa's *Due Figaro* as *Les deux Figaro* in 1827. A Prix de Rome laureate in 1820, he had spent the years 1820–23 in Italy and German-speaking states and returned to teach solfège at the Conservatoire. *Les deux Figaro* was his first exposure

114. Disentangling the Tolbecque family is nearly impossible. The careers of each may be pieced together from the issues of the *Almanach des spectacles* for 1825–27, and from *FétisB* 8: 238. See also the family tree in Christian Gendron, ed., *Auguste Tolbecque: luthier et musicien* (Niort: Musées de Niort, 1997), 8.

115. Pierre Constant, *Le Conservatoire national de musique et de déclamation: documents historiques et administratives* (Paris: Imprimerie nationale, 1900), 530; Guiraud won the premier grand prix and Gilbert the second grand prix. On the same occasion Berlioz's *Mort d'Orphée* was judged unplayable.

116. *FétisB* 4:5.

117. Ibid., supplément 1:436–38.

118. *FétisB* has no entry for Poisson, however. Perhaps *La jeune aveugle*'s premiere had been planned for 1 April 1826 but was brought forward into late March.

to the Parisian stage and was followed by *Le camp du drap d'Or* (1828; in collaboration with Désiré-Alexandre Batton and Louis-Victor-Étienne Rifaut to a libretto by Paul de Kock). By this time, however, Leborne had been appointed librarian of the Académie royale de musique (1829), and he was awarded a similar position at the king's chapel in 1834. He succeeded Reicha as professor of counterpoint and fugue and was to become one of the Conservatoire's most respected composition teachers after 1840.[119] Leborne's relationship with Carafa may well have started in the early 1820s when they were both in Italy (although Leborne arrived just as Carafa was leaving), and the former wrote the finales to acts 1 and 2 of the latter's *Violette* (Opéra-Comique, 1828) a year after he had arranged *I due Figaro*. The careers of the two men also followed similar paths: Carafa was director of music at the École militaire and in 1840 succeeded Leborne as professor of counterpoint and fugue.[120]

Panseron and Rolle, whose *École de Rome* was mounted in 1826, profited from the Odéon's attempts to mount new opéras comiques under the cover of state occasions. Panseron had been part of Parisian operatic circles since 1820. He had won the Prix de Rome in 1813, spent longer in Italy than he needed, and traveled in German-speaking lands and Russia before returning to Paris. Like Carafa and Leborne, he became absorbed into the Parisian musical establishment, and his potential career as a composer of opéra comique was eclipsed by his career as an influential teacher of singing, and noteworthy writer on the vocal arts.[121] Rolle, by contrast, married the widow of the novelist François-Guillaume Ducray-Duminil and retired to Ville d'Avray.[122]

Literary Collaborators

The range of literary figures who collaborated on music drama at the Odéon included established playwrights as well as men of letters whose works for the theater were just a part a part of their literary careers. Many works for the Odéon came from the pen of individuals who earned their living in nonliterary fields. The more established figures in Parisian theatrical circles contributed occasional texts for music drama at the Odéon and did not become embroiled in the business of translation or adaptation. Eugène Scribe, the most famous of these and the author of the Odéon's *Trois genres*, was at the height of his powers as a *vaudevilliste* in 1824. Although he had

119. *FétisB* 5:239–40.

120. Leborne also revised Catel's *Traité d'harmonie* (Paris: Brandus, 1848).

121. Jacques Feschotte, "Panseron, Auguste," *Die Musik in Geschichte und Gegenwart: allgemeine Enzyklopädie der Musik* (Kassel: Barenreiter-Verlag, 1949–79), 10:725–26.

122. *FétisB* 7:298.

yet to engage with the genre that was to establish his pan-European reputation (his first essay in grand opéra was *La muette de Portici* in 1828), he had been writing libretti for opéras comiques since 1813. The choice of Scribe to write the libretto for the opera scene in *Les trois genres* was an appeal to prestige and authority, and, as the manager of the Opéra-Comique wryly noted, must have cost the Odéon a great deal.[123]

Bayard, Carmouche, Rochefort-Luçay, and Dupin were all prolific and respected figures in the mid 1820s. Jean-François-Alfred Bayard had been a friend and collaborator of Scribe and married his niece in 1827. He collaborated with François-Auguste Romieu and Sauvage on *Le neveu de Monseigneur* in 1826, and many of his plays were mounted at the Odéon: *Molière au théâtre* (1824; in collaboration with Romieu), *Roman à vendre* (1825), *Le dernier jour de folies* (1825; with Romieu) and *L'Oncle Philibert* (1827; with Gabriel-Gustave de Wailly).[124] He also collaborated with de Wailly on *Anglais et français,* a response to the English season of 1827. Bayard's list of works runs to four columns in Larousse's *Grand dictionnaire universel du dix-neuvième siècle,* perhaps the most famous of which was the libretto to Donizetti's *Fille du régiment* (figure 19).[125]

Carmouche and Rochefort-Luçay may have collaborated with Charles-Augustin-Bassompierre Sewrin on *Charles V et Duguesclin* and with Gustave Vulpian and Espérance-Hippolyte Lassagne on *L'école de Rome.*[126] Both works were composed for the name day of Charles X, and this may be the reason why the authors were approached by the Odéon on those occasions. Although Rochefort-Luçay was an active collaborator on *Le drapeau blanc,* Dupin contributed much more directly to activities at the Odéon; he worked on two productions: *Les noces de Gamache* (1825) and *Les brigands de Schiller* (1828). Both works were pasticci, both were based on Germanic subjects (August Klingmann and Friedrich Schiller respectively), and both were executed in collaboration with Thomas Sauvage. *Les brigands de Schiller* was mounted when Sauvage was director of the theater, and this association resulted in a large number of further collaborations with Sauvage at other theaters.[127]

Three authors started their careers by writing for the Odéon. Jules-Henry Vernoy de Saint-Georges helped write *Louis XII ou La route de Reims,* but is much better known for his later collaboration with Théophile Gautier

123. F-Pan O^3 1791/VI.

124. Earlier works for the Odéon included *Une promenade à Vaucluse* (1821), *Mon ami Listrac* (1823; in collaboration with Dufau), and *Guillaume et Marianne* (1823).

125. *LDD-NS* 2:409–10.

126. For Carmouche, see ibid., 3:419 and for Rochefort-Luçay, 13:1277.

127. For a summary of Dupin's career, see ibid., 6:1409.

Figure 19. Jean-François-Alfred Bayard.
Lithograph by Pierre-Eugène Aubert.

on Adam's *Giselle,* and Bizet's *Jolie fille de Perth.* Similarly, Félix-Auguste Duvert's first theatrical success was in 1823, and his work on *La comédie à la campagne* and *L'eau de jouvence,* although more extensive than that of Saint-
Georges, still represented the very earliest stages in a career that was to last
until his death in 1876.[128] Jean-Pierre-François Lesguillon had his first theatrical experience at the Odéon a couple of years before he collaborated on
the translation of *Tancredi.* Born in 1799, he was working as a notary's clerk
when he wrote his first play; it was refused a reading by the Odéon in 1824.
Lesguillon then wrote an open letter to the writer Népomucène Lemercier,
who read the play to the Odéon, at which stage it was accepted for production. The open letter was however condemned by the censor for attacks on
royalty and religion, and Lesguillon was imprisoned and fined. The work
was eventually premiered at the Odéon as *Les nouveaux Adelphes* in 1825. In

128. Ibid., 14:68 and 6:1455.

addition to *Tancrède,* he also collaborated with Édouard d'Anglemont on *Le Cachemire* at the same theater.[129]

Many of the literary collaborators at the Odéon were not exclusively playwrights but were more widely involved in the profession of letters. Pierre-François Camus (known under his pseudonym, Merville) worked on the aborted production of *Fidelio* for the Odéon but also edited the *Almanach des Spectacles* between 1822 and 1835.[130] Romieu, in addition to contributing to the libretto of *Le neveu de Monseigneur,* wrote (under the pseudonym Augusta Kernoc) the *Code civil: manuel complet de la politesse, du ton, des manières* in 1828 and edited *Le Messager* from 1830 to 1833.[131] Before writing *L'eau de jouvence,* Joseph-Xavier Boniface (pseud., Saintine) won second prize at the Académie française in 1821 and at the same time published his novel *Picciola,* which made his name and his fortune. Under the name of Xavier, he wrote over two hundred works for the theater including the Odéon but he also worked extensively for the *Revue de Paris,* the *Musée des Familles, Le Siècle,* and *Le Constitutionnel.*[132] For many of the names that appeared on libretti at the Odéon, this was the only time they appeared in theatrical circles. Comtes Léonce de Saint-Geniez and Joseph-Henri de Saur also translated works by Friedrich Maximilian Klinger and Carl August Varnhagen von Ense as well as the libretto to Winter's *Das unterbrochene Opferfest.*[133] Joseph-François-Stanislas Maizony de Lauréal (*Louis XII ou La route de Reims*) made translations from the classics, as did Jean-Georges Ozaneaux (*Le dernier jour de Missolunghi*), while Alexandre Chalas translated August von Kotzebue and wrote a history of Jesuit conspiracies against the Bourbons.[134] Thomas Sauvage's career as a playwright lasted throughout the middle half of the nineteenth century. Émile Deschamps (*Ivanhoé*) was the best-known of the Odéon librettists; he was to collaborate with Meyerbeer on the later stages of the libretto of *Les huguenots* and would write the libretto of Abraham Louis Niedermeyer's *Stradella* (1837) and of Berlioz's *Roméo et Juliette* (1839).[135]

129. Ibid., 10:406.

130. Ibid., 11:98–99.

131. Ibid., 13:1359.

132. Ibid., 14:72–73.

133. Friedrich Maximilan Klinger's *Fausts Leben, Thaten und Höllenfahrt,* translated as *Les aventures de Faust* (1825); and Carl August Varnhagen Ense's *Die Sterner und die Psitticker* as *Les étoiles et le perroquet* (1823); neither has an entry in *LDD-NS.*

134. For Chalas, see *LDD-NS* 3:848, and for Ozaneaux, 11:1641; there is no entry for Maizony de Lauréal.

135. Deschamps, as a representative of the romantics, is much better documented than most of the authors discussed here. See Henri Girard, *Émile Deschamps dilettante: relations d'un poëte romantique avec les peintres, les sculpteurs et les musiciens de son temps* (1921; reprint, Geneva: Slatkine, 1977); G. Jean-Aubry, "A Romantic Dilettante: Émile Deschamps," *Music & Letters* 20 (1939): 250–65.

Patterns of Dispersal

When the opera troupe began to encounter difficulties in 1828, the vocal artists either left of their own accord when their unrenewed contracts expired at Easter that year, or they were laid off in the late summer when the opera trouped disbanded. Given the large turnover of vocal principals at the theater, closure did not affect soloists as much as it did the orchestra or chorus. The routine exchange of artists between the Odéon and other Parisian theaters or French theaters in the provinces and abroad enabled singers to develop careers elsewhere (Valère, Campenaut) or to escape from clearly difficult circumstances at the Odéon (Pouilley, Lecomte). Such departures and arrivals accelerated during the course of 1828, hastened by Sauvage's developing concern about the ability of the opera troupe to pay its way. Of the five men and four women whose contracts were canceled at Easter 1828, Sirand (*premier ténor*) and Leclerc (*premier basse-taille*) moved straight to the Opéra-Comique, and Mme Milen transferred to the Théâtre des Nouveautés.[136] Auguste and Mme Mondonville did survive the Easter cull to remain until August, whereupon they moved to the Opéra-Comique (Auguste had been one of the signatories to the letter withdrawing the company's confidence in Sauvage in July 1828). Saint-Preux, whose contract also was not to be renewed after Easter 1828, had been sixty in 1824 and presumably retired. The better known artists fared best in the final exodus from the Odéon: Schütz moved to the Théâtre italien; Duprez and Boulard joined their colleagues Sirand, Leclerc, and the Mondonvilles at the Opéra-Comique.[137] The administration of the Opéra-Comique was in similarly difficult circumstances, and those who had gone to other, perhaps less prestigious, theaters (Brice and Mme Milen had gone to the Théâtres de Nouveautés) might in the short term have fared better.

The dispersal of the vocal principals had been gradual, in part reflecting a policy in 1828 to run down the opera troupe. In contrast, when the opera company disbanded in 1828, there was an immediate breakup of the orchestra. For most of the orchestral players, there were homes in the Opéra-Comique, the Théâtre du Vaudeville, Théâtre des Nouveautés, Théâtre des Variétés, and the Théâtre des Jeunes Artistes.[138] A sizable number stayed behind at the Odéon and, in the immediate aftermath of the dispersal, represented an above-average theater orchestra responsible for the incidental

136. Ibid., 17 April and 6 September 1828.

137. *Le corsaire*, 6 August 1828 (Schütz); *Journal de Paris*, 1 and 9 September 1828 (Duprez and Boulard).

138. Pierre Crémont (conductor), Philippe and Dubois (violins), Alphonse Déjazet (cello), Alphonse (bass), Simon (trombone), and Prévot (timpani) were at the Opéra-Comique;

music for spoken drama.[139] It was only to be expected that, when the orchestra of the Société des Concerts du Conservatoire was gathered together in 1828, most of the positions for woodwind players went to players from the orchestra of the Académie royale de musique and other prestigious organizations, although one of the trumpets had seen service at the Odéon during the previous four years.[140] Yet among the strings, 20 percent of the violins in the Société des Concerts orchestra, 17 percent of the cellos, and one of the violas had played in the pit at the Odéon during the previous period.[141] One of the greatest strengths of the Odéon was to be continued in one of most prestigious musical organizations of the nineteenth century.

Among the personnel at the Odéon, the most coherent body, characterized by its youth, was the orchestra. Led by only a few experienced musicians, these young men succeeded in turning what might have been considered a liability into an asset. Again and again, the press singled out for approval qualities that a group of young instrumentalists exhibits: verve, drive, and dynamism. The rest of the artists associated with the Odéon were much more heterogeneous. The vocal soloists mixed provincial and Parisian, young and old, with the result that a lack of familiarity with Parisian theatrical and operatic customs sometimes marred performances or weakened the communicative ability of the artists. Although some of the most important contemporary composers of music drama were associated with the Odéon—Rossini, Weber, and Meyerbeer, for example—the lion's share of recomposition and arrangement was undertaken by musicians on the boundaries of Parisian compositional life. Auber, Boieldieu, and Hérold had very little to do with the theater, and the names that figure in association with productions at the Odéon were members of its own or other orchestras, or such polymaths as Castil-Blaze, Lemierre de Corvey, or Pacini. Its literary collaborators were similarly active on the margins of the Parisian literary world. Scribe appears only once as a librettist (and then solely for

---

Bruneau (1st violin), Gauthier (2d violin), and Billard *fils* (viola) transferred to the Théâtre du Vaudeville; the Nouveautés gave a home to Robinet (1st violin) and Rivière (2d violin); Cuvillon (1st violin), Vaillon and Roger (2d violins), Tilmans (cello), and Marconnot (bassoon) moved to the Théâtre des Variétés; Pitoux (bass) went to the Théâtre des Jeunes Artistes.

139. The 1829 *Almanach des spectacles* still lists 34 players. By 1830 however, only three of the opera orchestra were left at the Odéon: Trou (clarinet), Melchior (bassoon), and Bessière (trumpet).

140. Legros is listed in the *Almanach des spectacles* (1825) as an Odéon player, and in the volume for 1830 as a member of the Société des Concerts du Conservatoire.

141. Seghers, Rivals, and Cuvillon became 1st violins, Charles-Joseph Tolbecque, Philippe, and Manera 2d violins; Jean-Baptiste Tolbecque viola, and Tilmans and Alphonse Déjazet became cellists in the Société des Concerts.

the opening *pièce de circonstance*), while many of the individuals who later became well known were just beginning their careers.

The overriding characteristic of the personnel employed at the Odéon in the mid-1820s was that it was largely recruited opportunistically. Not only would artists wish to work at more prestigious right-bank theaters, but those theaters could call on the Odéon's artists whenever they wanted. Keeping a coherent opera troupe together was a challenge that called for constant vigilance and foresight, and for surefootedness in dealing with potential artistic and administrative disaster.

Chapter 4

La férule sévère et souvent capricieuse— Control and Consumption

The *jury de lecture*

The libretti of music drama produced at the Odéon were subject to the scrutiny of the theater's *jury de lecture* (reading committee) and the censor. In the eighteenth century, reading committees would summarily reach a decision on the quality of a play after they had listened to an author reading it aloud.[1] Such structures lasted well into the nineteenth century, and even experienced authors found themselves in front of the reading committee (*sociétaires:* the actors themselves) at the Comédie-Française.[2] Théophile Gautier's description of the reading committee at the Odéon in his *Histoire de l'art dramatique*—which included the manager running around the theater recruiting anyone he could find to sit on the committee—might possibly have reflected the position when Charles-Augustin Sainte-Beuve and Jules Janin were members and had to be replaced by random members of the public; it was however significantly at odds with the practice in the 1820s,[3] when a quorate committee met frequently. The reading committee at the Odéon was then made up of men of letters who represented scholarly, polemical, and dramatic literature and journalism. In early 1824, the committee consisted of André-René-Polydore Alissan de Chazet, François-Juste-Marie Raynouard, François-Xavier-Joseph Droz, D. Rothe de Nugent, François-Guillaume-Jean-Stanislas Andrieux, Jean-Marie Janin

---

1. Frederick William John Hemmings, *The Theatre Industry in Nineteenth-Century France* (Cambridge: Cambridge University Press, 1993), 259.

2. Ibid., 258–65.

3. Théophile Gautier, *Histoire de l'art dramatique en France depuis vingt-cinq ans* (Leipzig: Hetzel; Durr, 1858–59), 2:250–51. Gautier's description dates from the mid-1830s but Hemmings (*Theatre Industry,* 258) cites it as an accurate account of the Odéon's 1820s procedures.

(Mely-Janin), Gaillard de Murray, Michel-Ambroise de Gimel, and were joined by Bernard for the first time on 9 April 1824.[4] Raynouard, Droz, and Andrieux were academics. Raynouard, a linguist and philologist, was the permanent secretary at the Académie Française until he resigned in protest against the new press laws of 1826.[5] Droz was a moral philosopher who gained entry to the Académie française in 1824, and Andrieux professor of literature at the Collège de France until his death in 1833.[6] Alissan de Chazet and Mely-Janin were much more men of the theater: the former had written over one hundred plays by 1820, whereas the latter had produced *Oreste* at the Odéon in 1821 and would have *Louis XI à Péronne* mounted at the Comédie-Française in 1827.[7] Alissan de Chazet's membership in the committee was advantageous to the Odéon since, as well as holding the sinecure of the librarianship at Versailles and the Trianon, he was a censor. Mely-Janin had also been a journalist on the *Journal de l'Empire*, *Les Petites Affiches,* and *La Quotidienne.* Gimel, the ex-director of the Odéon, chaired the committee.[8] The inspector was Emmanuel-Louis-Nicolas Viollet-le-Duc, an author and scholar whose achievements were to be overshadowed by his son's reconstruction of Notre-Dame, Vézelay, and Carcassonne; Eugène-Emmanuel Viollet-le-Duc was ten years old in 1824.[9]

Meetings in April 1824, just before the reopening, were frequent; regular Saturday meetings took place on the 3, 10, and 17 April.[10] The meeting on Saturday 24 April was canceled because the committee met both the previous Friday and the following Monday. In addition, there were meetings on 9, 19, and 23 April. The committee therefore convened no fewer than seven times that month, and Viollet-le-Duc "examined" all three of the Saturday meetings. Under Bernard's management, copies of the plays were circulated to members of the committee who then wrote confidential reports; the Saturday meetings became discussions of these reports rather than readings of new plays by their authors; at this time, it was unique in the theatrical world of Paris.[11] New comedies and tragedies were assessed in this way, but it is difficult to know whether the libretti of public-domain opéras comiques were circulated to members of the reading committee, or if mu-

4. Reading committee records of attendance between 1824 and 1828 are preserved in F-Pan O³ 1791/IX and O³ 1792/IV.

5. *LDD-NS* 13:745–46.

6. Ibid., 6:1299–1300, 1:337.

7. Ibid., 3:1116 and 10:1489.

8. *Le Diable Boiteux,* 12 April 1824.

9. F-Pan O³ 1791/IX.

10. Ibid. Meetings were fixed for Saturdays and, as the signed *jetons de présence* clearly show (*pace* Gautier), on average, committee members attended 90 to 95 percent of the meetings to which they were called; the fee for attending was Fr 10 a day.

11. Bernard's new policy was announced in *Le Diable Boiteux,* 19 January 1824.

sic drama in translation was also put to this test. *Les trois journées* and *Le dernier jour de Missolunghi*—new works—were certainly received formally by the reading committee,[12] and it seems certain that such other new works as *L'eau de jouvence* (Kreutzer's opéra comique) and all the occasional works were also read by the committee. Libretti were read and considered independently of their music, as if they were plays. How interesting it would be to read the minutes of the meeting when the libretto of *Robin des bois* was discussed—not just because of the derision that the academics Raynouard, Droz, and Andrieux would have most likely heaped on it, but for any way in which the discussion of Weber's music—which could not in this sense be read—might have formed part of the decision on its fate. Despite the fact that the register of attendance of the Odéon's reading committee has been preserved almost in full, not a word of its deliberations survives.

Censorship

Unlike the minutes of the reading committee's meetings, large numbers of reports written by censors on music drama at the Odéon, along with submitted copies of the libretti, remain in the Archives nationales in Paris; the latter are often annotated with instructions on which parts to emend or excise.[13] Normal practice was to submit two copies of the libretto to the censor two weeks before the premiere; one copy of the text would remain in the censor's archives, the other was returned to the director of the theater concerned, unless the work had been rejected out of hand, in which case both copies were returned to the author.[14] A work might be accepted without correction or subject to modifications indicated by the censor. Any corrections had to be executed within forty-eight hours or the director would have to postpone the dress rehearsal; directors (who did not want to lose revenue) were therefore encouraged to collude with the censors in applying pressure on authors to execute changes promptly.[15]

The censors were men of letters who had interests in a wide range of diverse theatrical and literary activity in the city. They were headed by the director of the division de la Librairie, who from 1823 to 1828 was Jacques-Marie Lelarge, duc de Lourdouiex; he was assisted during the 1820s by Antoine-Marie Coupart. Lourdouiex was an *ultra* journalist during the Em-

---

12. *Le Diable Boiteux*, 12 April 1824; and *Le Courrier des Théâtres*, 4 May 1827.

13. For an outline of the sources on early nineteenth-century censorship, see Odile Krakovitch, *Les Pièces de théâtre soumises à la censure (1800–1830): inventaire des pièces (F^{18} 581 à 668) et les procès-verbaux des censeurs (F^{21} 966–95)* (Paris: Archives nationales, 1982), 42–45.

14. Ibid., 21.

15. Frederick William John Hemmings, *Theatre and State in France, 1760–1905* (Cambridge: Cambridge University Press, 1994), 216–17.

Figure 20. Antoine-Chrysostome
Quatremère de Quincy.
Lithograph by Émile-Pierre
Pichard after Giraldin fils.

pire, a position to which he returned (now as a legitimist) in 1828; he became editor of the *Gazette de France* in 1849 and died in 1860. Coupart had
been chef du bureau des théâtres since 1799, and would take over as *régisseur* at the Palais-Royal in 1831, where he would remain until 1864. While
a censor he also produced plays and collaborated on the *Almanach des Spectacles.*[16] Lourdouiex and Coupart were government officials, to whom the
other censors were responsible. During the 1820s they were Jean-Charles-
Dominique de Lacretelle and Pierre-Édouard Lemontey, both lawyers (the
latter died in 1826, the former resigned from the office in 1828), Antoine-
Chrysostome Quatremère de Quincy (figure 20), the archaeological historian (he resigned in 1827), and Alissan de Chazet, a member of the Odéon's
reading committee.[17]

   In early 1828 Jacques-Corentin Royou, Charles Briffaut, Jean-Louis Laya,
François Chéron, François Sauvo, and Delaforest were recruited as censors.
Royou was a censor with a background as an uncritical royalist historian
and playwright. He wrote *Zénobie* and *Phocion* (1820 and 1821, both for the
Comédie-Française) and *La mort de César* for the Odéon in 1825;[18] the lat-
ter was so badly received that Royou marched onto the stage, tore the man-

16. Krakovitch, *Pièces de théâtre,* 23–24.
17. Ibid., 24–26.
18. Ibid., 27–29.

uscript from the hands of the prompt, and—threatening the audience—
left the theater.[19] With the exception of the two lawyers and de Quincy, almost all the censors were themselves embedded, sometimes controversially,
in the theatrical culture of the Restoration. Briffaut and Chéron were playwrights, and Sauvo was attached to the *Moniteur Universel.*

Censors' reports for the Odéon survive for *Le sacrifice interrompu, Robin
des bois, Les noces de Gamache, Les deux Figaro, La folle de Glaris,* and *Le dernier
jour de Missolunghi.*[20] In general, censors troubled the theater hardly at all.
Lemontey's report on *Le sacrifice interrompu* showed that its author clearly
understood the musical importance of the work to the Odéon.[21] Although
he searched in vain in what he called this "musical frame" for correspondences between the libretto's insurrection in Peru and the current war in
Spain, all he found was unobjectionable praise for French bravery. Even for
Robin des bois, the censors could not generate a lot of enthusiasm: Royou
managed to say almost nothing in a bland, two-page report. Coupart, the intermediary between Royou and Lourdouiex, restricted his comments to
hostile, yet futile, criticism of its quality.[22]

The Odéon encountered serious difficulty with the censor only with a
work that it must have known would have been problematic. *Le dernier jour
de Missolunghi,* eventually premiered in 1828, was a three-act *drame héroïque*
by Ozaneaux with music by Hérold. Its history with the censors illustrates
well the relationship between the theater and this part of the government.
Ozaneaux's play tells the story of the final defense of Missolunghi by the
Greeks against the Turks as recently as 1824. The first act introduces the
Greek defenders of the city and a French mercenary, Gérard; they attempt
a final assault on the Turkish forces laying siege to the city, and Dryanis and
Chrysa (a young woman disguised as a soldier) are captured. Gérard arrives
in the Turkish camp as an envoy, and, in the second act, offers to swap him-
self for the two captives; the exchange is accepted in the knowledge that
Dryanis and Chrysa will die the following day when the Turks attack the city.
At the beginning of the third act, Chrysa marries her lover Capsali, and the
Greek defenders of the city plan a trap that involves mining the city, blow-
ing themselves up along with the Turks. At the last moment, Gérard escapes
and manages to join the Greeks in the cathedral, and the play ends with the
planned explosion and conflagration of Greek and Turk alike.[23]

19. *LDD-NS* 13:1487.
20. Censors' libretti for the Odéon are scattered among F-Pan F[18] 597[B] and 613–14.
21. F-Pan F[21]&& 967; the libretto itself is F-Pan F[18] 613/145.
22. F-Pan F[21] 967; the libretto is F-Pan F[18] 613.
23. *Le dernier jour de Missolunghi* (Paris: Barba, 1828). The censors' libretto also survives as
F-Pan F[18] 597[B].

Hérold's music consists of an overture, and three musical numbers, one in each act. The music in act I is a ballade for Dryanis (sung by Delaunay); there are three *couplets,* each with a choral refrain. In 2/4, and marked allegro moderato, the number exploits simple march topics. To balance this in act II is a *chanson turque.* Again, the number consists of *couplets;* in each, this time, the music moves from minor to major; the minor-mode music exploits idioms and scorings the audience had heard in "Turkish" music from Gluck to Mozart. The music of the main section is reused as part of the *musique militaire* later in the act. The most elaborate number is reserved for act III, which opens with the marriage of Capsali and Chrysa in the ruined cathedral of Missolunghi; Byron's tomb is stage left. Framing the number are two appearances of a *choeur général,* "Hymen, hymen, viens encore nous sourire"; the music is a chorale accompanied by the cantilena-style slow introduction to the overture. In between is a solo for a young woman and a warrior (sung by Duprez and his wife), and a brief interpolated chorus that shifts tempo and time as the chorus reminds the soloists of imminent defeat and death.[24]

The fate of *Le dernier jour de Missolunghi* was no less enmeshed in both domestic politics and foreign affairs in the second half of 1827 than was the city of Missolunghi itself in 1824.[25] The conflict in which the siege of Missolunghi was such an emotive event was still in progress in 1827. The war in the Balkans concerned much of western Europe; philhellene societies sprang up in most European countries, and various artistic enterprises reflected intellectual concern with the war between Greece and Turkey: Eugène Delacroix's *Massacres of Chios* and *Greece Expiring on the Ruins of Missolunghi,* Auguste Fabre's *Histoire du siège de Missolunghi,* Casimir Delavigne's *Messéniennes,* Berlioz's *Révolution grecque: scène héroïque* and even Rossini's *Siège de Corinthe* and the revival of Meyerbeer's *Crociato in Egitto* all point to a concern for the Greek revolution in the years 1824–27.[26]

Russia, France, and England signed the treaty of London on 6 July 1827; they agreed to compel the sultan to accept their mediation in setting up a Greek state and, in doing so, finally agreed to a confrontation with the

24. The autograph of Hérold's music is F-Pn Vm² 1341; a manuscript copy of the overture survives as F-Pn Rés. 11837. The three vocal numbers were published in *Le Dernier Jour de Missolunghi* (Paris: Meissonnier, [1828]), the third with substantial excisions.

25. The censors' libretto is F-Pan F¹⁸ 597ᴮ; the censors' reports are collected in F-Pan F²¹ 967. The eight documents that relate to *Le dernier jour de Missolunghi* are numbered separately in square brackets in the notes to the discussion that follows.

26. For a summary of these works within a philhellene context see Mark Everist, "Meyerbeer's *Il crociato in Egitto: Mélodrame,* Opera, Orientalism," *Cambridge Opera Journal* 8 (1996): 247–48.

Turks that would take place at Navarino in October.[27] On 11 August British and French admirals in Smyrna were empowered to enforce an armistice, and a formal note was passed to the Porte demanding an immediate truce with the Greeks. Although the Greek government accepted this idea with alacrity, the Turks treated it with scorn, and on 7 September the Egyptian fleet joined the Ottoman squadron in the harbor at Navarino. On 12 September the English admiral, Sir Edward Codrington, informed the Ottoman admiral that any attempt to leave Navarino would be met with force.[28] The next day, 13 September, the manuscripts of *Le dernier jour de Missolunghi* were deposited with the censor by the director of the Odéon; he could not have chosen a more inflammatory moment to present a play based on the conflict in the eastern Mediterranean.[29] The immediate response of the censors was panic and confusion. Both Royou and Lacretelle focused on the political implications of the work. The latter uncompromisingly pointed to twenty plays, all destined to demonstrate the exploits and misfortunes of the Greeks, that had appeared before the censor since the beginning of the war in the Balkans. His more wide-ranging principle was that events of modern history could not be, suitably and without danger, reproduced in the theater. He furthermore objected to the details of the Greek and Jewish religions and traditions that in any case would have been intolerable in Parisian theaters.[30] Royou placed political concerns second after a consideration of the propriety of showing a wedding according to the orthodox rite on the stage. He thought that it would be appropriate to await the outcome of the negotiations concerning Greece before authorizing the performance of the work.[31] He went on to advise deferring the decision. Three days later the matter was referred to the minister of the interior for special authorization from the king, where it remained in bureaucratic limbo.[32]

A month later, the situation had changed out of all recognition. The Egyptian fleet joined the Ottomans, and the Russian squadron joined those of France and England. A tripartite force sailed into the harbor at Navarino on 20 October and obliterated both the Ottoman fleet and any chances the Porte had of ever retaining control over Greece.[33] As soon as the news reached Paris, it can only be expected that the Odéon would immediately resubmit *Le dernier jour de Missolunghi,* unchanged, to the censor; this they

27. W. Alison Phillips, "Greece and the Balkan Peninsula," in *The Restoration*, ed. A. W. Ward, G. W. Prothero, and Stanley Leathes (Cambridge: Cambridge University Press, 1934), 195.

28. Ibid., 196.

29. F-Pan F²¹ 967.

30. F-Pan F²¹ 967 [2].

31. F-Pan F²¹ 967 [3].

32. F-Pan F²¹ 967 [2] addendum.

33. Phillips, "Greece and the Balkan Peninsula," 196.

did on 14 November 1827.[34] Lacretelle's is the only report that has survived from this phase of the proceedings; the author was adamant in his opposition to libretti drawn from modern history and politics;[35] he was unmoved, naturally, by any argument that the victory at Navarino made a difference to whether or not *Le dernier jour de Missolunghi* should be played. As far as the Odéon was concerned, nothing happened for two months, but behind the scenes much had changed: Lacretelle had resigned, and new censors had been appointed. Furthermore, the Villèle administration had fallen in January 1828, and Martignac's government had replaced it.[36] In late January, the matter of *Le dernier jour de Missolunghi* was back on the agenda. Royou now saw all his concerns from the previous September satisfied, Lacretelle's were no longer relevant, and Alissan de Chazet's report was a perfunctory authorization to allow the performance to take place. With this latter document countersigned by two of the new censors, Briffaut and Laya, Coupart could report to Lourdouiex that no fewer than four censors had agreed to approve the work.[37] When Sauvage wrote to the minister of the interior on 19 February to ask what had happened to *Le dernier jour de Missolunghi,* the decision to allow a performance of the work had already been taken, and it was premiered on 10 April.[38]

The Audience

The audience at the Théâtre-Royal de l'Odéon was heterodox. Alongside a petit bourgeois and very occasionally working-class element, the theater's largest, and most reliable, constituency was the student body from the Schools of Law and Medicine. These groups were occasionally joined by émigrés from the right-bank theaters, the so-called *ultra-pontins.* The students of the Schools of Law and Medicine made up a substantial proportion of the population of the arrondissement,[39] and in some neighborhoods they dominated the *cabinets de lecture* and the theater. Reading rooms were central to the students' work, and the Odéon area had the second-highest density of such establishments in the city (second only to the Palais-Royal);[40] the theater was the central locus of student entertainment. Both types of institution catered directly for the student body by offering sub-

34. According to F-Pan F^{21} 967 [9].

35. Ibid. Lacretelle's report was dated 15 November 1827.

36. André Jardin and André-Jean Tudesq, *Restoration and Reaction: 1815–1848,* trans. Elborg Forster (Cambridge: Cambridge University Press, 1983), 66–67.

37. F-Pan F^{21} 967 [7], [4], [1].

38. Sauvage's letter is F-Pan F^{21} 967 [8].

39. Jean-Claude Caron, *Générations romantiques: les étudiants de Paris et le quartier latin (1814–1851)* (Paris: Colin, 1993), 125–26 gives a breakdown of students per arrondissement.

40. Françoise Parent-Lardeur, *Les Cabinets de lecture: la lecture publique à Paris sous la restauration* (Paris: Payot, 1982), 22–24 and 54–55.

scriptions: 6 francs a month would gain a student access to a reading room,[41] 15 francs a month a pass to the parterre at the Odéon.[42] This compares with Fr 12 per month for the cheapest sort of room available and with between Fr 25 and Fr 50 for what most students spent monthly on food.[43]

The student body gave the audience at the Odéon its distinctive character. It was at its most generous when it heard singers making their debut at the theater. Even in cases where debutants were a little nervous or timid, the parterre would give them the benefit of the doubt. But when Duprez made his Parisian debut in December 1825, a critic was pleased that he should be made to "submit to the severe, and often capricious, discipline (*la férule sévère et souvent capricieuse*) of the Odéon's parterre."[44] The Odéon parterre could indeed be a rowdy place. When nothing more than a woman remaining standing before a performance of *La dame du lac* prompted an ugly disorder, the press took pains to make clear that the instigators of the disturbance were unknown to the usual audience, and that the students respected themselves too much to take part in such scenes.[45] In general, the students were noted for their assiduity and discrimination. During one of the accounts of disturbances by the claque, reviews distinguished it from the student body and praised the latter for its discernment.[46] Responses to both good and bad could be vociferous, but this did not mean that the parterre were deaf to the activity on stage. Whistling could easily stop a performance, as could enthusiastic applause; but more typical was a murmured approval for particular moments that gave real musical or dramatic pleasure.

The parterre had power. It not only consumed and responded to the music drama presented to it but controlled aspects of a performance. It engaged head to head with the manager, director, and artists and almost invariably won. In June 1826, a performance of *La pie voleuse* was stopped when the parterre demanded that a duet, sung as part of *La gazza ladra* at the Théâtre italien, should be sung—immediately. The director tried to explain that this duet was never sung at the Odéon, but the audience insisted. In the end, Belmont and Peronnet were called back to sing the duet, much to the satisfaction of the parterre, who (perhaps not surprisingly for a duet that many had never heard in the theater before) listened in total and admiring silence.[47] Similarly, at the premiere of Rossini's *Tancrède* in Septem-

41. Ibid., 54.
42. *Le Courrier des Théâtres*, 1 January 1826.
43. Caron, *Générations romantiques*, 135 and 137.
44. *Le Courrier des Théâtres*, 3 December 1825.
45. *La Pandore*, 30 May 1826; *Le Courrier des Théâtres*, 30 May 1826.
46. *L'Opinion*, 27 January 1826.
47. *Le Frondeur*, 2 June 1826; *L'Opinion*, 3 June 1826.

ber 1827, the parterre erupted with pleasure at the end of the performance and demanded that Amalia Schütz should return to the stage to acknowledge their applause. This was a difficult and potentially dangerous situation. Curtain calls were not allowed by law, and the theater would be answerable to the commissioner of police if one was allowed to take place.[48] Yet Schütz returned to the stage (whether the gendarmerie agreed is not known) three times, and the shouting turned into stamping.[49]

Confrontation with the police was to be avoided, since it almost always ended in violence. In June 1825 after a performance of Molière's *Tartuffe,* the Odéon audience demanded that a bust of Molière be brought onto the stage and be crowned with laurels. Bernard, then the manager, stepped onto the stage, apologized, and said that the theater did not own a bust of the playwright and implied that the audience might at this point want to go home. The parterre however responded by saying that the Café de Molière, in the street of the same name, possessed a bust, and that the director should go and get it in order to comply with their wishes. At this point, the commissioner of police ended the matter with the help of twelve gendarmes. As the press delicately put it, "Truth forces us to say that blows from rifle butts were not spared."[50]

The middle-class audience at the Odéon did not include individuals able to rent boxes but would instead wait in line for tickets: members of the legal, medical, and academic professions, intellectuals of all stripes, civil servants and merchants or wholesalers (*négociants*). This group included those who might not have been in a position to spend money on the theater during their working lives but might very well feel that in retirement they could allow themselves that luxury. These aspirants to the middle classes formed a not insubstantial part of the Odéon's audience.[51] The successful middle classes, those whose fortunes allowed them to leave urban professions for rural estates, had little to do with the theater.[52] Provincials in Paris were more likely to aim for the more prestigious entertainments than such a specifically local institution as the Odéon. Similarly, the manual laborers of the twelfth arrondissement were unlikely, except on the occasions of gratis

48. Curtain calls had been made illegal on 2 December 1824, although the ban fell into abeyance after 1830. For a summary of curtain calls in the nineteenth century, see Hemmings, *Theatre Industry,* 92–96.

49. *La Pandore,* 8 September 1827.

50. La vérité nous force à dire que les coups de crosse n'ont pas été épargnés (*Le Diable Boiteux,* 23 June 1825; see also *La Pandore,* 23 June 1825).

51. Adeline Daumard, *La Bourgeoisie parisienne de 1815 à 1848* (Paris: S.E.V.P.E.N., 1963), 29.

52. William Weber, "The Muddle of the Middle Classes," *19th-Century Music* 3 (1979): 178.

Figure 21. Hector Berlioz. Anonymous
engraving after de Pommaurne.

performances for the king's name days or coronation, to set foot inside the
theater.[53]

A number of individuals left accounts of their activities during the 1820s
that were sufficiently detailed to permit a reconstruction of at least part of
their opera-going experiences. Berlioz was a medical student, Hugo an as-
piring poet, and Achille Devéria and Delacroix on the verge of distinction
in the fine arts. All lived in the environs of the Odéon; for them, it was their
local theater and opera house.

From the time Hector Berlioz arrived in Paris in November 1821, he
lived in lodgings on the Left Bank and in many respects behaved very much
like any other of his medical contemporaries (figure 21). He first lodged
with Alphonse Robert at 104 rue St-Jacques but gave no. 71 on the same
street as his address when he was inscribed at the École de médecine; this
was the home of the surgeon and medical theorist François-Joseph-Victor
Broussais.[54] The move may well have been the result of Berlioz's father

53. For a fuller account of manual workers' penetration into theaters and opera houses,
see Hemmings, *Theatre Industry*, 117–32.

54. David Cairns, ed. and trans., *The Memoirs of Hector Berlioz, Member of the French Institute,
including His Travels to Italy, Germany, Russia and England* (London: Victor Gollanz, 1977),
53; David Cairns, *Berlioz, 1803–1832: The Making of an Artist*, 2d ed. (London: Penguin,
1999), 114.

placing his son under the supervision of a respected colleague whose son (Casimir-Anne-Marie Broussais) was also a medical student in the École de médecine. By February 1825 Berlioz had moved to 79 rue St-Jacques and, by the middle of the year, to "a tiny fifth-floor room in the Île-de-la-Cité at the corner of the rue de Harlay and the quai des Orfèvres"; this was 27 rue de Harlay.[55] A year later he moved to one of two rooms on the rue de la Harpe that he shared with Antoine Charbonel, a student of chemistry.[56] All the places that Berlioz chose to stay were entirely typical of students in his generation (see figure 1); for Berlioz, then, the Odéon ought to have been the logical theater of choice.

Berlioz's devotion to opera at the Académie royale de musique and his veneration of Gluck are well known.[57] From his arrival in Paris in 1821 until the premiere of *Robin des bois* at the Odéon in December 1824, his memoirs reflect a single-minded devotion to the newly opened Salle le Peletier; most of his accounts center on that institution.[58] Despite this enthusiasm, the lure of Weber at the Odéon was too great to resist, and in his own words, "I began to forsake the Opéra for the Odéon, where I had a pass to the pit. I never missed a performance, and soon knew *Der Freischütz*, or all of it that was given there, by heart."[59] Berlioz probably attended the Odéon well before it began to support music drama, since one of his abandoned—and now lost—projects, a *scena* from Bernard-Joseph Saurin's *Beverley ou Le joueur [sic]* (1768) for baritone and orchestra, was based on a work in repertory at the Odéon during 1823; Jean-Henri-Ferdinand Lamartelière's *Francs-juges* (1807), which provided Berlioz's starting point for his opera of the same name, was also performed at the theater in the same year as Saurin's play.[60] Exactly how much time Berlioz had for performances elsewhere after he starting work in the chorus at the Théâtre des Nouveautés on 1 March 1827 is unclear. He had to take time off for his Prix de Rome candidature in July and by September had been put in a financial position that allowed him to resign from his choral duties. Although he reports in his memoirs that he returned to the Académie royale de musique, he returned also to the Odéon where he would, later that month, see Harriet Smithson for the first time.[61]

55. Cairns, *Making of an Artist*, 172; Cairns, ed., *Memoirs of Berlioz*, 76.

56. Cairns, ed., *Memoirs of Berlioz*, 81–82.

57. See Mark Everist, "Gluck, Berlioz and Castil-Blaze: The Poetics and Reception of French Opera," in *Reading Critics Reading: Opera and Ballet Criticism in France, 1815–1848*, ed. Roger Parker and Mary Anne Smart (Oxford: Oxford University Press, 2001), 86–108.

58. Cairns, *Making of an Artist*, 151.

59. Cairns, ed., *Memoirs of Berlioz*, 100.

60. Cairns, *Making of an Artist*, 146–48, 197–99.

61. Berlioz's memorable account of his first sight of Harriet Smithson is in Cairns, ed., *Memoirs of Berlioz*, 109–13.

In his enthusiasm for Weber, and *Robin des bois* in particular, Berlioz had much in common with other romantics in literature and fine art. Victor and Adèle Hugo had moved in June 1824 to a first-floor apartment at 90 rue Vaugirard (see figure 1) a matter of weeks after the Odéon's opera troupe had opened for business; they naturally joined the audience of the theater. Later that year, the Odéon was the site of one of the key artistic meetings of the Restoration. Adèle Hugo tells how the romantics met at the Odéon to celebrate the success of *Der Freischütz,* and how she and her husband were standing in front of the theater when Devéria, waiting like them for the doors to open, offered his hand to the poet. The distinguished painter explained that he was coming for the second time to hear the Weber, and to demand encores for the drinking song, sung admirably by an artist called Valère.[62] Devéria lived not only close to the Odéon but more or less around the corner from the Hugos. He lived at 81 rue Notre-Dame-des-Champs and had moved to no. 45 by 1827; rue Notre-Dame-des-Champs runs into the rue de Vaugirard and parallel to the west edge of the Jardin du Luxembourg.[63]

By late 1824 Hugo had published a volume of *Odes* for which he received a royal pension, on the strength of which he had married Adèle Foucher; he held such a status that he wrote *Le sacre de Charles X* to celebrate the coronation of Charles X in 1825. The *Nouvelles odes* and *Les orientales* were still to be published, and *Cromwell* was still awaiting its preface. Devéria's lithographs of François-Joseph Talma and Benjamin Constant had brought him a degree of public approbation, but his more famous work, like Hugo's, was to come in the 1830s. He would illustrate scenes from the Théâtre anglais season in Paris in 1827 and in the 1830s produce lithographs of the entire *I puritani* quartet: Antonio Tamburini, Giovanni Battista Rubini, Giulia Grisi, and Luigi Lablache, as well as of Henri Herz and Liszt. The meeting outside the Odéon waiting to get into *Robin des bois* was of great significance for both Hugo and Devéria. Immediate collaborations were Devéria's frontispiece for Hugo's *Nouvelles odes* and ultimately a lithograph of the last scene of *Hernani.* Devéria was also a prominent member of the Hugo circle as it sought to distance itself from the cénacle of Charles Nodier in the years after 1826.

Another torchbearer of romanticism in the visual arts, Eugène Delacroix, aired his views on Italian music drama with some frequency in his journal (figure 22). Delacroix's friendship with Chopin is well known, and

62. Evelyne Blewer et al., eds., *Victor Hugo raconté par Adèle Hugo* (Paris: Plon, 1985), 372.

63. Dominique Morel, ed., *Achille Devéria: témoin du romantisme parisien 1800–1857,* exhibition catalog, 18 June–29 September 1985 (Paris: Musées de la ville de Paris, 1985), 57.

Figure 22. Eugène Delacroix. Anonymous
lithograph.

the letter from the former to the latter discussing the aesthetics of his music is often quoted.[64] Delacroix's preoccupation with music drama followed
different paths from those of Hugo and Devéria and juxtaposed Mozart—
particularly *Don Giovanni*—with Rossini. During the first half of 1824,
Delacroix recorded his impressions of three works by Rossini. He attended
a production of *Mosè in Egitto* at the Théâtre italien on 4 March 1824, where
he admired Bonsignori and—developing the romantic trope of concentrated listening—observed that it could be appreciated only if one went to
the opera alone; the same day he noted the possibility of producing a painting based on the work.[65] The next day, he wrote in his diary that "the impression of *Moïse* still remains, and I wish to see it again."[66] Whether he did
see the work again immediately is unclear; his journal shows that he saw it
on 17 July that year in company with Jean-Baptiste Pierret and one of the
four Fielding brothers.[67] Delacroix only moderately enjoyed a performance

64. See, most recently, Jean-Jacques Eigeldinger, "Placing Chopin: Reflections on a Compositional Aesthetic," *Chopin Studies* 2 (1994): 122–26.

65. André Jourbin, ed., *Journal d'Eugène Delacroix* (Paris: Plon, 1950), 1:57–58.

66. L'impression de *Moïse* reste encore, et j'ai le désir de le revoir (ibid., 1:58).

67. Ibid., 1:117. It is not clear which of the four brothers, Théodore, Copley, Thalès, or
Newton, accompanied Delacroix to the opera.

of *Tancredi* that he saw at the Théâtre italien on 8 April 1824.[68] Delacroix was then living at 118 rue de Grenelle St-Martin,[69] and a performance of Rossini on his own doorstep was therefore an event of some importance. He noted the premiere of *Le barbier de Séville* in his journal on 6 May 1824, but it is clear that he did not attend. He dined in the rue de la Harpe, visited Pierret, and returned home at 9:30 in the evening.[70] When he did get to the Odéon on 31 May, he described the performance as *fort satisfaisant* and related how—at the theater—he met an individual who had known Voltaire.[71]

Delacroix's increasing respect for Mozart tempered his devotion to Rossini. He saw *Don Giovanni* at the Théâtre italien with Carlo Zuchelli in the title role on 17 January 1824 and, reading Stendhal's *Vie de Rossini* a week later, noted (wrongly) that the composer was born the same year that Mozart died.[72] The artist was also at work on a canvas based on the final scene of *Don Giovanni*.[73] Opinions differ as to exactly when in 1824 the painting was executed, but on 11 April that year Delacroix noted a large number of potential projects: "*Mazeppa, Don Juan,* le *Tasse,* et cent autres."[74] Delacroix certainly must have engaged with Mozart and "the opera of all operas" between 1824 and 1847, when his journal resumes. There exist two critiques of *Don Giovanni* from 9 and 14 February 1847 (Delacroix had seen the work accompanied by George Sand); in the second of these, Delacroix still judged *Don Giovanni,* however favorably, by reference to Rossini: "Rossini does not vary his characters so much." In 1853, he noted that "all these charming motifs, those of *Semiramide* and *Le barbier,* are continually with me."[75]

Devéria and Delacroix were not the only artists to sample the delights of music drama at the Odéon. The art critic and author Étienne-Jean Delécluze traveled there to hear *Robin des bois*. He attended the third performance of the work on 17 December 1824 and disliked it intensely.[76] Although he admired Agathe's act II aria (he noted its use in the overture) and praised the orchestral playing of the Odéon orchestra, he attacked the libretto because it had no common sense and was based on a belief that

68. Ibid., 1:71.

69. Ibid., 1:16 n. 1.

70. Ibid., 1:93.

71. Ibid., 1:106.

72. Ibid., 1:45 and 46–47.

73. See Lee Johnson, "The Last Scene of *Don Giovanni:* A Newly Discovered Delacroix," *The Burlington Magazine* 138 (1996): 605–7.

74. See Jourbin, *Journal de Delacroix,* 1:73.

75. Rossini ne varie pas autant les caractères (ibid., 1:186–87); tous ces motifs charmants, ceux de la *Sémiramide* et du *Barbier* sont continuellement avec moi (2:15).

76. Robert Baschet, ed., *Journal de Delécluze, 1824–1828* (Paris: Grasset, 1948), 68–69.

was, in his view, completely foreign to the French.[77] Delécluze reserved his greatest scorn for the wolf's glen scene, where he thought the music was of a feeble sadness for which Weber compensated by intensified sorcery.[78] Such a negative view of Weber should not be taken as at all typical but needs to be read in the context of Delécluze's conservative and italophile preferences. He returned to the subject of "German" music and *Robin des bois* two and a half years later, when he wrote about the differences between Haydn, Mozart, and Beethoven and contrasted them to Italian music. In summarizing, he suggested that German music constantly harbors something religious, superstitious, or supremely fantastic, whereas in Italy, "it is necessary to hear in these allegros the joy of lovers for whom the pleasure of being together makes them forget the danger of the situation in which they find themselves."[79] This context makes explicable his ultimate dislike of *Der Freischütz,* centered on the one number he had praised in 1824—Agathe's act II aria. He contrasted what he called its lugubrious and often bizarre music to that of *La Cenerentola.*[80] Ultimately, for Delécluze, no German dramatic music could compete favorably with Rossini in its depiction of love.

Although Delécluze, like Berlioz and Delacroix, recorded his impressions of music drama at the Odéon, he was neither a habitué nor a local resident. He lived on the corner of the rue Chabanais and the rue Neuve-des-Petits-Champs, to the north of the Palais-Royal; his journey to the Odéon was perhaps ten times as long as that of Berlioz, Devéria, or Delacroix.[81] Delécluze was just one example of what the contemporary press called an *ultra-pontin*—an individual who either lived on the Right Bank or who was by inclination attracted to the right-bank theaters, the Académie royale de musique, the Opéra-Comique, or the Théâtre italien, but who could be persuaded—under the circumstances of a particularly interesting production—to attend performances at the Odéon.

Attracting *ultra-pontins* to music drama at the Odéon, despite the fact that they were not its natural audience, emerged as a central preoccupation for the management of the theater. If its financial difficulties were the result of its location, recruiting an *ultra-pontin* audience was the only way of supporting an opera troupe, and this was clearly possible only with works as successful as *Robin des bois.*[82] The presence of nontraditional audiences

77. Ibid., 68.

78. Ibid.

79. En Italie, il faut entendre ces allégros de joie d'amants, à qui le plaisir d'être ensemble fait oublier le danger de la situation où ils se trouvent (ibid., 433).

80. Ibid.

81. Robert Baschet, *E.-J. Delécluze: témoin de son temps, 1781–1863* (Paris: Boivin, 1942), 63 n. 1.

82. *Le Courrier des Théâtres,* 14 May 1827.

at the Odéon was assiduously described and categorized. For example, audiences from the Opéra-Comique were unlikely to cross the Seine to hear the *ancien répertoire* at the Odéon: some of the works were still in repertory at the Opéra-Comique, and in any case the theater could also mount productions of up-to-date works by Boieldieu and Auber that were forbidden to the Odéon. Audiences from the Académie royale de musique, used to the types of continuous opera forbidden to the Odéon, might however travel south to hear unfamiliar repertory.

Two types of work drew *ultra-pontins* to the Odéon: German music drama and works by Rossini. *Robin des bois* was repeatedly identified as a work that could bring audiences from the Right Bank to the Odéon;[83] so too were Winter's *Sacrifice interrompu* and *Les bohémiens,* the Weber pasticcio. In *Le sacrifice interrompu,* it was said, the charms of Elvire's third-act aria alone merited a journey "across the bridges," and the *Courrier des Théâtres* claimed that *Les bohémiens* attracted the *dilettanti* to the Odéon.[84] The extension of the Italian term *dilettanti* to audiences at a pasticcio of Weber is odd. During the Restoration, the term was usually reserved for the adherents of Italian music drama, and especially of Rossini. On 26 July 1825, *La Pandore* could write that "yesterday, the *dilettanti* of both banks were carried as a crowd to the Odéon to hear Rossini's *Otello*" there.[85] Staunch fans of German music drama at the Odéon, who might go out of their way to hear such works in the same way as the devotees of Rossini, were also grouped together with the *dilettanti.*

There were two reasons why audiences might forsake the Théâtre italien for the Odéon: volume and quality. Enthusiasts for Italian music drama, so the argument went, were simply not satisfied by the tri-weekly performances at the Théâtre italien, and on the evenings when there was no performance they would cross the river to hear Rossini at the Odéon. The press was anxious to promote the interest in Italian music drama as an obsession. On 18 August 1824, the *Courrier des Théâtres* reported the antics of the *dilettanti* on a night where *La gazza ladra* could be heard in Italian at the Salle Favart and in French, as *La pie voleuse,* at the Odéon. "We are assured," wrote their correspondent, "that the *dilettanti* were seen running pell-mell from one theater to other in order to hear the same piece twice in the evening."[86]

83. E.g., *Le Diable Boiteux,* 26 January 1826.

84. See, respectively, *La Pandore,* 23 October 1824; *Le Courrier des Théâtres,* 18 November 1824 *(Le sacrifice interrompu)*; and *Le Courrier des Théâtres,* 8 December 1826 *(Les bohémiens).*

85. Hier, les dilettanti des deux rives s'étaient portés en foule à l'Odéon pour y entendre l'*Otello* de M. Rossini (*La Pandore,* 26 July 1825).

86. On assure avoir rencontré des dilettanti courant bride abattue d'un théâtre à l'autre, pour entendre deux fois le même morceau dans la soirée (*Le Courrier des Théâtres,* 18 August 1824).

Rossini's works that attracted the *dilettanti* to the Odéon were *La gazza ladra, Otello, La donna del lago, Ivanhoé* (the Rossini pasticcio),[87] and *Il barbiere di Siviglia.* In the case of *Il barbiere,* it is clear that *dilettanti* who heard the work at the Odéon preferred the work sung in French there (with Schütz in the role of Rosine) to an Italian performance at the Salle Favart.[88]

One of the curious absences from the roster of Italian music drama performed in French at the Odéon that succeeded in attracting the *dilettanti* was the operatic output of Mozart. Productions of both *Don Giovanni* and *Le nozze di Figaro* were mounted at the theater, and both were successful. Mozart, as a composer of Italian music drama, could generate nothing like the excitement of Rossini however, and his "German" origins were insufficiently recognized to set him alongside Weber. Meyerbeer's *Marguerite d'Anjou* is a curious anomaly in this regard; like Mozart, he was a German-speaking composer writing Italian music drama that was in repertory at the Théâtre italien, yet *"Marguerite d'Anjou* has especially obtained public favor and the advantage of making music lovers from the opposite bank cross the bridges."[89] One of the attributes possessed by Meyerbeer but not by Mozart explains Meyerbeer's greater attraction. The recent success of *Il crociato in Egitto* at the Théâtre italien, had led enthusiastic fans and critics to call Meyerbeer a worthy successor to Rossini.

Les chevaliers de lustre

A frequent element of the heterodox audience at the Odéon was the claque. By the 1820s the claque, known also as the *chevaliers de lustre* or the *romains,* was a well-organized, fully professionalized, system that was as much in control of the destinies of soloists as it was of plays and music drama. It was unique to Paris, and seemed inexplicable to visitors.[90] The *chef de claque* assembled a team of as many as forty individuals who would agree to applaud a work or an artist or to ensure—by violent means if necessary—that the work or the artist succeeded or (if the *chef de claque* determined otherwise) failed. For a new work, or for the debut of an artist, the *chef de claque* would approach the playwright and demand a number of the free tickets the author had received from the administration. Some of these would be used to get the rest of the *claque* into the theater, and the rest would be sold outside the door; this, and straightforward cash payments made by artists, was the way in which extortion generated income. If the authors and artists

87. *Le Courrier des Théâtres,* 25 September 1826.

88. E.g., *Le Courrier des Théâtres,* 5 December 1826.

89. *Marguerite d'Anjou* a surtout obtenu la faveur publique et l'avantage de faire passer les ponts aux amateurs de l'autre rive (*Journal de Paris,* 1 January 1827).

90. This outline of the workings of the claque is indebted to the account in Hemmings, *Theatre Industry,* 101–10.

cooperated with the *chef de claque,* they could look forward to guaranteed applause throughout the premiere or debut; if not, the *chevaliers de lustre* would ensure that no member of the audience would express their approval of the performance. Such a freelance organization worked well until the moment when more than one *chef de claque* approached the authors or artists, as happened at the Théâtre-Français during the 1820s. The logical step, which was followed in most state theaters, was for the *chef de claque* to be placed on the theater's payroll. The resulting relationship between author, interpreter, and audience was very much at odds with current practices: "whereas today we regard a theatrical production as a matter of the dramatist addressing an audience through the medium of his interpreters, in Paris during at least the first half of the nineteenth century a play was in some ways analogous to a kind of profane mass, in which the priest (the actor) was supported by the server (the claque), while the audience corresponded to the congregation, witnessing but not vocally participating in the mystery being enacted."[91]

The audiences at the Odéon who had paid for their seats were less than enthusiastic about others telling them how to respond to the quality of the new works and artists with which they were confronted, and the theater became the center of opposition to the claque during this period.[92] Disturbances at performances of music drama were rare, although there was some talk of a disturbance at the premiere of Castil-Blaze's *Forêt de Sénart* that might have been the result of activity by the claque, and Louis Castel's account of his adventures at the Odéon centered on a performance of music drama.[93] Three works however, Voltaire's *Mérope,* Joseph-Isidore Samson's *Fête de Molière,* and the anonymous *Orphelin de Bethléem,* brought the issue to a head in 1825.

Just before the opera troupe opened for business in 1824, the Odéon had staged a performance of Voltaire's *Mérope;* Mlle Georges-Weimer had ill-advisedly walked off the stage in the face of hostile judgment animated

91. Ibid., 105–6.

92. Except at the Odéon, the claque was still a problem late in 1826: "One parterre, that at the Odéon, has rejected by force the insolent cabal that wanted to dictate its laws; such a crusade does not need to be preached in other theaters, wherever it takes place; it is up to the free citizens to purge the circus of the dogs that are loosed in order to bite them" (Un parterre, celui de l'Odéon, a repoussé par la force la cabale insolente qui voulait lui dicter des lois; une semblable croisade n'a pas besoin d'être prêchée dans les autres théâtres où qu'elle ait lieu; c'est aux citoyens libres à purger les Cirques des dogues qui y sont lâchés pour les mordre [*La Pandore,* 8 October 1826]).

93. *Le Frondeur,* 15 January 1826; Robert [Louis Castel], *Mémoires d'un claqueur contenant la théorie et la pratique de l'art des succès, des jugemens sur le talent de plusieurs auteurs, acteurs, actrices, danseurs, danseuses et un très-grand nombre d'anecdotes historiques toutes inédites* (Paris: Chantpie, Levasseur, 1829), 218–30.

by the claque. Although she was technically in the wrong, and in breach of the law, the audience at the Odéon recognized the difficulties created by the claque.[94] Less than a month later, the audience had taken the matter into their own hands and had come up with an ingenious—but simple— solution. The audience who had paid for their tickets possessed a piece of card—the ticket—whereas the members of the claque did not. It was a simple matter for it to be made clear to all bona-fide members of the audience that they should place their tickets in their hats; members of the claque were then in some difficulty since they were easily identifiable and could be—and were—expelled by members of *la jeunesse éclairée,* as the student members of the audience were called.[95] In the immediate aftermath of this coup, the claqueurs manufactured counterfeit tickets so that they could place them in their hats, but the claqueurs could not continue indefinitely to manufacture counterfeits for every performance, and, with occasional exceptions, the technique seemed to work well.[96] At the premiere of Samson's *Fête de Molière,* there was a disturbance before the beginning of the play. In his memoirs, Samson explains how the regular audience in their properly ticketed hats proceeded to expel the claque with some vigor.[97] The only difficulty with this process at a premiere was that friends and relatives of the author—the much-revered Samson—were in the audience and had received free tickets. They could not therefore be distinguished from members of the claque, and the resulting confusion saved the claque from a more comprehensive expulsion than the one it normally received.[98]

The outrage that resulted from claqueurs applauding a work of which the audience disapproved was one irritant. A further aggravation was that, having queued for perhaps two hours to get into the theater, the audience would arrive in the parterre to find that the best seats were either occupied by the claque or by their gloves, hats, or handkerchiefs, which were just as efficient at keeping the real audience out of the best seats. Such frustration would regularly lead to scuffles as the real audience came to terms with the false. An article in the *Diable Boiteux* described these difficulties exactly and gave a report on the resulting damage: three hats squashed, two noses broken, and one eye poked.[99]

A decisive confrontation between the claque and the audience at the Odéon took place at the premiere of *L'orphelin de Bethléem* on 1 February

---

94. *Le Courrier des Théâtres,* 3 May 1824, described the incident and on 5 May rebutted claims that the disturbance had *not* been the result of the claque.

95. *La Pandore,* 15 May 1824.

96. Ibid., 3 June 1824.

97. Ibid., 6 August 1824.

98. Hemmings, *Theatre Industry,* 111.

99. *Le Diable Boiteux,* 18 January 1825.

1825. Here, a work of which the audience disapproved was greatly applauded by the claque; the anonymous author had presumably delivered the necessary tickets and paid the obligatory fee. Once the play had started, it was difficult for the audience to deal with the claque. Unfortunately for the latter, a technical hitch meant that the performance had to be briefly interrupted while Herod apologized for the fact that the infant Jesus' foot had become stuck in a trapdoor. As one of the newspapers put it, the Massacre of the Claqueurs then began. The claque were expelled with such great violence that the orchestra were obliged to leave the building, and those members of the audience who were not involved in the expulsion took refuge on the stage.[100]

It must have been during 1827 when Castel (known simply as Robert) had the experience of being a claqueur expelled from the Odéon; he described his encounter with the Odéon audience in his *Mémoires d'un claqueur* (published in 1829). It is difficult to identify which performance he attended, since he says that it was the premiere of a pasticcio and that Schütz was singing; Schütz sang in no pasticci during her time at the Odéon, and the only premiere in which she took part was that of Conradin Kreutzer's *Folle de Glaris,* in April 1827; Castel's account may be an amalgam of various works and artists. Castel—an itinerant claqueur—was hired to ply his trade at the Odéon.[101] By 1827, the administration of the Odéon had begun to issue markers allowing members of the audience to come and go in the interval. When the expulsion began, Castel in his unticketed hat was lucky to escape uninjured, and his partner Thérèse concluded the episode with a request the he should never work as a claqueur at the Odéon again.[102]

The Odéon succeeded where almost all other Parisian theaters and opera houses had failed. It banished the claque without the intervention of the maison du Roi or the préfet de police. It may have done so because the audience was "composed of quick-tempered young men spoiling for a fight";[103] or perhaps the more disciplined students of law and medicine were prepared—as a result of their enthusiasm for the theater and music drama—to take the trouble to find an efficient way of getting rid of the claque. It is less easy to imagine the audience at the Académie royale de musique or the Théâtre italien coming up with, let alone implementing, such a solution. Whatever the results of the dealings with the claque, the passion for the works themselves and the skill with which they were performed says a great deal about the levels of listening and concentration exhibited at the Odéon in the 1820s.

100. Hemmings, *Theatre Industry,* 111–12.
101. Castel, *Mémoires d'un claqueur,* 227–29.
102. Ibid., 228.
103. Hemmings, *Theatre Industry,* 113.

Audiences have memories; at the Académie royale de musique's revivals of Gluck's operas in the 1820s there were members of the audience who had not only been present at the premieres but who also recalled members of the original audience who had not survived the Revolution. Similarly, some members of the audience at the Opéra-Comique could hear Grétry during the Restoration and compare the artists with those who had created the roles in the previous century. The Odéon was different. The youth of the student audience, the relatively recent affection for the theater and music drama on the part of the retired lower-middle classes and the imported enthusiasms for Rossini or Weber meant that a very small proportion of the audience could enjoy music drama at the Odéon with the same memory as their opposite numbers at the Académie royale de musique and Opéra-Comique. There may well have been some connection between this lack of aural memory and the engaged and passionate view of the stage that the Odéon audiences exhibited.

Benefit Performances

Benefit performances at the Odéon fell into two broad categories: those where the beneficiaries were employees at the theater (almost exclusively *premiers sujets,* and often as part of a contract) and those where an outside stimulus existed. Examples of the latter included national disasters and the urgent cases of theatrical colleagues in distress, or composers and others associated with he Odéon that the theater felt obliged to help. Benefits, even once agreed with the administration of the Odéon, were highly unpredictable events, and they rarely went according to plan. The benefit for Lecomte that took place on 18 January 1825 was entirely successful; music drama that evening was represented by *Le barbier de Séville,* and by all surviving accounts the takings were satisfactory; Lecomte was probably well pleased.[104] By contrast, the benefit for Schütz was a disaster, and no one attended. Given that the program for this benefit included *Tancrède,* the disappointing results could be the result either of Schütz's lack of popularity or the fact that music drama was going into steep decline in early 1828.[105] Although one of the plays was pulled at the last minute, the concert was well received.[106]

104. *Journal de Paris,* 20 January 1825.

105. The program consisted of two plays, the last two acts of *Tancrède,* and a concert in which Dabadie, Marinoni, and Schütz sang and Lafont, Herz, Farrenc, and Schult and his sons—a trio for two guitars and *eol-harmonica*—played; the evening closed with a divertissement performed by the Académie royale de musique soloists (*Le Corsaire,* 9 February 1828). See *Journal de Paris,* 11 February 1828.

106. *Le Corsaire,* 11 February 1828.

On two occasions, artists chose to adorn their benefits with premieres. When Jean-Bernard Brisebarre (known as Joanny) enjoyed a benefit in May 1825, it coincided with the premiere of *La mort de César;* the premiere was a debacle, and the takings were so poor that Bernard had to agree to take the box himself and to promise Joanny a benefit later in 1825.[107] Such generosity was apparently extended to Lecomte's second benefit, but accounts of this event in February 1827 differ radically; it took place on the same night that the pasticcio *Monsieur de Pourceaugnac* was premiered. According to *La Pandore,* Frédéric du Petit-Méré had promised Lecomte a minimum of Fr 2,500; since the house was only a quarter full, the takings fell short of this sum by around Fr 1,000, and the shortfall was to be made up by the administration of the Odéon;[108] however, the story related in the *Journal de Paris* was very different: the event was extremely successful and the premiere of *Monsieur de Pourceaugnac* was a credit to Castil-Blaze.[109] Whether the two reports are compatible—whether *Monsieur de Pourceaugnac* could have been a success and the box still only around Fr 1,500—remains an open question.

Lecomte, and perhaps Schütz, were entitled to benefits as part of their contracts. For Stéphanie Montano, this was not the case. She did however manage—or so she thought—to engineer a *concert spirituel* for her benefit during Holy Week 1825 and negotiated the release of two or three artists from other royal theaters to support her.[110] She was understandably dismayed when it became clear that she could put on this concert only in the Académie royale de musique and that it was assumed to be part of her work for the Théâtre-Royal de l'Odéon—that the proceeds from her performance at the *concert spirituel* were included in the salary she received from the theater. She had set up the concert for absolutely no remuneration whatsoever. Her barely contained anger may be read in every line of a letter she wrote to La Rochefoucauld in March 1825.[111]

Much more public than the benefits for artists at the theater were ones in support of worthy causes. Frédéric du Petit-Méré's unexpected death in the middle of 1827 left his wife close to destitute. The Odéon mounted a benefit for his widow the following November; the press recorded a disaster,[112] and Mme du Petit-Méré confirmed the scope of her affliction when she threw herself on the mercy of the maison du Roi the following month. The takings at the box office had been Fr 2,600 (well under half the maxi-

107. *Journal de Paris,* 10 May 1825.
108. *La Pandore,* 24 February 1827.
109. *Journal de Paris,* 26 February 1827.
110. *Le Diable Boiteux,* 17 March 1825.
111. Montano wrote to La Rochefoucauld, 11 March 1825 (F-Pan O^3 1792/VI).
112. *La Pandore,* 22 November 1827.

mum), but the new manager, Sauvage, had kept it all for the costs of the performance.[113] On 23 November 1826, Frédéric himself had scheduled a benefit for the Weber family. This was an extraordinary event, both in terms of its purpose, and in terms of its success. By the end of 1826, the Odéon could see just how much it owed to Weber's *Robin des bois.* The disastrous attempt to mount *Preciosa* in 1825 left this debt undiminished. Weber's death in London occurred right in the middle of negotiations with the Odéon to mount more of his works at the theater—and *Les bohémiens* had been the result. The fact that the Odéon felt inclined to offer a benefit to the Weber family is testimony to the fact that the theater was the capital's only home for his music. Most appropriately, the benefit included not only *Robin des bois*—with the decorations of the wolf's glen scene renewed—but also the premiere of *Les bohémiens,* in which the composer himself may have had a hand in planning. Not only was there a Weber premiere to be enjoyed at the Odéon benefit for the family, but Schütz—newly recruited to the Odéon— was to take the role of Anna in *Robin des bois* for the first time, and it was rumored that the duchesse de Berry and the family of Louis-Philippe, duc d'Orléans, were to attend.[114] Almost all expectations were fulfilled: Schütz was magnificent, the audience liked *Les bohémiens* (although some critics noticed the obvious correspondences with *Preciosa*), and the duchesse de Berry was indeed present.[115] Whether the duc d'Orléans appeared is unrecorded, but the takings were close to the maximum of Fr 6,000.

Two benefits at the Odéon were in support of the victims of fires at other theaters in the city. When the Ambigu comique was destroyed on 13 July 1827, the Odéon troupe led by Schütz put on *Le barbier de Séville;* neither the location (the Odéon was closed for repairs) nor the success of the enterprise is known.[116] In April 1826, the Franconi brothers' Cirque Olympique was destroyed, and the Odéon put on a performance that promised to include the last two acts of *La dame du lac* "in which the horses of the Cirque Olympique" were due to appear.[117] Clearly this was not a performance to be missed, and the takings for the benefit ran to Fr 6,200 to which were added Fr 500 apiece from the duchesse de Berry and the duc d'Orléans.[118]

Two events in 1825 prompted benefits either at the Odéon or by its troupe elsewhere. The fire at the Bazaar in January 1825 resulted in a benefit performance of *Le sacrifice interrompu.* It was prefaced by *Fiesque* by

113. Mme du Petit-Méré to La Rochefoucauld, 17 December 1827 (F-Pan O³ 1792/I).

114. *Le Courrier des Théâtres,* 23 November 1826.

115. *L'Opinion,* 24 November 1826.

116. *Le Courrier des Théâtres,* 16 July 1827.

117. Dans lesquelles paraîtront les chevaux du Cirque-Olympique (*La Pandore,* 24 April 1826).

118. *Le Courrier des Théâtres,* 3 May 1826.

Jacques-Arsène Ancelot, and between the two works Camus and Charles-François Jupin, the first flute and one of the first violins in the Odéon orchestra, played solos. Despite all these extra efforts, the box was a derisory Fr 2,000.[119] Later the same year, a fire in Salins elicited the same response from the theater, except that this time the performance was held at the Théâtre de la Porte-St-Martin, and *Robin des bois* was mounted. Although no figures are forthcoming for the box, newspaper reports described the event favorably.[120]

If the victims of the Salins and Bazaar fires benefited (albeit modestly) from the Odéon's efforts, the theater contributed regularly to the poor of the capital via the *droit des indigens.* The sums recorded at the box office were all net of this tax which took one eleventh of the gross takings, so that the box of Fr 6,200 at the Franconi benefit must have been the result of takings of Fr 6,820. One eleventh was then collected by the Hospices et secours à domicile de Paris for distribution to the poor.[121]

Publishers

Publishers were the ultimate beneficiary of almost all artistic and intellectual endeavor in nineteenth-century Paris. Even the most ephemeral production could assume that its libretto would be published and guarantee that some if not all of its numbers would be published in piano-vocal score; even moderately successful productions could reasonably expect the publication of a full score. Such luxuries were rare in German-speaking countries and—especially published full scores—were unheard of in Italy. The libretto of the most short-lived occasional work might well have been published; such music drama as *Louis XII ou La route de Reims* and *Le neveu de Monseigneur* make this clear. In cases where no libretto survives today, it is more likely that a copy has simply not survived rather than it was never published.

Libretti were published by houses who specialized in printing plays by authors prominent in early nineteenth-century theatrical history; in general these publishers had nothing to do with music. Barba, Bertrand, Bezou, Bouquin de la Souche, Duvernois, Gardet, Hautecoeur-Martinet, and Vente all profited from music drama at the Odéon during the 1820s. Only in one case did the publisher of music involve his enterprise in the printing of libretti; that was Castil-Blaze, who published the libretti as well as the

119. *La Pandore,* 21 January 125.

120. Ibid., 20 August 1825; *Le Frondeur,* 21 August 1825.

121. In the mid 1820s the *droit des indigens* became a major issue for the Académie royale de musique when the theater was trying to claim that the levy was not payable on free tickets. See John Drysdale, "Louis Véron and the Finances of the *Académie Royale de Musique, 1827–1835*" (Ph.D. diss., University of Southampton, 2000).

scores of *Robin des bois* and *Monsieur de Pourceaugnac*. Well-known publishing houses picked up some of the larger ventures, because they were able to buy the rights to them, and the translators or editors had no interest in publication themselves (unlike Castil-Blaze for instance): Troupenas (*Tancrède*), Schlesinger (*Emmeline ou La famille suisse*), Pacini (*Ivanhoé*), and Meissonnier (*Le dernier jour de Missolunghi*). These choices were predictable: Pacini and Troupenas sought out works by Rossini, in whatever state they were in, and Schlesinger took on Weigl's *Emmeline* as part of his collection of music drama by German-speaking composers.[122]

Four publishers were more closely involved in the activities of the Odéon: Castil-Blaze, Farrenc, Kretschmer, and Laffillé. Laffillé was the publisher of almost all of Castil-Blaze's early adaptations of Italian music drama, and the so-called *Répertoire d'opéras traduits,* which was produced in the very early 1820s, was originally published under his imprint. They were to become staples of the Odéon's repertory. After the successful productions of Castil-Blaze's arrangements of Cimarosa's *Mariage secret* and Mozart's *Noces de Figaro,* both in Nîmes, in 1817 and 1818, Castil-Blaze and Laffillé entered into a contract to publish the *Répertoire d'opéras traduits.*[123] The plan was to produce scores of Mozart's *Noces de Figaro, Don Juan,* and *La flûte enchantée;* Rossini's *Barbier de Séville* and *La pie voleuse;* and Cimarosa's *Mariage secret.* Castil-Blaze was contracted to deliver three scores by 20 February 1821, and three more by 15 May the same year. The first deadline was met with some ease, since two of the three arrangements had already been made. *Don Juan* and *Le barbier de Séville* followed, but outside the contracted time; they were coupled to performances in Lyon. Although the last two works were published by Laffillé,[124] the contract was broken, and Castil-Blaze struck out on his own. In August 1822 he created an association for the printing of music and published the score and libretto of *La pie voleuse* under his own imprint.[125] At this point, the structure of the *Répertoire d'opéras traduits* began to unravel. The libretto of *La pie voleuse* gives a revised listing of the *Répertoire* that puts an arrangement of Rossini's *Mosè in Egitto* in place of Mozart's *Flûte enchantée.*[126] By the time of the first performance of Castil-Blaze's *Folies*

122. For introductions to each of these publishers, see Anik Devriès and François Lesure, *Dictionnaire des éditeurs de musique française* (Geneva: Minkoff, 1979–88), 2:416–20 (Troupenas); 2:385–92 (Schlesinger); 2:332–34 (Pacini); 2:310–17 (Meissonnier).

123. For the premiere of Castil-Blaze's translation of *Le nozze di Figaro,* see *Journal du Gard, politique, administratif et littéraire,* 30 December 1818. The contract between Castil-Blaze and Laffillé survives as F-Pn L.a. XVIII, fols. 98^r–99^r.

124. *Le barbier de Séville* was premiered at the Grand Théâtre, Lyon, on 21 September 1821 and *Don Juan* was premiered on 22 December 1822.

125. F-Pn L.a. XVIII, fols. 99^v–100^r.

126. *La pie voleuse* (Paris: Barba, 1822). The libretto was listed in the *Bibliographie de la France,* 21 September 1822.

amoureuses in Lyon in 1823, Castil-Blaze had extended the *Répertoire* to ten items: the six items listed above (including *Moïse en Egypte*); *La flûte enchan-tée* itself was listed as the seventh item, followed by *Les folies amoureuses; Othello ou Le More de Venise;* and *Le château de Robion.*[127]

With the inclusion of *Les folies amoureuses,* the *Répertoire d'opéras traduits* was dead, confused with two other strands of Castil-Blaze's entrepreneurial activity: the pasticcio and the production of new and existing translations at the Odéon. *La flûte enchantée* never saw the light of day, *Les folies amoureuses* and *Othello* were duly published and premiered, but *Le château de Robion* never got beyond the listing described above.[128] Another pasticcio, *La fausse Agnès,* followed; by this time Castil-Blaze was committed to the music of Weber, with *Robin des bois* and *La forêt de Sénart.* Despite the fact that nearly every one of his arrangements and pasticci were used at the Odéon, it was only with these last two works that he began to arrange specifically for the theater.

Meanwhile, Laffillé had continued to publish smaller-scale works throughout the early 1820s and reentered the field of translated music drama to publish two works from the Odéon repertory in 1825: *Les noces de Gamache* and *La dame du lac.*[129] The two works were the product of different teams of musical and literary arrangers, and it seems unlikely that they were anything more than a pair of straightforward, one-off, agreements. This view is supported by the buying-out of Auguste Rousseau's interest in *La dame du lac* in May 1825.[130] Farrenc was a publisher who specialized in the work of German-speaking composers: Carl Gottlob Reissiger, Johann Nepomuk Hummel, Conradin Kreutzer, and Beethoven. He published five piano-vocal extracts from Kreutzer's *Eau de jouvence;* since this was a new work, Farrenc can have had little involvement beyond its publication. In the case of *Fidelio,* however, it seems likely that Farrenc was partially involved in the arrangement of the work as well as its edition.[131] Kretsch-mer was a key player at the Odéon, as well as one of its publishers. He shared the front desk of violas in the orchestra with Jean-Baptiste Tol-becque. While Tolbecque was paid Fr 1,300 per year, Kretschmer received Fr 2,000, nearly as much as the assistant conductor, Nathan Bloc. This was because he also functioned as a répétiteur, a position he could combine

127. *Le château de Robion* was probably a pasticcio planned, but never executed.

128. *Les folies amoureuses* was premiered on 1 March 1823 at the Lyon Grand Théâtre and *Othello* on 1 December 1823 in the same theater.

129. For a general account of Laffillé's publishing output, see Devriès and Lesure, *Diction-naire,* 2:251.

130. Paris, Archives municipales, DQ7.9140 fol. 5v.

131. See Devriès and Lesure, *Dictionnaire,* 2:169.

with his private teaching practice in the neighborhood (he lived and worked at 22 rue des Fossés-St-Germain-des-Prés). He was also the composer of a number of *romances* but from 1826 began to publish music. He began with piano-vocal numbers from Meyerbeer's *Marguerite d'Anjou,* which had been arranged by Pierre Crémont. And he paid Crémont the compliment of publishing piano-vocal extracts of *Les bohémiens* the following year.[132]

Various groups of individuals were expected, or took it upon themselves, to control the consumption of music drama at the Odéon. The censors, entirely external to the theater, were responsible for ensuring that public decency was not offended while other controlling forces were more closely related to the theater, but in different ways: the reading committee consisted of individuals who were not employed by the theater in any other capacity but who had the interests of the theater uppermost in their minds, whereas audiences had a keen sense of what they would like to see and hear, and how they would like it presented to them. They were rarely less than forceful in voicing their opinions. The claque cannot really be said to have been acting in anyone's interests apart from their own, and the theater was merely one of several locations where they could practice their questionable activity. Some publishers, similarly, stood in a symbiotic relationship to the theater: anxious to capitalize on any great success from which they could profit but with no interest in the theater if nothing marketable came forward; other publishers—Laffillé, Kretschmer, and Castil-Blaze are examples— had more of a stake in music drama at the Odéon, since the first was committed, in general terms at least—to the idea of publishing Italian and French music drama in translation, the second worked at the Odéon as its répétiteur, and the third was responsible for the original forms of many of the theater's most successful works. These last examples point clearly to the complex webs of what today appear to be conflicting interests; such overlaps of activity in the nineteenth century were regarded much more in terms of complementarity than conflict.

Chapters 1 to 4 have described a number of threads in the web of culture in which the Odéon was embedded: the city of Paris and its institutions that supported music drama, the bureaucracy of the maison du Roi and its dependent offices, the theater's license that controlled its repertory and the resulting works promoted. Further elements of this thick description are the individuals who made up these threads: the administrators within and

132. Ibid., 2:247.

outside the theater, its performers and audience; and those who controlled its activities: the reading committee, the censors, the claque, and publishers. The interaction between all these elements is already clear in the descriptions given of them in this and previous chapters; as the discussion focuses on particular aspects of repertory in the following chapters, it shows the web of culture in more complex and finely woven detail.

PART TWO

The Repertory

Chapter 5

Une heure à l'opéra-comique—
Occasional Works

Some music drama mounted at the Odéon was a response to particular events in Restoration Paris. The name days of the monarch and the coronation of Charles X generated new works that at once benefited the theater's repertory of music drama and the French royal family (which used, and was used by, the theater). The management seized the opportunity for mounting occasional works to smuggle in opéras comiques by young Parisian composers that infringed its license. The official nature of royal name days and the coronation limited competing theaters in their scope for criticism of the Odéon for these breaches of its license. Despite the importance of royal celebrations, the most significant occasion for the theater itself was its opening under Bernard's direction in April 1824 with *Les trois genres*.

Opening the Theater: *Les trois genres*

On 13 February 1824, a rumor circulated that the new régime at the Odéon would be inaugurated by a new composition, that the author would be well known, and that the composer would be a figure who had however produced little in recent years.[1] This work was *Les trois genres;* the well-known author was Eugène Scribe, and the reticent composer was François-Adrien Boieldieu; his last works for the Opéra-Comique had been *Le petit chaperon rouge* (1818) and the revision of *Les voitures versées* (1820).[2] Apart from the

---

1. *Journal de Paris,* 13 February 1824.
2. *Les voitures versées* was first produced in 1808 at the Hermitage in Saint Petersburg; along with it and *Le petit chaperon rouge,* Boieldieu had been engaged in two collaborations: *Blanche de Provence ou La cour des fées* (1821, Académie royale de musique) and *La France et l'Espagne* (1823, Hôtel de Ville). His next work, *Pharamond* (1825, Académie royale de musique), was also a collaboration.

fact that the music was the work of more than one composer—the other was Daniel-François-Esprit Auber—this description was accurate. By 12 April, the reading committee at the Odéon had received and approved the work,[3] and it was premiered on 27 April 1824.

The title was at the same time a description, a manifesto, and an advertisement. It described the activities of the new régime at the Odéon that mounted productions of three genres and promoted the fact that these three genres now included music drama; it advertised the three genres by including an example of each in the work itself. *Les trois genres* was called a prologue in one act. It was cast in the form of three set-pieces—one for each of the three genres—between which were mingled scenes between the two protagonists: M. d'Herbelin and his friend, Simon. Each of the three embedded scenes had its own cast of characters (the comedy had dialogue only). In the connecting parts of the work, various themes were adumbrated: the geography of the Odéon vis-à-vis other theaters and neighborhoods, the benefits of playing three genres at the same theater, and the shortcomings of other theaters, as a synopsis of *Les trois genres* will show.

M. d'Herbelin lives in the neighborhood of the Odéon and his friend Simon has just bought property in the quarter. They express regret that when Simon lived in the faubourg Poissonnière, he rarely came to see his friend in the rue Vaugirard. At the time when the play is set, they had not seen each other for nearly a year. Simon sings the praises of their local theater—the Odéon—where he has rented a box for the year. D'Herbelin explains his hatred of the theater: an incident that had befallen him personally had been related to a member of the Odéon staff and had ended up dramatized on the stage of the theater; the humiliation had troubled him a great deal. Simon asks where he goes to the theater, and d'Herbelin speaks disparagingly of the Théâtre-Français and the Opéra-Comique, as well as the Odéon. He concludes, "Thus, for example, I would consider myself a very happy member of the audience if I could, in the same evening, spend an hour with tragedy, an hour with opéra comique, and an hour with comedy (*une heure à l'opéra comique*)."[4] Such a declaration sets up the play's outcome.

Simon takes him to rehearsals at the Odéon (claiming that it is first the Théâtre-Français and then the Opéra-Comique). D'Herbelin is of course delighted and claims that—after rehearsals of each of the three genres—he will attend the premiere of each later that week. Simon tempts d'Herbe-

3. *Le Diable Boiteux,* 12 April 1824.

4. Ainsi, par exemple, je m'estimerais un spectateur très-heureux, si je pouvais dans la même soirée passer une heure à la tragédie, une heure à l'opéra-comique et une heure à la comédie (*Les trois genres* [Paris: Blosse, 1824], 7).

lin throughout with the possibility of pleasures to be enjoyed later. When the latter asks the name of the author of the tragedy, *Turnus,* Simon tells him that he will have to wait two days until the work has been premiered before he can know that. At the end of the comedy, Simon drags his friend away just as he is beginning to enjoy the play; the pretext is of course that d'Herbelin wants to see music drama on the same evening and they have to travel to the Opéra-Comique. The title of the comedy, *Les deux quartiers ou La chaussée d'Antin dans la rue St-Jacques,* contrasts the traditional theater quarter of Paris (la chaussée d'Antin) with the Left Bank (symbolized by the rue St-Jacques) which was the home of the Odéon and its audiences. The denouement is propelled forward by the appearance of d'Herbelin's stepdaughter in the role of Franchette in the opéra comique; she explains that far from being taken from the Théâtre-Français to the Opéra-Comique, d'Herbelin has simply been taken out of one door of the Odéon, spun around the Jardin du Luxembourg, and brought back through another entrance to the theater. The outcome is predictable. When d'Herbelin expresses outrage at the trick that has been played on him, his friend objects and points out all the advantages of the Odéon that have been made manifest during the previous scenes.[5] The libretto's text throughout talks up the Odéon in no uncertain terms. It sets the agenda for a number of issues that were to characterize the opera seasons at the Odéon: the migration of audiences from the chaussée d'Antin to the faubourg St-Germain, the coexistence of three genres, and the commercial acumen that the theater had to exhibit to survive.

No music survives for *Les trois genres,* and the contributions of Auber are difficult to distinguish from those of Boieldieu.[6] The opera scene consisted of an aria for Verte-Allure, "La belle chose qu'un tournois," followed by *couplets* for Hildegonde, "J'en tremble encore lorsque j'y pense." Hildegonde and Fernand then join forces in a recitative and duet, "Dans ce noble castel, séjour d'opulence"—"Daignez dans ce manoir antique." Since Verte-Allure's aria may be shown to have been composed by Boieldieu, one or both of the remaining numbers must have been by Auber.[7] A fortunate coincidence means that it is possible to reconstruct one of the numbers in the opéra-comique scene and to attribute it. The aria "La belle chose qu'un tournois" was composed for *Les trois genres* (1824) by Boieldieu and then reused for his phenomenally successful *Dame blanche* the following year; it

5. Ibid., 51.

6. See Herbert Schneider, *Chronologisch-thematisches Verzeichnis sämtlicher Werke von Daniel François Esprit Auber* (Hildesheim: Olms, 1994), 1:89–90.

7. See Wolfgang Börner, "Die Opern von Daniel-François-Esprit Auber" (Ph.D. diss., Universität Leipzig, 1962), 38 for the claim, made without citing evidence, that Auber composed "Dans ce noble castel, séjour d'opulence"—"Daignez dans ce manoir antique."

became Georges's act I aria, "Ah! quel plaisir d'être soldat." The openings of the two texts with their common rhyme schemes are as follows:

La belle chose qu'un tournois	8a	Ah! quel plaisir d'être soldat	8a
C'est là que pour sa belle	6b′	On sert par sa vaillance	6b′
Un chevalier courtois	6a	Et son prince et l'état	6a
Fait en amant fidèle	6b′	Et gaiement on s'élance	6b′
Admirer ses exploits.	6a	De l'amour au combat.	6a
La belle chose qu'un tournois	8a	Ah! quel plaisir d'être soldat	8a

The structure of the two poems is similar, and there can be no doubt that Boieldieu did indeed model the one on the other; a reconstruction of this part of the aria, effectively a refrain, is unproblematic (example 2).[8]

Reconstruction of the rest of the aria is more complex. The section from *La dame blanche*'s introduction follows an ABACC pattern in which the final C element merges into a passage with chorus and recitative before the aria for Jenny that follows; as part of a larger introduction, its beginning and ending are more fluid than if they had belonged to a self-contained aria. The text of the aria from *Les trois genres* seems to have the structure AB[A]CA. This first reprise of the A section seems logical although the cue is missing (perhaps because it is the same as the last line of the A section). The B section is unproblematic and may be reconstructed in the same way (example 3).

The C section resists reconstruction. The structure of the poetry in *Les trois genres* does not match that of the corresponding section in "Ah! quel plaisir d'être soldat"; the reworking of the number in *La dame blanche* must have been at its most extensive here.

Boieldieu encountered two separate problems with *La dame blanche* in the wake of its premiere, and both were concerned with the aria that had its origins in *Les trois genres*. First, there was a sense in the press that the rights to the music for *Les trois genres* still belonged to the Odéon at the time Boieldieu turned "La belle chose qu'un tournois" into "Ah! quel plaisir d'être soldat" in *La dame blanche*. This was settled quite readily however by recourse to the longstanding principle that the work reverted to the author if it had not been performed for a year and a day: the last performance of *Les trois genres* had been on 24 May 1824, and the premiere of *La dame*

---

8. Example 2 reconstructs the setting of lines 1–3 by mapping the libretto from *Les trois genres* onto the music from *La dame blanche*. But in line 4 the music for the word repetition in *La dame blanche* ("Et gaiement, gaiement, on s'élance") is difficult to fit to the *Trois genres* text ("Fait en a-, en a-, mant fidèle"). In this case Boieldieu must have done more than replace the text.

Example 2. Auber/Boieldieu, *Les trois genres*. Aria "La belle chose qu'un tournois," bars 13–21 (opening of A section).

blanche was on 10 December 1825. Boieldieu's other difficulty concerned the similarity between themes in "Ah! quel plaisir d'être soldat" and the overture to Castil-Blaze's pasticcio *La fausse Agnès,* premiered at the Odéon on 13 June 1826 but familiar also to audiences at the Gymnase dramatique, where it had been played in its one-act form since 6 July 1824. In its published three-act (Odéon) version, the overture was taken from Meyerbeer's *Romilde e Constanza.*[9] Reports after the premiere of the one-act (Gymnase

9. Meyerbeer's opera was premiered at the Teatro Nuovo, Padua, on 19 July 1817.

Example 3. Auber/Boieldieu, *Les trois genres*. Aria "La belle chose qu'un tournois," bars 48–56 (opening of B section).

dramatique) version that Meyerbeer had written the overture to the work may have misled readers to assume that the composer had *originally* written the overture for *La fausse Agnès*. Boieldieu alluded to this matter in an undated letter written to Castil-Blaze after the premiere of *La dame blanche*, and after a press report to the effect that *La fausse Agnès* began with an overture that included motifs from *La dame blanche*.[10] Boieldieu asked Castil-Blaze to exculpate him from potential charges of plagiarism, and he used as evidence the fact that the music to "Ah quel plaisir d'être soldat" was a reworking of the aria he had originally written for *Les trois genres;* he could not therefore have plagiarized Meyerbeer's overture.[11] None of the first, second, or closing themes in the overture to *Romilde e Constanza* resemble "Quel plaisir d'être soldat"/"La belle chose qu'un tournois" in anything more than a very superficial way, and a serious claim of plagiarism could never have been pursued on technical or indeed legal grounds.

Such a work as *Les trois genres* might seem to break a condition of the license of the theater that it was not to mount productions of new opéras comiques. This was certainly the view of the Louis-Marie-Céleste, duc d'Aumont, the manager of the provisional administration at the Opéra-Comique. He wrote to the marquis de Lauriston and drew attention to what he considered an infringement of the Odéon's license and his own interests.[12] This ought to have been a watertight case. Bernard had however second-guessed the Opéra-Comique's intentions, and his own letter arrived on Lauriston's desk the same day as the duc d'Aumont's. He wrote that it was a question merely of a single scene that was justified by the particular circumstances of the opera troupe's opening.[13] Lauriston was entirely swayed by this argument. His response to Bernard however makes it clear that his decision represented a single exception to a general rule and that no precedent was to be set.[14]

Les trois genres was well received by an audience already well disposed to the success of their theater. Ideas in the work were picked up in the press, most obviously the encouragement to audiences at other theaters to cross the river to the Odéon: "Let the inhabitants beyond the bridge leave behind their prejudices and their neighborhoods!" was typical of commentary in

10. *La Pandore,* 14 June 1826.

11. Boieldieu's letter to Castil-Blaze is F-Pn L.a. XI, fols. 275[r–v]. See also, Paul-Louis Robert, "Correspondance de Boïeldieu," *Rivista musicale italiana* 22 (1915): 522–23. I am grateful to Valerie Neveu of the Bibliothèque municipale in Rouen for effectively recataloguing the entire Boieldieu correspondence still held in Rouen ("Correspondance de Boïeldieu/état au 20 III 1991" [typescript, 1991]).

12. F-Pan O³ 1791/VI.

13. Ibid.

14. Ibid.

the press.[15] The presence of the claque was noticed, but it was also noted that it failed to do any damage.[16] Audiences were large, and the doors were besieged.[17] There was a general view that the theater had changed out of all recognition—and that had to be for the better: "The Odéon [was] no longer the Odéon."[18]

The Monarchy and the Theater

Louis XVIII and Charles X were brothers of the executed Louis XVI. By the 1820s they exhibited little of the enthusiasm for the stage and its music that had characterized the reign of their predecessors, and especially that of Louis XIV. Indeed, it was Napoléon who had, for very different reasons to those of Louis XIV, become involved with theater and music drama.[19] During the Empire, Napoléon attended the opera twenty times; on average he went twice a year. In 1810, he set up the Decennial Prize for opera and in that year attended the opera no fewer than ten times. Not only was he present at performances at the Académie impériale de musique (as it was then called) but he involved himself greatly in the organization and administration of the institution.[20] Napoléon's interest in French music drama has however to be set in the context of his real enthusiasm for Italian opera, which he preferred to hear at the court theater in the Tuileries. His interest in the Académie impériale de musique was much more an acknowledgement of the possible enhancement to his prestige and power offered by the institution. His carefully stage-managed appearances at performances often involved calling a halt to the performance while the audience recovered from its excitement, and often such appearances were timed to follow major military victories.[21] Some works in the imperial repertory were unashamed propaganda; *Le triomphe de Trajan* and *La fête de Mars* are good examples.[22] Even works with libretti that could be read at one level as classical

---

15. Puissent les habitants d'outre-pont sortir de leurs préjugés et de leurs quartiers! (*Le Diable Boiteux,* 28 April 1824).

16. *Journal de Paris,* 28 April 1824.

17. *La Pandore,* 28 April 1824.

18. Ibid.

19. Patrick Barbier, *Opera in Paris 1800–1850: A Lively History,* trans. Robert Luoma (Portland Or.: Amadeus, 1995), 5–6.

20. Ibid., 6–12.

21. James H. Johnson, *Listening in Paris: A Cultural History* (Berkeley: University of California Press, 1995), 166–69.

22. *Le triomphe de Trajan* was composed by Louis-Luc Loiseau de Persuis and Jean-François Le Sueur to a libretto by Joseph-Alphonse Esménard, premiered at the Académie impériale de musique, 23 October 1807; *La fête de Mars,* composed by Rodolphe Kreutzer with *divertissements* by Pierre-Gabriel Gardel, was premiered at the Académie impériale de musique, 26 December 1809.

or early modern history could also be seen as thinly veiled—and positive—commentaries on the qualities of the emperor. Licinius in Spontini's *Vestale* and the eponym of the same composer's *Fernand Cortez* could be seen as barely concealed shadows of the emperor.[23]

The restored Bourbons neither liked music drama nor saw the immense political value of the renamed Académie royale de musique. Furthermore, the alacrity with which they resumed the ceremonial of the *ancien régime*, only slightly modified as a result of imperial practice, resulted in a disinclination to leave the cycle of receptions and presentations at the Tuileries or St-Cloud.[24] Neither Louis XVIII nor Charles X was a young man, and Louis XVIII was in serious ill health for much of his reign. His figure did not bear comparison with Napoléon's or indeed with that of the average gentleman who attended the Académie royale de musique. Although the opera represented an opportunity for the meeting of the court and the society of the faubourg St-Germain, it also represented an opportunity—never taken—for the monarch to enhance his prestige.

During the celebrations of Charles X's coronation, Rossini's *Viaggio a Reims* was given a command performance and premiere. Castil-Blaze's often-quoted account of the monarch's behavior at the performance gives the clearest idea of how Charles X personally failed to respond to the opportunities presented to him by a public presence at the opera.

> King Charles X, who was fêted in the most brilliant and sumptuous manner, did not have a good time at all. Sitting in one of the front boxes between the duchesses of Angoulême and Berry, His Majesty at first endured the extravaganza patiently but, like Dido at the stake, soon raised his eyes to heaven, sought the gaslight, and groaned. This expressive pantomime was evidence of royal boredom. I saw the monarch lean toward the duchess of Berry and ask if the drudgery was still far from ending. Without a word, the princess responded by showing him the open libretto. One third was done, two thirds remained to be endured: he had to take his medicine in three doses![25]

Exactly how the audience, who had so admired and applauded the emperor at the opera only a little over a decade earlier, responded to this behavior is open to conjecture. His conduct at the Théâtre italien was typical of attitudes of almost all the royal family and betrays the restored Bourbons' dis-

23. Johnson, *Listening in Paris,* 178.

24. Barbier, *Opera in Paris,* 16. For an outline of the restored Bourbons' attitude to the court and the city see Philip Mansel, *The Court of France 1789–1830* (Cambridge: Cambridge University Press, 1988), 151–53.

25. Castil-Blaze, *L'Opéra-Italien de 1548 à 1856* (1856), quoted in Barbier, *Opera in Paris,* 17; and discussed in Johnson, *Listening in Paris,* 182.

inclination to take the pulse of public opinion that prefaced the *trois glorieuses* and the suicide of the monarchy.[26]

The Monarch's Name Day

State occasions that were celebrated by the theaters of Paris fell into two categories: the monarch's name day, and the occasional command performance. In addition, the theaters participated in the coronation of Charles X in May–June 1825.[27] Normal practice at all Parisian theaters except the Académie royale de musique was to reflect the nature of the royal name day. This took a variety of forms that ranged from simply reviving a work on a royal theme to offering a newly commissioned work that directly reflected either the holiday itself or the historical context of kingship. By and large, these latter works were not designed to have a life span of longer than a week or so; it was rare to see them appear on the stage again. During the period in which the Odéon produced music drama, Parisian theaters had the opportunity to celebrate the name day of the monarch five times: the feast of Saint Louis on August 25, 1824, and the feasts of Saint Charles (4 November) in 1824–27. By the time of the feast of Saint Charles in 1828, the opera troupe at the Odéon had ceased to exist.

On the feast of Saint Louis 1824 (25 August), the dying Louis XVIII dragged himself from St-Cloud to the Tuileries to preside over the celebration of his name day for one last time.[28] The theaters of Paris, including the Odéon, rose to the occasion and presented specially composed or revived works that, as normal, were presented gratis. The principal (and usual) exception was the Académie royale de musique, which did not mount an appropriate work; even the Opéra-Comique managed to mount *Le roi René* (as it usually did for these occasions). The Odéon's contribution, *Le théâtre dans la caserne,* was entrusted to the drama troupe. Given the fact that the opera troupe had been functioning only for a few weeks, the absence of an operatic celebration of the king's name day is hardly surprising.

The feast of Saint Charles 1824 (4 November) was a muted affair, perhaps because the burial of Louis XVIII had taken place at St-Denis the previous week. Nevertheless, the Comédie-Française premiered *Une Journée de Charles V* on 2 November, and the Théâtre du Vaudeville produced a verse prologue entitled *Le dernier des Romains* on 4 November. On 7 November

---

26. The events leading up to July 1830 have been described as the "suicide of the Monarchy" by André Jardin and André-Jean Tudesq (*Restoration and Reaction: 1815–1848,* trans. Elborg Forster [Cambridge: Cambridge University Press, 1983], 94).

27. Françoise Waquet, *Les Fêtes royales sous la restauration, ou l'ancien régime retrouvé* (Geneva: Droz, 1981), 60–63 and 109–18.

28. Évelyne Lever, *Louis XVIII* (Paris: Fayard, 1988), 555.

was a performance at the Académie royale de musique in which Gluck's *Orphée* opened the program and Berton's *Aline, reine de Golconde* closed it; in between was a vocal and instrumental concert to celebrate the inauguration of the bust of Charles X. None of the events was presented gratis, and the Odéon felt unable to contribute to the festivities. For the feast day of Saint Charles in 1825–27, normal celebrations were resumed, although 1825 was a little less active than the two following years since it fell several months after theatrical responses to the coronation.

Two types of work emerge for the celebration of the king's name day: compositions that display the royalty of the past as main or subordinate characters, and works that are set on the holiday of the Feast of Saint Charles. Popular French history during the Bourbon Restoration laid out kingship in terms of four figures: Charles V, Louis XII, François I, and Henri IV. Each was invested with a particular characteristic: Louis XII was the last medieval king, François I was the first renaissance king, and Henri IV was the first Bourbon; Charles V was the most acceptable figure to whom allusion might be made on behalf of a nineteenth-century monarch of the same name. Each king therefore could serve as the subject of a *pièce de circonstance*—of whatever genre—as a means of praising the restored Bourbon monarchy. Thus, similar subject matter could be worked into an opera at the Académie royale de musique, an opéra comique, a vaudeville, a play without music, or one of the more popular forms of entertainment on the city's boulevards. When in November 1827 Parisian theaters celebrated Charles X's name day, they invoked Charles V (*Une Journée de Charles V* at the Comédie-Française; *Charles V et Duguesclin* at the Odéon), Henri IV (*Le Roi et le batelier* at the Opéra-Comique), or the duchesse de Berry (*La fête des marins ou La St-Charles à Dieppe* at the Gymnase dramatique).[29] More popular at the secondary theaters was the type of work that simply set its action during a holiday. At the Théâtre de la Gaîté in 1826, *La salle de police* conformed to a pattern that was followed by the Gymnase dramatique (*La fée du voisinage ou La St-Charles au village*), the Théâtre du Vaudeville (*Le bourgeois d'Essonne*), and the Théâtre des Variétés (*La fête à la guinguette*).

Against this background the Odéon prepared two works for the name days of Charles X in 1826 and 1827: *L'école de Rome* and *Charles V et Duguesclin*. Although the latter is the more typical of the two, it is perhaps one of the most ephemeral of all the works discussed in this book; no material,

---

29. *La fête des marins* has a complex history. The Gymnase dramatique had been known since 8 September 1824 as the Théâtre de Son Altesse royale, Madame, duchesse de Berry— or simply as the Théâtre de Madame—after a performance given in Dieppe in front of her. *La fête des marins* both celebrates the monarch's name day and alludes to the duchesse's patronage of the theater (see Nicole Wild, *Dictionnaire des théâtres parisiens au XIXe siècle: les théâtres et la musique* [Paris: Amateurs des Livres, 1989], 181).

musical or literary, survives, but the names of the composers and librettists are known, and the action of the piece can be deduced from a summary published in the press.[30] *Charles V et Duguesclin* tells the story of how, in the fourteenth century, a village celebrates the king's name day. The villagers want, according to custom, to elect a neighborhood noble to represent the king, and their choice is Duguesclin. The English unfortunately hold him prisoner (a not uncommon occurrence) and decline to participate in the celebrations but nevertheless agree to allow Duguesclin to take part. Meanwhile the real Charles V arrives incognito in the village and assumes, in the guise of Duguesclin, the "role" of Charles V; the sire de Beaujeu, who has accompanied Charles, rounds up the necessary money to free Duguesclin and takes all the English prisoner. This satisfactory outcome reaches a climax as Charles V makes his identity known and all fall at his feet.

Exactly of what the opéra consisted is open to question. The libretto is attributed to various authors. All authorities agree on Pierre-François-Adolphe Carmouche as one, but sources differ on the second: both of the candidates, Charles-Augustin-Bassompierre Sewrin and Jean-Baptiste-Charles Vial, might have been somehow involved. The three composers of *Charles V et Duguesclin* were all members of the Odéon orchestra: Gilbert, Guiraud, and Tolbecque. One can only guess at what musical numbers featured in this one-act work, and which composers contributed which numbers. The fact that the work is called an opéra rather than a *propos mêlée d'ariettes* (the generic title of *L'école de Rome,* for example) suggests that it might have had a larger proportion of musical items to spoken dialogue. All reports point to the fact that music was newly composed for the work. *Charles V et Duguesclin* was well received. Of the three planned performances, the last (on 6 November 1827) was canceled and replaced by a performance of Dalayrac's *Adolphe et Clara.* No reason was given, but it was probably because of indisposition on the part of one of the performers. As with most such *pièces de circonstance,* no revival was ever proposed.

The previous year's work for the feast of Saint Charles was *L'école de Rome.* Little more survives than for *Charles V et Duguesclin,* but there is extant a manuscript copy of the libretto submitted to the censor on 26 October 1826. The work was premiered on 4 November the same year, and, like *Charles V et Duguesclin,* ran for very few performances; the work was taken off the stage after its fifth presentation on 16 November.[31] *L'école de Rome* is more than an occasional piece; in addition to the royal celebrations of the monarch's name day, its context is embedded in Parisian theatrical politics of late 1826. *L'école de Rome* may have been read as part of the campaign to

---

30. *Le Courrier des Théâtres,* 4 November 1827. The journal gave similar summaries of all *pièces de circonstance.*

31. The censor's libretto is F-Pan F[18] 614/163.

give a platform to returning Prix de Rome composers that had resulted in a petition to La Rochefoucauld only a week before. Its young composers were Auguste Panseron and Pierre-Gaspard Rolle, laureates for the years 1813 and 1814 respectively, and both signatories to the petition presented to La Rochefoucauld. For the libretto's three authors (Claude-Louis-Marie de Rochefort-Luçay, Gustave Vulpian, and Espérance-Hippolyte Lassagne), this was their only collaboration with the opera troupe at the Odéon. Having chosen to use the opportunity of an occasional work to make a political point about the status of young composers returning from Rome, the authors were careful, even oblique, in their handling of the text. The scene is set in Rome just before the painter (Auguste) and the sculptor (Armand) are to return to Paris after their sojourn as Prix de Rome laureates. In the opening scene, surrounded by admirers, Auguste and Armand are putting the finishing touches to their respective works, a portrait and a bust of Charles X. The text of the opening chorus runs as follows, "Travaillons, amis, travaillons/De notre Prince c'est la fête./Nos pinceaux, notre palette/Et nos coeurs sont aux Bourbons." The musician, Charles, does not appear until scene ii; although his musical activity is at the center of the action in scene vi (the duet "Quoi! Vous voulez que je chante?"), the text does not address his difficulties as a Prix de Rome composer; these are dwarfed by the fact that he is the desperate lover of Fiorella, who is likely to be married off to the aging antiquarian Signor Vétusti. At the dénouement, Auguste and Armand return to presumably successful careers in Paris; significantly, Charles—together with Fiorella—remains in Rome: love is, apparently, a satisfactory substitute for a successful career on the lyric stage. Just to remind the Odéon audience that it is indeed the feast of Saint Charles (because the action might easily have eclipsed the date), the work ends with a short chorus: "Chantons! Célébrons ce beau jour!/Et que nos chants, dans ce séjour/franchissant la distance,/Portent aux pieds du Roi de France/Le doux tribut de la reconnaissance/Et les accès de notre amour."

L'école de Rome belongs to the second category of occasional works: those that simply take the opportunity of the feast of Saint Charles as a pretext for a largely unrelated story. Those in the know at the Odéon would have appreciated the work's eventual outcome; after all, it was the consistent argument of the Odéon and its adherents that Prix de Rome composers had no future on their return to Paris from Rome. Charles's decision to remain in Rome would have seemed the logical outcome of the status quo that the Odéon was trying to change. The composers of *L'école de Rome* had been trying to make their way for nearly a decade in the world of Parisian music drama and were probably grateful for the opportunity to compose some theater music that would actually go into rehearsal and performance. The music for *L'école de Rome* consisted, in addition to the opening and closing choruses, of four solos and a duet. None of the musical material is attributed in the single surviving source, but press reports confirm that it is the original work of the two composers, Panseron and Rolle. *La Pandore* attributed an *air bouffe* to Rolle that must surely be Vétusti's aria "J'ai le bandeau de Darius."[32] The *romance* sung by Peronnet was also praised, and this could only have been Charles's "Ma Fiorella." More perplexing is the identification of a *nocturne* by Panseron. This is not a work that belongs to the instrumental *notturno-nocturne* tradition; it is tempting to read this as a reference to an evening event—the concert that takes place in scene vi—and therefore to attribute the duet "Quoi! Vous voulez que je chante" to Panseron.

On 9 December 1826, a month after *L'école de Rome* had been taken off, Panseron was reported to have published three numbers from the work with the publisher Pacini.[33] This is entirely credible since Pacini was also the publisher of other Odéon music drama: *Le neveu de Monseigneur* and *Ivanhoé*. However, there is no record in the *Bibliographie de France* of any publication by Pacini of music by Panseron during 1826 or 1827. Curiously, there is a reference on 13 December 1826 to a *nocturne à deux voix* entitled "Le voleur et le passant" jointly composed by Panseron and Charles-Henri Plantade; it was written for two equal voices and published by Frère and cannot therefore be "Quoi! Vous voulez que je chante?" Panseron and Rolle's music for *L'école de Rome* remains to be discovered.

The Odéon took a calculated risk in mounting *Charles V et Duguesclin* and *L'école de Rome*. The latter consisted of seven newly composed musical numbers, and *Charles V et Duguesclin* might have included more. The theater got away with making a clear breach of its license. Although *Les trois genres*, which opened the opera seasons at the Odéon, was subject to criticism from the duc d'Aumont and defended for that occasion only by the marquis de Lauriston, no record of any complaint about either of the two works for the feast of Saint Charles survives. It might have appeared unseemly on the part of the Opéra-Comique to criticize a work that was mounted gratis specifically to celebrate the name day of the king. Selecting such a work as *L'école de Rome* that drew attention to the issue of opéra comique by young composers and giving the libretto to two Prix de Rome laureates seems, at nearly two centuries' distance, to be close to inflammatory but, as with all the Odéon's attempts to broaden its repertory, the efforts were fruitless.

Crowning Charles X

Undoubtedly the most memorable state event in which the Théâtre-Royal de l'Odéon participated during the 1820s was the coronation of Charles X.

32. *La Pandore,* 5 November 1826.
33. Ibid., 9 November 1826.

Although Louis XVIII had died on 16 September 1824, his brother Charles was not crowned until 29 May 1825. Various difficulties during the early part of the reign of Louis XVIII—the hundred days of 1814–15, the assassination of the duc de Berry at the Académie royale de musique in 1820—had contributed to the collapse of projects to mount a coronation in the style of the *ancien régime*.[34] Hence Charles X made his intentions clear on 22 December 1824 from the throne: he would be crowned in Reims at the same altar as Clovis "in the presence of He who judges peoples and kings."[35]

The splendor of Charles X's coronation is well known. The event fell into four phases: the journey from Paris to Reims, the ceremonies in Reims itself, the return to and entry into Paris, and the celebrations in the capital.[36] The king and his entourage left Paris on 24 May 1825 for Compiègne, where they stayed until the twenty-seventh. The journey to Reims was via Soissons and Fismes, and the king arrived in Reims on 28 May. He was crowned the following day and returned to Compiègne on 1 June; he rested there for a few days and made his entrance into Paris on the sixth.[37] Many of the images of royalty that may be witnessed in the texts of occasional works at Parisian theaters characterize all four of these phases, and allusions to the monarchy of the past were much in evidence. On the journey to Reims, at the entrance to the commune of Buson in Fismes was an *arc de triomphe* on which was written: "Long live the King! Long live our Henri IV, and long live Charles X!"[38] As part of the decorations of the cathedral in Reims, a gallery was formed of twenty-four arcades, part of the decoration of each were portraits of every king of France from Clovis to Louis XVIII.[39] There was no doubt that Charles X's coronation was to be seen as the defining moment when the ruptured dynasty of the Bourbons was to be repaired.

34. Waquet, *Fêtes royales,* 109.

35. En présence de Celui qui juge les peuples et les rois (ibid.).

36. For an account of the coronation ceremony's musical characteristics see Jean Mongrédien, "La musique aux fêtes du sacre de Charles X," *Recherches sur la musique française classique* 10 (1970): 87–100.

37. The literature on Charles X's coronation is extensive. For primary sources see Jean Jérôme Achille Darmaing, *Relation complète du sacre de Charles X avec toutes les modifications introduites dans les prières et le cérémonies et la liste de tous les fonctionnaires publics qui ont été appelés au sacre par lettres closes* (Paris: Baudouin, 1825); *Journal historique des cérémonies et fêtes du sacre de Sa Majesté Charles X* (Paris: Imprimerie royale, 1827); Alexandre Le Noble, *Relation du sacre de S. M. Charles X* (Paris: Pochet, 1825); Edme François Antoine Marie Miel, *Histoire du sacre de Charles X dans ses rapports avec les beaux-arts et les libertés publiques de la France* (Paris: Panckoucke, 1825). For a view from Reims, see Charles Joseph Christophe Siret, *Précis historique du sacre de S. M. Charles X* (Reims: Regnier, 1826).

38. Le Noble, *Relation du sacre,* 10.

39. Ibid., 30.

On 6 June 1825, Charles X and his entourage arrived at la Villette, on the outskirts of Paris, at one in the afternoon. At his arrival at the barrière St-Martin, the king was met by the *corps municipal* of the city headed by Gilbert-Joseph Gaspard, comte de Chabrol de Volvic (the prefet de la Seine) and Guy Delavau (the prefet de police); to the accompaniment of a 100-gun salute, he was given the keys of the city. The royal itinerary went via Notre-Dame, where the king met his ministers and the archbishop of Paris, and thence to the Tuileries. Along the route were public and unofficial manifestations of the city's enthusiasm: all the trees on the boulevard from the Porte-St-Martin to the Porte-St-Denis were joined by garlands, interspersed with flags bearing fleurs de lys. The drapers on the rue St-Honoré and the rue St-Denis decorated their houses with the fabrics they had made, as Parisian industry paid homage to its monarch.[40] The diary of celebrations that followed Charles X's entry in Paris divides clearly into the public and the court: there were public royal presences at the Académie royale de musique, the Comédie-Française, the Opéra-Comique, the Odéon, and the Théâtre italien (10, 11, 14, 17, and 19 June); court events included the balls on the 12 and 13 June, performances at the theater in the Tuileries (16, 20, and 21 June) and the amusements in the royal apartments on 18 June. The premiere of Rossini's *Viaggio a Reims* on 19 June was the last of five command performances at the royal theaters.[41]

There were two types of involvement in the coronation for the Parisian theaters: the presentation of a *spectacle gratis* on Tuesday 7 June, and the command performances in the two weeks following. Almost all theaters in the capital—royal and secondary—participated in the performances on 7 June, but only the royal theaters gave command performances. Most mounted a work that reflected the pageantry of the day in question. The relationship between the spectacles gratis and the command performances differed from theater to theater. The Académie royale de musique and the Théâtre-Royal italien offered no spectacle gratis and saved their *pièces de circonstance* for the command performances (*Pharamond* and *Il viaggio a Reims* respectively); it was in this respect only that the Théâtre italien's performance of *Il viaggio a Reims* differed from others. The Opéra-Comique and Théâtre-Français simply repeated their spectacles gratis (*Le bourgeois de Reims* and *La clémence de David*). The Odéon's spectacle gratis had included *Louis XII ou La route de Reims* and the play *Adélaide Duguesclin,* whereas for its command performance it included *Robin des bois* alongside *Louis XII.*

40. *Journal historique,* 78–81.

41. Ibid., 86. See Janet Johnson, "A Lost Rossini Opera Recovered: *Il viaggio a Reims,*" *Bollettino del Centro Rossiniano di studi* (1983): 19–20.

All that survives of *Louis XII ou La route de Reims* is a printed libretto.[42] Yet given the fact that the work is a pasticcio of compositions by Mozart, it is possible to reconstruct at least parts of the work. Setting the action in the period of an earlier monarch, the pasticcio falls into the first of the two categories of occasional works, as a synopsis of the libretto makes clear.

Background
Louis de La Trimouille, victor of St-Aubin, has yet to appear at the court of Louis XII, who is grieved by his absence. De La Trimouille, his wife, and daughter, Clotilde, have recently been entertaining young knights who are disaffected with the court because they have received no position (Jean Marot, d'Albiac, d'Albert, and Duplessis).

ACT I (THE VALLEY OF JONCHERY; SEVEN LEAGUES FROM REIMS)
The villagers of Jonchery look forward to the arrival of Louis XII on his way to Reims (chorus "Travaillons, gens du village"). To make the day even more of a celebration, the local magistrate (*le grand bailli*) has refused to allow any marriages in the neighborhood for three months, in the hope that the king will officiate as he passes through. The king's majordomo, Desbatignolles, arrives to make arrangements and suggests that the magistrate make no speech, but that one of the village girls, Marguerite (the protégée of Mme de La Trimouille), should speak to the king; the magistrate agrees. Olivier de Surville arrives (air "Voyez sa marche altière"); he is the king's page and delighted to be so close to the de La Trimouille castle, because he is Clotilde's admirer. Olivier is disturbed by news given to him by Marguerite (duo "Près de ma belle"), of the disaffected knights in the de La Trimouille castle. The king arrives with General Aubigni (chorus "Quelle ivresse nous presse!"); the former receives Marguerite with enthusiasm. The king and Aubigni discuss the reasons for de La Trimouille's absence from court. The king decides to go the castle of de La Trimouille (chorus "Ah! d'un si beau voyage").

ACT II (SALON IN THE CHÂTEAU DE LA TRIMOUILLE)
De La Trimouille, Mme de La Trimouille, and Clotilde lament the situation in which they find themselves (trio "Parlons, plus de crainte") and are disturbed by an off-stage chorus ("Dans le vin, plus de tristesse"), and are then interrupted by the arrival of the young knights, who explain to de La Trimouille that they are on their way to take up places with the duc de Guise. In disgust, de La Trimouille orders them to leave but Olivier arrives, an-

42. *Louis XII ou La route de Reims* (Paris: Bouquin de la Souche, 1825).

nouncing that it is too late, and that the king's retinue is outside the castle. De La Trimouille agrees to hide the knights in a forgotten wing of the castle (ensemble "Fuyons tous"). Mme de La Trimouille wrestles with her conscience: to protect her husband or to confess to the king; she chooses the former (recitative and aria "Il est donc vrai"—"Douce espérance"). Louis XII arrives and immediately seeks an interview with de La Trimouille, where the two reestablish their friendship; de La Trimouille is afraid that the king will find out about the miscreant nobles. Aubigni presents the king with the documents taken from the duc de Guise's intercepted messenger: it is clear that the nobles are in the castle, and that they intend to defect to the duc de Guise. Louis confronts Clotilde with this knowledge but makes it clear that he exonerates her father (duo "Allez, laissez-moi mon enfant"). The king instructs Olivier to tell the nobles to leave the castle—at the signal of a song with words by Marot—and to go to Reims, where they should present themselves at court with the same enthusiasm that they were prepared to present themselves at the court of the Guise. Just before dinner, the king invites Olivier to sing a ballad. As he sings, the nobles disappear across the back of the stage, observed by the king and Aubigni (finale "Venons, loin du fardeau"). The company goes to dine.

ACT III (THE *SALLE D'HONNEUR* OF THE PALACE AT REIMS)
Aubigni asks the king if he will pardon or punish the young nobles. The offstage chorus ("Quelle ivresse/Nous presse") convinces the king to take the former path. Desbatignolles admires the palace (*couplets* "Quel effet, tantôt à la fête") and encounters the young nobles. Desbatignolles leaves and de La Trimouille enters and explains that he had nothing to do with their escape; the nobles realize that they have been tricked. The king, Aubigni, and the court enter; Louis XII pardons the nobles and makes Jean Marot his historian. The king's reception begins (chorus "Guidés par l'espérance"), and the theater changes into the great square in Reims (prayer "O grand Dieu, dont la puissance" and *choeur général* "Français, voilà de la patrie").

The libretto of *Louis XII* gives clear indications from which of Mozart's works each number was taken. The majority are from *La clemenza di Tito,* one number from *Idomeneo,* and two from *Die Entführung aus dem Serail.* The libretto does not indicate which specific numbers were reworked for *Louis XII.* However, the prosody of the French libretto, when compared with that of the German or Italian original models, allows the identification of the source of five of the fourteen numbers with some security. All the numbers in *Louis XII ou La route de Reims* that were taken from *Die Entführung aus dem Serail* are recoverable in part, as are three of the numbers adapted from *La clemenza di Tito.*
    The first number, the chorus "Travaillons, gens de village," is modeled

on the Janisseries' chorus from act I of *Die Entführung aus dem Serail.* Mozart's chorus takes the form of a simple ABA structure in which the B section is devoted to choral soloists. As can be seen from the libretto's text, the number in *Louis XII* follows this closely:

CHOEUR	CHOR
Travaillons, gens de village	Singt dem großen Bassa Lieder
Pour fêter un si beau jour:	Töne, feuriger Gesang;
Que le Roi, sur son passage,	Und vom Ufer halle wider
Trouv' le gage de notre amour.	Unsrer Lieder Jubelklang.
LE BAILLI	SOLO
Chut! paix! silence!	Weht ihm entgegen,
Quelle importance!	Kühlende Winde,
Un Roi de France	Ebne dich sanfter,
S'arrête ici!	Wallende Flut!
J'en perds la tête:	Singt ihm entgegen,
Pareille fête	Fliegende Chöre
N'fut jamais faite	Singt ihm der Liebe
A Jonchery.	Freuden ins Herz!
CHOEUR	CHOR
Travaillons, gens de village	Singt dem großen Basse Lieder

The libretto indicates a single soloist in the B section of the chorus whereas Mozart's original uses chorus members. Although it is possible to reconstruct most of the A section of this chorus, this is not the case for the B section. Even in the case of the A section, there are difficulties. The presentation of the two texts masks the fact that Mozart's chorus makes use of, and perhaps depends for its effect on, the repetition of certain words in the text. The discrepancies between the two libretti are evident in the very first line where the words "dem großen Bassa Lieder" are repeated (example 4).

Executing a similar repeat of the words in the French version would not be possible. The text would have to read: "Travaillons, gens du village, -aillons, gens du village"; although the repeat's omission of the first syllable (and word) in the German libretto is satisfactory, it is not so in the French.

In act II of *Louis XII,* the king and Clotilde sing a duet during the course of which Clotilde admits her love for Olivier ("Allez, laissez-moi mon enfant"). Its model is the act II duet from *Die Entführung aus dem Serail* for Osmin and Blonde. It begins very simply and closely follows Mozart's word-repetitions and changes of voice (example 5). Even when the exchanges pick up velocity, the French version requires no change (example 6).

The andante middle section of this duet is missing from *Louis XII,* and the final section is difficult to reconstruct. The two lines of poetry assigned

Example 4. Mozart, *Die Entführung aus dem Serail.* Chorus "Singt dem großen Bassa Lieder," bars 10–20.

to the king and Clotilde for this section do not correspond clearly to those in *Die Entführung,* and this passage in *Louis XII* must have been subject to considerable reworking.

The duet for Olivier and Marguerite in act i of *Louis XII* ("Près de ma belle") is based on Servilia's act ii aria, "S'altro che lacrime," from *La clemenza di Tito.* Mozart's aria is a setting of an eight-line poem. The music of the first four lines modulates to the dominant and the next four lines remain there. The first four lines are then repeated with their music but changed so as to end with a coda in the tonic. Vergne and perhaps Crémont turned out a duet with the sixteen lines of poetry that are found in the li-

Example 5. Mozart/Vergne, *Louis XII ou La route de Reims*. Duet "Allez, laissez-moi," bars 1–12.

bretto. There are two identical stanzas of eight lines each, so the last four lines (13–16) may have been used for the repeat of Mozart's first four lines. New text could also have been given to the repetitions in the coda of the text "Tutto il piangere/Non gioverà," but this does not account for all the text in the libretto. Again, this final section must have been reworked (pos-

Example 6. Mozart/Vergne, *Louis XII ou La route de Reims*. Duet "Allez, laissez-moi," bars 17–23.

sibly with the inclusion of a transposition of lines 5–8 into the tonic to end the work).

The first 13 bars of the act I quintet "Deh conservate, oh Dei" from *La clemenza di Tito* serve as the basis for the chorus that ends act I of *Louis XII* ("Ah! D'un si beau voyage"). They are the only lines in the libretto that correspond to those in *La clemenza di Tito* in terms of their scansion. The libretto of *Louis XII* gives five identical four-line stanzas to *la cour* (as chorus), *les villageois* (also as chorus), Aubigni, Olivier, and the king. None of these could be used alongside the music from bar 14 onward in Mozart's original, and the rest of the chorus must have proceeded differently.

Vitellia's act II *recitativo accompagnato e rondo* "Ecco il punto"—"Non più di fiori" from *La clemenza di Tito* becomes the recitative and aria sung by

Mme de La Trimouille, in act II of *Louis XII*, as she wrestles with her decision whether or not to betray her husband to the king ("Il est donc vrai"—"Douce espérance"). "Ecco il punto"—"Non più di fiori" is the only *recitativo accompagnato* in *La clemenza di Tito* that leads into an aria for the same soloist. Sesto's accompanied recitative leads into the quintet that closes act I, Tito's into a *recitativo semplice* with Publio, and his second recitative straight into the closing sextet with chorus at the end of the work. The internal structuring of both poems confirms that the one is modeled on the other. The structure of "Non più di fiori" is well known:[43] Mozart sets the first eight lines of the poem (*quinari*) in a 6/8 F major larghetto that modulates to the dominant. The first four lines of the poem are then repeated so as to return to the tonic. The following allegro in common time sets four *ottonari;* in turn this is followed by a return of the opening music and text recast in the prevailing 4/4 allegro; all twelve lines are then repeated in this configuration, at which point the structure begins to break down with nonsequential references to various parts of the poem. The version of "Non più di fiori" in *Louis XII* is rather simpler. The opening section matches very easily: Lauréal's and Saint-Georges's words fit Mozart's music perfectly (example 7).

The move into the common-time allegro, while difficult to track exactly, seems to be mirrored in *Louis XII*, and the *ottonari* of the lines "Chi vedesse il mio dolore/Pur avria di me pietà" are exactly matched by the octosyllables in French: "Épargne une fille chère/Destin, ne frappe que moi." The reprise of the opening text is difficult to assess. The cue "Douce espérance" is simple enough, but the next four lines of text match those of the opening and would make sense if they followed the first four lines that are cued. Lines five to eight of the original poem, when they are repeated in the allegro section, are replaced by four new lines. The rondo in *Louis XII* may have ended with the reprise reengineered to return to the 6/8 larghetto with which it opened, although this would however have resulted in some further tonal difficulties. The recitative is even more problematic because in recitatives (*accompagnato* or *semplice*), French translations and reworkings diverge more widely than is the case in arias and ensembles. The recitative "Ecco il punto" formed the basis of the one for Mme de La Trimouille, but many of the vocal details must have been changed quite markedly in *Louis XII*. The length of both recitatives is similar, and points of articulation fall in the same place. The end of the recitative, as it moves into the rondo, is a point where the two recitatives approach each other most closely.

43. John A. Rice, *W. A. Mozart: La clemenza di Tito* (Cambridge: Cambridge University Press, 1991), 34, 49–51, and 99–100; James Parakilas, "Mozart's Mad Scene," *Soundings* 10 (1983): 3–17.

Example 7. Mozart/Vergne, *Louis XII ou La route de Reims.* Duet "Près de ma belle," bars 9–30.

Example 7 *(continued)*

Command Performances

Louis XVIII and Charles X hardly ever went to the opera. The only member of the royal family who seems to have made an impression on Parisian theatrical life was the duchesse de Berry. Marie-Caroline, formerly princess of the Two Sicilies, had been widowed by the assassination of her husband the duc de Berry at the Académie royale de musique in 1820. Her interest in the theater was remarkable. She was the patron of the Gymnase dramatique (which had accordingly changed its name to the Théâtre de Madame) and was a regular member of the audience at most of the royal theaters in the capital. As far as can be established, the duchesse de Berry attended performances at the Odéon nine times (in addition to the 1825 coronation performance) during the period 1824–28. Of these nine performances, only four included music drama, and it is clear that the duchesse de Berry attended events that were of theatrical interest or significance and—with the exception of two performances of *Robin des bois*—not necessarily of operatic importance. Three of the command performances were for nights when there was no music drama staged at all; given the relative rarity of such evenings, this may possibly betray a preference on the part of the duchesse for spoken drama or an indifference to the music drama mounted at the Odéon. Her presence in the audience of *Ivanhoé* on 28 October 1828 was perhaps motivated more by a desire to be familiar with the work of the novelist who was to arrive in Paris within the week rather than by a wish to see the work itself. It is however possible that the two German works—*Robin des bois* and *Le sacrifice interrompu*—were the reason for the duchesse's attendance at the Odéon on those evenings.

Descriptions of the command performance at the Odéon on 17 June 1825 identify the occasion as one of the most spectacular in the theater's history and as one with striking resemblance to the premiere of *Il viaggio a Reims* at the Théâtre-Royal italien two days later. As early as 13 June, Bernard warned his audiences in an announcement in *La Pandore* that all seats had been reserved for the 17 June command performance. On the day of the performance it was announced that no seats would be available on the night. Crowds had already assembled by 4:00 in the afternoon for the performance that was due to begin after the arrival of the royal party at 7:30. The rue de l'Odéon was decorated with illuminated trees, and the facade of the theater was decorated with paper lanterns under the colonnade. "Everything that was opulent, powerful, or ambitious in Paris, in the provinces, and abroad appeared to be at the Odéon."[44] The inside of the auditorium

---

44. Tout ce qu'il y a d'opulent, de puissant ou d'ambitieux à Paris, en province et à l'étranger semblait s'être donné rendez-vous dans la salle de l'Odéon (*Le Diable Boiteux,* 19 June 1825).

had been modified in deference to the prestige of the occasion.[45] Three-quarters of the parterre were equipped with stalls and veterans handed out bouquets to the women as they entered. When the royal party arrived, everyone waved flowers at the king in greeting. The command performance consisted of a repeat of *Louis XII ou La route de Reims* and the sixty-ninth performance of *Robin des bois*. An additional stanza was added to Richard's act I aria in praise of the king. This came in for a certain amount of criticism from those who thought that such praise ought to come from someone else in the cast. Richard (Caspar) was perhaps the least suitable character, but his strophic aria was the most obvious number to which to add an additional stanza. In the description in the *Moniteur Universel,* this ambiguity is diplomatically skated over. If Charles X was as little interested in *Robin des bois* as he later was in *Il viaggio a Reims,* he never learned the ultimate fate of the character who sang his praises.

Mounting occasional performances for the royal celebrations of the Bourbons after the Restoration cannot have been a particularly rewarding experience. The structures for celebration were in place but the principal objects of celebration, the royal family, exhibited little or no interest. Audiences were probably unconcerned about the monarch's lack of interest in music drama; it was the structures themselves that guaranteed free performances and novel operatic productions. The Odéon succeeded in turning this situation to its advantage. The official structures for celebration were used to cloak new works by young French composers that were banned by the Odéon's license; although these attempts were successful in their own terms, they failed to shift the prevailing official view that the Odéon's license should remain unchanged, and that it should be forbidden to mount new opéra comique.

As in other Parisian theaters during the Restoration, occasional works figured larger in the performance calendar than they did in the later nineteenth or twentieth centuries. Rather than selecting a well-known classic to announce the beginning of music drama at the Odéon, the management commissioned a new and idiosyncratic composition from the capital's best-known playwright, and from two of its most prestigious composers. In doing so, the theater's management advertised the radically different profile of its repertory and fought off claims from the Opéra-Comique that it was transgressing the terms of its license—an exemplum of the way in which the complex bureaucratic network of which the Odéon was part developed and contained pressures between rival institutions.

45. *Journal des Débats,* 19 June 1825.

In its responses to public celebrations of the power of the monarchy—the king's name day, Charles X's coronation and command performances—the Odéon closely approached to the practices of other theaters in Paris. All, by custom, found a way of honoring the king by adapting a small number of dramatic themes and subjects to the generic constraints of the individual theater, and the Odéon was no exception. It shared in the tangle of tales related to French history and more or less comic events based on the Feast of Saint Charles, and—significantly—chose music drama as its medium for this activity rather than spoken drama. Command performances represented ways in which the monarchy could (but did not) exercise a degree of personal taste in matters relating to the stage.

Using performances at public occasions to smuggle into its repertory new numbers or works by younger composers, the Odéon eased the difficulties of a ban on new opéra comique. Yet such occasional works were by their very nature guaranteed only a very few performances and never subject to revival. The pasticcio was the genre of preference in occasional works, and the next chapter spins out this particular thread in the Odéon's repertorial web.

Chapter 6

Rendre service à notre scène lyrique—
The Pasticcio

The Pasticcio in Paris

The pasticcio today occupies a precarious position. A work formed out of compositions by a range of composers, out of different works by the same composer, or even out of extraneous interpolations in one single-composer work offends against modern prejudices in favor of unified works by single composers; the genre is marginalized if not ridiculed as a result. Yet in the eighteenth century, the pasticcio was an important part of operatic culture, "the prevailing form of Italian music drama in London from 1704 until the beginning of the nineteenth century";[1] and "without the pasticcio, Italian opera could never have gained a foothold in France."[2] In the 1820s the status of the pasticcio was ambiguous and confused. Still in vogue as an operatic modus operandi, it had less and less to do with rapidly developing ideas of a work's unity and artistry. In France, these views are most obviously associated with Berlioz.

Eighteenth-century patterns of producing pasticci have to be separated from the so-called "medley" opera, where more than one individual contributed a new act to a collaborative enterprise.[3] Genuine pasticci inserted new compositions into an existing score, set an existing libretto to preexisting arias, or created a libretto to accommodate well-known music. The list of those who occupied themselves with the pasticcio, either as arrangers or contributors, is a roll call of eighteenth-century composers of music drama:

---

1. Curtis Alexander Price, "Unity, Originality, and the London Pasticcio," *Harvard Library Bulletin*, n.s. 2–4 (1991): 17.

2. Reinhard Strohm, "Pasticcio," *The New Grove Dictionary of Music and Musicians*, ed. Stanley Sadie (London: Macmillan, 1980), 14:289.

3. Ibid., 288; Price, "Unity," 18.

Handel, Vivaldi, Hasse, Gluck, Mozart, and Haydn. Crossing the boundary of the nineteenth century, Beethoven contributed finales to two pasticci by Treitschke, and Weber wrote numbers for revivals of music drama by Haydn, Méhul, Cherubini, and Spontini. In turn, Méhul, Cherubini, and Spontini also contributed to revivals of works by others and to other types of pasticcio.

Three pasticci produced in Paris in the fifty years before the Odéon opened its doors to music drama illustrate the particular qualities of French eighteenth-century pasticci and their early-nineteenth-century successors. Grétry's *Trois âges de l'opéra* was created to open the 1778 season at the height of the Gluckiste-Ramiste debate. Writing the history of French opera within an opera, it included music by Lully, Rameau, and Gluck as part of an entirely new libretto. In this respect, it was in line with other French pasticci: music by other composers were brought into service to set a new libretto.[4] Two other pasticci represent a different trend: the setting of a new libretto with music from different works by the same composer. Both *Les mystères d'Isis* (1801) and *Le laboureur chinois* (1803) were pasticci of works by Mozart.[5] *Les mystères d'Isis,* although ostensibly an arrangement of *Die Zauberflöte,* included numbers from *La clemenza di Tito, Don Giovanni,* and *Le nozze di Figaro; Le laboureur chinois* chose more eclectically from *Così fan tutte, La clemenza di Tito,* and *Idomeneo.*[6]

The opera troupe at the Odéon mounted both single-composer and multiple-composer pasticci (appendix 1). On at least one occasion in 1826, critics tried to draw a qualitative distinction between the two, and usually in favor of the former.[7] Confusions occurred, however, as to what constituted a pasticcio, especially when it was made up from the works of Rossini. Some

---

4. In its occasional nature, it also is closely allied with such pasticci at the Odéon as *Louis XII ou La route de Reims.* See M. Elizabeth C. Bartlet, "A Musician's View of the French Baroque after the Advent of Gluck: Grétry's *Les Trois Âges de l'Opéra* in Its Context," in *Jean-Baptiste Lully and the Music of the French Baroque: Essays in Honor of James R. Anthony,* ed. John Hajdu Heyer (Cambridge: Cambridge University Press, 1989), 291–318.

5. For *Les mystères d'Isis,* see Rudolph Angermüller, "'Les Mystères d'Isis' (1801) und 'Don Juan' (1805, 1834) auf der Bühne der Pariser Oper," in *Mozart-Jahrbuch 1980–83 des Zentralinstitutes für Mozartforschung der Internationalen Stiftung Mozarteum Salzburg* (Kassel: Bärenreiter, 1983), 32–97; and Jean Mongrédien, "*Les Mystères d'Isis* (1801) and Reflections on Mozart from the Parisian Press at the Beginning of the Nineteenth Century," in *Music in the Classic Period: Essays in Honor of Barry S. Brook,* ed. Allan W. Atlas (New York: Pendragon, 1985), 195–211. For *Le laboureur chinois,* see Peter Revers, "Mozart und China: Henri-Montan Bertons Pasticcio *Le laboureur chinois:* Ein Beitrag zur französischen Mozart-Rezeption des frühen 19. Jahrhunderts," in *Mozart-Jahrbuch 1991 des Zentralinstitutes für Mozartforschung der Internationalen Stiftung Mozarteum Salzburg* (Kassel: Bärenreiter, 1991), 777–86.

6. Both *Le laboureur chinois* (arr. Henri-Montan Berton) and *Les mystères d'Isis* (arr., Ludwig Welzel Lachnith) include a single number from Haydn, as does *Louis XII ou La route de Reims.*

7. E.g., *Le Courrier des Théâtres,* 28 September 1826 (on the single-composer pasticcio *Ivanhoé*).

critics had no difficulty in separating out pasticci from other works, for example in praising one pasticcio over another.[8] Others clearly thought that all Rossini's works at the Odéon were pasticci.[9]

The pasticcio was coming to the end of a long and distinguished career during the 1820s, and questions of unity and value moved to the center of the concerns of critics and audiences at the Odéon. It was recognized that a pasticcio could be put together well or badly, an echo of François Raguenet's 1709 distinction between the haphazard selection of material and a pasticcio "prepar'd by a Person that is capable of uniting different Styles so artfully as to make 'em pass for one."[10] Even in reviews that were beginning to lose patience with the pasticcio as a genre, writers praised the ability of a musician to select preexisting music skillfully.[11] But Parisian critics were indeed losing patience. Even in 1824, critics were noting unfavorably that pasticci did not have "that process and unity (*cette gradation et cet ensemble*)" found in complete scores.[12]

The 1826 Plan

In early 1826, the Odéon was evolving a plan to bring three foreign composers to the theater to direct pasticci of their own music: Weber for *Les bohémiens,* Meyerbeer for *La nymphe du Danube,* and Rossini for *Ivanhoé.* The nationalities of the three pasticci were carefully balanced: one Italian, one German, and the third a pasticcio of Italian music composed by a German. Meyerbeer was already well known because of the work on *Marguerite d'Anjou,* and the proposed *La nymphe du Danube* ought to have been the least problematic of the three works. Paradoxically, it was the only one to have had no reflection on the Odéon stage. *Les bohémiens* went ahead in November 1826. Although it was staged without the cachet of Weber's supervision, the Odéon strongly suggested to their audiences that his participation had been intended, and the correspondence between Crémont and Weber suggests that the press release was not entirely fictitious. Rossini's *Ivanhoé,* like *Les bohémiens,* was advertised as a performance in part supervised by Rossini and surviving materials make it clear that he was involved in the preparation of the score if not in the production itself.

The Odéon had planned the three pasticci that made up the 1826 plan with some care. *La nymphe du Danube* was originally timed to follow *Les noces*

8. *Le Frondeur,* 14 June 1826, where *La fausse Agnès* was rated as Castil-Blaze's best pasticcio.

9. *Le barbier de Séville* was described as a pasticcio in *La Pandore,* 25 September 1824.

10. *A Critical Discourse on Opera and Musick in England* (1709), cited in Price, "Unity," 18.

11. See, among many others, *Le Diable Boiteux,* 6 June 1824; *Le Courrier des Théâtres,* 10 August 1824.

12. Ibid.

de Figaro in July 1826, *Ivanhoé* was premiered in September, and *Les bohémiens* in November the same year. The original Odéon proposal was to mount the pasticci at approximately two-month intervals. The plan collapsed quickly with initial postponements for *La nymphe du Danube,* but the two other productions went ahead, and *Ivanhoé,* at least, achieved the objectives both of a satisfactory artistic production and of a box-office success. The Odéon's 1826 plan was ambitious in the extreme. When compared, for example, to the Académie royale de musique's efforts to recruit Rossini and to get him to compose music drama in French, to have brought three projects so close to fruition in a single year (and two of them into performance) is an astonishing achievement for a theater with nothing like the resources of such competitors as the Académie royale de musique or the Théâtre italien.

Les bohémiens

The idea of resuscitating *Preciosa* and reworking it with numbers from Weber's *Silvana* arose out of discussions between Crémont and Weber himself. Crémont wrote to Sauvage on 30 November 1825 asking permission to reuse material from the failed *Preciosa* arrangement.[13] Crémont wrote rather elliptically about adapting "a few numbers from *Preciosa* to a libretto offered to me that might be a very great success."[14] Exactly what happened after that request is difficult to determine. Although Crémont's plan was certainly to squeeze Sauvage out of the revision of *Preciosa,* as the correspondence with Weber reveals, it was Sauvage who reworked the *Preciosa* libretto as *Les bohémiens* for a production in November 1826. Crémont wrote again to Sauvage on 7 September 1826, with a desperate demand for Sauvage's revised versions of parts of the libretto, and printed material associated with *Les bohémiens* bears Sauvage's name.[15] As things turned out, the revised *Les bohémiens* included nine numbers from another work by Weber, *Silvana,* but only four from *Preciosa.* The result of this activity is a complex generic hybrid. The libretto of the 1826 pasticcio *Les bohémiens* is ultimately derived from Sauvage's reworking of Pius Alexander Wolff's play *Preciosa.* The basis of the 1825 *Preciosa* had been Weber's incidental music, and this was unprecedented and unsuccessful. Using numbers from *Silvana* set to a

---

13. F-Pn L.a. XXIII, fol. 317[r-v].

14. Quelques morceaux de *Préciosa* à une pièce qu'on m'offre et qui peut être susceptible d'un grand succès (ibid., fol. 317[r]).

15. Crémont's letter to Sauvage is in ibid., fol. 319[r]; surviving material for the production of *Les bohémiens* includes a censors' libretto (F-Pan F[18] 614 G/187) and a collection of extracts in vocal score, *Les bohémiens* (Paris: Kretschmer, [1826]). This edition has only the overture and nine out of the sixteen numbers (2–3, 7–10, 12–13, 15), but the *table thématique* makes it possible to identify the remaining numbers without difficulty.

more conventional libretto brought *Les bohémiens* more directly into line with practices for translations and pasticci at the Odéon.

The premiere of *Les bohémiens* took place on 23 November 1826 as part of a benefit for the Weber family. It was performed alongside a renewed production of *Robin des bois* and benefited a great deal from this pairing. The significant musical changes to *Les bohémiens* received little acknowledgment, but the press recognized that its libretto consisted of more or less the same story as that of *Preciosa*.[16] More striking was the fact that most of the press believed that Weber had been involved in the reworking of *Preciosa* as *Les bohémiens* to the extent of adding numbers from *Silvana* to it.[17] When the composer was in Paris, he had apparently advised the authors of *Les bohémiens* to reinstate all the music to the work, and to complete the score with fragments from *Silvana*. Although Crémont did anything but restore all the music of *Preciosa* to *Les bohémiens*, the Weber benefit was a golden opportunity to relaunch *Robin des bois*, smuggle in the reworking of *Preciosa* under Weber's semi-authorial imprimatur, and rebuild some of the bridges burned as a result of the exchanges between Weber and Castil-Blaze earlier that year. *Les bohémiens* ran for eight nights during November and December 1826; then the indisposition of several principals halted the performances and it was never seen again.

La nymphe du Danube

The idea of conflating the *Undine* story with a pasticcio of Meyerbeer's earlier Italian music drama had been conceived by Crémont and Sauvage during the earliest stages of work on *Marguerite d'Anjou*.[18] On 5 July 1825, Crémont had intimated to Sauvage that *La nymphe du Danube* could be a second *Robin des bois*, in other words a work that could—almost single-handedly— sustain the Odéon's financial position.[19] The supernatural element in *Robin des bois* was an obvious point of contact with *La nymphe du Danube*. Crémont was anxious to move as quickly as possible with the project, and encouraged Sauvage to approach Meyerbeer—whose name, he said, "would have a magic effect at the Odéon"—to provide the music. Although this was not the first time that Crémont and Sauvage had discussed the project, it remained untouched until the spring of 1826. Approaches were made to

---

16. E.g., the report published in the *Journal de Paris*, 9 November 1826.

17. *La Pandore*, 24 November 1826. Similar reports were carried in the *Journal de Paris* and *Le Courrier des Théâtres* on 19 November 1826.

18. Reiner Zimmermann's speculation (*Giacomo Meyerbeer: eine Biographie nach Dokumenten* [Berlin: Henschel, 1991], 145–46) on Meyerbeer's interest in the *Undine* story is thus largely redundant.

19. F-Pn L.a. XXIII, fols. 311^{r-v}.

Meyerbeer, who wrote from Berlin to Sauvage and agreed to work on the project on 2 April 1826. His enthusiasm was clear from the start. He immediately wrote to Vienna for parts two and three of the libretto to Ferdinand Kauer's *Donauweibchen,* since Sauvage had only the first part, and also requested another unidentified libretto—a *comédie féerie*—that he thought might be of use to the work.[20]

Sauvage was responsible for translating the libretto by Karl Friedrich Hensler, molding the narrative sections into spoken dialogue and translated or paraphrasing the lyric sections into French; Meyerbeer selected the specific music to form the basis of the pasticcio and drafted linking material, and Crémont was then responsible for the exact setting of Sauvage's translations or paraphrases to Meyerbeer's music. Most of the music was to be taken from *Romilde e Constanza, Semiramide riconosciuta, Emma di Resburgo, Margherita d'Anjou,* and *L'esule di Granata. Il crociato in Egitto* appears once only in Meyerbeer's plan for the work and then only with an alternative from *Semiramide.*[21] Given the success of *Il crociato* at the end of the previous year, and the prospect of further productions at the Théâtre italien, Meyerbeer was presumably reluctant to expose extracts elsewhere.[22] The surviving autograph material for *La nymphe du Danube* (a plan and some musical sketches) shows that Meyerbeer supplemented his plans for the reuse of material from his earlier music dramas with the composition of new numbers.[23] In the light of his prose notes for the work, the musical sketches, and his earlier enthusiasm for the project, it was perhaps inevitable that he should be closely involved in rehearsals. His participation in these preparations was reported in the press in July 1826.[24]

Initial plans for the staging of *La nymphe* were ambitious. Crémont, presumably with Frédéric's approval, had suggested that the work should be given after *Les noces de Figaro,* which was performed for the first time at the

20. Letter from Meyerbeer in Berlin to Sauvage in Paris, 2 April 1826 (Heinz Becker and Gudrun Becker, *Giacomo Meyerbeer: Briefwechsel und Tagebücher* [Berlin: De Gruyter, 1960–], 2: 26–28).

21. D-Bds N. Mus. Nachl. 97 X/47. Heinz Becker, "Eine *Undine*-Oper Meyerbeers für Paris," in *Festschrift Martin Ruhnke zum 65. Geburtstag* (Neuhausen-Stuttgart: Hänssler, 1986), 41.

22. On the French reception of *Il crociato in Egitto,* see Jean Mongrédien, "Les débuts de Meyerbeer à Paris: *Il Crociato in Egitto* au Théâtre Royal Italien," in *Meyerbeer und das europäische Musiktheater,* ed. Sieghart Döhring and Arnold Jacobshagen (Laaber: Laaber, 1998), 64–72; and on the work's French background see Mark Everist, "Meyerbeer's *Il crociato in Egitto: Mélodrame,* Opera, Orientalism," *Cambridge Opera Journal* 8 (1996): 215–50.

23. The sketches are now F-Po Rés. A. 500.a¹. For a full account of the compositional history of *La nymphe du Danube,* see Mark Everist, "Giacomo Meyerbeer and Music Drama at the Paris Odéon during the Bourbon Restoration," *19th-Century Music* 16 (1993): 124–48, esp. 136–42.

24. *Le Courrier des Théâtres,* 22 July 1826, 4.

Odéon on 22 July 1826.[25] On the same day, however, it was announced that *La nymphe du Danube* could not be mounted until October. By this stage, Meyerbeer may have been working with singers on those numbers for which the translation was already complete. Yet as late as the end of August or early September, he was still receiving outstanding fragments from Sauvage.[26] The latter also asked Meyerbeer to return Frédéric's copies of the first two acts of the work (presumably of Hensler's libretto). Although much of the lyric poetry had been composed or translated by early September, Sauvage had not even begun the spoken dialogue.

With the work in this condition, it was unlikely to meet its postponed deadline of October 1826. Crémont threatened that *Emmeline ou La famille Suisse* might go into rehearsal after *Ivanhoé* if material for *La nymphe du Danube* was not forthcoming. *Ivanhoé* was premiered at the Odéon on 15 September 1826, by which time *La nymphe du Danube* was in no position to go into rehearsal. Crémont's threat was carried out, and *Emmeline* indeed went into rehearsal immediately after *Ivanhoé*. It was premiered at the Odéon on 6 February 1827. The Odéon's need for a new work and Sauvage's tardiness had sounded the death knell of *La nymphe du Danube* in September 1826. Despite Sauvage's hope in November that Schütz's arrival at the Odéon might promote the fortunes of the work, these plans came to nothing. They were briefly resuscitated in the summer of 1827 when Sauvage took over as manager of the Odéon and closed the theater for repairs between 1 June and 17 August that year. One report suggested that *La nymphe du Danube* was to reopen the theater in August.[27] The work was not performed, and Sauvage's debut as manager at the Odéon was marked by such better-known works as *Le barbier de Séville* and *Robin des bois*. Apart from the mélodrame by René Charles Guilbert de Pixérécourt, entitled *Ondine ou La nymphe des eaux*, which was premiered in 1830 (and might have been modeled on what Sauvage completed of *La nymphe du Danube*), the Meyerbeer pasticcio sank without trace.[28]

Ivanhoé

Early in 1825, there was talk in Parisian theatrical circles of music drama based on Sir Walter Scott's novel to be performed at the Odéon. Although

---

25. F-Pn L.a. XXIII, fol. 318ʳ.
26. Becker and Becker, *Briefwechsel und Tagebücher*, 2:31.
27. *Le Courrier des Théâtres*, 10 June 1827, 2.
28. *Ondine ou La nymphe des eaux* (Paris: Barba, 1830). Act IV.xix–xx take place in a palace of crystal that may well have had its origins in the stage design for *La nymphe du Danube*. Such a scene had a large part in the plan to produce the work at the beginning of Sauvage's managerial career in 1827 (*Le Courrier des Théâtres*, 10 June 1827).

Figure 23. Anne-Honoré-Joseph
Duveyrier (pseud. Mélesville). Lithograph
by Pierre-Eugène Aubert.

plans for the Rossini pasticcio were at that stage embryonic or nonexistent, the tenor of one report speaks volumes for Parisian attitudes to Scott in the theater: "*La Gazette* announced, the day before yesterday, that an opera taken from the novel *Ivanhoe* will shortly be played at the Odéon. Might this journal be badly informed? It appears to us that every work of this sort has to originate in Italy, in Germany or with the Hurons (*d'Huronie*)."[29] Scott's work was exotic and popular. Auber's *Leicester ou Le château de Kenilworth* set a libretto by Eugène Scribe and Anne-Honoré-Joseph Duveyrier had been based on Scott's *Kenilworth* and was still in repertory at the Opéra-Comique (figure 23).[30]

Rossini's *Donna del lago,* premiered in Paris the previous September, had brought a dramatization of *The Lady of the Lake* to Parisian audiences. In the case of *Ivanhoe,* the exotic was central to the plot, and the Odéon *Ivanhoé* re-

29. *La Gazette* annonçait avant-hier qu'un opéra, tiré du roman d'*Ivanhoé*, serait joué incessamment à l'Odéon. Cette feuille ne serait-elle pas mal informée? Il nous semble que tout ouvrage de ce genre doit être originaire d'Italie, d'Allemagne ou d'Huronie (*La Pandore*, 24 January 1825).

30. Although played three times a month during 1823, *Leicester* was only played once in 1824, and only seven times in the whole of 1825. *La donna del lago* had only played seven times since its September 1824 premiere and would not appear until 3 March in 1825.

THE PASTICCIO *179*

oriented it. Key figures in Scott's novel are the Jewish silversmith Isaac, and his daughter, Rebecca. In the pasticcio, these characters are changed from Jews to Turks: Ismaël and Léila. This translation aligns the libretto more clearly with Parisian models of self and other that go back to the eighteenth century; as operatic protagonists, Jews do not have a significant profile on the French stage until Halévy's *Juive* of 1835.

Parisians were aware of the changes that had been made to Scott's story and were intrigued by its motivation. Arbitrating between Jewry and the Turkish question in 1826 was not easy. One observer put the matter very well: "According to the modifications, it seems the Turks are not yet under the protection of my lords the dramatic censors; but since they might acquire this important protection before the deadline for the mise-en-scène, the manager would do well to hurry up, for the day the Turks are protected, only the Greeks will be left to the authors."[31] Six months later, when the work was still waiting for its premiere a critic returned to the charge: "The censor has not allowed the role of the Jew Isaac to stand, in the opera *Ivanhoé*. The authors have transformed the Israelite into a Saracen; but it is said that the pasha, Mehmed-Ali, informed by his chargé d'affaires, le marquis de L———, has complained to the censor and has formally asked for an amendment. The authors no longer know to which religion to devote their character: one censor has suggested making him a schismatic Greek."[32] None of these reports had any basis in fact and were probably meant to stir up interest in a work that should have been premiered weeks before. The context for these comments is the Greek war of independence and French philhellenism; the same issue of the journal in which the ironic comments of the press appeared had a report of a Jew being burned in the town of Valence.[33] Closer to home, the change of Boisguilbert from a Knight Templar to a secular knight was fancifully explained by reference to the fact that his original short cloak too much resembled those of magistrates, and that

31. Il paraît, d'après des modifications, que les Turcs ne sont pas encore sous la protection de Messieurs les censeurs dramatiques; mais, comme il pourrait arriver que cette haute protection leur fût acquise avant le délai de la mise en scène, le directeur fera bien de se hâter, car le jour où les Turcs seront protégés, il ne restera plus aux auteurs que les Grecs (*La Pandore*, 9 March 1826).

32. La censure n'a pas voulu laisser subsister, dans l'opéra d'*Ivanhoé*, le rôle du juif Isaac. Les auteurs ont transformé l'Israélite en un Sarrazin; mais on dit que le Mehemed, ali-pacha, informé de ce fait par son chargé d'affaires, le marquis de L———, s'est plaint à la censure et a formellement exigé un amendement. Les auteurs ne savent plus à quel culte vouer leur personnage: un censeur a proposé d'en faire un Grec schismatique (*La Pandore*, 5 September 1826).

33. Ibid. Shortly after the premiere of *Ivanhoé*, *L'Opinion* reprinted an article from *Le Courrier Français* claiming that the change from Jews into Turks reflected the large Jewish interest in Parisian finance (*L'Opinion*, 5 October 1826).

Figure 24. Émile Deschamps. Lithograph
by Johannes Pieter de Frey after Mlle de
La Morinière.

comparisons between Boisguilbert's dissolute behavior and that of members of the legal profession might be dangerously apposite.[34] Unfortunately,
the censors' reports on the libretto do not survive, but the copy of the libretto presented to the censor gives some idea of the changes that were
made to the original draft of the text and add detail to the general changes
of color to the libretto.

The 1826 Odéon *Ivanhoé* brought together some of the central players
in French romanticism, notably Rossini and Émile Deschamps (figure 24).
The production remains therefore at some distance from much of the music drama mounted by the Odéon, where Hugoesque romanticism found it
hard to gain a foothold. Deschamps wrote a letter to Victor Hugo that discussed *Ivanhoé* in particular and music drama in general. The letter is dated
22 September 1826, a week after the premiere of *Ivanhoé*.

> It is very good of you, my dear Victor, to occupy yourself a little with *Ivanhoé*.
> You know that these sorts of works are only pretexts for tasteful music. True,
> these pretexts can be more or less reasonable.
>   In this regard, there is art and taste in the new opera's arrangement. These
> are situations and tableaux that follow one another, Rossini's music is their
> text. The work is therefore marvelously written. . . . Furthermore, many men

34. *La Pandore,* 9 March 1826.

of letters, and even *gens d'esprit,* know nothing about limits and relative rank in the arts. Because poetry is far above music, they want it to dominate everywhere and always. It is an absurdity. In opera the author is subordinate to the musician, as in turn the musician in ballet is subordinate to the choreographer, and nevertheless dance is much inferior to music.

If you want poetry, go and hear *Athalie* or *Saul.* But do not ask of one art the emotions of another. . . . Each genre of work aims to benefit art and thus in relation to it the other arts are secondary, whatever their absolute superiority.[35]

In its rigorous separation of genres, this letter cannot have appealed to the author who published a preface to *Cromwell* the following year. In most of Deschamps's collaborations with musicians, he seems to have taken the same view; even when working with Berlioz in the 1830s—and however enthusiastic Berlioz might have been about *Roméo et Juliette*'s literary dimension—Deschamps was happy to provide poetry that could be set according to the composer's fantasy. As a librettist, Deschamps holds an anomalous position. He was at the forefront of the development of historical drama and a translator and proponent of Shakespeare, and his musical collaborations were all with romantic subjects: Scott (*Ivanhoé*), the conception of genius (Niedemeyer's *Stradella*), and Shakespeare but, as eighteenth-century house poets did, he yielded to the musical impulses of composers.

The music for *Ivanhoé* was assembled by Antonio Francesco Gaetano Saverio Pacini in collaboration with Rossini himself. The Odéon considered that the composer's presence at the center of preparations was an asset for this work, and Rossini did indeed participate. He was not as much involved in the construction of the pasticcio as was Meyerbeer in *La nymphe du Danube,* but he wrote new linking material for parts of the work and appar-

35. Vous êtes bien bon, cher Victor, de vous occuper un peu d'*Ivanhoé.* Vous savez que ces sortes d'ouvrages ne sont que des prétextes à une musique délicieuse. Il est vrai que ces prétextes peuvent être plus ou moins raisonnables.

Sous ce rapport, il y a de l'art et du goût dans la disposition du nouvel opéra. Ce sont des situations et des tableaux qui se succèdent, les notes de Rossini en sont les paroles. L'ouvrage est donc merveilleusement écrit. . . . Au surplus, beaucoup de gens de lettres, et même des gens d'esprit, ne connaissent rien aux limites et aux préséances des arts. Parce que la poésie est fort au-dessus de la musique, ils veulent qu'elle domine partout et toujours. C'est une absurdité. L'auteur, dans un opéra, est subordonné au musicien, comme dans un ballet le musicien à son tour est subordonné au chorégraphe, et cependant la danse est fort inférieure à la musique.

Si vous voulez de la poésie, allez entendre *Athalie* ou *Saul.* Mais ne demandez pas à un art les émotions d'un autre. . . . Chaque genre de spectacle est donné au bénéfice de l'art, et alors les autres arts sont secondaires relativement, quelle que soit leur supériorité absolue (Henri Girard, *Émile Deschamps dilettante: relations d'un poète romantique avec les peintres, les sculpteurs et les musiciens de son temps* [Geneva: Slatkine, 1977], 45).

ently supervised rehearsals;[36] Rossini's position was more distant than that of Meyerbeer, but the Odéon must have been delighted to have secured his services, especially after Weber's death. Pacini must have set the numbers to Deschamps and Gabriel-Gustave de Wailly's libretto, with or without Rossini's cooperation (table 7).[37]

Many of the most obvious cuts in the source texts are made because they are preceded or interrupted by a dramatic scena or recitative that, however logical in the original, has no place in the libretto of *Ivanhoé*. In nos. 4 and 7, for example, the scenes that precede the quartet in *Armida* and the aria from *Sigismondo* are cut for dramatic reasons, and the beginning of no. 10, based on the quintet from *La gazza ladra,* omits the opening section that is concerned with the establishment of Ninette's guilt. Some cuts are the result of abandoning formal conventions in the translation into a French theatrical and operatic milieu: cabalette in nos. 3 and 13 are given in a truncated form (in both cases, the opening statement is omitted and the second, more extensive, statement is retained). Tempi di mezzo are excised from the *Sigismondo* (no. 7) and *Semiramide* (no. 13) arias for the same reasons. The introduction, made up of three separate numbers from *La Cenerentola,* requires a degree of rewriting of the second section (the end of "Un tantin di carità") to effect a logical modulation to the dominant of C major, whereas the following section in the original is in G major.

Ivanhoé takes music without chorus and adds vocal lines, borrows arias with chorus, and excises choral sections. The first part of the introduction is based on the instrumental temporale from *La Cenerentola* and adds choral parts to the instrumental ones. The aria and chorus "Boisguilbert dont la

36. Rossini's autograph sketches for linking material for *Ivanhoé* are in London, British Library, MS Additional 30426, fols. 24^r–27^v. The work was consistently described during the long rehearsal period as Rossini's *Ivanhoé* (e.g., *Le Courrier des Théâtres,* 26 August 1826). A little over a week earlier, the *Journal de Paris* definitively stated that *"Ivanhoé,* Rossini's pasticcio, is in rehearsal at the Odéon, and the famous maestro is taking charge of the mise-en-scène himself" (On répète à l'Odéon *Ivanhoé,* pastiche de Rossini, dont le célèbre maestro soigne lui-même la mise en scène [ibid., 19 August 1826]). There is also a letter of thanks from Rossini (18 September 1826) to Frédéric or one of his directors applauding the care with which *Ivanhoé* was mounted and the skill of the orchestra (see Marc Pincherle, *Musiciens peints par eux-mêmes; lettres de compositeurs écrites en français [1771–1910]* [1939], reprinted in *Gioachino Rossini: lettere e documenti,* vol. 2, *21 marzo 1822–11 ottobre 1826,* ed. Bruno Caglo and Sergio Ragni [Pesaro: Fondazione Rossini, 1992], 619–20).

37. On various attempts to assemble this set of correspondences, see Reto Müller, *"Ivanhoé:* eine authentische Rossini-Oper?" *Mitteilungsblatt der Verein der Freunde der Musik Gaetano Donizettis* (May 1990) [unpaginated]; Bernd-Rüdiger Kern and Reto Müller, "Originalwerk oder Machwerk? *Ivanhoe* mit Musik von Rossini," *Neue Zeitschrift für Musik* 151 (1990): 44–45; and Fiamma Nicolodi, "Un *pastiche* di Rossini: *Ivanhoé* e il medioevo reinventato," in *49a Settimana Musicale Senese: 23–29 luglio 1992* (Siena: Fondazione Accademia Musicale Chigiana, 1992), 135–57.

TABLE 7. Sources of *Ivanhoé*

Ivanhoé (1826)	Source
Overture (allegro vivace; 6/8—allegro; 4/4; D:), 1–61	*Semiramide*, overture

ACT I

Ivanhoé (1826)	Source
1. Introduction, "Quel tems affreux" (62–104)	
(allegro; 3/4; d:—D:), 62–73	*La Cenerentola*, no. 12, temporale, 196–98 [instrumental]
(moderato; 4/4; B♭), 74–82	*La Cenerentola*, no. 1, "Un tantin di carità," 18–21
(stratta [*sic*]; allegro vivace; 3/4; C:), 83–104	*La Cenerentola*, no. 5, final section of quintet, 91–103
2. [Aria and chorus], "Boisguilbert dont la vengeance" (Ismaël) (allegro; 4/4; D:), 105–23	*La Cenerentola*, no. 8 (complete), "S'ia qua lunque" (Magnifico), 165–72
3. Aria, "Blessé sur la terre étrangère" (Ivanhoé) (andante; 3/4; A♭:), 124–142	*Bianca e Falliero*, no. 11, "Figlia mia" (Contareno [primo tenore]), 112–16
4. Quartet and chorus, "Ah point d'alarmes"	
(andante; 2/4; G:), 143–48	*Armida*, no. 5, scena and quartet, "Or che farò?" 57–60
Recitative (allegro; 4/4; G:V), 149	*GB-Lbl* Add.30426, fols. 24ʳ–25ʳ
(allegretto; 4/4; G:), 150–57	*Armida*, no. 5, 61–64
(allegro; 4/4; E:), 158–85	*Armida*, no. 5, 65–88
5. Chorus (allegro; 4/4; A:), 186–96	*Maometto II*, no. 23, chorus
6. Finale, "Que vois-je"	
(allegro; 4/4; C:), 197–203	*Aureliano in Palmira*, no. 4 "Senti ahimè"
(largo; 3/4; G:), 203–6	*La gazza ladra*, no. 14, andante sostenuto "Che abisso" from quintet, 215–20
(allegro vivace; 4/4; C:), 207–25	*Armida*, no. 12, stretta to act I finale, "Amica la sorte," 166–91

ACT II

Ivanhoé (1826)	Source
7. Aria, "En vain mon âme" (Léila) (andante—allegro maestoso; 4/4; G:), 227–37	*Sigismondo*, no. 30, grand scena and aria, "Alma rea! il più infelice" (Sigismondo); 257–73

(continued)

TABLE 7 *(continued)*

Ivanhoé (1826)	*Source*
8. Duet, "Que vois-je?" (Léila, Boisguilbert) (andante; 4/4; C:— largo; 3/4; E♭:—allegro; 4/4; C:), 238–62	*Torvaldo e Dorliska*, no. 7 (I.v; Dorliska, Duca), 72–87
9. Trio, "Souffrance cruelle" (andante; 3/4; A♭:), 263–67	*Mosè in Egitto*, act II quartet, no. 10, 136–43 (1st section of 3)
Chorus, "Suivez-nous" (vivace; 4/4; C:), 268–85	*Mosè in Egitto*, act II quartet, no. 10, 145–57 (3d section of 3)
10. Finale, "Race infidèle," 286–345 (maestoso; 3/4; C:), 286–95	*La gazza ladra*, no. 15, "Tremate o populi," 193–202
([largo]; 4/4; a♭:), 296–313	*Semiramide*, no. 24, finale I largo, "Qual mesto gemito," 237–54
(allegro assai; 3/4; c:), 324–45	*Mosè in Egitto*, no. 7, finale I, 83–96
11. Entr'acte of act III (allegro vivace; 2/4; F:), 347–60	*Semiramide*, no. 3, coro festivo, "Belo si celebri" without text, 26–38

ACT III

12. Chorus, "Faisons silence" (allegro; 3/4; E♭:), 361–71	*Tancredi*, no. 20, chorus, "Regno il terro nella città," 139–43
13. Scena and aria, "Combat terrible" (allegro; 4/4; C:—andante; 4/4; f:— allegro; 4/4; F:), 372–95	*Semiramide*, no. 33, scena, delirium, and aria, "Si vi sarà," 435–55
14. March and chorus, "Dieu signale ta clémence" (tempo di marcia; 4/4; a:), 396–404	*Bianca e Falliero*, no. 25, chorus, "Ah! Qual notte di squallore," 285–88
Fanfare (vivace; 2/4; C:), 405	"Passo doppio" for military band
15. Finale, "Victoire"	
"Qu'entends-je" (Ismaël, Ivanhoé, Cedric) (moderato; 2/4; D:), 406–11	*Torvaldo e Dorliska*, no. 13 (I.x; Dorliska, Carlotta), 157–63
(rapido; 4/4; D:), 412–27	*Torvaldo e Dorliska*, no. 16 (stretta del finale I), 182–83 cut; 183–206

SOURCES: Giaochino Rossini, *Ivanhoé* (Paris: Pacini, n.d.); and piano-vocal scores for *Semiramide* (Milan: Ricordi, n.d.), *La Cenerentola* (Paris: Pacini, n.d.), *La gazza ladra* (Paris: Pacini, n.d.), *Sigismondo* (Milan: Ricordi, n.d.), *Bianca e Falliero* (Milan: Ricordi, n.d.); *Zelmira* (Paris: Pacini, n.d.), *Mosè in Egitto* (Paris: Pacini, n.d.), *Armida* (Milan: Ricordi, n.d.), *Tancredi* (Paris: Pacini, n.d.), and *Torvaldo e Dorliska* (Milan: Ricordi, n.d.).

vengeance" (no. 2) is taken from Magnifico's aria "S'ia qua lunque," and the chorus parts are again added in the French version. Conversely, Contareno's aria "Figlia mia" from *Bianca e Falliero* (the first part of whose cabaletta is cut) removes the choral lines from the second part of the cabaletta.

The redistribution of voices, as source texts are reworked for the 1826

French pasticcio, is one of the most complex characteristics of the compositional history of *Ivanhoé*. Pacini, and perhaps Rossini, adopted as many different strategies for reworking combinations of voice parts as there were such combinations in the source texts. In the act I finale, derived from three numbers from *Aureliano in Palmira, La gazza ladra,* and *Armida,* the source for the middle section is the quintet "Che abisso" from *La gazza ladra.* This is converted into a quartet in *Ivanhoé* simply by conflating the two bass roles (Podesta and Fernando) in *La gazza ladra* into a single one in *Ivanhoé.* Other changes simply involve the redistribution of roles via transposition; in the second part of the introduction, it might be expected that parts with similar ranges (Ismaël in *Ivanhoé* and Alidoro in *La Cenerentola;* both F_4) might map onto one another. However, when the original voice parts from *La Cenerentola* are used (and they are, for example, completely rewritten at the beginning of this section), they follow much more elaborate patterns of transposition than might be expected: Ivanhoé (C_4) takes Cenerentola's lines (G_2) and Léila (C_1) takes Alidoro's lines (F_4). More complex reductions in the number of voices are found in the act II finale (no. 10), and in the trio (no. 9); the latter is based on the quartet from *Mosè in Egitto,* a four-part canonic structure modified simply by removing one of the voice parts, leaving only three-quarters of Rossini's musical text. The addition of voice parts takes place only in chorus numbers, the best example of which is no. 14, "Dieu signale ta clémence." The source for this is a three-part chorus from *Bianca e Falliero* to which are added two additional voice parts. The resulting five-part texture enables the development of antiphonal effects (soprano and alto against two tenors and bass).

Ivanhoé presents the opportunity to reconsider the issue that underpins most criticism of pasticci: to what extent a pasticcio is a competent reworking of preexisting material or, to restate the issue in Raguenet's phraseology, whether a musician has taken a variety of different styles and made them into one. The adaptation of numbers in *Ivanhoé* betrays a real concern for matching not just appropriate music for dramatic situations but also mapping dramatic situations in the source text onto those in *Ivanhoé.*[38] In its context of kidnap, detention, and seduction the duet "Que vois-je?" sung by Boisguilbert and Léila in *Ivanhoé* matches well the context of the Duca's capture of Dorliska in the version of this duet in *Torvaldo e Dorliska.* Likewise the scena and aria with chorus "Combat terrible" takes a desperate Assur and his encouraging soldiers out of *Semiramide* and gives the same music to Boisguilbert and his own encouraging men.

Early performances of *Ivanhoé* were successful. The premiere was characterized by the presence of "the most distinguished men of letters and

---

38. These are outlined in Nicolodi, "Un *pastiche*," 145–46.

artists,"[39] who belonged to the circles in which the librettists—especially Deschamps—moved. In the light of Deschamps's letter quoted earlier and of Hugo's predilection for the Odéon, it seems reasonable to assume that Hugo might well have been in the audience; if so, he might well have been accompanied by others in his circle.[40] On the second night, the manager was forced to return Fr 500–600 to members of the audience who had been unable to get in, and it was rumored that Frédéric might have to call in the police to maintain order.[41] The work certainly rated among those responsible for attracting audiences from much wider afield than the eleventh arrondissement.[42] In its summary of theatrical events of September, *Le Journal de Paris* considered *Ivanhoé* the only work of any interest, and it was one of the few operatic performances graced by the presence of the duchesse de Berry; she attended on 25 October.[43]

The author of *Ivanhoe* also attended a performance at the Odéon on 31 October 1826. Scott and his wife crossed the Channel on 26 October and, after four days reaching Paris from Calais, via Montreuil and Grandvilliers, stayed at the Hôtel de Winsor, rue de Rivoli.[44] They went to four performances during their stay in Paris. On 30 October, they went to hear Émile de Bonnechose's *Rosamonde* at the Comédie-Française, where Scott was impressed by the play and noted that "two or three ladies were carried out in hysterick."[45] On 2 November Scott wrote in his journal: "Went to the Italian opera and saw Figaro. Anne liked the music; to me it was all caviare."[46] On the following day, they went to the Gymnase dramatique (Théâtre de Madame) where they heard *Le mariage de raison* and *Le plus beau jour de ma vie*, both excellently played.[47] The highlight of their tour was however on 31 October. Scott wrote in his journal as follows:

> In the evening at the Odéon where we saw *Ivanhoe*. It was superbly got up, the Norman soldiers wearing pointed helmets and what resembled much hauberks of mail which looked very well. The number of the attendants and

39. Les hommes de lettres et les artistes les plus distingués (*Le Courrier des Théâtres,* 16 September 1826).

40. See further concerning Hugo, page 124.

41. *Le Courrier des Théâtres,* 20 September 1826.

42. Ibid., 25 September 1826.

43. *Journal de Paris,* 1 and 30 October 1826. The royal presence had been (wrongly) trailed for several weeks in advance. See one account in *Le Courrier des Théâtres,* 25 September 1826.

44. W. E. K. Anderson, ed., *The Journal of Sir Walter Scott* (Oxford: Clarendon, 1972), 222–23.

45. Ibid., 224.

46. Ibid., 230.

47. Ibid., 231.

the skill with which they are moved and grouped on the stage is well worthy of notice. It was an opera, and of course the story greatly mangled, and the dialogue in a great part nonsense. Yet it was strange to hear anything like the words, which I (then in an agony of pain with spasms in my stomach) dictated to William Laidlaw at Abbotsford, now recited in a foreign tongue and for the amusement of a strange people. I little thought to have survived the completing of the novel.[48]

It is certainly true that the libretto of *Ivanhoé* came in for much criticism; none of it was however consistent. Some critics simply blamed its weaknesses on the changes required by the censor (a familiar trope in 1826).[49] Others were unhappy that the scenes from Scott had been placed "in a frame that constantly offends against the requirements of our [Parisian] stage."[50] Word must have circulated quickly concerning Scott's judgment— that the work had little to do with his story. A fictional anecdote was reported in the journal *L'Opinion:* "Are they going to play *Ivanhoé* now? asked an Englishman seated in the *premières loges* at the Odéon, at the end of an opera. Now, the opera that had just been played was *Ivanhoé,* and the questioner?. . . Sir Walter Scott."[51] But Scott's own commentary was clear: the story was mangled and the dialogue nonsense *because* the work was music drama, and—for Scott—this would always have been the case. Translated into the critical hothouse of Restoration Paris, this became a critique of Wailly's and Deschamps's libretto, to be set alongside the more serious literary moralizing of the latter's romantic colleagues.

The 1826 plan to mount three pasticci by Europe's three most important living composers for the stage was founded on a tradition of single-composer pasticci that ran throughout the history of the Odéon's opera company. The music of Rossini, Mercadante, Mozart, and Dalayrac was all pressed into service for other works at the Odéon. The surviving sources for the Rossini and Mercadante pasticci—*Le testament* and *Les noces de Gamache*—allow a view of how these pieces sounded; so too does the Mozart pasticcio, *Louis XII ou La route des Reims,* assembled for the coronation of Charles X. Dalayrac's *Brigands de Schiller* and *Le neveu de Monseigneur,*

48. Ibid., 226.

49. *La Pandore,* 16 September 1826.

50. Dans un cadre qui viole constamment les exigences de notre scène (*Le Courrier des Théâtres,* 16 September 1826). It is possible that this view is attributable to the "hommes de lettres et artistes les plus distingués" mentioned earlier.

51. Va-t-on jouer maintenant *Ivanhoé?* demandait à la fin d'un opéra, un Anglais assis aux premières loges de l'Odéon. Or l'opéra qu'on venait de jouer c'était *Ivanhoé,* et le questionneur? Sir Walter Scott (*L'Opinion,* 5 November 1826).

works whose construction is doubtful, conclude this discussion of single-composer pasticci.

Single-Composer Pasticci

Le testament

Little survives of *Le testament*. The libretto was by the comtes de Saur and de Saint-Geniez, and the music was adapted by Lemierre de Corvey from music by Rossini.[52] The manuscript censors' libretto provides the text of the spoken dialogue along with the words for the sung items, as well as generic indications for each of the sung numbers.[53] Given that the casting was listed in the press, it is possible to identify the voice for which each of the numbers was written.[54] Furthermore, a review that listed the sources in greater or lesser detail makes it possible to outline the structure of the work.[55] The range of its sources is wide, and the work is built up out of extracts from ten separate works, all by Rossini, ranging from *L'inganno felice* (1812) to *Semiramide* (1823). The work prompts comparison in this respect with *Ivanhoé*. The range of sources is very similar, with *Ivanhoé* drawing on eleven music dramas as its source (it has fifteen numbers as opposed to *Le testament*'s eleven). However, de Corvey's treatment of Rossini's music is much more circumspect than Pacini's and perhaps Rossini's own: *Le testament* clings much more closely to the principle of simply putting new text to Rossini's music than does *Ivanhoé*, which reworks Rossini's original material to a substantial degree. Most numbers in *Le testament*, as far as it is possible to judge, adhere closely to the vocal scoring of the original (the surviving sources make it impossible to judge the instrumentation). Two exceptions only need to be noted to prove the rule. The quartet from *Semiramide* "Di plausi qual clamor" that closes the act I finale in *Le testament* uses only the first section of its original and also redistributes the ranges of voices of the original to fit the new context. In one further instance, the duet for le colonel and Julie in act II of *Le testament* is based on the act I duet for Isabella and Taddeo from *L'italiana in Algeri*, "Ai capricci della sorte." The original is clearly for contralto and bass, but the roles of le colonel and Julie were

52. *FétisB* (5:265) wrongly lists it as an original work by Lemierre de Corvey.
53. The censors' libretto is F-Pan F[18] 614.
54. The cast of *Le testament* (given in *Le Courrier des Théâtres*, 22 January 1827): le colonel, Leclerc (première basse-taille); Malvitz, Duprez (tenor); Walter, Mondonville (baritone); Mme Dahl, Mme Durand (contralto); Henriette, Mme Mondonville (première chanteuse); Julie, Mlle Pouilley (soprano).
55. Ibid., 23 January 1827.

taken respectively by Leclerc—a bass, certainly—and Mlle Pouilley, who was without a doubt a soprano. In this duet, "Dieux! Pourrais-je fuir," at least one of the voices must have been reconfigured.

Le testament was not well received. The music by Rossini was praised, but the libretto, based on a play by Kotzebue—and therefore German—was savaged in the press.[56] On the first night (22 January 1827), the performance was greeted with "a pasticcio of applause and whistles": the applause, one infers, for the music, the whistles for the libretto.[57] Although Duprez was reported as having sung his act I aria well ("Animé par l'espoir"—little more than a translation of "Ah! Dove il cimento" from *Semiramide*), the work ran to four performances and disappeared.[58]

Les noces de Gamache

The music of Saverio Mercadante figured most prominently in a single work at the Théâtre-Royal de l'Odéon. Too recent for any of Castil-Blaze's pasticci, and still lacking the stature of Rossini or Mozart, his work emerged in a single-composer pasticcio, *Les noces de Gamache*, in May 1825. The libretto, by Sauvage and Dupin, was based on Klingmann's *Don Quijote und Sancho Panza, oder die Hochzeit des Camacho* (modeled in turn on an incident in Cervantes's *Don Quixote*).

Les noces de Gamache bears comparison with other treatments of Italian sources at the Odéon. Only two of Mercadante's twenty music dramas completed by 1825, *Elisa e Claudio* and *L'apoteosi di Ercole*, were selected as sources for *Les noces de Gamache*. In this respect, it differs from *Ivanhoé* and *Le testament*, where up to a dozen works were used as sources, and seems to align itself more closely with Meyerbeer's *Marguerite d'Anjou*. This translation, however, is based on a version of the libretto of one of the two pieces that are used for it, and the sections from *Margherita d'Anjou* and *Emma di Resburgo* are placed together in such a way that numbers that had followed one another in the original also follow one another in the translation. By contrast, individual numbers from *Elisa e Claudio* and *L'apoteosi di Ercole* are entirely reshuffled in *Les noces de Gamache* without any regard to their original order: sections of act II of *L'apoteosi* rub shoulders with act I of *Elisa*, while parts of act II of *Elisa* precede parts of act I of the same work.

---

56. See *Journal de Paris,* 23 January 1827; *La Pandore,* 23 January 1827. The identification of the libretto's source had been made the previous November (*Journal de Paris,* 30 November 1826).

57. *Le Courrier des Théâtres,* 23 January 1827.

58. *La Pandore,* 23 January 1827.

In its selection of music, and in the relation between music, libretto, and the source's libretto, *Les noces de Gamache* resembles *Louis XII ou La route de Reims,* premiered only a month later, which is also a single-composer pasticcio that makes use of two works by the same composer adapted to a new libretto: in this case, *Die Entführung aus dem Serail* and *La clemenza di Tito.* Furthermore, the musical arranger, Alphonse Vergne—like Luc Guénée—also slipped in a couple of his own compositions. The scope of the two works is also similar: fifteen numbers in *Louis XII ou La route de Reims,* fourteen in *Les noces de Gamache.*

Nothing in the libretti of *L'apoteosi* or *Elisa* has anything to do with Cervantes's or Klingmann's vision of Spain; and there are no Iberian topics in any of the music appropriated for *Les noces de Gamache.* In addition to recasting the music, Guénée added three numbers (two of which were marked "ajouté" in the published score). Of the three, the entr'acte between the second and third acts is the least interesting. However, the *couplets* in act I "Si par hasard à travers la campagne" and the *choeur final* that ends act III, "Oui, malgré votre mésaventure," add substantially to the range of musical topics. Both numbers exploit the dance rhythm of the fandango (albeit in different tonalities), injecting a degree of the exotic into Mercadante's score (example 8).

Mercadante's music was little known in Paris in 1825, and the premiere of *Les noces de Gamache* on 9 May gave the composer's music its first continuous exposure in the capital. The work was subject to a range of changes of cast during the period, and performances were heard well into 1828. Initial reactions were favorable, and by the end of May 1825 it was playing to full houses.[59] Although the work is cast in three acts in the published full score and libretto, it was swiftly reduced to two acts, and this reduction contributed substantially to its success.[60]

Les brigands de Schiller is a play within a play that features—as the title suggests—Schiller's *Raüber,* and *Le neveu de Monseigneur* is based on the *Mémoires* of Mme de Hausset.[61] All that survives of each work is a libretto and in some cases conflicting accounts in the press as to the nature of the music. *Les brigands de Schiller* is a pasticcio of the works of Dalayrac. This in itself is remarkable as the only attempt made at the Odéon to assemble a pasticcio out of works by a French composer. Although the authors of

59. As with many Odéon premieres, the first night was untidy; reviews of the second night were entirely positive (see *La Pandore,* 10 May and 30 May 1825).

60. Ibid., 2 June 1825. Curiously, the same journal had described the work, before its premiere, as an *opéra bouffon* in *two* acts (5 May 1825). Given that the description was otherwise correct down to the last detail (genre, composer, and translation from from German), this discrepancy points to ambiguity about the work's earlier structure.

61. *Mémoires de Mme du Hausset, femme de chambre de Mme de Pompadour, avec des notes et des éclaircissements historiques* (Paris: Baudouin, 1824).

Example 8. Beginning of *couplets* in *Les noces de Gamache*.

a. "Si par hasard à travers la campagne"

(continued)

the libretto are known (Sauvage and Dupin), the arranger of the music is nowhere recorded. However, although the musical arranger of *Le neveu de Monseigneur* was Guénée (the libretto was by Bayard, Romieu, and Sauvage), there were conflicting views on the musical sources of what was certainly a pasticcio: the censors' libretto stated that the music was all by Francesco Morlacchi (i.e., a single-composer pasticcio), and this attribution

Example 8 *(continued)*

b. "Oui, malgré votre mésaventure"

was duplicated in the press.[62] However, the same newspaper claimed less than a month later that the music was by Rossini and Pacini.[63] Both were well received: *Le neveu de Monseigneur* ran for twenty performances well into 1828, and *Les brigands des Schiller* ran until the opera troupe at the Odéon closed.

Castil-Blaze

Castil-Blaze wrote four pasticci that were performed at the Odéon. Of these, *Les folies amoureuses* had originally been composed for the Grand Théâtre in Lyon, and *La fausse Agnès* had been written for the Gymnase dramatique.[64] Both works were subject to significant change. *La fausse Agnès* started out during the summer of 1824 as a work for the Gymnase dramatique in one act and was reworked in three acts for its premiere at the Odéon two years later.[65] *Les folies amoureuses* had originally been constructed as a three-act pasticcio for Lyon but was reworked in one act for the Gymnase dramatique in order to conform to the restrictions of that theater's license; it was then returned to three acts when it was produced at the Odéon on 5 June 1824.[66] The printed score reflects its original three-act state, and the version heard at the Odéon, also in three acts, was probably the same as the one heard in Lyon and published.[67] During the course of its career at the Odéon, *Les folies amoureuses* was reduced in scale by two substantial cuts: the duet from *Tancredi* "Ah se de mali miei" ("Il faudra du canon" in the pasticcio), and the sextet from *La Cenerentola* "Questo è un nodo inviluppato" ("Juste ciel" in the pasticcio).[68] In the versions in which they were performed at the Odéon, the composer best represented in both *Les folies amoureuses* and *La fausse Agnès* was Rossini; Cimarosa was a poor second.

62. *Journal de Paris,* 15 July 1826.

63. Ibid., 8 August 1826. Just to complicate the matter further, Franz Stieger (*Opernlexikon* [Tutzing: Schneider, 1975–83], 2:860) describes the work as a pasticcio by Rossini, Morlacchi, and Fioravanti.

64. The printed editions of pasticci made Parisian productions available in the provinces but do not reflect the substantial changes during performance at the Odéon.

65. In their one-act versions at the Gymnase dramatique, *Les folies amoureuses* was rated more highly than *La fausse Agnès,* and Rossini was preferred to Cimarosa or Meyerbeer (*Journal de Paris,* 8 July 1824); there was in fact no Meyerbeer in *Les folies amoureuses,* and Meyerbeer's overture to *Romilde et Constanza* was rumored (wrongly) to have been written for the Gymnase dramatique—or, as the critic put it, for "l'opéra du boulevard de Bonne-Nouvelle" (*Le Courrier des Théâtres,* 9 July 1824).

66. *Journal de Paris,* 10 May 1824.

67. *Les folies amoureuses* (Paris: Castil-Blaze, 1823).

68. *Le Courrier des Théâtres,* 1 December 1824; *La Pandore,* 28 May 1825.

Other composers represented were Paër, Mozart, Pavesi, Steibelt, and Generali (*Les folies amoureuses*), and Meyerbeer and Pucitta (*La fausse Agnès*). Central to judgments of these two works was the relation of French theatrical classics to Italian music drama. Both *Les folies amoureuses* and *La fausse Agnès* were the subject of hostile commentary in this regard; *Le Diable Boiteux*'s critic disliked what he called a mixture of sacred and profane—Jean-François Regnard's play, *Les folies amoureuses*, and *any* sort of music drama—and the correspondent in *L'Opinion* was happy that Castil-Blaze should be allowed to import foreign libretti and their music into *La fausse Agnès* but argued strongly that he should not be allowed to mutilate the classics: in this case, Philippe Destouches's play.[69] One critic took the more pragmatic view that Regnard's play was a poor choice because it "presented fewer situations favorable to the different numbers that made up an opéra comique."[70]

Whatever views critics might have had of the suitability of particular plays as the basis of an opéra comique, they liked Rossini and thought that Castil-Blaze had succeeded in his choice of compositions to adorn the plays.[71] A line that he had inserted into the libretto of *Les folies amoureuses*, "Rossini fut toujours mon guide et mon patron" met with universal approval; one critic thought it could well have served as a motto for Castil-Blaze himself.[72] Exactly how *Les folies amoureuses* and *La fausse Agnès* fitted into the Parisian view of the Rossini canon is unclear; although always identified as a pasticcio, *Les folies amoureuses* was compared to his *Pie voleuse* and *Le barbier de Séville:* "[La pie voleuse is] superior to the pasticcio, *Les folies amoureuses*, but much inferior to *Le barbier*."[73] In the wake of the premiere of *La fausse Agnès*, by contrast, comparisons were drawn exclusively from Castil-Blaze's pasticci.[74] To compare the musical content of *Les folies amoureuses* with that of *La fausse Agnès* was to witness a move from the eclectic to the specific, and a greater concentration on Rossini. By the time Castil-Blaze came to assemble *La fausse Agnès*, two out of the six Rossini numbers from *Les folies amoureuses* had been cut. *La fausse Agnès* therefore doubled the number of Rossini items, and it was the Rossini numbers that were singled out for praise in reviews,

69. *Le Diable Boiteux*, 6 June 1824; *L'Opinion*, 15 June 1826.

70. Présentent moins de situations favorables aux divers morceaux qui constituent un opéra-comique (*Le Courrier des Théâtres*, 10 July 1824).

71. Ibid.; *Le Diable Boiteux*, 6 June 1824.

72. *Le Diable Boiteux*, 7 June 1826.

73. [*La pie voleuse* est] supérieur au pasticcio des *Folies amoureuses*, mais bien inférieur au *Barbier* (*La Pandore*, 3 August 1824).

74. See the conflicting opinions in the *Journal de Paris*, 8 July 1824 (comparing the one-act versions of *Les folies amoureuses* and *La fausse Agnès*) and *Le Frondeur*, 14 June 1826 (comparing the three-act versions of the two works).

and one critic made explicit the Parisian preference for Rossini over Cimarosa or Meyerbeer.[75]

Castil-Blaze wrote two pasticci expressly for the Odéon: *Monsieur de Pourceaugnac* and *La forêt de Sénart*. *Monsieur de Pourceaugnac* followed in the tradition of *Les folies amoureuses* and *La fausse Agnès,* and here Castil-Blaze narrowed his frame of reference to four composers only (Rossini, Borghi, Mosca, and Weber) and boosted the number of works by Rossini to eleven (from no fewer than seven different works). Not only was the construction of *Monsieur de Pourceaugnac* in line with the Odéon arrangements of Castil-Blaze's two earlier pasticci, but the work's reception followed similar themes: *Le Courrier des Théâtres* asked what crime Molière had committed to be associated with Rossini, although there were none of the eulogies for Rossini's music that had characterized *Les folies amoureuses* and *La fausse Agnès*. Nevertheless, Castil-Blaze was praised for his ability to suit the music to the situation.[76]

The second of Castil-Blaze's pasticci to be premiered at the Odéon was the first that he wrote specifically for the theater. In its subject matter *La forêt de Sénart* stands apart from its fellows. Like *Les folies amoureuses,* it is eclectic in its range of music (works by six different composers), but it needs to be considered in the context of the enthusiasm for Weber that swept Paris in the wake of *Robin des bois,* along with the abortive production of *Preciosa* and *Les bohémiens*—all part of the 1826 plan. Weber's music makes up half of *La forêt de Sénart,* although the range of reference to the composer is narrow: numbers from *Der Freischütz, Euryanthe,* and the incidental music to Eduard Gehe's *Heinrich IV, König von Frankreich.* The predominant source is *Euryanthe,* from which four out the seven Weber numbers were taken.[77] Even in such a work as this, Rossini could not be entirely sidelined, and *La forêt de Sénart* makes reference to three works by the composer, from *Il turco in Italia, La pietra del paragone,* and *La Cenerentola.*[78] Responses to *La forêt de Sénart* were predictably different to those for the Rossini-dominated pasticci. In a long review of the work, *Le Journal de Paris* expressed the opinion that Parisian audiences did not appreciate Beethoven, which is why the work had so much Weber and Rossini in it.[79] Indeed, Beethoven's position in the piece was

75. *La Pandore,* 14 June 1826; *Journal de Paris,* 8 July 1824.

76. *Le Courrier des Théâtres,* 22 and 27 February 1827.

77. The evidence does not support Adolphe Boschot's claim (*La Jeunesse d'un romantique: Hector Berlioz, 1803–1831* [Paris: Plon, 1906], 214), repeated by Frank Heidlberger (*Carl Maria von Weber und Hector Berlioz: Studien zur französischen Weber-Rezeption* [Tützing: Schneider, 1994], 337), that *La forêt de Sénart* was, or was viewed by its contemporaries as, effectively a French version of *Euryanthe.*

78. For a fuller account of the sources for *La forêt de Sénart,* see Heidlberger, *Weber und Berlioz,* 336–43.

79. *Journal de Paris,* 17 January 1826.

marginal; the overture and perhaps one other number are his. Yet according to at least one other review, it was the numbers by Beethoven and Weber that produced the greatest effect.[80]

All four Castil-Blaze pasticci shared a trait that set them apart from others mounted at the Odéon. Each included at least one number that fell outside the repertorial field of German or Italian music drama from the previous half century. *Les folies amoureuses* had an *air espagnol* of indeterminate origin, "Plus fraîche que l'aurore," and *Monsieur de Pourceaugnac* included an *air languedocien*, "M'en souvené d'ou jour." *La fausse Agnès* contained two numbers from the sixteenth and seventeenth centuries, and *La forêt de Sénart* had a song by Thibaut de Champagne and one attributed to Lully in the published full score but described as a song from the time of François I in the libretto. All have so far resisted identification.

Judgments on Castil-Blaze's activities varied dramatically and focused on his monopoly status as arranger, the quality of his literary work, the decisions he took in making his arrangements and pasticci, and his assimilation of foreign music drama, especially Rossini, on behalf of Parisian audiences. The press was constantly keeping him up to the mark: one particularly weak translation in *La pie voleuse* was ridiculed at the premiere, and it disappeared immediately afterward and never appeared in the published libretto.[81] More generally, he was criticized for his treatment of the mute *e:* "Forced to put a note on the mute *e*, M. Castil-Blaze thus substitutes a muffled sound for a brilliant one; he might as well have put mutes on the lips of his singers."[82] In general, his contemporaries did not traduce Castil-Blaze for his activities per se (as later critics would) but criticized technical shortcomings when he fell short of his usual quality. Pasticci were however different: "What would one say of a literary work written by pens as different as MM. Chateaubriand, Royer-Collard, Benjamin Constant, Jouy, and a few other writers whose styles do not resemble one another in any way?"[83] The critic addressed the issue head-on by asking about the suitability of juxtaposing Cimarosa and Rossini "who, if we dare make use of a comparison commonly made today, represents classic and romantic genres."[84] In undertaking the construction of pasticci, Castil-Blaze was opening himself up to criticism

---

80. *La Pandore*, 18 January 1826.

81. *Le Courrier des Théâtres*, 3 August 1824.

82. Forcé de mettre la note sur la terminaison muette, M. Castil-Blaze substitue ainsi un son étouffé à un son brillant; autant vaudrait qu'il plaçât des sourdines sur les lèvres de ses chanteurs (*La Pandore*, 12 August 1824).

83. Que dirait-on d'un ouvrage de littérature qui serait écrit par les plumes si différentes de MM. Chateaubriand, Royer-Collard, Benjamin Constant, Jouy et quelques autres écrivains dont le style ne se ressemble en aucune manière? (*Le Courrier des Théâtres*, 28 June 1826).

84. Qui, si nous osions nous servir d'une comparaison bien usitée aujourd'hui, représentent en musique les genres classique et romantique (ibid.).

that was directed largely at a genre that was in a state of flux, if not of decline. Even so, while he was being described as a monopolist, his earlier pasticcio, *Les folies amoureuses,* was praised for its judicious choice of music.[85] Castil-Blaze's assimilation of Rossini was the subject of a further *apologia* at the end of 1825.

> Castil-Blaze's franco-barbarian translations have often and justly been criticized. But having paid this debt to good taste, and setting aside literary style, we must admit that he has been of service to our lyric stage (*il a rendu service à notre scène lyrique*) by making us familiar with masterpieces only up till then admired in France by those amateurs who frequented the Italian Opera. Success has legitimated M Castil-Blaze's enterprise, and the public has made its way to the Odéon despite the gibes of some people who have seen only poetic deficiencies but who have not taken into account the difficulties he had to overcome in order to adapt words with the same number of syllables as those in the Italian scores to a given piece of music.[86]

Castil-Blaze would have been pleased with such a verdict on his attempts to assimilate foreign music drama to the rigid context of Parisian theater and music drama. Despite the ever-present criticism of his use of language, the Parisian debt to him was too great to be ignored.

Ignoring the opprobrium that unfamiliar pasticci carry today, a rational account of their place in the Odéon repertory of music drama focuses on two main types described above: a pasticcio with music based on the work of a single composer, and one derived from several composers' output. The second category is largely associated with Castil-Blaze although only two of his four pasticci were written with the Odéon in mind. Both types of work point up the remarkable possibilities of intertextuality and fragmentation that the pasticcio allows, while providing an extreme view of the status of the autonomous artwork. At a time when a critique of music drama that prized authorial voice and structural integrity was beginning to evolve (most obviously at the hands of Berlioz and like-minded critics), the pasticcio—as a

---

85. *Le Diable Boiteux,* 6 June 1824.

86. On a beaucoup et justement blâmé les traductions franco-barbares de M. Castil-Blaze. Mais cette dette au bon goût étant une fois payée, et abstraction faite du style de l'écrivain, on doit avouer qu'il a rendu service à notre scène lyrique, en nous faisant connaître des chefs-d'oeuvre admirés jusqu'alors en France des amateurs qui fréquentent l'Opéra Italien. Le succès a légitimé l'entreprise de M. Castil-Blaze, et le public a repris le chemin de l'Odéon malgré les brocards de quelque personnes qui n'ont pas vu que les défauts de vers, mais qui n'ont point tenu compte des difficultés qu'il fallait surmonter pour adapter à une musique donnée, des paroles du même nombre de syllabes que celles des partitions italiennes (*Le Courrier des Théâtres,* 9 November 1825).

relic of eighteenth-century and earlier practices represented the opposite polarity.

For the Odéon, pasticci were central to one of the most ambitious strategies it adopted: the 1826 plan to mount pasticci of the works of Rossini, Weber, and Meyerbeer. Trying to attract contemporary composers of distinction was problematic given its license; to offer the opportunity to major composers to write a new work for the theater was to court the possibility of further claims that it was breaking its license. The attraction of the pasticcio was that it presented no such difficulty and, being well integrated into the repertorial profile of the Odéon—with critics sometimes confusing pasticcio and other types of music drama—the theater's strategy seemed a logical one. It owed its limited success to the effect of Weber's death and a certain dilatoriness on the part of one of the librettists, who, paradoxically, was eventually to manage the theater.

Chapter 7

Le fruit défendu—Opéra Comique and the French Tradition

The *ancien répertoire*

The clearest and most succinct definition of the types of music drama permitted at the Odéon lies in the contract agreed between La Rochefoucauld and Bernard, which stipulated that Bernard had the right to mount productions of the Odéon's traditional repertory—tragedy and comedy—and "if he wishes, opéra comique, but for this last genre works taken solely from the public domain, and works taken from the Italian and French repertory [translations], and *comédie mêlée de chant.*"[1] The clause "opéra comique . . . taken solely from the public domain" pointed to a crucial element of the Odéon's profile during the 1820s, and one that aroused great controversy. Works in the public domain were so identified when both the composer and the librettist had been dead for ten years. During the four years that the opera company was active at the Odéon, twenty-five productions of opéras comique*s* were drawn from the public domain. This often meant works up to fifty years old (appendix 1).

During the first year of the Odéon's existence as a venue for music drama, fifteen works from the public domain included music by André-Ernest-Modeste Grétry (d. 1813) and Nicolas-Marie Dalayrac (d. 1809), with libretti by Louis Anseaume (d. 1784), Jean-François Marmontel (d. 1799), and Michel-Jean Sédaine (d. 1797). Despite the fact that some of these composers and librettists continued to write and compose during the Revolution and Empire, the works mounted at the Odéon all dated from the *ancien régime.* Of the five opéras comiques produced during May 1824, four were

---

1. Bernard's revised contract is in F-Pan O³ 1791/VII.

Figure 25. Set design for act II of Grétry's *Richard Coeur-de-Lion* at the Odéon. From Pierre-Luc Ciceri and Léger-Larbouillat, *Recueil des décorations théâtrales et autres objets d'ornement* (Paris: Léger-Larbouillat, 1830), no. 18.

by Grétry: *Le tableau parlant* (1769), *La fausse magie* (1775), *L'épreuve villageoise* (1784), and, from the same year, *Richard Coeur-de-Lion* (figure 25).

Such a concentration on works over half a century old met with general approval; a reviewer for the *Journal de Paris* suggested à propos Grétry's *Tableau parlant* that "On the whole, these little operas that form part of the old repertory give the administration [of the Odéon] an excellent means of varying the entertainment of the public, and they will be always be well received, especially after a tragedy."[2] A month later, Grétry's work was contrasted with *un concert,* a derogatory journalistic reference to the works of Rossini and the "Italian school": "Grétry does honor to opéra comique almost alone at the Odéon. So much the better for the theater and for the public. It is always to the works of this great composer that one returns when

2. En dernier résultat, ces petits opéras de l'ancien répertoire fournissent à la direction un excellent moyen de varier les plaisirs du public, et ils seront toujours bien reçus, surtout après une tragédie (*Journal de Paris,* 15 May 1824).

one wants to find something in an opera *more than a concert,* and when one looks for dramatic truth joined to all the charms of melody [emphasis added]."[3]

Despite such generally enthusiastic testimonials, the Odéon was anxious to broaden its repertory of classic opéra comique but was unable to do so. Many obvious examples especially from the revolutionary period were outside the public domain. Such works as Luigi Cherubini's *Lodoïska* and *Les deux journées* (1791 and 1800 respectively) must have seemed attractive additions to the Odéon repertory, but Cherubini was still alive (he died in 1842). Étienne-Nicolas Méhul died in October 1817, and his works did not therefore become available to the Odéon until the opera troupe was in decline; *Les deux aveugles de Tolède* (1806) was the only one of his works to be mounted at the Odéon but did not appear until February 1828.[4] Gaveaux, Isouard, and Boieldieu (to say nothing of Auber) were, since they were yet to fall into the public domain, beyond the Odéon's grasp.

The opéras comiques of Dalayrac, also logical acquisitions for the Odéon repertory, were tantalizingly out of the public domain because the librettist with whom the composer worked most frequently, Benoît-Joseph Marsollier de Vivetières, lived until 22 April 1817. Within days of the tenth anniversary of Marsollier's death, Dalayrac's *Adolphe et Clara* found its way onto the Odéon stage. It was premiered on 14 May 1827. Such a close proximity of these two dates strongly suggests that the Odéon was—pragmatically—prepared to exploit such good fortune as soon as possible. Other works by Dalayrac and Marsollier followed: *La maison isolée* (20 August 1827), *Camille ou Le souterrain* (23 October 1827), and *Les deux mots ou Une nuit dans la forêt* (4 May 1828); *Gulnare ou L'esclave persane* (18 May 1828) was a rare example of a "Turkish captivity" opera at the Odéon.[5] Perhaps the most frustrating work for the Odéon was Pierre-Alexandre Monsigny's *Déserteur.* It had been premiered in 1769 and would have been the oldest work of the *ancien répertoire* on the boards of the Odéon. It still appeared every month or so at the

3. Grétry fait presqu' à lui seul les honneurs de l'Opéra-Comique à l'Odéon. Tant mieux pour le théâtre et pour le public. C'est toujours aux ouvrages de ce grand compositeur qu'il faudra en revenir lorsqu'on voudra trouver dans un opéra autre chose qu'un concert, et qu'on cherchera la vérité dramatique unie à tous les charmes de la mélodie (*La Pandore,* 17 June 1824).

4. The press was aware when Méhul's works had just fallen into the public domain. See the *Journal de Paris,* 7 January 1828.

5. These works and original production dates are *Adolphe et Clara* (10 February 1799), *La maison isolée* (11 May 1797), *Camille ou Le souterrain* (19 March 1791), *Les deux mots ou Une nuit dans la forêt* (9 June 1806), and *Gulnare ou L'esclave persane* (30 December 1797). The term "Turkish captivity opera" is borrowed from and discussed at length in James Parakilas, "The Soldier and the Exotic: Operatic Variations on a Theme of Racial Encounter," *Opera Quarterly* 10 (1993–94): 33–56.

rival Opéra-Comique during the 1820s. The Odéon was unable to produce the work until 1828 since Monsigny did not die until January 1817. It was given six frantic performances in late May and June 1828, just as the opera troupe was entering its last financial crisis.

As far as it is possible to tell, the works taken from the public domain repertory were performed at the Odéon more or less as they were published. Unlike music drama taken from Italian or German originals, neither scores nor libretti were published to accompany productions of public domain opéra comique at the Odéon, and no press report suggests that substantive changes beyond the very occasional were made to the published versions of these works. An exception is François Devienne's *Visitandines*. Originally composed to a libretto by Louis-François Picard and premiered at the Opéra-Comique in August 1792, it was mounted at the Odéon on 30 June 1825 as *Les Français au sérail*. The history of this work is complicated by three facts: the Opéra-Comique was also planning a version of *Les visitandines* for production in early 1825 entitled *Le pensionnat de jeunes demoiselles*, *Les visitandines* survives in 1792 two-act and 1793 three-act versions, and the librettist was still alive (Picard died in 1828).[6]

The original plot of *Les visitandines* consists of the arrival of two characters, Belfort and Frontin, during a storm at a convent, their admission, and the discovery that one of the sisters, Euphémie, is Belfort's long-lost lover. The subject matter was clearly popular in the wave of anticlericalism on which the Revolution was riding in 1792 and 1793. By 1825, such a subject created many more problems. The Opéra-Comique and the Odéon responded in two different ways to this problem: the Opéra-Comique transferred the action from a convent to a boarding school for young ladies (the *Pensionnat de jeunes demoiselles* of the title); the Odéon turned the work into a Turkish captivity opera.[7] Both versions of *Les visitandines* from 1825 follow the action of Devienne's and Picard's 1792 original plan. In the case of the Odéon version, *Les Français au sérail*, the poetry and prose of the libretto

6. For a summary biography of Picard, see *LDD-NS* 12:937–38. For the two original versions (1792 and 1793) of Devienne's *Visitandines* see William Montgomery, "The Life and Works of François Devienne, 1759–1803" (Ph.D. diss., Catholic University of America, 1975). The differences between the two versions from the 1790s have no effect on this discussion. See also Karin Pendle, "'*A bas les couvents!*': Anticlerical Sentiment in French Opera of the 1790s," *Music Review* 42 (1981): 22–45.

7. The surviving sources for these two productions are slight. For *Le pensionnat de jeunes demoiselles*, there is a printed libretto (Paris: Barba, 1825), and the censors' libretto in F-Pan F[18] 613. The status of the censors' report in F-Pan F[21] 980 is unclear. Odile Krakovitch incorrectly claims (*Les Pièces de théâtre soumises à la censure [1800–1830]: inventaire des pièces [F[18] 581 à 668] et les procès-verbaux des censeurs [F[21] 966–995]* [Paris: Archives nationales, 1982], 209) that *Le Pensionnat de jeunes demoiselles* was never published. The sole source for the Odéon *Français au sérail* is the censors' libretto (F-Pan F[18] 613/157).

were completely rewritten, although the plot remained unchanged in its overall shape. Both 1825 versions add new music to Devienne's original. In the Opéra-Comique's *Pensionnat de jeunes demoiselles,* Frontin's aria from II.viii, "Le ciel, mes soeurs," is replaced with two songs. The first is sung *à la manière italienne* ("Jé viens, aimables damizelles/Tutté quanté fraîches et belles"), and the second consists of *trois couplets de la gasconne* in which each six-line stanza includes a two-line refrain ("Un jour de cet automne/ De bordeaux revenant,/Je vois nymphe mignonne/Qui s'en allait chan-tant:/On rit, on jase, on raisonne,/On s'amuse un moment"). Since the only traces of the 1825 Opéra-Comique version of the piece are the printed libretto and the censors' libretto from which it is taken, it is impossible to say what music would have accompanied this poetry.

The verbal incipit of every number in the libretto of *Les Français au sérail* differs from the original. However, the structure of the poetry (number of lines, line-lengths, and rhyme) is identical, and there can be little doubt that the music was essentially the same as in *Les visitandines. Les Français au sérail* departs from the Devienne/Picard original in another way. The Odéon's version kept Frontin's aria "Le ciel, mes soeurs" but added two new numbers at the beginning of the second act. On either side of Euphémie's aria "O toi dont ma mémoire" were placed *couplets* ("Si vous voulez nous plaire") and a recitative and aria ("Sous un berceau"). Both numbers are for the character Zélia, who has no counterpart in either *Visitandines* or, for that matter, *Le pensionnat de jeunes demoiselles.* This character had been created for almost exclusively musical reasons, to allow the participation of Mme Montano.[8] That these two musical interpolations were Italian is clear from press reports, and according to one they were by Rossini.[9] Writing much later after the event, Paul Porel and Georges Monval claimed that one of them was an aria from *Elisabetta, regina d'Inghilterra.*[10] The censors' libretto for *Les Français au sérail* includes "Si vous voulez nous plaire" as an addition; of the recitative and aria, only four lines of the recitative are included and the aria is marked "to be done" (*à faire*). The sense of this latter comment could include composition of the poetry, music, or both. Nevertheless, it is entirely possible that Zélia's *couplets* could have been set to Elisabetta's aria from the act II finale of *Elisabetta, regina d'Inghilterra.* The Italian original consists of three *settenari piani* followed by a single *settenario tronco,* and the French matches perfectly with three six-syllable feminine-ending rhymes followed by one six-syllable masculine rhyme. Since the number from *Les Français au sérail* is strophic, it is reasonable to assume that the music for

8. See *La Pandore,* 1 July 1825.
9. *Journal de Paris,* 29 June 1825.
10. Paul Porel and Georges Monval, *L'Odéon: histoire administrative, anecdotique et littéraire du second théâtre français* (Paris: Lemerre, 1876–82), 1:70.

Example 9. Reconstruction of "Si vous voulez nous plaire" (*Les Français au sérail*).

the first four lines of Rossini's aria would have been repeated. Porel and Monval may well have been right, and what Zélia (Montano) sang may have been what is given as example 9, although contemporary sources are silent concerning exactly which Rossini aria served as the basis for this number.[11]

Because no published materials for *Les Français au sérail* survive, identifying the authors of the arrangement of music and libretto is difficult. Some

---

11. Example 9 is an amalgam of Rossini's score with the text from F-Pan F^{18} 613/157.

contemporary accounts state that the arrangement of *Les Français au sérail* originated in Lyon and, by the time it was premiered at the Odéon, was already at its fifteenth performance there.[12] It is possible that at least one of the authors was Hyacinthe Albertin, who was certainly Lyonnais and whose works were often heard in Paris.[13] Strictly speaking, *Les Français au sérail* was an opéra comique that had not yet fallen into the public domain. A report in the *Journal de Paris* at the end of 1824, however, mentions the fact that the work had been arranged by two Lyonnais from Devienne's opéra comique, and that it had been accepted by the Odéon on the condition that Picard would get half the royalties.[14] The fact that this report mentions that the work had been arranged *à l'italienne,* and that *Les Français au sérail* was in fact an arrangement, in turn, of an Italian version of *Les visitandines,* might have enabled the Odéon to mount the work while keeping to the spirit, but hardly to the letter of its license.[15] Stitching together such a complex production was probably helped by the fact that Picard was an ex-manager of the Odéon.[16]

The competition between the two arrangements of *Les visitandines—Le pensionnat de jeunes demoiselles* at the Opéra-Comique and *Les Français au sérail* at the Odéon—was noticed in the press well before either work reached the theater; the former was premiered on 2 March 1825 and the latter on 30 June the same year. Two months before the Opéra-Comique premiered the work, the critic for *La Pandore* had put it succinctly:

> The Odéon are rehearsing *Les Français au sérail,* but it appears that the production of these disguised Sisters of the Visitation (*ces Visitandines travesties*) will encounter some obstacle if the Opéra-Comique, as everyone says, persists in wanting to oppose it. Nevertheless, what makes us believe that these difficulties are only imaginary is that the Opéra-Comique is thinking, for its part, of mounting a production of *Les visitandines* under the title *Le pensionnat de demoiselles* [*sic*]. That is the nature of forbidden fruit (*le fruit défendu*): everyone grabs onto its branches.[17]

12. *La Pandore,* 9 June 1825.

13. Porel and Monval, *L'Odéon,* 1:70.

14. *Journal de Paris,* 27 December 1824.

15. The phrase *à l'italienne,* on the other hand, might have signified nothing more than the addition of a single Rossini number to the work.

16. Picard had been manager of the Odéon from 1816 to 1821 (Nicole Wild, *Dictionnaire des théâtres parisiens au XIXe siècle: les théâtres et la musique* [Paris: Amateurs des Livres, 1989], 290).

17. L'Odéon répète les *Français au serail;* mail il paraît que la représentation de ces Visitandines travesties éprouvera quelqu'obstacle, si Feydeau, comme on l'assure, persiste à vouloir s'y opposer. Cependant, ce qui nous ferait croire que ces difficultés ne sont qu'imaginaires, c'est que l'Opéra-Comique pense, de son côté, à jouer les *Visitandines* sous le titre du *Pensionnat de demoiselles.* Voilà ce que c'est que le fruit défendu, tout le monde s'accroche aux branches (*La Pandore,* 22 January 1825).

The Opéra-Comique does not seem to have tried to prevent *Les Français au sérail* from being produced, but there is ample evidence of their acting similarly in other instances.[18] *Les Français au sérail* ran only for five nights whereas the Opéra-Comique's *Pensionnat de jeunes demoiselles* played for forty-five nights in 1825 alone and was a regular part of the institution's repertory throughout the second half of the decade. Whether the failure of *Les Français au sérail* was the result of intrigue from the Opéra-Comique that has left no documentary trace or the result of a poor critical response to the mixture of Italian music with French lies within the realm of conjecture. Hostile responses in the press concentrated exclusively on what was seen as the inappropriate inclusion of Italian music.[19]

Although the Odéon viewed public domain opéra comique as a less exciting part of its repertory and took greater trouble to promote foreign music drama, the view of its audience was that both were types of music drama, and that each should be judged according to its intrinsic merits. To an extent, the press shared this view. Almost a dozen opéras comiques had been performed during the summer of 1824 by the time Dalayrac's *Philippe et Georgette* came to the Odéon. It was badly received. The principal objection was that the story lacked verisimilitude but did not counteract this flaw with interesting dramatic and musical situations.[20] Views on the *ancien répertoire* conflicted: some thought that such music drama needed rejuvenating by skilled actors, and that it was correspondingly harder to perform, whereas others chastised the actors for including plays on words that were not present in the original libretto—in other words for attempting to rejuvenate it; even though *Le tonnelier,* for example, was not perhaps an important work, it carried a weight of tradition that needed to be respected.[21] Exactly what constituted insignificant works was a good question: *Le tonnelier* and Dalayrac's *Ambroise* were, for one journalist, "of too little importance to excite a great deal of interest."[22] Such questions became pressing when, because of the conditions that governed public-domain works, there was a perception that the Odéon might run out of opéras comiques.[23] Grétry, however, was never out of favor.

Opéra Comique

Throughout the 1820s, the managers of the theater campaigned vigorously to be permitted to mount new opéras comiques. Claude Bernard tried re-

18. E.g., the discussion of *Les trois genres* (page 149).
19. See *La Pandore,* 29 June and 1 July 1825.
20. *Le Diable Boiteux,* 27 July 1824.
21. Ibid., 27 May 1825; *Le Courrier des Théâtres,* 30 May 1825.
22. *Le Courrier des Théâtres,* 4 June 1824.
23. *La Pandore,* 3 June 1824.

peatedly in the year before the theater began its opera seasons to change the license (which effectively formed part of his contract) and tried again in October-November 1824. Both Frédéric du Petit-Méré and Thomas Sauvage tried, from April to November 1826 and from March to May 1828 respectively, to obtain permission to play new opéra comique. Frédéric was fortunate enough to have the support of all the winners of the Prix de Rome in his attempt; Sauvage recruited even more weighty support. At no time, however, were any of the managers successful. The Odéon occasionally responded in practice to the stipulation that it could play public domain opéra comique only by subterfuge. The arrangement of *Les visitandines* may have come close to infringing the conditions of the license, and in the case of *Les trois genres,* the Odéon fought off an energetic claim from the Opéra-Comique that the license had been ignored as early as the opening night of the Odéon's opera enterprise. Other occasional works came close to breaking the terms of its license by including new music within preexisting opéras comiques. Despite the fact that the Odéon scrupulously adhered to the conditions laid down for its repertory, the question of broadening its license was rarely far from the minds of its administrators and devotees, both behind the scenes and occasionally in the press.

The reason for the restriction of the theater's license, never clearly stated, was the potential competition with the Opéra-Comique. This, like the Odéon, was a royal theater and, again like the Odéon, was responsible to the maison du Roi. The mechanisms for altering the Odéon's license consisted of making representations to the relevant official at the maison du Roi (initially La Ferté, then Lauriston, and La Rochefoucauld), who would then invite responses from other interested parties before reaching a decision. After the defeat on the issue of mounting new opéras comiques as part of his original contract negotiations (discussed in chapter 2), Bernard opened his next campaign on 13 October 1824. By this time, the Odéon had mounted only two Rossini translations (*La dame du lac* and *Le barbier de Séville*), its opening occasional work, *Les trois genres,* and the first of Castil-Blaze's pasticci, *Les folies amoureuses.* These translations were supplemented by no fewer than twelve productions of public domain opéras comiques. The success of the French translations of Peter von Winter's *Das unterbrochene Opferfest* and Carl Maria von Weber's *Der Freischütz* was still to come. Bernard was less than sanguine about the future. He began his request in a style that would become familiar to the maison du Roi: "I have learned by a fatal experience that the exploitation of the Odéon can only, despite my zeal and my activity, drag me into total ruin."[24] Bernard sug-

---

24. J'apprends par une fatale expérience que l'exploitation de l'Odéon ne peut malgré mon zèle, mon activité, que m'entraîner dans une ruine totale (F-Pan O^3 1791/VI).

gested two remedies to La Rochefoucauld. The first of these was an increase in subvention; the second was permission to produce opéra comique at the Odéon. His request was cunningly tempered with the suggestion that the Odéon should be allowed to mount productions of all works that were at least five years old and that had received the permission of the composers and librettists. Such a procedure would have stopped him putting on such opéras comiques as Auber's *Neige* and *Leicester,* Carafa's *Chambre,* and Hérold's *Muletier* (all premiered in 1823), because they were too recent. Bernard's proposal represented a clear compromise between the ten years of the public domain requirement, and the complete abolition of the restrictive clause in the contract and license. Because he had carefully not reiterated his stipulation that the works need be in only one or two acts, he would have been able to put on Hérold's *Troqueurs* (1819), Batton's *Fenêtre secrète,* Boieldieu's *Petit chaperon rouge* (1818), Hérold's *Clochette* and *Les rosières,* and Catel's *Wallace* (all 1817). Furthermore, all Méhul would have been open to the Odéon, as would have been Cherubini, if it could have been assumed that the composer would have cooperated in the venture.

The problem with Bernard's suggestion was that many of the works that he proposed including in the Odéon repertory were still performed at the Opéra-Comique, albeit infrequently. *Le petit chaperon rouge,* for example, had been played there eight times the previous year and would enjoy a run of five performances just after La Rochefoucauld had received Bernard's letter. Although *La clochette* had not been performed at the Opéra-Comique since October 1822, it would also have a successful run in the second half of 1827. It can have come as no surprise to La Rochefoucauld that the administration of the Opéra-Comique would take a less than enthusiastic view of extending the Odéon's license. The duc d'Aumont, who had directed the provisional administration of the Opéra-Comique from September 1823 to April 1824 wrote twice to La Rochefoucauld in November 1824. D'Aumont was angry that he had not been consulted about the establishment of an opera troupe at the Odéon in the first place and was adamantly against changing the Odéon's license now. He pointed to works currently in repertory at the Opéra-Comique and suggested that Cherubini's *Elisa* and Méhul's *Ariodant* were scheduled for performance in the near future.[25] Despite this claim, there is no indication that either of these works were performed during the 1820s.

Bernard could be very persuasive in his attempts to convince La Rochefoucauld that the Odéon should be allowed the extension to its license, and he threatened the closure of the theater if he did not get his way. His rea-

25. Both letters from the duc d'Aumont to La Rochefoucauld are in F-Pan O^3 1791/VI. This is a specific response to a list of works that he wanted to mount at the Odéon mentioned by Bernard to La Rochefoucauld.

sons were, first, that the Odéon was sufficiently far from the main areas of theatrical interest not to damage performances at the Opéra-Comique, Académie royale de musique and Théâtre italien; second, that the theater was close to the Chambre de Pairs, at the Palais du Luxembourg; third, that as the theater was close the university, young people needed a place of assembly where they could hear lyric and dramatic masterpieces, both French and foreign; and, finally, that the Odéon was the only theater on the Left Bank and its closure would precipitate a fall in tax income of Fr 1,000,000. This last argument, claimed Bernard, had already been won in the Chambre des Pairs.

Bernard's letter of 13 October 1824 was ambiguously worded and spoke about works (*ouvrages*) without specifying opéras comiques. Whether the effect on La Rochefoucauld was intended or not, the latter considered that Bernard was asking for the right to produce grand opéra; accordingly he referred the matter to François-Antoine Habeneck at the Académie royale de musique.[26] As in the case of the duc d'Aumont, Habeneck's response was predictably negative: after repeating at length the definition of public domain, he drew an analogy between the Odéon and the Gymnase dramatique. Both institutions, he said, were allowed to play all genres (in other words, plays as well as music drama; he did not mean a finer distinction between opéra comique and grand opéra), but both were subject to restriction. At the Gymnase, all works had to be reduced to one act and, at the Odéon, the repertory was limited to public domain works. Habeneck thought this entirely fair and saw no reason to change the status quo. In the responses from the duc d'Aumont and Habeneck can be seen typically Parisian responses to what they saw as essentially a bureaucratic problem. Each theater in Paris had its license, and this system was designed to avoid rivalry and the overlapping of repertory. Neither could see any reason why changes should be made to increase the receipts of a single theater, not because there was a serious chance of the Odéon competing with either of them (although in the case of *Robin des bois,* it came close) but because it would disturb the system of licenses. In a world where the royal court still had powers of patronage and control, such a disturbance was unthinkable. Bernard, the outsider, found these conventions irksome.

When Frédéric du Petit-Méré took over the direction of the Odéon, he immediately took over where Bernard had left off. He approached La Rochefoucauld and pointed to the possibility of the closure of the Odéon and his own possible ruin. During April and June 1826, he offered exactly the same remedies for the situation as Bernard: an increase in subvention and the extension of the theater's license to include new opéras comiques.

26. Habeneck's response to La Rochefoucauld, dated 17 October 1824, is ibid.

Like Bernard, he wanted to avoid competition with the Opéra-Comique, so he offered a restriction that he would not put on any works by composers who had works currently in repertory at the Opéra-Comique (rather than, as Bernard suggested, restricting the Odéon to works that were at least five years old).[27] These representations came to nothing. An additional piece of business transacted by Frédéric around this time was a successful request to the Chambre de Pairs to continue its protection of its local theater. The support of the marquis de Sémonville, *grand référendaire* of the Chambre des Pairs, would prove relevant for Frédéric's successor, Thomas Sauvage, in future years.[28]

Later in 1826 Frédéric received support from a powerful lobby. Fourteen Prix de Rome laureates signed a letter addressed to La Rochefoucauld; the signatories represented prizewinners from as long ago as 1805 and from as recently as 1826.[29] The petition pointed out the fact that painters, sculptors, and architects who had won the Prix de Rome received work from the government whereas composers were left to fend for themselves, and to earn their living by means other than their musical talent. The government might have spent a large amount of money on keeping its best students in Italy and Germany for five years, but this money was wasted if they could not then use the skills that they had acquired. The text continued with a reference to the wishes of the manager of the Odéon to be allowed to include opéra comique in the theater's repertory and explained exactly how such a course of action would satisfy the needs of the debutant composers. The arguments in the composers' letter were strong, and they were increased in strength by the comments added by three of the most respected senior composers and musicians in the capital. Charles-Simon Catel was joined by two of the Conservatoire's composers, Jean-François Le Sueur and Henri-Montan Berton, in offering support to the roster of young composers who were in turn supporting the Odéon. The request made, and the situation described, was one that would recur throughout the nineteenth century in a variety of contexts.

However eloquent the petition, and however impressive the cosignatories, La Rochefoucauld's immediate response was noncommittal. By the beginning of the next month, the result was clear. Frédéric was invited by La Rochefoucauld, and with the approval of both the duc d'Aumont and the new manager of the Opéra-Comique, René Charles Guilbert de Pixéré-

27. Both letters are in F-Pan O^3 1792/I.

28. The dossier of materials relating to the transactions between Petit-Méré, La Rochefoucauld, and the marquis de Sémonville are in F-Pan O^3 1792/V.

29. The document is preserved, along with La Rochefoucauld's response, in F-Pan O^3 1792/I, and is transcribed as appendix 2. Two of these composers, Panseron and Rolle, wrote the music of *L'école de Rome,* discussed in chapter 5.

court, to attend a meeting of the *conseil judiciaire* of the Opéra-Comique on 9 November 1826. This was a step forward for Frédéric in his campaign, and his rumored success was reported by the press early in December 1826.[30] However, the absence of any documentary consequence of the meeting with the Opéra-Comique, and the fact that no change is detectable in the Odéon's programming, makes it abundantly clear that the outcome was not the one desired.

The marquis de Sémonville had long been a supporter of the Odéon. In March 1828, a rumor was circulating concerning the building of a second theater for Opéra-Comique, also in the Right Bank's traditional theater district. The apparent consequence of such an action would have been the closure of the Odéon. Sémonville wrote to his subordinate, the baron de La Bouillerie (the intendant général of the maison du Roi) about the matter. His opening lines made it clear where he thought the power lay: "M. le baron, it is much less as *grand référendaire* than as a neighbor of the Odéon, and as a good servant of the King, that I allow myself the honor of approaching you again concerning this establishment." The demands of the Odéon, as restated by Sémonville, were the same: further financial support and the permission to play new opéra comique.[31] The day before Sémonville had written his letter, Sauvage had written one of his own. Rather than addressing La Rochefoucauld, the manager of the Intendance des beaux-arts, he could have applied to the baron de La Bouillerie, La Rochefoucauld's immediate superior. However, Sauvage in fact went one step higher and wrote to the vicomte de Martignac, secrétaire de l'état au département de l'Intérieur (of which the maison du Roi was part).[32] Sauvage could do this because he had the support of the mayor of the eleventh arrondissement of Paris, Antoine-Marie Fieffé, who wrote a letter to Martignac the day after Sauvage (1 March 1828). While Sauvage's letter contained the usual requests, Fieffé's was more wide ranging.[33] Since by early March 1828, Sauvage had recruited the support of two of the most powerful and influential individuals representing the district in which the Odéon was situated, he bypassed the appropriate channels to get his voice heard well outside the maison du Roi. Pressure was accordingly brought to bear on La Bouillerie from above by Martignac, and from below by La Rochefoucauld.[34] However promising the position might have been for the Odéon, the matter was unsatisfactorily settled on 13 June 1828 when La Bouillerie wrote to Martignac's office. In the shortest of notes, La Bouillerie wrote: "I regret to have

30. See *Le Courrier des Théâtres*, 14 December 1826.
31. F-Pan O³ 1793/I.
32. F-Pan O³ 1792/V.
33. Ibid.
34. Letter of 29 May 1828 (ibid.); letter of 11 March 1828 (F-Pan O³ 1793/I).

to announce to your excellency that it is impossible to agree to the extension of the Odéon's license at the moment."[35]

Although individual works from the public domain repertory found favor with the press, public support for allowing the Odéon to play new opéras comiques was widespread. In Castil-Blaze's initial article on the Odéon's opera troupe, he seemed to think that the theater would be allowed to include new opéra comique in its repertory. When it had been made clear that this was not the case, *La Pandore*'s critic quickly came to the support of the theater and cited the same arguments.[36] Almost three years later, *Le Courrier des Théâtres* came out in support of the same cause.[37] Whatever weight the press could add to the Odéon's arguments however, it could not compete with the Opéra-Comique's vigorous defense of its license against threats from the Odéon.

The Opéra-Comique was not entirely in the wrong in its dealings with the Odéon. True, it not only struggled effectively against the theater but was merciless with the Théâtre des Nouveautés when the latter looked like it was going to infringe the Opéra-Comique's license in March 1827.[38] Such action, however, was entirely normal in the theatrical world of Restoration Paris, and the Odéon itself acted in exactly the same way as the Opéra-Comique when it served its purpose to do so. Indeed, the Odéon's administration was significantly more relentless in pursuit of its rivals than the Opéra-Comique. The element in the Odéon's license that it guarded most preciously was the right to play foreign music drama in translation. Well before the Odéon's opera troupe began work, the theater was seeking to ensure that no others could mount French translations of Italian and German music drama. The Gymnase dramatique was particularly singled out for attention. On the Odéon's behalf, the marquis de Lauriston approached the minister of the interior, comte Corbière, and asked him to act against the Gymnase dramatique and in favor of the Odéon.[39] Corbière replied that he could not act in this regard, and that it was up to the theater itself to act if it saw its license being infringed.[40] No evidence survives of the Odéon's taking any action against the Gymnase dramatique, although attempting to gain sole rights to foreign music drama in translation may have had something to do with the projected arrangement of *Der Freischütz* as *Le chasseur noir* at the Gymnase the previous year.

35. F-Pan O³ 1792/V.
36. *La Pandore,* 27 May 1824.
37. 22 March 1828.
38. See *La Pandore,* 3 March 1827.
39. Letter of 21 January 1824 (F-Pan O³ 1790/VI).
40. Letter of 9 February 1824 (ibid.).

Within weeks of opening the opera season at the Odéon, Bernard was already taking a hard look at the local opposition. Pierre-Jacques Séveste was the manager of several suburban theaters that were allowed to operate outside the city walls. Bernard's complaint was that Séveste was posting bills within the walls, alongside the posters for the royal and secondary theaters.[41] Three years later, Sauvage was still filing the same complaint, although by now Pierre-Jacques had died and had been succeeded by his two sons, Edmond and Jules Séveste.[42] Sauvage's request to La Rochefoucauld in 1827 was only part of much longer complaint about theaters competing with the Odéon. Another victim was the Théâtre du Luxembourg, otherwise known as the Théâtre Bobino. This theater had grown from nothing in 1816 with no license, tolerated by the prefet de police as long as it was the source of no disturbance, to a venue for high-wire acts, feats of strength, and marionettes. The theater had already tried to extend its repertory in 1817 to include vaudevilles and short plays; it was promptly shut down for two years after a request from the Odéon's manager, Picard.[43] Ten years later, Sauvage repeated Picard's request in exactly the same terms. The theater was by then playing vaudevilles and even mélodrames, and the high wire was hardly of any importance there at all. Its ability to attract audiences, especially on Sunday and Monday, was, according to Sauvage, to the detriment of the Odéon.[44] Within a week, La Rochefoucauld had received orders that these transgressions would be ended.[45] However difficult working within a license might be, it was substantially better than working, as in the case of the Théâtre du Luxembourg, without one, when the theater could simply be closed, without appeal, by the prefet de police.

Berlioz

The only French composer who actively attempted to compose a new work for the Odéon was Hector Berlioz. As was the case with so many of his compositions from the 1820s, the composition and subsequent fate of the work caused the composer large amounts of difficulty. Berlioz had got to know the librettist of *Les francs-juges,* Humbert Ferrand, in November 1825.[46] Less than six months later, he referred in a letter to Léon Compaignon, the li-

41. F-Pan O^3 1791/III (3 May 1824). For an account of Séveste's activities, see Wild, *Dictionnaire,* 47–50.

42. .F-Pan O^3 1793/III.

43. Wild, *Dictionnaire,* 232–36.

44. F-Pan O^3 1793/III.

45. Ibid., letter of 6 September 1827.

46. David Cairns, ed. and trans., *The Memoirs of Hector Berlioz, Member of the French Institute, including His Travels to Italy, Germany, Russia and England* (London: Victor Gollanz, 1977), 77.

brettist of the even more incomplete *Richard en Palestine,* to errands he had to run *pour notre opéra de l'Odéon.*[47] Six weeks later, when he wrote to Édouard Rocher, he not only admitted to being in the process of completing *Les francs-juges* but outlined some of the difficulties he envisaged with the Odéon.[48] When set against the Odéon's campaign to be allowed to mount productions of opéras comiques, Berlioz's conviction that *Les francs-juges* would be premiered at the Odéon shows just how far from the center of musical and theatrical life he really was in the 1820s.

Berlioz's letter to Rocher (15 July 1826) describes *Les francs-juges* as an opéra in three acts for the Odéon and mistakenly claimed that "the manager has at last obtained permission to produce new operas there composed by Frenchmen." The score was to be presented in two months' time, and the libretto was apparently as good as agreed with the manager, to whose suggestions for changes Berlioz had agreed. Le Sueur was happy with the first two acts. Later in the letter, Berlioz returned to the subject of the Odéon, its audiences, and Berlioz's own superiority to both: "Let my opéra be given and may it succeed (this I have cause to hope for at least as far as the libretto, which is infinitely better than all those than have been presented at the Odéon so far). . . . [The libretto is] extremely severe and dramatic, and the Odéon audience is in such a state of stupor since it has had to swallow *Marguerite d'Anjou* and *La dame du lac,* etc., etc., that if I counted on its understanding and good taste I would be counting on *providence* [Berlioz's emphasis]."[49] Two months later, *Les francs-juges* was complete, although Berlioz was still tinkering with it. He also reported (in a letter to Léon Compaignon, 14 October 1826) that permission to produce new music drama in French at the Odéon had not yet been obtained.[50] Berlioz was still following this matter closely, but knew relatively little beyond what could be gleaned from the press; public information about this matter was confused and contradictory. Berlioz did know however about the composers' plan to write to La Rochefoucauld.[51] To Compaignon in provincial Chartres, he could ally himself with the composers: "we have put together a petition

47. Pierre Citron, ed., *Hector Berlioz: correspondance générale, 1803–1832* (Paris: Flammarion, 1972), 1:113 (letter of 30 May 1826).

48. Ibid., 127 (letter of 15 July 1826).

49. Que mon opéra se donne et réussisse (ce que j'ai lieu d'espérer du moins quant au poème qui est infiniment meilleur que tous ceux qu'on a donné à l'Odéon jusqu'à présent). . . . [Le poème est] extrêmement sévère et dramatique, et le public de l'Odéon est si stupide depuis qu'on lui a fait avaler des *Marguerite d'Anjou,* des *Dames du lac,* etc., etc., que si je compte sur ses connaissances et son bon goût, c'est comme si je comptais sur la *providence* (ibid., 128).

50. Ibid., 139.

51. Ibid. See note 29 above.

signed by all the young composers and addressed to Sosthène de La Roche-foucauld; so far, it has remained without response."[52] This is the letter La Rochefoucauld received on 23 October 1826; because its authors were prizewinners of the Prix de Rome, Berlioz's name was not among them (the young composer did not comment on this point).

By the beginning of the following year, Berlioz's enthusiasm for pro-ducing *Les francs-juges* at the Odéon was undiminished. Writing to Com-paignon, he spoke of preparing parts for some kind of performance at the Odéon.[53] Given what is known of performing practices at the theater, this was probably nothing more than a run-through in the foyer at best; concerts did not take place there, and Berlioz was unlikely to allow fragments of *Les francs-juges* to sit alongside works of other composers. It is possible that he had in mind some sort of public audition of the music, since in a letter to his sister on 20 January 1827 he said he was still copying parts of the work he wanted to have heard *pour la réception de l'ouvrage.* This would have been an anomalous procedure at the Odéon, since the reading committee was not ever required to judge new music because of the conditions of the Odéon's license, and no evidence exists of judging a work by its music dur-ing this period. In the same letter to Nanci Berlioz, her brother announced that the Odéon was again on the verge of being allowed to play new opéras comiques, and his endeavors were directed toward being ready to be one of the first French composers represented there.

As a tiny codicil to the history of *Les francs-juges,* Berlioz told his sister about a banquet offered by the members of the Odéon orchestra to Nathan Bloc, who had so ably looked after their interests during the summer of 1828. At this event, which took place in October 1828, Bloc—according to Berlioz—toasted him: "Gentlemen, I drink to the success of an artist who does not form part of the establishment of the Odéon, but whom we would be proud to possess; that is M. Berlioz."[54] Berlioz responded in his inim-itable style with a toast to the memory of Weber and Beethoven. It is difficult to know how to interpret this bonhomie. By November 1828 the Odéon had ceased to host an opera troupe, and many of the participants at the banquet can no longer have been working there. Furthermore, Bloc's comment con-cerns Berlioz as a member of the establishment of the Odéon—not solely as a composer for the stage—and it may well be that this has more to do with Berlioz's energy in mounting concerts of his music (reflected in his ap-

52. Nous avons fait une pétition signée par tous les jeunes compositeurs, et adressée à Sosthène [de La Rochefoucauld]; elle est restée jusqu'à présent sans réponse (ibid.).

53. Ibid., 147 (letter of 12 January 1827) and 149.

54. Messieurs, je bois aux succès d'un artiste qui ne fait pas partie de l'administration de l'Odéon, mais que nous serions fiers de posséder, c'est M. Berlioz (letter to Nanci Berlioz, 1 November 1828 [ibid., 211]).

pointment as commissaire de la Société du Gymnase lyrique the following month, which amounted to very little) than with *Les francs-juges*.

Berlioz's music for *Les francs-juges* was carved up, used in concert performances—most notably at the Conservatoire on 26 May 1828—and reworked for other purposes.[55] Well before its final arrangement as *Le cri de guerre de Brisgaw* in 1833–34, Ferrand had reworked the libretto during 1828 and 1829, and in June 1829 Berlioz informed his collaborator that the revised libretto had been finally refused by the Académie royale de musique.[56] The only libretto that survives from *Les francs-juges* dates from 1829, and it is clearly in a form that would have been suitable for the Académie royale de musique in that it has loosely rhyming recitative poetry rather than spoken dialogue.[57] It disguises much of the form of the 1826 Odéon libretto.[58]

The surviving musical fragments of *Les francs-juges* permit a partial reconstruction of the music of the 1826 work:[59] a total of fourteen numbers and an overture. Some sort of music survives for the overture and eight numbers.[60] However, the generic profile of the 1826 *Les francs-juges* is far from clear. Although there are no precedents for new music drama by a French composer at the Odéon, the discussions both in the press and between the Odéon's managers and the maison du Roi were almost all about opéra comique. The question then is whether Ferrand and Berlioz, in 1826, had written an opéra comique (with spoken dialogue) and changed it into a grand opéra for the Académie royale de musique in 1829, or whether they had tried to foist a work more suitable for the Académie royale de musique onto the Odéon from the beginning.

A useful analogy here is Meyerbeer's *Robert le diable,* which was planned as an opéra comique for the institution of the same name in 1825–27 and reworked for the Académie royale de musique during 1829–31.[61] The correlation between these dates and those of the composition and reworking

55. The best summary of the sources and reworking of *Les francs-juges* is in D. Kern Holoman, *The Creative Process in the Autograph Musical Documents of Hector Berlioz, c.1818–1840,* 2d ed. (Ann Arbor, Mich.: UMI Research Press, 1980), 215–36; see also idem, *Catalogue of the Works of Hector Berlioz* (Kassel: Bärenreiter, 1987), 34–45.

56. Citron, ed., *Berlioz: correspondance* (letter of 3 June 1829), 1:256.

57. The manuscript is now in F-Pn papiers divers de Berlioz, 45.

58. The loss of the manuscript mentioned by Adolphe Boschot (*Une Vie romantique: Hector Berlioz* [Paris: Plon, 1919], 1:206) is great indeed; this could well have been the original version that predated the revisions for the Académie royale de musique.

59. The musical fragments are now F-Pn Rés. Vm² 177; an outline of the manuscript's contents is in Holoman, *Catalogue of Works of Berlioz,* 38.

60. D. Kern Holoman, "Les Fragments de l'opéra perdu de Berlioz: *Les Francs-Juges,*" *Revue de musicologie* 63 (1977): 84–85.

61. See Mark Everist, "The Name of the Rose: Meyerbeer's *opéra comique, Robert le Diable,*" *Revue de musicologie* 80 (1992): 211–50.

of *Les francs-juges* is remarkable. Broadly speaking, Eugène Scribe and Germain Delavigne took the libretto of their opéra comique, replaced all the dialogue with poetry that could be set as accompanied recitative, spread the action out over five acts rather than the three of the opéra comique, and restructured some parts to adjust the tone for a more serious environment. Meyerbeer then had to rework large parts of the score; some of these changes related to changes in the libretto, and others to the different singers available at the Académie royale de musique. He also had to write a ballet.

All that survives of *Les francs-juges* is Ferrand's revised libretto of 1829, the musical fragments mentioned above, and the presence of parts of the work in other compositions. Inferences about either the structure of the 1826 *Les francs-juges* or the result of Berlioz's revisions (if he made them at all) are dangerous. Meyerbeer was an experienced man of the theater, sensitive to questions of genre and convention; Berlioz was young and headstrong, and the words genre and convention were uncongenial to him. It is far from clear that Berlioz would have meekly written an opéra comique on the model of Boieldieu's *Dame blanche,* for example. Even so, nothing in the list of musical numbers that made up the 1826 *Les francs-juges* contradicts the idea that he did indeed write an opéra comique. The two numbers prefaced with recitatives (no. 3, recitative and aria "Va! Je t'abhorre" and no. 11, recitative and invocation "Voici l'endroit fatal") would hardly be out of place in an opéra comique from the middle of the decade; *La dame blanche,* for example, includes a massive recitative for Anna and Georges before the duet "Toujours soumis" in act II. Perhaps more interesting are the two items that preface the final *choeur du peuple:* the "Hymne des francs-juges" (no. 12) and the mélodrame and reprise of the hymn (no. 13). Mélodrame would be an interesting inclusion in an opéra comique at this period, but not so much, perhaps, for an opéra comique at the Odéon. One passage in mélodrame stood out from the entire repertory of music drama at the Odéon in the 1820s: the wolf's glen scene from *Der Freischütz,* well known throughout 1825 and 1826 as *Robin des bois,* and one of the Odéon's greatest successes. A mélodrame, even in an opéra comique, would be the obvious homage for Berlioz to offer the recently deceased Weber.

Ferrand either reworked the libretto of the hypothetical opéra comique he and Berlioz wrote in 1826 as an opéra three years later, or the style of its 1826 libretto was much closer to the 1829 version and changes in it reflected the pair's dissatisfaction with the work. In the latter case, even if the Odéon gained permission to mount opéras comiques by living French composers, the theater could never produce them. Even if Ferrand and Berlioz wrote an opéra comique, they were gambling on the maison du Roi's making a massive shift in policy that nearly the entire Parisian operatic and theatrical establishment opposed. Like other young composers and librettists trying to break into the world of Parisian music drama, Berlioz and Ferrand were doomed to fail.

French Origins of Odéon Compositions

The French tradition at the Odéon during the 1820s is most obviously represented by its cultivation of opéra comique from the *ancien régime,* Revolution, and Empire. Yet every work—whatever its original language—that was produced at the Odéon during these years was in French. At the time, translations from Italian and German were described as being performed *en opéra comique.* At a deeper level, this was a misnomer: conventions that governed the patterns of scene, aria, duet, introduzione, and finale in an Italian opera semiseria, say, were left as they were and contrasted with the conventions of opéra comique. In broader terms—the facts that the drama was mainly conducted in spoken dialogue and that the work was in French—to describe the Odéon translations as *en opéra comique* was not far off the mark.

Many of the works translated from German and Italian originally had libretti based on French models; Cesare Sterbini's libretto for *Il barbiere di Siviglia* was based on Beaumarchais's *Barbier de Séville,* for example. Wherever possible, a French translation for the Odéon returned to the French model for the original libretto. When Castil-Blaze came to translate Sterbini's libretto into French, wherever possible he returned to Beaumarchais for the spoken dialogue.[62] Indeed, for many Parisian audiences, Castil-Blaze's translation of the Rossini/Sterbini work *was* Beaumarchais's *Barbier de Séville.* On some nights, Beaumarchais's play could be heard at the Théâtre italien in the guise of *Il barbiere di Siviglia,* at the Odéon in Castil-Blaze's French translation of the same work, and at the Comédie-Française in Beaumarchais's original version. For the press, there were many respects in which all three performances were presentations of the same work.[63]

The origins of each work were different and called forth different responses from the Odéon arrangers. The works can be grouped into four: Castil-Blaze's pasticci, translations from Italian, translations from German, and the francophone rerouting of English sources. Castil-Blaze's four pasticci were not translations but adaptations of seventeenth- and eighteenth-century classics. His practice was to construct a libretto for an opéra comique out of a French play, either creating opportunities for arias, duets, finales, and so on, and then to rework individual numbers by other composers to accompany the libretto he had written, or to build the libretto

---

62. The relationship between Castil-Blaze, Rossini, Sterbini, and Beaumarchais is discussed at greater length in idem, "Lindoro in Lyon: Rossini's *Le Barbier de Séville,*" *Acta musicologica* 44 (1992): 50–85.

63. Ibid., 84.

around particular numbers that he wanted to include. His sources were Charles Collé (*La forêt de Sénart*, 1775), Destouches (*La fausse Agnès*, 1759), Regnard (*Les folies amoureuses*, 1704), and Molière (*Monsieur de Pourceaugnac*, 1669). At almost every level Castil-Blaze tries to keep to his original as closely as possible, given the generic constraints of opéra comique, which mean that abridgement of the original text is essential in order to allow space for the extensive pauses in dramatic time for sung numbers. This is necessarily an important part of the process of creating any libretto from a preexistent literary source, and such abridgement can result in scenes being cut or carefully pruned to reduce their length. Act II of *Les folies amoureuses* is a good example not only of how musical numbers are worked into the original, but also of how some scenes are unchanged, some slightly shortened, some resequenced, and others cut.[64] Scenes i, vi, and vii are unchanged, and viii–xiii omitted entirely. Scenes iii–iv are reworked around Cimarosa's quintet "Stanco ma no ferito" from *I nemici generosi*, and other scenes are modified to allow the incorporation of music.

In terms of the overall structure of the drama, the number and sequence of acts and scenes, three out of the four pasticci retain the pattern of the original. The exception is *La forêt de Sénart*, where the whole of act I is omitted. The resulting pattern is as follows:[65]

La partie de chasse de Henri IV (1775)	*La forêt de Sénart* (1826)
I	
II.i–v	I.i–viii
II.vi–xi	II.i–vi
III.i–xiv	III.i–xiii

In general, Castil-Blaze follows the exact language of his source wherever possible. In three of the four plays that serve as Castil-Blaze's models, the dialogue is in prose, and in many respects already indistinguishable from the dialogue in opéra comique. By contrast, Regnard's *Folies amoureuses* is cast in alexandrines, and Castil-Blaze follows suit. Although this was something of a rarity in opéra comique, it was not remarked on in the press, who did however notice that *Les folies amoureuses* could have been heard both at the Odéon (as an opéra comique) and at the Comédie-Française (as spoken drama) on 6 September 1824.[66]

---

64. *Les folies amoureuses* (Paris: Castil-Blaze, 1823); an early-nineteenth-century print of Regnard's text that might have served as Castil-Blaze's model is *Les folies amoureuses* (Paris: Fages, 1806).

65. *La forêt de Sénart* (Paris: Castil-Blaze, 1826); Collé's original is *La partie de chasse de Henri IV* (Paris: Gueffier, 1775).

66. *Le Courrier des Théâtres*, 7 September 1824.

Castil-Blaze's respect for his model even goes as far as his treatment of the texts for the lyric items. Normally, this is a place where a librettist or arranger is allowed a degree of license, but Castil-Blaze's clear preference is to use the vocabulary and content of the model (whether in prose or alexandrines) as the basis for the poetry of numbers destined wherever possible to be sung. To exemplify this adherence to his model, the construction of the first number from *La fausse Agnès* may be considered.[67] The baron has requested a delay to the marriage of des Masures and his daughter, Angélique, and is developing the idea that although he is his wife's master, he is not a tyrant and will therefore obey her orders. Destouches's original reads as follows:

Le Baron: Je suis votre *maître,* mais je ne suis pas votre *tyran.* Je vous *confie tous mes droits; ordonnez,* ma chère *baronne,* ordonnez, et faites bien valoir mon autorité [I am your master, but I am not your tyrant; command, my dear baroness, command and assert my authority].

Castil-Blaze turns this line into poetry of seven syllables (3 feminine followed by a single masculine) to match the *ottonari* of the original poetry of the Italian music ("Il vecchiotto cerca moglie" from Rossini's *Barbiere di Siviglia*):

Ah! J'en ai trop dit peut-être,	Ah! I have perhaps said too much about it,
Mais je vous ferai connaître	But I will have you know,
Qu'un époux est *votre maître*	That a husband is your master
Mais non pas *votre tyran.*	But not your tyrant.
Vraiment, vraiment,	Indeed, indeed,
Un époux est *votre maître,*	A husband is your master,
Mais non pas *votre tyran.*	But not your tyrant.
Ordonnez, chère baronne,	Command, dear baroness,
Tous mes droits je vous les donne;	I give you all my rights;
Puis-je mieux les *confier?*	Could I entrust them better?
Digne mère de famille,	Worthy mother of the family,
Disposez de notre fille!	Our daughter is at your service!
Oui, vous devez à votre gré la marier.	Yes, you must marry her to your liking.

Almost all the keywords from Destouches find their way into Castil-Blaze's lyric (italicized in both versions); the only exception is the baron's final instruction to the baroness to assert his authority. In addition to the close adherence to the source text, there is a certain congruence in the choice of

---

67. *La fausse Agnès* (Paris: Castil-Blaze, 1824); Destouches's original is *La fausse Agnès ou Le poete campagnard* (Paris: Fages, 1802).

music that would not have gone unnoticed at the Odéon. Berta's aria from *Il barbiere di Siviglia* concerns Rosina and her unwanted suitor, Dr. Bartolo; the similarity of their respective positions to those of Angélique and des Masures in *La fausse Agnès* must surely have provided the prompt for the selection of this number for this particular scene. Although "Ah! J'en ai trop dit peut-être" well illustrates Castil-Blaze's normal working practices in this regard, it does not approach his practice in *Monsieur de Pourceaugnac*, where the text of some numbers consists precisely of Molière's original set to music selected by Castil-Blaze.

Castil-Blaze's translations from Italian libretti exhibit, as far as possible, the same fidelity to the French sources of the works. *Le barbier de Séville*, *Le mariage de Figaro*, and *Don Juan* behave in a similar fashion. Lorenzo da Ponte's most obvious changes to Beaumarchais's *Mariage de Figaro*—the compression of five acts into four—is not reinstated (the musical ramifications would have been too great). In acts that correspond, act I for example, Castil-Blaze follows Beaumarchais closely, even slavishly. In *Don Juan*, Molière plays only one role among other contributors to the literary tradition (Tirso de Molina, Goldoni, and Bertati, for example) but his lines form the basis of much of the dialogue in Castil-Blaze's version. Castil-Blaze also translated *La pie voleuse*. Giovanni Gherardini's libretto *La gazza ladra*, set by Rossini, was based on a mélodrame by Louis-Charles Cagniez and Théodore Baudouin d'Aubigny, and Castil-Blaze again returned to the model for as much of his translation as possible.[68]

Two other Odéon translations from Italian music drama were not the product of Castil-Blaze's pen: *Marguerite d'Anjou* and *Les deux Figaro*. Despite the complexities of *Marguerite d'Anjou*'s musical arrangement, its libretto adhered as closely as possible to the mélodrame source for Felice Romani's original libretto for Meyerbeer. In this respect, the textual tradition of the libretto and its translation is similar to that of *La pie voleuse*. *Les deux Figaro* is analogous to *Le mariage de Figaro*. The libretto of Michel Carafa's *Due Figaro, ossia il soggetto di una commedia* is also by Romani and based on Honoré-Antoine Richaud Martelly's *Deux Figaro ou Le sujet de comédie*. Martelly's play in three acts was reduced to two by Romani, and although Victor Tirpenne's arrangement and translation carefully returns to the text of Martelly's play, he did not reinstate the original three-act plan and left Martelly's first two acts condensed into the Italian version's one.

Édouard d'Anglemont and Jean-Pierre-François Lesguillon translated Gaetano Rossi's libretto for Rossini's *Tancredi* into French for the Odéon.

68. See Emilio Sala, "Alla ricerca della *Pie Voleuse*," in *Gioachino Rossini, 1792–1992: il testo e la scena: Convegno internazionale di studi, Pesaro 25–28 giugno 1992*, ed. Paolo Fabbri (Pesaro: Fondazione Rossini, 1994), 205–53.

The French tradition is here represented by Voltaire's *Tancrède* of 1760, and this is regularly cited as the source for Rossi's libretto. However, between 1760 and Rossini's premiere in 1813, there had been at least four Italian works with libretti derived from Voltaire's text. The libretto by Silvio Saverio Blabis had been set by Ferdinando Bertoni (Turin, 1767) and again by Ignaz Holzbauer with shortened recitative and other small changes (Munich, 1783). Alessandro Pepoli's libretto was set by Francesco Gardi in Venice in 1799 and Luigi Romanelli's by Stefano Pavesi in 1812 in Milan. Exactly how much Voltaire and how much Italian libretto tradition remains in Rossi's libretto is unclear; Voltaire's *Tancrède* was written in alexandrines, and eighteenth-century Italian translations were in 11-syllable *versi piani*.[69] Anglemont and Lesguillon simply translated Rossi's libretto. There is no trace of Voltaire's alexandrines in their prose translation, and this absence of language from the model is unique in the treatments of Italian music drama based on French literary models at the Odéon during this period. True, the only other model in verse was Regnard's *Folies amoureuses,* but Castil-Blaze's treatment of this text was very different. *Tancrède's* translation back into French was recognized as having turned its back on Voltaire.[70]

Although almost all Italian music drama at the Odéon could claim some French in its pedigree, the same could not be said for German works. The libretto of *Robin des bois* (*Der Freischütz*) was based on Apel and Laun's *Gespensterbuch,* and that of *Preciosa* and *Les bohémiens* originally started out as a play by Pius Alexander Wolff. Winter's *Sacrifice interrompu* (*Das unterbrochene Opferfest*) is problematic since no source has yet been identified for Franz Xaver Huber's libretto. Only two Odéon works translated from German music drama had French models as their source. These were the translations of Johann Baptist Weigl's *Schweizerfamilie* as *Emmeline ou La famille suisse* and of Adalbert Gyrowetz's *Augenarzt* as *La jeune aveugle.*

Ignaz Franz Castelli's libretto for Weigl's *Schweizerfamilie* was based on a vaudeville entitled *Pauvre Jacques* by Sewrin and Chazet; it had been premiered at the Théâtre du Vaudeville in October 1807.[71] A French translation of the Weigl had been given in 1812, first at St-Cloud in front of the empress and then at the Opéra-Comique; no editors or translators are named on the libretto, although a group of three extracts cites Henri Tourterelle (pseud., Herdlizka), pianist and répétiteur at the Opéra-Comique,

---

69. Philip Gossett, ed., *Tancredi: melodramma eroico in due atti di Gaetano Rossi, musica di Gioachino Rossini* (Pesaro: Fondazione Rossini, 1984), 1:xxii–iii.

70. *La Pandore,* 9 September 1827.

71. It is difficult to understand the claim made by Elizabeth Norman McKay (*Grove Opera* 4:1123) that the source for Castelli's libretto—and a *lyrische Oper* in three acts—was Saint-Just's libretto for Boieldieu's *Famille suisse,* in one act only. Comparison of the two works makes such a claim impossible.

as the arranger and translator.[72] The dialogue from *Pauvre Jacques* served for much of that of *La vallée suisse* five years later. However, the 1812 production at St-Cloud and at the Opéra-Comique omitted numbers from Weigl's original score,[73] and this is presumably why the 1827 Odéon version (*Emmeline ou La famille suisse*) was described as "exactement conforme à la partition de l'auteur." Unique among the Odéon translators, Sewrin was both the arranger of the libretto and one of the authors of the model for the foreign libretto; hence he left the vaudeville dialogue untouched and sanctioned its use. Furthermore, the other author of the vaudeville, Chazet, was still alive and had been one of the royal censors since 1822.[74] Sewrin's contribution to the arrangement consisted of touching almost nothing of his 1807 vaudeville, and of retranslating the sung numbers (since they are almost entirely different to the 1812 version).

Gyrowetz's opera *Der Augenarzt*, premiered in Vienna in 1811, had a libretto based in turn on an earlier text by Armand Croizette and Armand-François Chateauvieux entitled *Les aveugles de Franconville*, composed as an opéra comique by Louis-Sébastien Lebrun and premiered in 1802.[75] When reworked for the Odéon in March 1826, it was retitled *La jeune aveugle*.[76] The translators and arrangers of the libretto—Alexandre Chalas and Maurice Dufresne—appear not to have made use of the 1802 libretto at all. The matter is complicated by frequent references in the press to *La jeune aveugle* as being effectively the same story as *Valérie*. The day after its premiere the *Journal de Paris* described the libretto as being a poor imitation of *Valérie* while, the same day, *Le Frondeur* more charitably suggested that the story was taken from the same source as *Valérie*. It is not entirely clear to which text these two reports refer. *Valérie* was a play by Scribe and Mélesville, premiered at the Comédie-Française in 1822, but the reports could have been referring to *Valérien ou Le jeune aveugle*, a mélodrame by André-Henri-François Victor de Carrion-Nisas and Sauvage, given for the first time at the Théâtre de la Porte-St-Martin in 1823.[77] Neither text, however, shows any signs of ever having served as a source for Chalas and Dufresne's translation.

72. *Chassant les ennuis, je chante, je ris* (Paris: Pacini, n.d.). Henri Tourterelle was accompanist at the Opéra-Comique between 1808 and 1814 (Wild, *Dictionnaire*, 333); according to *FétisB* (4:302), his date of birth was 1796 (thus Tourterelle was sixteen when the arrangement was made) and his career at the Opéra-Comique ended in 1818.

73. The duet "Avance donc" from act I, the duet "J'ai donné mon coeur," and *couplets* "J'avais un champ, une patrie" from act II, and the chorus "Pour contenter" and trio "L'ombre fuit" from act III.

74. The censors' libretto, presumably seen by Chazet, is F-Pan F^{18} 614/188.

75. *Les aveugles de Franconville* (Paris: Barba, 1802).

76. The only surviving source of *La jeune aveugle* is the censors' libretto (F-Pan F^{18} 614/176).

77. *Valérie* (Paris: Ladvocat, 1822); *Valérien ou Le jeune aveugle* (Paris: Pollet, 1823).

Other works from a German-speaking tradition were considered for production at the Odéon. Beethoven's *Fidelio* and the French source for its libretto are discussed below. Two works by Spohr that were considered for
performance were *Jessonda* and *Der Berggeist*. The libretto to the first of these
was based on a French model—*La veuve de Malabar*—and there is every
likelihood that the arrangers would have returned to this text as the basis of
their translation. The source for the libretto of *Der Berggeist* was German,
and any French version would—like *Robin des bois*—have been a translation
without the benefit of a French model.

The libretti of three works by Rossini have their origins in English literature; each was routed via some kind of French intermediary or served as the
basis for a French work and exhibits different characteristics. Although Sir
Walter Scott's novel *Ivanhoe* had been available since 1820 in a translation
by Auguste-Jean-Baptiste Defauconpret, there is nothing in the libretto of
Ivanhoé that suggests that Émile Deschamps or Gabriel-Gustave de Wailly
found anything in the translation of the novel to help them.[78] The claim
made by Henri Girard that Deschamps's text alludes to a tale by E. T. A.
Hoffmann is difficult to substantiate.[79] There is no internal evidence of a
specific borrowing from Hoffmann in the *Ivanhoé* libretto, and the earliest
attempts at a complete French translation of Hoffmann do not date from
before 1829.[80] The circle in which Deschamps grew up, as well as including Hugo (with whom he founded *La Muse Française* in 1824), encompassed
Alphonse Lamartine, Alfred de Vigny, Charles Nodier, and Alexandre
Soumet;[81] any one of these could have introduced Deschamps to the works
of Hoffmann in German before 1826.

Rossini's *Otello* had been arranged for the French stage by Castil-Blaze for
a production in Lyon in late 1823 and was given at the Odéon in July 1825.
Well before the Paris premiere, the press was already asking questions about
the French libretto on the basis of the Lyon performance. *La Pandore* asked
the perhaps obvious question: why had Castil-Blaze not used Jean-François
Ducis's translation of Shakespeare?[82] Answers are not hard to find. One
is that Ducis's 1792 translation of Shakespeare was in alexandrines, and

78. Defauconpret's translation was reprinted in 1821 (in his collected works) and revised
in 1826, by which time the Chaillot brothers had produced a further translation. It is unclear
whether Deschamps knew of either Defauconpret's new translation or the Chaillots' (both
from 1826) before he worked on *Ivanhoé*.

79. Henri Girard, *Émile Deschamps dilettante: relations d'un poëte romantique avec les peintres, les
sculpteurs et les musiciens de son temps* (Geneva: Slatkine, 1977), 45.

80. The earliest attempt at a complete French translation of E. T. A. Hoffmann was the edition of the collected works published as *Oeuvres complètes de E. T. A. Hoffmann, traduites de l'allemand par M. Théodore Toussenel et par le traducteur des romans de Veit-Weber* (Paris: Lefebvre, 1830).

81. *LDD-NS* 6:538–39.

82. *La Pandore*, 8 January 1824.

although Castil-Blaze did once retain original alexandrines in an Odéon pasticcio (in *Les folies amoureuses*), this was not a normal working method at the theater. The real answer however lies in the degree of change that Francesco Maria Berio, marchese di Salza had effected in reworking *Otello* for his libretto. So much had been altered that it would have been impossible for Castil-Blaze to do anything apart from translate the Italian as he found it. This did not stop the press from savaging Castil-Blaze's efforts; the most vitriolic of these was *Le Courrier des Théâtres'* specific complaint that Castil-Blaze had indeed translated Berio's libretto and not made use of Ducis or Shakespeare.[83]

La donna del lago was the first music drama to be based on a work by Scott; there is still, however, a certain amount of doubt concerning the origins of Andrea Leone Tottola's libretto. Giuseppe Radiciotti related an anecdote concerning Rossini's first encounter with *The Lady of the Lake*.[84] Apparently, the Prix de Rome laureate, Batton, showed Rossini a French translation of Scott, and Rossini was so impressed that he passed the translation to Tottola to serve as the basis for *La donna del lago*. Despite the fact that Radiciotti claimed to have heard the story from Batton himself (impossible because Radiciotti was born in 1858, three years after Batton's death), the story has the ring of truth.[85] Batton had won the Prix de Rome in 1817 and left for Rome after the premiere of his *Fenêtre secrète* at the Opéra-Comique in November 1818 (staying there presumably until around 1821 and going on to Munich where he stayed, at the expense of the French government, until 1823). After his return to Paris, he was one of the signatories of the laureates' petition to La Rochefoucauld in October 1826. It is entirely possible that he was in Naples in the late summer or autumn of 1819 at an appropriate time to suggest Scott in translation to Rossini. Further evidence of the veracity of Radiciotti's account—and the variant given by Alexis Azevedo—lies in the fact that no Italian translation of Scott's *Lady of the Lake* was pub-

83. 28 December 1826. The criticism in the *Courrier des Théâtres* was unduly harsh because Schütz was playing Édelmone, and, as far as the journal was concerned, she could do nothing right. Only slightly less charitably, *Le Diable Boiteux* had suggested merely that Castil-Blaze was not as good as Ducis (26 July 1825).

84. Giuseppe Radiciotti, *Gioacchino Rossini: vita documentata opere ed influenza su l'arte* (Tivoli: Chicca, 1927), 1:376–77.

85. Herbert Weinstock (*Rossini: A Biography* [London, 1968], 96) translates Radiciotti's anecdote and repeats the latter's claim that he heard the story from Batton. Richard Osborne (*Rossini* [London: Macmillan, 1986], 223–24) summarizes Radiciotti without comment or acknowledgment. H. Colin Slim (ed., *La donna del lago, melodramma in due atti de Andrea Leone Tottola, musica di Gioachino Rossini*, Edizione critica delle opere di Gioachino Rossini, Sezione prima 20 [Pesaro: Fondazione Rossini, 1990], 1:xxi–iii) summarizes previous literature and adds important comments on the Ossianic influences on the libretto (taken from unpublished work by Stefano Castelvecchi, published separately [see below note 88]).

lished before 1821.[86] Missing from the story so far is the text that Batton passed to Rossini. A two-volume prose version of Scott's poem was published in Paris, and it seems possible that this was the text that Batton brought with him from Paris to Rome, and thence to Naples.[87] It is described on its title page as a novel, however, and its bulky prose character fits badly with the descriptions in Radiciotti's anecdote as an *opusculo* and *poema;* it may be that these discrepancies do not count for a great deal, given the doubtful nature of the detail of Radiciotti's anecdote. Whatever the relationship between *La dame du lac* (1813) and Tottola's *Donna del lago*,[88] none of the four arrangers made any use of the 1813 French novel for the version performed at the Odéon.

The French tradition at the Odéon during the years 1823–28 can be separated into three strands: the role that eighteenth-century opéra comique played in the theater's opera seasons, the attempt to gain permission to play new opéras comiques, and the almost omnipresent French literary background to the translations of foreign music drama mounted at the theater. The first and third of these strands constitute central aspects of the theater's artistic policy during the period under review. The second—the campaign to mount new opéras comiques at the theater—represents one of the theater's most salient financial and artistic failures during the 1820s.

The Odéon's recourse to a French model for a libretto to Italian or German music drama was the consequence of actions taken by the literary arranger of the work linked to what he thought the audience would endorse, and to three related texts: the Italian or German libretto, the French original, and his own "translation." The presentation of public domain opéras comiques from before 1820 similarly represented an engagement with texts that embodied tradition and continuity. By contrast, the campaign for permission to mount new opéra comique, is one that can be explained only by an examination of the interconnections between the theater's management, the maison du Roi, and the belief that Prix de Rome laureates should receive some sort of institutional support while giving some financial help to the Odéon.

---

86. Slim, *La donna del lago,* xxii n. 5, and the source cited there.

87. *La dame du lac* (Paris: Galignani, 1813).

88. This comparison is surprisingly not undertaken in Stefano Castelvecchi, "Walter Scott, Rossini e la *couleur ossianique:* il contesto culturale della donna del lago," *Bollettino del Centro Rossiniano di studi* 33 (1993): 59 n. 10; in addition, the text is described erroneously as "una traduzione francese di *The Lady of the Lake.*"

Chapter 8

Les heureux étrangers—
Italian Music Drama

Rossini

Gioachino Rossini's music featured at the Odéon either as part of a pasticcio or as a complete work in French translation, of which five were presented during the period 1824–28: *Le barbier de Séville* (*Il barbiere di Siviglia*), *La pie voleuse* (*La gazza ladra*), *Othello* (*Otello*), *La dame du lac* (*La donna del lago*), and *Tancrède* (*Tancredi*).[1] In addition, there were rumors that Rossini had written choruses for Alexandre Soumet's tragedy *Saül* (figure 26).[2] These translations of Rossini dramatize the difference between the contribution of Castil-Blaze and that of other arrangers, and they also point up the differences between works arranged and translated specifically for the Odéon and those prepared originally for other theaters.

Rossini's status in Paris in the summer of 1824 when the Odéon began mounting productions of music drama—*cet heureux étranger,* one reviewer would label him the following year—depends on the sources used. Modern accounts speak of his prudence in delaying the composition and presentation of new works well into 1825.[3] According to this view, the composer

---

1. *Il barbiere di Siviglia,* Rome, Teatro Argentina, 1816; *La gazza ladra,* Milan, Teatro alla Scala, 1817; *Otello,* Naples, Teatro del Fondo, 1816; *La donna del lago,* Naples, Teatro San Carlo, 1819; *Tancredi,* Venice, Teatro la Fenice, 1813 (see appendix 1).

2. "The Odéon is currently rehearsing M. Soumet's *Saül* with choruses whose music is by Rossini" (On répète en ce moment, à l'Odéon, le *Saül* de M. Soumet, avec des choeurs, dont la musique a été composée par Rossini [*Le Frondeur,* 14 March 1826]). There is no evidence to support this rumor, and it may be a confusion with Soumet's authorship of the libretto to *Le siège de Corinthe.*

3. Rossini's contract with the Département des beaux-arts de la maison du Roi, signed in February 1824, required him to produce a grand opéra and an opera buffa within the first year of his engagement (see Osborne, *Rossini,* 69).

Figure 26. Gioachino Rossini. Engraving
by Ambroise Tardieu after Léopold Beyer.

needed to develop his skills in French prosody, in compositional technique,
and in the training of new singers; the result is an absence of new compositions and sporadic premieres of old works in the original Italian. Such a
state of affairs meant that there was adequate opportunity for such a theater as the Odéon to mount productions of some of Rossini's best-known
works in French translation, and to benefit both financially and artistically
from them.

Of the five works by Rossini produced by the Odéon, three were translated and arranged by Castil-Blaze. The two other works were translated into
French by different teams, but the music was arranged in both cases by
Lemierre de Corvey. Significantly, all three Castil-Blaze arrangements had
been prepared for provincial theaters well before the Odéon was even considered as a home for music drama.[4] *Le barbier de Séville* and *Othello* had been
premiered in Lyon and *La pie voleuse* in Lille; the three works had appeared
at annual intervals between 1821 and 1823.[5] Public opinion confused much

4. See the specifically Lyonnais context for Castil-Blaze's *Barbier de Séville* in Mark Everist,
"Lindoro in Lyon: Rossini's *Le Barbier de Séville*," *Acta musicologica* 44 (1992): 73–85 (and 56–
61, a full account of the work's textual and publication history).

5. *Le barbier de Séville*, Lyon, 1821; *La pie voleuse*, Lille, 1822; *Othello*, Lyon 1823.

of this information and assumed—as the capital's press was only too fond of doing—that no new Parisian production could be a mere revival of a provincial performance. For example, the *Courrier des Théâtres* reported on 15 December 1824 that Castil-Blaze was working on an arrangement of *Otello* for the Odéon.[6] Although the Paris premiere of Castil-Blaze's arrangement was six months away (*Othello* was produced there for the first time on 25 July 1825), the arrangement was in fact eighteen months old and had already received a successful production in Lyon in the summer of 1823.

Le barbier de Séville

Le barbier de Séville clearly exemplifies Castil-Blaze's normal working methods; he adheres closely to Beaumarchais's plot and restructures Rossini's music accordingly. The changes resulting from eliding Rossini's musical compositions with Beaumarchais's comedy make the libretto substantially different from the one written by Sterbini for Rossini (table 8). A translation of Berta's aria "Il vecchiotto cerca moglie" is relegated to an optional appendix in the published edition. Berta has a singing role in Sterbini and Rossini's opera buffa but, with Ambrogio, replaces Beaumarchais's characters la Jeunesse and l'Éveillé. Presumably to give some semblance of congruity with Beaumarchais, Berta appears as Marceline in Castil-Blaze's translation; however, she retains her singing role in the act II finale (act I in Rossini). Marceline has to sing in the French version of the piece, so her apparent absence from Beaumarchais's original play is no reason to excise the aria. Yet if Castil-Blaze kept the aria at the end of act III, rather than the more impressive quintet, he would have had to link the end of the quintet to Marceline's aria, and his preference for reusing material rather than incorporating new matter is clear from other instances in his work on *Le barbier*.[7] Dramatic reasons may explain the excision of "Il vecchiotto cerca moglie," or it may reflect considerations of duration or technical competence on the part of the singer taking the role of Marceline at the Lyon premiere.[8]

6. Cet intrépide arrangeur [Castil-Blaze] s'exerce pour le moment sur l'*Otello* de M. Rossini qu'il destine au théâtre du faubourg St-Germain (*Le Courrier des Théâtres,* 15 December 1824).

7. Castil-Blaze himself remarked that he had arranged Beaumarchais's work rather than translating Sterbini's (*Molière musicien: notes sur les oeuvres de cet illustre maître et sur les drames de Corneille . . . Beaumarchais, etc, où se mêlent des considérations sur l'harmonie de la langue française* [Paris, 1852], 2:428).

8. Later, in a review of the Italian version of *Il barbiere di Siviglia,* Castil-Blaze made it plain that he thought that the melody of "Il vecchiotto cerca moglie" was Russian. He wrote, "Mme Rossi chante l'air russe, *Il vecchiotto cerca moglie,* que M. Rossini a transporté en Espagne, on ne sait trop pourquoi" (*Journal des Débats,* 6 August 1825). Toward the end of his life, Castil-Blaze

TABLE 8. Comparison of *Il barbiere di Siviglia* and *Le barbier de Séville*

Il barbiere di Siviglia (1816)	*Le barbier de Séville* (1824)
Overture	Overture
I.i Introduction	I.i Introduction
I.ii Cavatina, "Largo al factotum"	I.ii Aria, "Place au factotum"
I.iv Canzone, "Se il mio nome"	———
I.iv Duet, "All'idea di quel metallo"	I.viii Duet, "D'un métal si précieux"
I.v Cavatina, "Une voce poco fa"	II.i Aria, "Rien ne peut changer"
I.viii Aria, "La calunnia"	II.ii Duet, "Je suis donc"
I.ix Duet, "Dunque io son"	II.iv Aria, "C'est d'abord"
I.x Aria, "A un dottor della mia sorte"	II.vi Aria, "Pensez-vous qu'il soit"
I.xiii–xvi Finale I, "Ehi, di casa!"	II.viii–xii Finale, "Hola, quelqu'un!"
II.ii Duet, "Pace e gioia"	III.ii Duet, "Que le ciel"
II.iii Aria, "Contro un cor"	III.iv Aria, "Tout se tait"
	[O patria! Dolce e ingrata patria (*Tancredi*)]
II.iii Arietta, "Quando me sei vicina"	III.iv Arietta, "Près de ma Rosinette"
II.iv Quintet, "Don Basilio!"	III.ix Quintet, "Don Basile!"
II.vi Aria, "Il vecchiotto cerca moglie"	———
II.viii–ix Temporale	III–IV Entr'acte—Storm
II.ix Trio, "Ah, qual colpo!"	IV.vi Trio, "O surprise"
II.ix Recitativo strumentato, "Il conte!"	———
II.ix Aria, "Cessa di più resistere"	———
II.ix Finaletto II, "Di si felice"	IV.viii Final chorus, "Chantons cette journée"

SOURCES: Alberto Zedda, ed., *Gioacchino Rossini: Il barbiere di Siviglia* (Milan: Ricordi, 1969); Gioachino Rossini, *Le barbier de Séville* (Paris: Petit, n.d.).

In Rossini and Sterbini's account of the story, Basilio suggests besmirching Almaviva's name to Bartolo ("La calunnia") in I.viii before Figaro tells Rosina the name of her admirer ("Dunque io son") in I.ix. But in Beaumarchais, and hence in Castil-Blaze's translation, these two events take place in the opposite order: "Dunque io son"/"Je suis donc" in II.ii, and "La calunnia"/"C'est d'abord" in II.iv. Petrosellini had reduced Beaumarchais's four acts to two for Paisiello, and Sterbini followed this plan;[9] the original

took pride in having adhered so closely to Beaumarchais in some cases that vocabulary and rhyme words were borrowed; he cited the "calumny" aria (*Molière musicien*, 2:428).

9. Comparisons of Beaumarchais, Petrosellini/Paisiello, and Sterbini/Rossini have often been made. For a selection of opinions see Alfred Loewenberg, "Paisiello's and Rossini's 'Barbiere di Siviglia,'" *Music & Letters* 20 (1939): 157–67; Marvin Tartak, "The Two 'Barbieri,'" *Music & Letters* 50 (1969): 453–69; Ricky Ricardo Little, "A Comparative Study of *Le Barbier de*

structure is restored in Castil-Blaze's opéra comique, with the result that the storm in Rossini's act II reverts to its original function as an entr'acte.[10]

In all works at the Odéon, kinetic sections in *recitativo semplice* were reworked as spoken dialogue. Problems are created where a musical composition begins with an unaccompanied vocal line after an extended passage of spoken dialogue. In all three cases where this happens, the technique used by Rossini of concluding a passage in recitative with a perfect cadence in either the tonic or dominant of the following number is no longer available as a compositional resource. Rather than simply allowing the musical compositions to begin as Rossini wrote them, which would have created moments of danger for singers searching for their notes, Castil-Blaze provides either a unison or a tonic chord at the beginning as in example 10, the beginning of "A un dottor della mia sorte"/"Pensez-vous qu'il soit."

In the lesson scene (III.iv in Castil-Blaze's translation), the arietta sung by Bartolo is interspersed with recitative in which he explains that he has changed the name of the lady in the song from Giannina to Rosina (Franchette to Rosine in the French version). This portion of the text is marked "parlé" in the translation and separates the two stanzas of the arietta. This part of Bartolo's dialogue is borrowed from Sterbini, because simple borrowing from Beaumarchais at this point would be complicated by the presence of a song, and recourse to Sterbini appears as a suitable intermediary option between following Beaumarchais and writing original dialogue. A final complication of this order involves Figaro's very first appearance in the drama. While Almaviva contemplates Rosina's qualities after Fiorello and the musicians have disappeared, Figaro is heard singing; he interrupts and changes the direction of Almaviva's recitative. What he sings are the first two and half bars of the following cavatina/aria, "Largo al factotum"/"Place au factotum," and since the recitative and Figaro's interruption are cast in dialogue in the opéra comique, this overt correspondence that is dramatically so successful is apparently lost. And indeed in Beaumarchais, there is nothing but a brief pause in Almaviva's speech at this point; however, in his transmission of Beaumarchais, Castil-Blaze effectively incorporates part of Sterbini's action to give Figaro a chance to sing the line and prefigure his cavatina as is specified in Rossini's version (example 11).

Such returns to Sterbini are rare in *Le barbier de Séville*. The only other major borrowing is in I.iv where Rosine's letter to Almaviva is read out loud. In Beaumarchais, she asks him to "sing something or other, to the music of this tune, something that will inform her of his name, his status, and his

---

Séville: The Original Play, and the Two Operas, *Il barbiere di Siviglia* by Giovanni Paisiello and Gioachino Rossini" (Doctor of Musical Arts diss., Ohio State University, 1985).

10. Castil-Blaze discussed the same point himself in an article in the *Journal des Débats* (19 October 1824, 4).

Example 10. Context for duet "Non più, tacete" (*Il barbiere di Siviglia*) and aria "Pensez-vous qu'il soit" (*Le barbier de Séville*).

a. Rossini, *Il barbiere di Siviglia*

b. Castil-Blaze / Rossini, *Le barbier de Séville*

Rosine: Et qui ne rougirait pas, monsieur,
de voir tirer des conséquences
aussi malignes des choses *les plus*
innocemment faites?

Bartolo: Pen - sez- vous

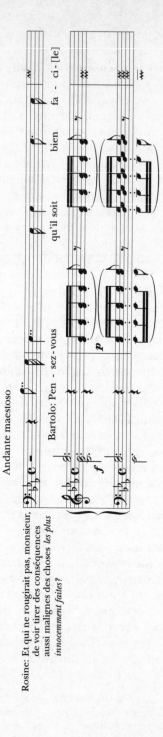

Example 11. Relation of cavatina "Largo al factotum" (*Il barbiere di Siviglia*) and aria "Place au factotum" (*Le barbier de Séville*) to preceding recitative and dialogue.

a. Rossini, *Il barbiere di Siviglia*

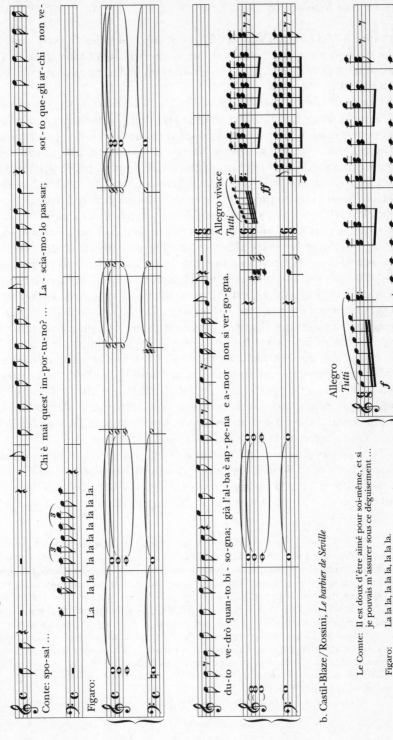

b. Castil-Blaze/Rossini, *Le barbier de Séville*

Le Comte: Il est doux d'être aimé pour soi-même, et si
je pouvais m'assurer sous ce déguisement …

Figaro: La la la, la la la, la la la.

Le Comte: *Au diable l'importun.*

intentions." In Sterbini and in the translation, she is less specific, and asks him to "find some ingenious method to inform [her] of his name, his status, and his intentions." This corresponds well with the omission of Almaviva's canzone "Se il mio nome."

One of the major tasks facing Castil-Blaze was reducing the combination of Rossini's music and Beaumarchais's play to proportions acceptable for an opéra comique. Beaumarchais himself recognized the need to prune inessential elements, for when his *Mariage de Figaro* was amalgamated with Mozart's *Nozze di Figaro* at the Académie royale de musique in 1793 in a version put together by Notaris, Beaumarchais was brought in after the second performance to revise the drama because the work suffered from being too long.[11] Nearly thirty years later, Castil-Blaze was placed in a similar position, although he was more aware of the problem than had been Notaris. In the initial exchanges between Almaviva and Figaro early in act I (scene ii in Beaumarchais, corresponding to scene iv in Castil-Blaze). Beaumarchais's fifty-two exchanges between the two characters are cut to sixteen; much of the dialogue omitted by Castil-Blaze consists of a systematic exposition of Figaro's movements since he and Almaviva last met, as well as some gratuitous jibes at Galicians, Catalans, and Auvergnats. The omissions result in a loss of some of Beaumarchais's humor, although the ultimate balance between the inclusion of Rossini's music and the loss of some of Beaumarchais's lines was—at least according to accounts of the work in the press—well struck. Some scenes in Beaumarchais disappear simply because they duplicate Rossini's larger-scale compositions: the scenes replaced by the introduction and the finale I, for example, or the scenes that featured Beaumarchais's characters la Jeunesse and l'Éveillé (II.vi–vii).

The 1821 translation of *Le barbier de Séville* involved the suppression of two compositions and the substitution of a third. The omission of "Se il mio nome," Almaviva's act I canzona, comes as less of a surprise in the light of its earlier history.[12] This number was probably cut soon after the first night in

11. Léon Guichard, "Beaumarchais et Mozart: note sur la première représentation à Paris des *Noces de Figaro*," *Revue d'histoire littéraire de la France* 55 (1955): 341–43; Jacques Roulleaux-Dugage, "Un livret d'opéra inédit de Beaumarchais," *Nouvelles littéraires*, 3 November 1966, 12; and Jacques Proust, "Beaumarchais et Mozart: une mise au point," *Studi francesi* 46 (January–April 1972): 34–45, have all addressed this subject. For Beaumarchais's exact relationship to this production, see Sherwood Dudley, "Les premières versions françaises du *Mariage de Figaro* de Mozart," *Revue de musicologie* 59 (1983): 57–58 and 62. Castil-Blaze was also scathing about earlier attempts to translate Italian music drama. He had unrestrained contempt for the 1784 translation of Paisiello's *Barbier de Séville*: "Comment Framery a-t-il osé les [= his own translations] substituer aux brillants récits de Beaumarchais, et les faire précéder et suivre par un dialogue scintillant d'esprit et de gaîté? (*De l'opéra en France*, 2d ed. [1820; Paris: Sautelot, 1826], 2:160).

12. Alberto Zedda, ed., *Gioacchino Rossini: Il barbiere di Siviglia* (Milan: Ricordi, 1969).

1816 and may not have been heard in Paris until 1831 (when Rubini sang it).[13] Castil-Blaze's source did not include this composition, so neither did performances in Lyon or at the Odéon. The *recitativo strumentato* "Il conte" with its following aria "Cessa di più resistere," omitted at the Odéon, was often cut from early Italian performances, and the aria had in fact been taken from Almaviva and given to Rosina in the September 1816 revival in Bologna.[14] Its textual instability and uncertain performance tradition may have had some role to play in its suppression. Given the number of substitutions for the aria in the lesson scene, the 1821 print, and presumably performances during the 1820s, quite understandably did not include Rossini's original "Contro un cor." If Stendhal is to be believed, and the aria "Di tanti palpiti" from *Tancredi* had been used by Joséphine Fodor-Mainvielle in Paris at the Théâtre italien,[15] its appearance in Castil-Blaze's version of the work is hardly unexpected. Both the recitative and aria are changed in many respects, and the French text is taken from an aria in Méhul's *Bion* of 1800.

Minor variations in ornamentation and scoring characterize large parts of Castil-Blaze's arrangement. In one instance, the published edition of the duet "Je suis donc"/"Dunque io son" includes ornamentation of the vocal lines for both Rosine and Figaro that should be added to the growing body of evidence for early-nineteenth-century ornamentation of operatic vocal lines (example 12).[16]

---

13. Philip Edward Gossett, "The Operas of Rossini: Problems of Textual Criticism in Nineteenth-Century Opera" (Ph.D. diss., Princeton University, 1970), 286.

14. Ibid., 293–94.

15. Dans un théâtre bien réglé, Rosine changerait l'air de sa leçon à toutes les deux ou trois représentations. A Paris, madame Fodor, qui du reste chantait ce rôle à ravir, et comme probablement il ne l'a jamais été, nous donnait toujours l'air de *Tancrède:* "Di tanti palpiti," arrangé en contredanse, ce qui ravissait les têtes à perruque; on voyait à cet air toutes les têtes poudrées de la salle s'agiter en cadence (Victor del Litto et Ernest Abravanel, eds., *Stendhal: vie de Rossini suivie des Notes d'un dilettante,* vol. 22 of *Stendhal: oeuvres complètes* [Geneva: Edito-Service, 1968], 257).

16. E.g., Austin Caswell, "Mme Cinti-Damoureau and the Embellishment of Italian Opera in Paris: 1820–1845," *Journal of the American Musicological Society* 28 (1975): 459–92; and idem, "Vocal Embellishment in Rossini's Paris Operas: French Style or Italian?" *Bollettino del Centro Rossiniano di studi,* n.s. 1–2 [bound as one] (1975): 5–21. In his edition, Caswell (*Embellished Opera Arias* [Madison, Wis.: A-R Editions, 1989], 91–101) gives embellishments of the same duet from Manuel Garcia, *École de Garcia: traité complet de l'art de chant* (Mainz: Schott, 1847), 2:57; from its English edition, *Hints on Singing,* trans. Beata Garcia (London: Ascherberg, 1894), 65 (three versions from each); and from Barbara Marchisio, "Cadenze e variante composte e eseguite dalle sorelle Marchisio" (New York, Pierpont Morgan Library, Cary Collection 142, two versions dated 1900). The version in Castil-Blaze's edition is substantially more elaborate than those of Garcia and Marchisio, as example 12 shows. It also has a change in tessitura: Rossini's mezzo soprano original requires a range of b to a'' whereas Castil-Blaze's version entails d' to b''.

Example 12. Ornamentation in duets "Je suis donc" (*Le barbier de Séville*) and "Dunque io son" (*Il barbiere di Siviglia*).

In matters of dynamics, articulation, tempo indications, trills, solo-tutti designations, the edition is no more or less reliable than any other nineteenth-century edition that was not authorized by the composer or overseen, in whole or in part, by him.[17]

Castil-Blaze's reworking of *Le barbier de Séville* was not the first time that Rossini and Sterbini's version had been translated into French. For the performances at the Théâtre italien throughout the 1820s, libretti were published that translated both the recitative and Rossini's musical compositions and placed French and Italian side by side. Whatever the accuracy of these translations, their purpose was to provide a succinct and comprehensible translation, not to offer something that was singable. In this respect, they differed widely from Castil-Blaze's translations of Rossini's compositions, and indeed it is quite clear that, although he must have been familiar with these libretti,[18] he made no use of them whatsoever.

The version of *Le barbier de Séville* that Castil-Blaze made for Lyon remained more or less intact during its run at the Odéon. Apart from near-catastrophes, such as the night that Camoin was unable to sing at all, so that all his music was excised, the only change concerned the lesson scene.[19] The version of *Il barbiere di Siviglia* that reached Paris via Lyon included "Di tanti

17. Zedda's view of Castil-Blaze's work in general is relevant here: "Castil-Blaze ha dedicato un lavoro di musicista appassionato, ricco di gusto e di buon senso pratico, anche se non proprio irreprensibile dal punto di vista del rispetto filologico dovuto ai testi" (*Rossini*, 29; cf. similar sentiments on 15). One problem in Castil-Blaze's translation of Rossini concerns the entr'acte between acts I and II. Gossett ("Operas of Rossini," 303) writes, "Act 2 begins with an entr'acte based on the thematic material of the second finale, no. 19. This was first added by Castil-Blaze for his provincial performances of *Il barbiere di Siviglia* throughout France in 1819. From here it passed into most French and German printed editions. It occurs in no Italian editions at all, however, and is surely not authentic." The vocal score (*Le barbier de Séville* [Paris: Petit, n.d.])—apparently prepared after Petit took over Laffillé's business on 15 September 1825—has the 54-bar entr'acte, between pp. 197–98. The origins of the entr'acte probably lie in the early German vocal scores of the work, all of which (listed in Gossett, "Operas of Rossini," 273) have the interpolation and two, perhaps three, of which (see James J. Fuld, *The Book of World-Famous Music: Classical, Popular and Folk*, 3d ed. [New York: Dover, 1985], 124) predate the mid-1821 publication of Castil-Blaze/Laffillé's full score. The presence of a manuscript addition of part of the entr'acte in a copy of the published full score (F-Po A.796a[2]) reinforces the idea that these German vocal scores are the source for Castil-Blaze's arrangement of the entr'acte.

18. By 1825, he was granted an *entrée de faveur* at the Théâtre italien (Janet Johnson, "The Théâtre Italien and Opera and Theatrical Life in Restoration Paris" [Ph.D. diss., University of Chicago, 1988], 3:459). Whether the anecdote offered by Alexis Azevedo (*G. Rossini: sa vie et ses oeuvres*, Notice publié par *Le Ménestrel* [Paris: Heugel, 1864], 209) that Castil-Blaze had contracted with Gambaro to collaborate on a translation in 1819, and that Gambaro had backed out, is true is an open question (but Azevedo's claim that Castil-Blaze followed activities at that theater assiduously is very plausible).

19. Bartholo's act 2 aria was simply cut and the sextet performed as a quintet (*Le Courrier des Théâtres*, 25 June 1824).

palpiti"; it was a popular favorite, and Stéphanie Montano's attempt to substitute a French *romance* met with little support.[20] When the arrangement of *Le barbier de Séville* was mounted at the Odéon on 6 May 1824, the work was not only immediately successful but remained so until 1828. Opinions were divided about Castil-Blaze's arrangement: *Le Diable Boiteux* felt that the success of the work was the result of Castil-Blaze's sensitive handling, whereas *La Pandore* thought that the work had been successful because of Rossini's music but in spite of Castil-Blaze's poetry.[21] Other authors made more specifically technical observations. In the Rossini/Sterbini original, repeating musical phrases corresponded to repeating lines of poetry, but *Le Courrier des Théâtres* noticed that Castil-Blaze's translation provided new text for these lines.[22] Impressive as this may sound, from the mouth of a critic at a performance, it must be remembered that the score had been available since 1821, and the tone of these comments has the air of study rather than instinctive response.

During the four years that the Odéon competed on the Parisian operatic stage, *Le barbier de Séville* was one of its mainstays. During its career it would have to negotiate both the work in the original language at the Théâtre italien and the original Beaumarchais play at the Comédie-Française. Its appearance in the early summer of 1824 at the Odéon was however propitious. The work had not been given at the Théâtre italien for six months—not, in fact since Manuel Garcia had left the capital. For a favorite work to be missing from the Théâtre italien's repertory and then mounted albeit in a French translation at the Odéon lured many audiences who would not have otherwise made the journey to the theater.

La dame du lac

It might be expected that Rossini would have a view on performances of his works in translation, especially since they often differed from those whose performance and text he could control at the Théâtre italien. However, the history of his involvement with the Odéon is contradictory and inconsistent. He seems to have collaborated enthusiastically with the theater on the project to mount *Ivanhoé* but was apparently unconcerned about the success

20. "*Le barbier de Séville* was given on Sunday at the Odéon. Mme Montano substituted a French *romance* for the aria 'Di tanti palpiti.' This innovation did not meet with approval. Someone shouted 'the Italian aria!' . . . The poor French!" (On donnait, dimanche [5 July], à l'Odéon le *Barbier de Séville*. Mme Montano a substitué à l'air de *Tancredi* "O patria!" [Di tanti palpiti], une romance française. Cette innovation n'a pas été goûtée. On a crié: "L'air italien!" . . . Pauvres Français! [*Le Diable Boiteux*, 6 July 1824]).

21. *Le Diable Boiteux*, 7 May 1824; *La Pandore*, 7 May 1824.

22. *Le Courrier des Théâtres*, 8 May 1824.

of *Le barbier de Séville, La pie voleuse, Othello,* and *Tancrède,* all old works.[23] Yet in the case of the arrangement of *La donna del lago* as *La dame du lac,* the Odéon, its direction, and its collaborators found themselves in as much direct competition with Rossini and the Théâtre italien as they had been with the Opéra-Comique in early 1824, and on other occasions.[24]

Jean-Fréderic-Auguste Lemierre de Corvey was the musical arranger of *La dame du lac* as well as *Le testament* and *Tancrède.* Jean-Baptiste Rose Bonaventure Violet d'Épagny and Auguste Rousseau were the arrangers of the libretto; for both authors, this was the only occasion that they worked for the Odéon. In many respects, the team put together a reworking of *La donna del lago* that was much in line with other productions at the Odéon: all *recitativo semplice* was either omitted or recast as spoken dialogue in French. Act I of *La dame du lac* consists of the introduzione to act I of *La donna del lago.* Malcolm's cavatina and Duglas's aria are moved from act I and are found at the beginning of act III of *La dame du lac,* the chorus and cavatina for Rodrigo are abbreviated and followed by the duet from *Semiramide* for Arsace and the eponym "Ebben! A te feresci"; act II of *La dame du lac* closes with Rossini's original act I finale much truncated. After the resequenced material from act I, act III concludes with the trio that opened act II of *La donna del lago.* Elena's rondo that closed act II of *La donna del lago* is replaced by a chorus that duplicates material from the original act I finale.

The libretto of *La dame du lac* had been authorized on 27 May 1825, and the work was premiered on 31 October. In many ways, its reception was predictable: Rossiniphiles enjoyed the work but Rossiniphobes disliked it; devotees of Castil-Blaze claimed that d'Épagny, Rousseau, and Lemierre de Corvey's arrangement was not as good as Castil-Blaze's version of *La gazza ladra,* whereas Castil-Blaze's critics were quick to show how others were better at arranging Italian music drama for the French stage. Most of the staff and audience at the Odéon would have thought that this was business as usual.[25]

Word soon reached Rossini and the administration of the Théâtre italien that what they thought was simply an arrangement of *La donna del lago* included a translation of a duet from *Semiramide.* This work did not fall into

23. Rossini apparently attended a performance of *La pie voleuse* shortly after its premiere (press accounts conflict: *Le Courrier des Théâtres,* 4 August 1824, reports his presence; the *Journal de Paris,* 6 August 1824, denies it). Positive reviews are summarized in *Le Courrier des Théâtres,* 18 August 1824; the work was revived on 7 June 1825.

24. This was not the first time that a translation into French of *La donna del lago* had been proposed. A version for the Opéra-Comique, translated by Dupaty with a musical arrangement by Félix Bodin, had been prepared but rejected in early 1824.

25. Reviews of the premiere of *La dame du lac* are in *La Lorgnette* (1 November 1825), *La Pandore, Journal des Débats,* and *Journal de Paris* (2 November 1825); and *Le Frondeur* (4 November 1825).

the same category as the others that had either been translated or used as the basis for a pasticcio at the Odéon. Premiered only in 1823 at La Fenice, *Semiramide* had yet to appear on any Parisian stage, and the Théâtre italien was anxious to preserve its novelty. Accordingly, the day after the premiere of *La dame du lac,* La Rochefoucauld wrote to Bernard asking him to excise the number. Unfortunately, in the rush to police the theater, La Rochefoucauld identified not a duet but a chorus; that, and the late arrival of the letter gave Bernard a chance to prevaricate. In a letter dated 2 November 1825 at 8:00 P.M., he was able to write that "having checked the score of *La dame du lac,* I am convinced that there is no *chorus* from *Sémiramis.* Monsieur Rossini himself will be able to verify this. I find it impossible, then, to make the cuts that you require of me."[26] Bernard then continued to make the point that, in any case, his license allowed him to play translated foreign works and concluded by reminding La Rochefoucauld—at length—of how successful Bernard had been in turning around the theater, and how unwise La Rochefoucauld would be to risk damaging its current success.

La Rochefoucauld's reply was angry and frustrated. In the draft of his letter, his opening line—"Your license is as well known to me as it is to you"[27]—was crossed out and replaced with something more diplomatic; he also simply referred to "un morceau" from *Semiramide* so that Bernard could not avoid the direct request to cut the number that La Rochefoucauld now repeated. Five days later, Bernard received a letter from d'Épagny, which he forwarded to La Rochefoucauld. At a stage where Rossini had yet to write any sort of music drama in French, d'Épagny was already displeased with Rossini's behavior: "Monsieur Rossini, who scorns all our librettists and has not the slightest wish to give them any new music, at least should not complain when new words are written in order to assimilate his music already known here. But let us leave aside the peculiar caprice of the Swan of Pesaro who excepts only the Odéon from singing his music sold by him all over Europe."[28] D'Épagny missed the point and was in error, however, when he went on to write that the duet in question had been on sale for ten years. Much more important for Bernard and the Odéon was the fact that d'Épagny claimed that he could not simply excise the duet and therefore

26. Après avoir compulsé la partition de *la Dame du lac,* je me suis convaincu qu'il n'y éxiste aucun *choeur* de la *Sémiramis.* M. Rossini lui même peut vous l'attester. Je me trouve donc dans l'impossibilité de faire la coupure que vous exigez (F-Pan O³ 1792/VI).

27. Votre privilège m'est aussi connu qu'à vous même (ibid.).

28. Monsieur Rossini, qui dédaigne tous nos poètes, et ne veut point leur donner de musique nouvelle devrait au moins ne pas se plaindre lors qu'on fait des paroles *nouvelles* qui servent à nationaliser chez nous sa musique déjà connue. Mais laissons de côté notre droit et le singulier caprice du Cygne de Pezzaro qui n'excepte que l'Odéon pour la faculté de chanter sa musique vendue par lui-même à toute l'Europe (ibid.).

requested the withdrawal of the work. A marginal note at the bottom of the letter seemed definitive: "return to my servant the manuscript of the opera *La dame du lac* for the printer; I want it to be seen that the work is not copied or translated from the Italian."[29] Bernard's covering letter to La Rochefoucauld used d'Épagny's request to withdraw the work in trying to force La Rochefoucauld's hand. The latter proposed that either the duet be cut or that the performances of *La dame du lac* be suspended until after the Paris premiere of *Semiramide,* which took place on 8 December 1825.

The maison du Roi's decision outraged the press. Part of a report in *La Lorgnette* reads as follows: "Vainly has M. Rossini, this happy foreigner (*cet heureux étranger*) paid handsomely to compose music in France as if we had no more composers, become angry at the scandalous mixture of two of his works; vainly, in the access of an entirely Italian fugue, has he obtained from the little heir with a great name the excision of numbers extracted from the score of *Semiramide.*"[30] In the wake of the conspiracy—as *La Lorgnette* saw it—between the foreign Rossini and the unworthy La Rochefoucauld, *Semiramide* was premiered at the Théâtre italien. The offending duet was printed in the score of *La dame du lac* and the corresponding text appeared in the printed libretto; the premiere took place at the Odéon on 31 October (as noted earlier, a particularly poor day in the theatrical year), and the production ran throughout November. It ran for fifteen performances in December 1825, effectively every other night in alternation with *Robin des bois.* Nothing in this reflects the compromise proposed by La Rochefoucauld. The gap in performances in November might have been because Lecomte was ill,[31] but it may also have been because the Odéon had agreed to La Rochefoucauld's original request and—in the teeth of d'Épagny's opposition—cut the duet and suspended performances until after the 8 December premiere of *Semiramide.*

Despite the difficulties with Rossini and the maison du Roi, *La dame du lac* was well received. The performance was judged very favorably, and journalists noted the work's success despite the fact that it was well known.[32] What adverse criticism that appeared was of a ritual nature: the French libretto was greatly distanced from the Italian original, and—according to

29. Faites remettre à mon domestique le manuscrit de l'opéra de *la Dame du lac,* pour l'imprimeur, je veux que l'on voie que la pièce n'est pas copiée ni traduite de l'italien (ibid.).

30. Vainement M. Rossini, cet heureux étranger payé grassement pour faire de la musique en France comme si nous n'avions plus de compositeurs, a-t-il jeté feu et flamme contre le mélange scandaleux de deux de ses partitions; vainement dans l'accès d'une fugue toute italienne a-t-il obtenu du petit héritier d'un grand nom le retranchement des morceaux extraits de la partition de *Sémiramis* (*La Lorgnette,* 9 November 1825).

31. *La Pandore,* 22 November 1825.

32. *La Lorgnette,* 1 November 1825; *Journal de Paris,* 2 November 1825.

Castil-Blaze writing in the *Journal des Débats*—the arrangers were not as good as Castil-Blaze (not an uncommon complaint from this particular quarter).[33] The lavishness of the sets and costumes drew approving comments.[34]

Meyerbeer

In June 1825 Giacomo Meyerbeer was in Padua and sent a copy of the libretto of *Margherita d'Anjou* to his brother, Michael Beer, then in Paris, giving instructions that it was to be passed to the publisher Laffillé.[35] Although Laffillé had published the first group of Castil-Blaze's translations of Italian music drama early in the decade and was publishing other Odéon arrangements in 1825, he had little or no experience of carrying out arrangements himself.[36] He had difficulty in projecting himself as a particularly sympathetic character. Meyerbeer had written, "I have had it up to here with that bourgeois tyrant,"[37] and by September, Laffillé had become a serious impediment to the preparation of what was to become Meyerbeer's first music drama in French: the arrangement of *Marguerite d'Anjou*. On 29 July 1825, Pierre Crémont outlined the Odéon plans for the late summer and autumn to Sauvage; he suggested that the arrangement of *Marguerite d'Anjou* should appear at the end of October.[38] By the middle of August, Crémont had however received nothing of the translation from Sauvage and asked the latter to bring to Paris a copy of the Pixérécourt mélodrame so that he could familiarize himself with it before he set to work on the music. The tone of his letter, sent to Sauvage's Paris home with instructions to forward it as soon as possible to his country address, gives some idea of the working relationship between the two men: "When you come [to Paris], bring me, I beg you, Pixérécourt's mélodrame, *Marguerite d'Anjou*. I need to know the play a little before I set to work. But hurry, for the love of God! Hurry! You'll kill me within a year if I have to work like this again."[39] By the time Crémont

33. *Le Frondeur*, 1 November 1825; *Journal des Débats*, 2 November 1825.

34. *La Pandore*, 2 November 1825.

35. Heinz Becker and Gudrun Becker, *Giacomo Meyerbeer: Briefwechsel und Tagebücher* (Berlin: De Gruyter, 1960–), 2:20 (letter of 6 June 1825).

36. Laffillé's publications of Odéon works included the Mercadante pasticcio, *Les noces de Gamache,* and the translation of Rossini's *Donna del lago* as *La dame du lac*. Both works were premiered, and probably published, in 1825.

37. "Über den Tyran bourgeois bin ich außer mir" (Becker and Becker, *Briefwechsel und Tagebücher,* 2:20).

38. F-Pn L.a. XXIII, fols. 312^{r-v}.

39. Quand vous viendrez, apportez-moi, je vous prie, le mélodrame (tel que l'a fait Pixérécourt) de *Marguerite d'Anjou*. Il faut que je connaisse la pièce à peu près avant d'y mettre la main. Mais dépêchez-vous pour l'amour de dieu! Dépêchez-vous! Vous me feriez mourir avant

had begun work on the music of *Marguerite d'Anjou,* he had succeeded in squeezing Laffillé out of the affair, and by 13 September, he could chastise Sauvage with the fact that he was three pieces ahead of him;[40] by 30 September, he had reached the act II finale and stopped dead. Laffillé had appeared at his door, furious that he had apparently been excluded from the work on *Marguerite* without agreement.[41] The matter was resolved only by a meeting between Crémont, Sauvage, Bernard, Meyerbeer, and Pixérécourt; they offered Laffillé the publication rights to the work.[42] Crémont was having problems with the act II finale on 11 October, and as late as 30 November was still claiming that he could not see the end of his work.[43] The libretto was passed by the censor on 23 February 1826, and the work was put into rehearsal by 2 March and premiered on 11 March.[44] Meyerbeer evidently participated in the early stages of this project and was active in the preparations. As long as his model was sufficiently comprehensible, Crémont was capable of producing an arrangement without assistance, and he had the musical and dramatic imagination to edit intelligently. Yet, he insisted, the arrangement should carry the authority of the composer himself—even if the result was a slowing down in the pace of work—and Crémont's own suggestions should guide Meyerbeer in detail.[45]

The playwright and manager, Pixérécourt, was not directly associated with the administration of the Odéon, but he was of importance for Meyerbeer's work there. He was the author of the *mélodrame historique* that had received its premiere at the Théâtre de la Gaîté on 11 January 1810 and that had served as the model for Felice Romani's libretto of Meyerbeer's *Margherita d'Anjou* (premiered at La Scala on 14 November 1820).[46] This

un an s'il me fallait travailler encore de cette manière (letter dated 19 August 1825 [F-Pn L.a. XXIII, fol. 314^{v}]).

40. Ibid., fols. 315$^{\text{r–v}}$.

41. Ibid., fols. 328$^{\text{r–v}}$.

42. Ibid., fols. 334$^{\text{r–v}}$ (undated letter from Crémont to Pixérécourt, written after 30 September but before 15 November 1825).

43. Ibid., fols. 316$^{\text{r–v}}$; ibid., fols. 317$^{\text{r–v}}$.

44. F-Pan F^{18} 613/158. Weber was reported as having made generous observations on *Marguerite d'Anjou* as he passed through Paris in early March 1826 (*Le Courrier des Théâtres,* 2 March 1826, 4).

45. See the detailed letter preserved in F-Pn L.a. XXIII, fols. 315$^{\text{r–v}}$.

46. *Marguerite d'Anjou, mélodrame historique* (Paris: Barba, 1810). Romani's libretto is *Margherita d'Anjou: melodramma semiserio* (Milan: Pirola, [1820]). Sources for Meyerbeer's music are severely problematic. The autograph is lost. Manuscript copies of uncertain authority are listed in the entry "Margherita d'Anjou," in *Pipers Enzyklopädie des Musiktheaters: Oper, Operette, Musical, Ballet,* ed. Carl Dahlhaus and Sieghart Döhring (Munich: Piper, 1986–97), 4: 117. A contemporary piano-vocal score was published by Schlesinger: *Margherita d'Anjou: opera semiseria* (Paris, n.d.). Romani's libretto may have been based on a translation of Pixérécourt by Francesco Gandini (*Opere teatrali: traduzione* [Milan: Destefanis, 1813], 1:187–285). Ac-

background in earlier French mélodrame was significant for the Paris version, since in the period in which it was reworked—June 1825–March 1826—Pixérécourt was manager of the Opéra-Comique and one of the most powerful figures in the Parisian lyric theater. Furthermore, he was still there when Eugène Scribe and Meyerbeer planned the original version of *Robert le diable,* and the relationship that developed between Meyerbeer and Pixérécourt during work on *Marguerite d'Anjou* influenced the work on *Robert le diable.*[47]

At the end of September 1825 Meyerbeer attempted to show Pixérécourt the translation of *Marguerite d'Anjou.*[48] On 11 October, Crémont was still missing translations of Lavarenne's aria and that of one of the duets, so Meyerbeer could not have been in a position to show Pixérécourt all the lyric items.[49] The spoken dialogue (a part of the work in which Pixérécourt would be especially interested) was therefore probably mostly complete at the end of September. Pixérécourt was not only consulted about the translation of Romani's libretto but was partially responsible for removing the difficulties with Laffillé in September 1825. Furthermore, Crémont had needed Pixérécourt's permission in order to undertake the arrangement.[50] This seems to point to the anomalous position of the arrangement of *Marguerite d'Anjou* with regard to Romani's libretto and Pixérécourt's 1810 mélodrame. Normally, since copyright law carried no weight over national boundaries, an Italian librettist could rework a French pre-Restoration mélodrame with impunity, even if the original author was still alive and entitled to royalties in his own country. Yet it is unclear whether Pixérécourt had any legal rights to the mélodrame when the Italian work on which it was based found its way back to Paris. If he had, some kind of agreement was indeed necessary. Even if he had not, it is highly unlikely that Crémont and

cording to Döhring ("Margherita d'Anjou," *Pipers Enzyklopädie* 4:117; and private communication 11 March 1993), the translation was performed in Milan in September 1812.

47. Pixérécourt's tenure as manager of the Opéra-Comique ran from April 1824 to August 1827 (Nicole Wild, *Dictionnaire des théâtres parisiens au XIXe siècle: les théâtres et la musique* [Paris: Amateurs des Livres, 1989], 329). From 5 July 1825 until 1 April 1835, he was also the *directeur privilégié* of the Théâtre de la Gaîté (ibid., 168). The bibliography on Pixérécourt is extensive. See Karin Pendle, "Pixérécourt, René Charles Guilbert de," *The New Grove Dictionary of Opera,* ed. Stanley Sadie (London: Macmillan, 1992), 3:1024–25.

48. Becker and Becker, *Briefwechsel und Tagebücher,* 2:578 (letter of 27 September 1825). The Beckers' source for this letter is René Charles Guilbert de Pixérécourt, *Théâtre choisi* (Paris, 1841–43), 2:581.

49. The postscript to the letter of 11 October 1825 makes this clear: "I'm addressing this note to you in the hope that you are not dead, although I've had no word of you for at least a week. *And the duet? And the duke's aria? And? And? And?*" (Je vous adresse ce billet espérant que vous n'êtes pas mort quoi'que je n'aye point entendu parler de vous depuis huit jours au moins. *Et le duo? Et l'air du duc?* Et? Et? Et? [F-Pn L.a. XXIII, fol. 316ᵛ]).

50. Ibid., fol.328ᵛ (letter of 30 September 1825).

Sauvage would want to antagonize him. He was the manager of a theater with which, to a certain extent, they were in competition, and with which they had to maintain reasonable relations.

Pixérécourt's mélodrame is in three acts whereas the Romani libretto is in two. The 1826 Paris version reverts to the three acts of its earlier French model. The mélodrame *Marguerite d'Anjou* is substantially longer than the Italian version and remedies this shortage of music by grafting additional parts of the story onto music from another Italian work by Meyerbeer: *Emma di Resburgo,* first performed at Venice's San Benedetto theater in June 1819.[51] Put simply, most of act I of *Marguerite* comes from Meyerbeer's original except the finale, which is taken from the act I finale to *Emma.* The first part of act II is from act II of *Emma,* and the finale is the act I finale from *Margherita.* Act III of *Marguerite* is taken from act II of the Italian original. The overture comes from *Emma di Resburgo.* This procedure must have been authorized by Meyerbeer. Indeed, since *Emma di Resburgo* was unknown to Parisian audiences, and perhaps to Crémont and Sauvage, Meyerbeer may have suggested such a course of action himself.

Such a ground plan required a number of strategies from the musical and literary arrangers of the work. Sauvage had to translate Romani's libretto, and Crémont had to adjust the music to fit. Numbers from *Margherita d'Anjou* remain mostly in their original context, paralleling the practices evolved by Castil-Blaze earlier in the decade and those employed by other arrangers for the Odéon. However, corresponding parts of the libretto were of little value as the basis for a translation of music from *Emma,* and Sauvage had to replace them with paraphrases based on the Pixérécourt mélodrame. All of Romani's recitative text had to be replaced with spoken dialogue, as was the convention at the Odéon. Replacing it verbatim with the dialogue from Pixérécourt's mélodrame was impractical because some of the turns in the action of the Paris 1826 *Marguerite* were already determined, especially those in some of the larger sections, by those that had been borrowed from the Italian version.[52] Nevertheless, wherever dramatically feasible—for example where Romani had cut scenes from Pixérécourt—

51. As the work's published piano-vocal score explained, "In arranging M. Meyerbeer's Italian *Marguerite d'Anjou* for the French stage, for the sake of dramatic consistency the poem's authors have had to extend certain parts of their work beyond what is present in the *Italian libretto.* Several pieces of music then became necessary: they were taken from another score by M. Meyerbeer (*Em[m]a di Resburgo*)" (En arrangeant pour la scène française la *Marguerite d'Anjou* italienne de M. Meyerbeer, les auteurs du poème ont dû pour la regularité du drame donner à certaines parties de leur travail plus de développements que dans le *libretto italien.* Plusieurs morceaux de musique devenaient alors nécessaires: on les a puisés dans une autre partition de M. Meyerbeer [*Em(m)a di Resburgo*] [F-Pc Rés. 1187]).

52. Most obviously in the act I introduction, and the finales to acts II and III.

Sauvage was able to reinstate the dialogue from the mélodrame word for word.[53]

Crémont's concerns about the length of the act II finale were based on the fact that it was originally the first of only two finales in the original Italian work. He was anxious to reduce the length of the finale by at least half without cutting the trio that began it. He suggested doing so by reducing levels of repetition and development. The cuts are identified in the published Parisian full score, and Meyerbeer, prompted by Crémont, presumably executed or authorized the changes in late October or early November 1825.[54] Comparison with finales in such works as Auber's *Maçon,* premiered on 3 May 1825, and Boieldieu's *Dame blanche,* a work that received its premiere while revision of *Marguerite d'Anjou* was taking place, shows that extended act II finales were not uncommon in opéra comique. Changes in action, mood, key, and tempo are in general just as frequent as in the original act I finale to *Margherita d'Anjou.* The one exception is that extended ensemble numbers in a slow tempo—as in the case of the A-flat andante sostenuto from *Margherita d'Anjou*—are almost entirely unknown. Although removal of this section from the Odéon version did not form part of Crémont's original idea, its excision brings the finale more into line with Parisian practices. In general however Crémont's plans were thwarted either because of his own second thoughts or because the negotiations with Meyerbeer entailed compromise. Certainly, the reductions of length fall far short of Crémont's hope to reduce the finale by half. Indeed, the enthusiastic critical response to the work pointed to some overlengthy passages, both in the music and the dialogue. Some critics went as far as to identify which scenes should go, but their complaints were directed at act I, and not the act II finale.[55]

Marguerite d'Anjou was a success for the Odéon and an important boost to Meyerbeer's reputation. For the Odéon, the work not only meant good box-office receipts and critical approbation, it lured audiences from the other side of the Seine—from the Académie royale de musique and the Théâtre italien. It had not been able to do that since the heady days of late 1824 and early 1825 when *Robin des bois* was the talk of Paris.[56] For Meyerbeer, it meant exposure in a city that had heard six performances of *Il cro-*

---

53. Examples are I.xi in both the Pixérécourt mélodrame and *Marguerite d'Anjou,* before the duet for Isaure and Lavarenne, and the exchange between Barville and Lavarenne in I.xii of *Marguerite,* that corresponds to I.xiv in Pixérécourt.

54. *Marguerite d'Anjou: drame lyrique* (Paris: Kretschmer, n.d).

55. *Journal de Paris,* 12 March 1826, 3–4; 16 March 1826, 3.

56. See page 129 and note 89.

ciato six months previously and was clamoring for more. *Marguerite* was performed regularly for a year at the Odéon, and kept Meyerbeer's name in audiences' minds, especially when a revival of *Il crociato* planned for October 1826 had to be aborted at the last minute. In November, Sauvage wrote to Meyerbeer suggesting that he rewrite the title role of *Marguerite d'Anjou* as a mezzo role for Schütz.[57] It is unclear how much work Meyerbeer did in response to this suggestion. Frédéric du Petit-Méré, who had taken on the Odéon in February 1826, was anxious to mount the work with Schütz early in 1827. Meyerbeer held three meetings with Sauvage during January that year.[58] Crémont and Sauvage began to put pressure on Meyerbeer at the end of January and beginning of February 1827.[59] Meyerbeer had wanted to include an extra aria and duet in the production, and Crémont was specific about the parts of the role of Marguerite that needed rewriting: the introduction and the act II finale. Meyerbeer's diary records work on *Marguerite d'Anjou* in February and March 1827.[60] These may have been for performances in April 1827 but may also have been associated with the work's publication by Kretschmer in early 1827. Schütz, however, never played the title role of *Marguerite d'Anjou* at the Odéon.

Mozart

Two complete works by Wolfgang Amadeus Mozart were presented to the audience of the Odéon during the 1820s, *Le nozze di Figaro* and *Don Giovanni*. The arrangement of *Les noces de Figaro* had been given for the first time in Nîmes in 1819 and *Don Juan* in Lyon in 1822. Neither work seems to have been a priority at the Odéon; *Don Juan*, for example, was not given at the theater until 24 December 1827, only a few months before the opera troupe disbanded. The reasons lie only partly with the ambivalent position that Mozart occupied in Restoration Paris; the two works were both staples of the Théâtre italien, and the Odéon seemed unwilling to engage in competition as it did for the works of Rossini.

Mozart had a significant place in the musical and theatrical culture of imperial Paris, as Rossini did during the Restoration. The difference between

---

57. Becker and Becker, *Briefwechsel und Tagebücher,* 2:48.
58. 3, 5, and 10 January (ibid., 2:53).
59. Crémont wrote to Sauvage at Petit-Méré's behest just before 1 February 1827, asking him to approach Meyerbeer (D-Bds N. Mus. Nachl. 97 E/51 [a]; partially summarized in Becker and Becker, *Briefwechsel und Tagebücher,* 2:584); Sauvage transmitted the request to Meyerbeer on 1 February (2:57).
60. 23 February 1827: "Coda zum Terzett von Margherete" (Becker and Becker, *Briefwechsel und Tagebücher,* 2:58); 3 March 1827: "2 Stücke von Margherete" (2:59).

the two was that Mozart's music dramas had been adopted more than a decade after the composer's death whereas Rossini was still alive during the Restoration, present in the capital, and able to whip up enthusiasm and contempt in equal measure. By 1820, Mozart's music dramas had lost their status as contested ground; as canonical works, they ranked with works by Spontini and Gluck. Whether Mozart was considered Italian or German was a confusion that remained throughout the 1820s.

Castil-Blaze adhered to Beaumarchais's original text in his translation of *Le nozze di Figaro,* much to the satisfaction of the press.[61] *Le Courrier des Théâtres* noted that audiences came to hear Beaumarchais first and Mozart second.[62] Premiered at the Odéon in July 1826, it was surprisingly successful; during the summer months, it was not expected to fill the theater but *Les noces de Figaro* protected the Odéon box-office receipts. By contrast, the Académie royale de musique kept putting the premiere of *Le siège de Corinthe* back until the hot weather abated. Castil-Blaze's insistence on Beaumarchais's dialogue resulted in a number of changes to Mozart's score. In act I, the duet "Via resti servita," and the repeat of the chorus "Giovanni lieti fiori spargete" were cut, as were in act II the trio "Susanna or via sortite" and the duet "Aprite presto aprite." Apart from the fact that it opened with "Dove sono," act III was largely unchanged but in act IV the first three numbers were omitted.

The version of *Don Giovanni* heard at the Odéon was in four acts. In act I, Masetto's "Ho capito," Elvira's "Ah fuggi," and the recitative before "Or sai che l'onore" were omitted, and the act closed with Don Giovanni's "Fin ch'han dal vino." Act II included only Zerlina's "Batti, batti" and the original act I finale. Act III omitted Leporello's "Ah pietà" and Anna's "Non mir dir bell'idol mio" and ended after the cemetery scene. Act IV comprised the original act II finale but omitted the last scena. Although *Don Juan* did not play a significant role at the Odéon, Castil-Blaze's arrangement formed the basis of the production at the Académie royale de musique in 1834. Although the production required the addition of recitatives and entr'actes, and although Vigny and Hoffmann influenced the libretto, the working model for the 1834 arrangement was Castil-Blaze's edition.[63]

In Restoration Paris, Italian music drama meant Rossini, and so it was at the Odéon. Of the thirteen Italian works mounted there more or less intact,

61. *Gazette de France,* 27 July 1826.
62. 23 July 1826.
63. Sabine Henze-Döhring, "E. T. A. Hoffmann-'Kult' und 'Don Giovanni'-Rezeption im Paris des 19. Jahrhunderts: Castil-Blazes 'Don Juan' im Théâtre de l'Académie Royale de Musique am 10 März 1834," in *Mozart-Jahrbuch 1984–5 des Zentralinstitutes für Mozartforschung*

eight were by Rossini, two by Mozart, and one each by Meyerbeer, Cimarosa, and Carafa. Two works form the basis of the account of Rossini given in this chapter, *Le barbier de Séville* and *La dame du lac*. *Le barbier* provides an excellent example of Castil-Blaze's working practices as he translated the libretto "back" into French via Beaumarchais in accordance with conventions discussed in the previous chapter and resequenced accordingly, whereupon he adjusted the numbers to fit the newly configured spoken dialogue. *La dame du lac*, in contrast, exemplifies the web of culture in a particularly striking and concentrated way. The conflict over the inclusion of a duet from *Semiramide* in the arrangement involved Rossini himself, the maison du Roi, the press, the manager of the Odéon, and one of the authors of the arrangement. Each individual represented a particular interest—a particular knot in the web of culture—and broader concerns further complicate the affair: the concept of novelty (which underpinned Rossini's complaint) and the question of power, since the decision by the maison du Roi upheld the primacy of the Théâtre italien over the Odéon rather than any a priori argument.

Although *Le nozze di Figaro* and *Don Giovanni* together represent the next largest group of Italian music dramas at the Odéon, they never really received the profile they might have deserved, and their discussion here is as much for a sense of completeness as much as a concession to modern senses of the position that such a composer as Mozart might hold in a study like this. By contrast, Meyerbeer's *Marguerite d'Anjou* was a sturdy link in the chain of premieres and revivals that would culminate in 1831 in *Robert le diable*. *Marguerite* was performed a great deal and was influential, remarkably so given that its extraordinary merging of two works into one offends to such a degree against the emerging concept of *Werktreue*. But it offends less, perhaps, than Mercadante's *Noces de Gamache*, a similar instance of two works being merged into one; the subject of Meyerbeer's libretto remains the same, and the sections taken from the two works are larger than in the Mercadante, with the result that the points of disjunction are fewer. Modern adherents to Berlioz's view that any sort of "meddling" is indefensible will probably not distinguish, but there is a very real difference between the procedures in *Marguerite d'Anjou* and *Les noces de Gamache* that illustrates the complexity of working and reworking music drama in this period.

Chapter 9

Une leçon de morale—
German Music Drama

German music drama never had the same impact as Italian stage music on Parisian theatrical culture. Apart from performances before 1800 of *Die Entführung aus dem Serail* (one of them in German), French audiences knew German music drama mostly through the arrangement of *Die Zauberflöte* as *Les mystères d'Isis.*[1] Premiered in 1801 at the Opéra (then the Théâtre des arts), it received over a hundred performances up to 1827. It was a familiar work during the 1820s and appeared three or four times a year until it finally disappeared after a performance on 2 May 1827. Its arranger, Ludwig Wenzel Lachnith, had planned it as a work for the Théâtre Feydeau—a more logical choice since the arrangement would then keep the original spoken dialogue rather than substitute accompanied recitative.[2] Much of the success of *Les mystères d'Isis* drew on the current interest in the culture of the Middle East—an emergent Egyptomania—and especially on rites of initiation reflected in its libretto.[3] Because it interpolated numbers from *Don Giovanni* and *La clemenza di Tito,* or because it had Mozart's name attached to the score, contemporary press accounts did not rate the German

---

1. For *Les mystères d'Isis,* see Rudolph Angermüller, "'Les Mystères d'Isis' (1801) und 'Don Juan' (1805, 1834) auf der Bühne der Pariser Oper," in *Mozart-Jahrbuch 1980–83 des Zentralinstitutes für Mozartforschung der Internationalen Stiftung Mozarteum Salzburg* (Kassel: Bärenreiter, 1983), 32–97; Jean Mongrédien, "*Les Mystères d'Isis* (1801) and Reflections on Mozart from the Parisian Press at the Beginning of the Nineteenth Century," in *Music in the Classic Period: Essays in Honor of Barry S. Brook,* ed. Allan W. Atlas (New York: Pendragon, 1985), 195–211.

2. Mongrédien, "*Mystères* and Reflections," 199–200.

3. Ibid., 201–4.

work's intellectual or musical challenges any higher than those of an Italian or a French one.[4]

A quarter of a century later, things were a little different. Shortly after the Odéon opened for operatic business, two German works were mounted: Winter's *Das unterbrochene Opferfest* and Weber's *Der Freischütz*. These were much more straightforward translations of their German originals than *Les mystères d'Isis*, and the German origins of their libretti far more in evidence in 1824 than those of Mozart's in 1801. The success of *Le sacrifice interrompu* (*Das unterbrochene Opferfest*) has undoubtedly been overshadowed by that of *Robin des bois*. But its premiere on 21 October 1824 was well attended and well received; six hundred people were turned away from the second performance, and—said the press—if *Le sacrifice interrompu* were played every night, the *dilettanti* from the Right Bank would sleep in the Odéon district.[5] For those skeptical of translations, it was deemed a model of how such works might contribute to the culture of stage music in the capital.[6] *Le sacrifice interrompu* immediately called attention to the complex subject of German libretti; it was simply considered to be weak, and the trope of a weak libretto coexisting with fine music was repeated in the critique of *Robin des bois* two months later and characterized many of the translations or adaptations of German stage music mounted at the Odéon.[7] One response to *Le sacrifice interrompu* recurred throughout the commentary on German music drama at the Odéon: it was difficult to grasp and required multiple hearings to assimilate.[8] The production of *Le sacrifice interrompu* prompted a comparison of French, Italian, and German stage music at the Odéon that is valuable for contextualizing not only Winter but also other German composers:

> French music, full of light motifs that are little developed, appears more particularly to appeal to the spirit; that of the Italians charms the heart and the ear at the same time; the Germans, party to the secrets of harmonic science, appear to have as their object the loftiness of the soul, and to arouse the most noble ideas in the intellect. The Frenchman seeks a distraction, the Italian a pleasure, and the German a lesson in ethics (*une leçon de morale*).[9]

4. Angermüller, "Les Mystères," 40–41.

5. *Le Courrier des Théâtres,* 26 October and 26 November 1824.

6. *La Pandore,* 23 October 1824.

7. *Le Courrier des Théâtres,* 22 October 1824; *Journal des Débats,* 9 December 1824.

8. *Le Courrier des Théâtres,* 23 November 1824; *Le Diable Boiteux,* 26 January 1825.

9. La musique des Français, pleine de motifs légers et peu développés, semble plus particulièrement s'adresser à l'esprit; celle des Italiens charme à-la-fois le coeur et l'oreille; les Allemands, initiés à tous les secrets de la science harmonique, paraissent avoir pour but d'élever l'âme, et de réveiller dans l'intelligence les idées les plus nobles: le Français cherche une distraction, l'Italien un plaisir et l'Allemand une leçon de morale (*Le Diable Boiteux,* 25 October 1824).

Weber

Critical Trajectories

If a single production at the Odéon during the 1820s has taken root in the history of nineteenth-century music, it is the version of *Der Freischütz* that was given as *Robin des bois* from late 1824 until the collapse of the opera troupe in 1828. The production has often been read as a paradigm of the ways in which canonic works have been bowdlerized to suit the require-ments of audiences unable to appreciate the value of such works.[10] This was not the view of critics and audiences in the 1820s; neither was it the view of most composers of the period. Views of the authority and integrity of works of art were however changing very quickly. The tension between the tradi-tional view—that music drama could be rearranged to suit local conven-tions and the newer view that works of art were sacrosanct explains much of the later controversy surrounding the Odéon production of *Robin des bois*. It is a particularly striking example because of the work's colossal success—the greatest in Paris in 1825 and probably 1826 as well—and because of the large box-office receipts that resulted.

Two critical traditions spring from the 1824 Odéon production of *Robin des bois:* one based on Weber's own response, and a French tradition that started with Berlioz; both have colored the tone of subsequent critical lit-erature and therefore the value attributed to it. Carl Maria von Weber's case was straightforward. His complaint lay largely with the fact that he had missed the chance to exploit the financial possibilities of *Der Freischütz* and *Euryanthe* in Paris and was anxious not to miss similar opportunities in the future (figure 27). The origin of this particular problem lay quite simply in the fact that French law did not protect foreign authors' interests; Weber's claim to the Parisian rights to his works was therefore futile. Berlioz and the French tradition is more complex, and in many ways much more reveal-ing. Berlioz's *Memoirs,* in which *Robin des bois* is most fully discussed, were printed in 1865, distributed posthumously in 1870, but had been drafted between 1848 and 1854. His commentary on *Robin des bois* dates from the beginning of this period and surfaces in a diatribe against Habeneck's and François-Joseph Fétis's modifications of Beethoven's symphonies, Lach-nith's *Mystères d'Isis,* and Colley Cibber's and David Garrick's reworkings of

---

10. For a view that lays the blame at the public's door, see Catherine Nazloglou, "Castil-Blaze [Blaze, François-Henri-Joseph]," *The New Grove Dictionary of Music and Musicians,* ed. Stanley Sadie (London: Macmillan, 1980), 3:872. See also the commentary in Mark Everist, "Gluck, Berlioz and Castil-Blaze: The Poetics and Reception of French Opera," in *Reading Crit-ics Reading: French Music Criticism, 1789–1848,* ed. Roger Parker and Mary Ann Smart (Oxford: Oxford University Press, 2001), 86–108.

Figure 27. Carl Maria von Weber. Lithograph by
Bove after Ludwig Theodor Zollner.

Shakespeare.[11] Berlioz does not distinguish between his own priorities—
the complete authority of the composer and his compositions—and those
of Weber's:

> Weber was naturally incensed when he discovered what Castil-Blaze, veteri-
> nary surgeon of music, had done with his *Freischütz,* and he aired his just griev-
> ance in a vigorous letter which was published in the Press before he left Paris.
> Castil-Blaze had the audacity to reply that it was precisely the changes of which
> the composer complained which had ensured the success of *Robin des bois,* and
> that it was most ungrateful of M. Weber to reproach the man who had popu-
> larised his music in France.
>   Villain! And a wretched sailor gets fifty lashes for a minor act of insub-
> ordination![12]

Berlioz's implication that Weber was angered solely for artistic reasons is
wrong. In his published writings, Weber admits—albeit reluctantly, and

11. David Cairns, ed. and trans., *The Memoirs of Hector Berlioz, Member of the French Institute,
Including His Travels in Italy, Germany, Russia and England: 1803–1865* (London: Victor Gollanz, 1977), 99–106.

12. Ibid., 102.

only in the case of French music drama—the necessity of reworking stage music for different local circumstances.[13]

Published in 1866, around the same time as Berlioz's memoirs but written after them, was an extraordinary article by one of the arrangers of the libretto of *Robin des bois,* Thomas Sauvage.[14] It was written forty years after the event and had been characterized as a "public confession."[15] It emerges as a product of a world where attitudes to artistic authority had changed in favor of the views set forth by the avant-garde of the 1820s. By the 1860s, views hostile to nonauthorial intervention in autonomous works of art were more orthodox. The overall tenor of Sauvage's article was to play down the author's role in the production of *Robin des bois* forty years earlier and to lay the blame (as it was then seen) for *Robin des bois* at Castil-Blaze's door.

Berlioz and Sauvage served as key sources for late-nineteenth- and early-twentieth-century attempts to excoriate those responsible for *Robin des bois* and Castil-Blaze in particular. The only dissenting voice seems to have been Adolphe Jullien, whose *Weber à Paris* offers the only reasonably balanced view of the subject.[16] Both the article by Jacques-Gabriel Prod'homme and the introduction to Georges Servières's own translation of *Der Freischütz* (the latter perhaps predictably) lean heavily and uncritically on Berlioz and Sauvage.[17] Their intemperate views of Castil-Blaze and the Odéon have

13. In a review of Pierre Gaveaux's *Échelle de soie,* published in the *Königliche kaiserliche priviligierte Prager Zeitung,* 11 February 1816, Weber summed up a common—but contradictory—view: "Only a few of Gaveaux's musical numbers remain in this version, as four other numbers [by Weigl, Spontini, Isouard, and Gyrowetz] were substituted for the originals in Vienna. But these extraneous additions are so well chosen, belonging . . . to the same musical world and forming together such a charming bouquet, that on this occasion we can only applaud what is, in principle, deplorable and unhappily becoming increasingly common—I mean the prejudicing of the uninstructed against a composer by inserting what are often the most alien pieces into his works" (*Carl Maria von Weber: Writings on Music,* trans. Martin Cooper, ed. John Warrack [Cambridge: Cambridge University Press, 1981], 163).

14. Thomas Sauvage, "Histoire de *Robin des bois:* opéra fantastique imité du *Freischütz,* représenté sur le Théâtre de l'Odéon le 7 décembre 1824," *Revue et gazette musicale de Paris* 33 (1866): 385–87 and 393–95.

15. Georges Servières, *Freischütz: opéra romantique en 3 actes, musique de Carl-Maria von Weber, traduction du poème de Friedrich Kind précédée d'une histoire de l'oeuvre et de ses adaptations françaises* (Paris: Fischbacher and Floury, 1913), 32–33. The same formulation is used in John Warrack, *Carl Maria von Weber* (Cambridge: Cambridge University Press, 1968; 2d ed. 1976), 263 n. 3. Twentieth-century treatments of *Robin des bois* typically characterize its arrangement as a crime.

16. Adolphe Jullien, *Weber à Paris en 1826, son voyage de Dresde à Londres par la France: la musique et les théâtres, le monde et la presse pendant son séjour* (1877); reprinted in *Paris dilettante au commencement du siècle* (Paris: Firmin-Didot, 1884), 7–66.

17. Jacques-Gabriel Prod'homme, "'Robin des Bois' et 'le Freyschütz,'" *Le Ménestrel* 88 (1926): 437–40 and 449–51. Sevrières's use of a 1841 motto taken from Théophile Gautier illustrates his attitude to authority (though Servières ignores the disparity between this date and that of the events described): "Genius may be handled only with respect, as the priest does

been repeated in a variety of scholarly contexts up to the present, and both the evidence on which they depended and a quantity of new information invite review.[18]

Robin des bois: Production and Publication

The history of *Der Freischütz* in Paris is complicated by three different productions and three separate attempts at publication. Although some of these left little trace, others led to some of the most important musical and dramatic events in Paris during the Bourbon Restoration. Of the three productions, one was initiated by Weber himself in collaboration with François-Antoine Habeneck at the Académie royale de musique, a second was driven by Castil-Blaze and Sauvage at the Gymnase dramatique, and the third was *Robin des bois* itself.

A letter from Weber to Maurice Schlesinger, dated 15 March 1823, discusses methods of sending a score of *Der Freischütz* to Habeneck, presumably with an eye to a performance at the Académie royale de musique.[19] Weber wrote, "My view of this opera is still the same, and I cannot persuade myself that the Parisian public will relish the libretto of this opera."[20] Weber's subsequent comments suggest that he was aware of the conditions under which his work would have been performed at the Académie royale de musique, "conditions . . . that will be, I am sure, of a sort mutually to honor artists and the temple of arts erected in the capital of France."[21] Whether at this stage this was a serious undertaking or simply a way of smoothing the path toward obtaining a commission for Weber to write an opéra for the Académie royale de musique (with which the substance of the letter is concerned) is difficult to tell. Certainly, by the end of 1825 and early 1826, Weber was prepared to say that he was planning a Parisian performance of *Euryanthe,* but there is little evidence that he was ever seriously committed to a production of *Der Freischütz* at the Académie royale de musique.

---

when he holds up the Host. Each note is sacred, and the words that have awakened the master's inspiration may not be changed lightly" (On ne doit toucher le génie qu'avec des mains respectueuses, comme le prêtre quand il tient l'hostie. Chaque note est sacrée, et les paroles qui ont éveillé l'inspiration du maître ne doivent pas être changées à la légère [Servières, *Freischütz,* 29]).

18. Warrack (*Carl Maria von Weber,* 236–37) draws indiscriminately on Berlioz, Sauvage, and Servières.

19. The letter is published incompletely in Jullien, *Weber à Paris,* 29–30, and more fully in Prod'homme, "Robin des Bois," 437.

20. Mes vues sur cet opéra sont toujours encore les mêmes, et je ne puis me persuader que le public parisien goûtera le poème de cet opéra (Prod'homme, "Robin des Bois," 437).

21. Conditions . . . qui seront, j'en suis sûr, de sorte à honorer mutuellement les artistes et le temple des arts édifié dans la capitale de la France (ibid.).

At the same time that Weber was negotiating with Habeneck through Schlesinger, Castil-Blaze and Sauvage were planning a production of *Der Freischütz*. This was a year before the beginning of opera production at the Odéon, and the production of the work under the title *Le chasseur noir* was destined for the Gymnase dramatique.[22] Most relevant for the Castil-Blaze/ Sauvage production of *Der Freischütz* was the second clause in the Gymnase dramatique's license that outlined the repertory it was allowed to play. "Plays of the *ancien répertoire* that form part of the public domain may be played by the actors of the Gymnase dramatique, but in fragments only: in one act for plays in several acts, and in one scene for those in one act."[23] *Der Freischütz*, as far as French law was concerned, was in the public domain, but to comply with their license the arrangers were forced to reduce Weber's three acts to one. Very little of the Gymnase arrangement survives, and it is impossible to tell just how the reduction was executed. There is no libretto, printed or manuscript, and nothing in the archives of the Gymnase dramatique mentions the production.[24] Two sources, extracts in vocal score published by Castil-Blaze, and Sauvage's "public confession," put a little more flesh on the bones of this skeletal production.

Sauvage gives a cast list for the projected Gymnase production. Although full of errors, it identifies Mme Dormeuil as Ännchen, her husband as Max, Émile Cottenet as Caspar, and Mme Méric-Lalande as Agathe.[25] Henriette Méric-Lalande had joined the Gymnase dramatique and made her debut there on 3 April 1823. She was to make her name in Italy in the second half of the decade and was to participate in the premieres of Meyerbeer's *Crociato in Egitto,* four works by Bellini, and finally Donizetti's *Lucrezia Borgia*.[26] She must have been in Venice by the beginning of 1824, because Meyerbeer's *Crociato,* in which she sang the role of Palmide, was premiered on 7 March at La Fenice. Furthermore, she must soon have yielded the role of Agathe to Mlle Florigny, whose name appears in the Castil-Blaze print. Méric-Lalande may have been the preferred artist in mid-1823, replaced once it was clear that she was leaving for Italy.

22. Very little information is readily available about the Gymnase dramatique in this period. The best summary is Nicole Wild, *Dictionnaire des théâtres parisiens au XIXe siècle: les théâtres et la musique* (Paris: Amateurs des Livres, 1989), 178–83.

23. Les pièces de l'ancien répertoire qui font partie du domaine public, pourront être jouées par les acteurs du Gymnase, mais par fragments seulement, composés au plu d'un acte pour les pièces en plusieurs actes, d'une scène pour les pièces en un acte (Wild, *Dictionnaire,* 181).

24. Archival sources for the theater are F-Pan F^{21} 1137 and 1138.

25. Sauvage, "Histoire de *Robin des bois,*" 385.

26. For summaries of Méric-Lalande's career see *GroveOpera* 3:341; and Karl-Josef Kutsch and Leo Riemens, *Großes Sängerlexikon* (Bern: Francke, 1987–94), *s.v.* Méric-Lalande.

Only four numbers of the Gymnase arrangement published by Castil-Blaze survive: Max's scena from act I, the act II trio, and Agathe's act II and act III arias.[27] Although the last mentioned was radically different in the Gymnase version, the translations of the rest were the same as those that would be used at the Odéon, and Castil-Blaze's vocal score of the Odéon version (*Robin des bois*) used, where possible, the same plates as the extracts from the Gymnase version (*Le chasseur noir*). The Gymnase extracts were advertised for sale in the *Bibliographie de la France* on 14 February 1824. The dialogue's history is much less clear. Sauvage was responsible for a first draft with assistance, he claimed, from François-Adolphe Loève-Veimars.[28] After the collapse of the Gymnase project, Sauvage said that he approached Scribe, who required six months to bring the work to fruition, and then Duveyrier, who refused to assist. It is difficult to believe that the spoken dialogue of the one-act arrangement for the Gymnase could have been of any use for a three-act arrangement for the Odéon, so serious revision and retranslation must have taken place during the course of 1824.

The production of *Le chasseur noir* at the Gymnase dramatique came to nothing. Sauvage reported that the scenery for the wolf's glen scene was completed and also, after the production was abandoned, that it was used in two vaudevilles: *Le dîner sur l'herbe* and *Le bal champêtre*.[29] The manager of the Gymnase, Delestre-Poirson, was certainly interested in stretching the terms of the theater's license (as the Odéon feared) but not in the direction of translations; it would encompass comédie-vaudeville in collaboration with Scribe.[30] Furthermore, a three-act translation at the Odéon must have seemed a much more attractive possibility to Castil-Blaze than a one-act version at the Gymnase. His column in the *Journal des Débats* for 9 April 1824, however, still described *Le chasseur noir* as the property of the Gymnase and therefore unavailable to the Odéon.[31] The early success of the opera troupe at the Odéon and the switch in direction at the Gymnase brought the possibility into production at the Odéon in December 1824.

Schlesinger, meanwhile, had been anxious to counter the incursions of Castil-Blaze and Sauvage by producing a vocal score of *Der Freischütz* in

27. The surviving extracts are *Le chasseur noir: opéra en un acte, imité de Der Freischütz* (Paris, n.d.).

28. Sauvage ("Histoire de *Robin des bois*," 386) styles the name Loève-Weimer. However spelled, Loève-Veimars would have been a good choice for advice with a translation. He had translated Wieland's *Mélanges littéraires* of 1824 and *Oberon ou Huon de Bordeaux* of 1825. Later in the decade, he translated E. T. A. Hoffmann's *Contes fantastiques et contes nocturnes* (see the biography and list of works in *LDD-NS* 10:617).

29. Sauvage, "Histoire de *Robin des bois*," 385.

30. Wild, *Dictionnaire*, 181.

31. *Journal des Débats*, 9 April 1824.

French. Under the same title as the Gymnase arrangement, he produced an edition in French that differed from the Berlin Schlesinger vocal score and Castil-Blaze's French versions as well. The translator was nowhere named, nor was the edition ever listed in the *Bibliographie de France*.[32] It is therefore difficult to say whether Schlesinger's or Castil-Blaze's edition appeared first.[33] Whether Castil-Blaze or Schlesinger was the first to produce a French version of *Der Freischütz* seems to have worried some earlier commentators but is beside the point, since neither were the first to produce such an edition. Laffillé published a single extract of *Der Freischütz* translated into French in April 1823, well before either Schlesinger or Castil-Blaze. The extract was advertised in the *Bibliographie de France* on 5 April 1823 and is an arrangement of "Und ob die Wolke" with a French translation ("Quoique voilé par un nuage") distinct from those published by Schlesinger and Castil-Blaze. A single copy of the extract survives; its title page claims that Laffillé had arranged both the words and the music himself, and it seems reasonable to assume that the publisher's plans were to produce a complete set of extracts and an entire piano-vocal score.[34]

The traditional view of the Parisian premiere of *Der Freischütz,* and its accompanying demonization of Castil-Blaze, gives an incomplete view of the reception of the work in Paris. Ignoring the vocal scores of a French version that Schlesinger and Laffillé put on sale, and two early aborted productions projected by Weber himself and by Sauvage, Scribe, and Castil-Blaze, it too centers on the December 1824 production at the Odéon.

Robin des bois at the Odéon

Criticism of the Odéon production of *Der Freischütz* as *Robin des bois* goes into detailed bar-by-bar and line-by-line comparisons between Weber's 1821 Berlin version of the work and the Odéon production, as printed in

32. *Le chasseur noir / Freischütz: opéra romantique en trois actes* (Paris: Schlesinger, n.d.).

33. Logically, the plate number M.S.148 for *Le chasseur noir* should have been assigned before the one for Ries's second divertissement, which bore the plate number 166 and had been announced in the *Bibliographie de la France* on 21 February 1824. Since *Le chasseur noir* was so obviously a larger project than the Ries piano work, M.S.148 could not have been published before 21 February 1824 (and therefore possibly after Castil-Blaze's extracts advertised on 14 February in the *Bibliographie de la France*). The entries for Schlesinger's plate numbers M.S.112 and M.S.155 have already been discussed à propos the publisher's Beethoven prints by Alan Tyson, "Maurice Schlesinger as a Publisher of Beethoven: 1822–1827," *Acta musicologica* 35 (1963): 186.

34. *Der Freischütz ou Le franc-chasseur* (Paris: Laffillé, n.d.). Although the advertisement in the *Bibliographie de la France* (5 April 1823) clearly refers to this extract, the wording of the advertisement warrants quotation: "*Der Freishats,* ou *le franc Chasseur* [*sic*]."

Castil-Blaze's edition of the score.[35] The action shifts from Friedrich Kind's German mountains at the end of the Thirty Years' War to Sauvage and Castil-Blaze's Wentworth in Yorkshire at the end of the reign of Charles I. The characters take on new names. Agathe becomes Annette, Ännchen Nancy, Max Tony, Caspar Richard, and Kilian Dick. Both Ottokar and the hermit disappear. Their omission from the 1824 Odéon production is the result of the complete reworking of Weber and Kind's act III finale. Musical changes include moving the trio with chorus ("O diese Sonne!") to after Caspar's song ("Hier im ird'schen Jammerthal") in act I, and putting the same character's act I aria ("Schweig! Damit dich Niemand warnt") into act III. The most notable musical change is in the insertion of a duet in act II for Tony and Annette (Max and Agathe). This is a retexting of the duet for Euryanthe and Adolar ("Hin nimm die Seele mein") from act II of Weber's *Euryanthe*. This addition aroused the ire of commentators perhaps because of Weber's own concern with this number. In Weber's open letters to Castil-Blaze he drew special attention to the addition of this duo (example 13). Weber was particularly sensitive to this matter because he believed that Castil-Blaze had orchestrated the duo from a piano-vocal score.[36] Finally, the French production cut large parts of the so-called wolf's glen scene (something of a misnomer for a scene reset in the ruins of Saint Dunstan's): a comparison between Castil-Blaze's print of 1824 and Weber's original shows the detail of this abridgement of the act II finale (table 9).

Apart from some choral additions, from the casting of the third bullet onward the Odéon version is essentially the same as Weber's, though Robin des bois (Samiel) delivers the bullets by hand at the moment where the seventh is forged in *Der Freischütz* (figure 28). The earlier parts of the scene are different: a short monologue for Richard (Caspar) replaces the exchanges between Caspar and Samiel, into which Weber puts so much of the truly innovative in his score; the exchanges between Max and Caspar after the former's arrival receive similar treatment, and the forging of the first two bullets is cut entirely. The finale ends in Castil-Blaze's published version of *Robin des bois* with a chorus.

The foregoing summary does not complete the textual history of *Robin des bois* on the stage of the Odéon. The production underwent a number of

---

35. Warrack (*Carl Maria von Weber,* 236–37) gives an excellent short account; the fullest account of the changes is in Servières, *Freischütz,* 38–49. See also Frank Heidlberger, *Carl Maria von Weber und Hector Berlioz: Studien zur französischen Weber-Rezeption* (Tützing: Schneider, 1994), 314–36.

36. A comparison of Castil-Blaze's version with Weber's original suggests that Weber was correct, and Castil-Blaze apparently made no attempt to contradict him. Weber seemed not to mind that Castil-Blaze had reduced the orchestral introduction from 22 to 10 bars.

Example 13. Duet "Non plus d'alarmes" from *Euryanthe* (*Robin des bois*).

TABLE 9. Comparison of *Robin des bois* and *Der Freischütz*, act II finale

Robin des bois (1824)	*Der Freischütz* (1821)
Chorus, "Le sang de sa mère" (166–71)	Chorus, "Milch des Mondes" (138–41)
Dialogue (Richard—alone; 172)	Caspar's invocation to Samiel (melodrama; 141–42)
	Exchanges between Caspar and Samiel (composed; 143–149)
	Caspar prepares the furnace (melodrama; 150–53)
Tony's arrival and visions of his mother and Annette (172–84)	Max's arrival and visions (153–64)
Dialogue (Tony, Richard)	Casting of the first two bullets (dialogue, melodrama and composed; 165–67)
Orchestral sequence 1; B♭ (185)	Casting of the third bullet; B♭ (168–69)
Orchestral sequence 2; d (186–88)	Casting of the fourth bullet; d (169–70)
Orchestral sequence 3; c:V (188–89)	Casting of the fifth bullet; c:V (171)
Orchestral sequence 4; c:V; with chorus "Robin des bois" and dialogue invocation (190–93)	Casting of the sixth bullet; c:V with chorus "Durch Berg und Thal" (172–74)
Orchestral sequence 5; c with appearance of Robin des bois, delivery of the bullets, and chorus, "Non aux tourmens" [this lengthens the section] (194–207)	Casting of the seventh bullet. Appearance of Samiel to assist in its forging (175–80)

SOURCES: Carl Maria von Weber, *Der Freischütz* (Leipzig: Breitkopf und Härtel, n.d.; reprint, New York: Dover, 1977); Castil-Blaze, *Robin des bois: opéra-féerie en trois actes* (Paris: Castil-Blaze, 1824).

changes; some brought the version of the work heard at the Odéon closer to Weber's original, while others reflected local circumstances. The libretto was printed several times during the course of the run at the Odéon (three separate editions within the first year), and the different editions are useful for identifying practices in the theater.[37] Nancy's *romance* and air "Un soir rêvant" (Ännchen's "Einst träumte meiner sel'gen Base"), present in the full and vocal scores of the arrangement, is absent from all libretti and never

37. The first-edition libretto (*Robin des bois ou Les trois balles: opera-féerie en trois actes* [Paris: Barba, 1824]) appeared in the *Bibliographie de la France,* 25 December 1824, and the second (essentially the same) on 28 May 1825. The third edition was completely reset and listed in the *Bibliographie de la France* on 15 October 1825.

Figure 28. Set design for act II of Weber's *Robin des bois. Album théâtrale* (Paris: Osterwald, n.d.), no. 7.

mentioned in reviews, for example. It was presumably printed to add to the authority of Castil-Blaze's edition but seems never to have been sung at the Odéon.

Premieres at the Odéon were usually badly organized dress rehearsals, and the theater was often criticized for it. *Robin des bois* was no exception.[38] Indeed, it was agreed both by the press and by the administration that the work had been miscast at the first performance, and between the premiere on 7 December 1824 and the second performance on 18 December many changes of role were made. The casting for these two performances, the roles given in the published libretto, and an important change of cast for the sixth performance are in table 10.[39]

The most pressing concern after the premiere was to replace Campe-naut, who was insufficiently well to sing, and to replace Maire in the role of

38. See *Le Courrier des Théâtres,* 16 December 1824; *Journal de Paris,* 18 December 1824. Castil-Blaze was more cautious. He described all the performances up to 26 December 1824 as *Generalproben* (*Journal des Débats,* 26 December 1824).

39. The sources for table 10 consist of press notices, castings given in theatrical journals, and the first-edition libretto.

TABLE 10. Cast changes for 1824 performances of *Robin des bois*

Role	Premiere (7 December)	2d Performance (18 December)	6th Performance (30 December)	Libretto (1st ed.)
Annette (Agathe)	Mlle Florigny	Florigny	Mlle Pouilley	Florigny
Nancy (Ännchen)	Mme Letellier	Letellier	Letellier	Letellier
Tony (Max)	Campenaut	Lecomte	Lecomte	Campenaut/Lecomte
Reynold (Cuno)	Maire	Bernard	Bernard	Bernard/Maire
Richard (Caspar)	Valère	Valère	Valère	Valère
Dick (Kilian)	Latappy	Latappy	Latappy	Latappy
Robin des bois (Samiel)	Édouard	Édouard	Édouard	Édouard

Reynold. The latter task was easily accomplished by the manager's agreeing to deputize in a not very arduous part. Replacing the principal tenor was a different matter, and the fact that Lecomte would have to prepare the role, quite possibly from scratch, was one of the main reasons why eleven days elapsed between the premiere and the second performance. The final principal change concerned Latappy, who had been heavily criticized. The solution affected the textual tradition of the work. Replacing him was impossible because the only other candidate, Léon, had been indisposed since well before the *Robin des bois* premiere. The role of Dick (Kilian) is not extensive, and his most exposed music is in the act 1 introduction, where he leads off the strophic song with chorus "Schau der Herr mich an als König" ("Admirez tous son adresse"). The solution for the Odéon was to give this number to Valère—a simple answer in terms of voice-type; the result was perhaps more problematic in characterization, for Richard (Caspar) now sang the music that Weber had written for Kilian.

The delay to the second performance gave the arrangers of the music and the libretto (Castil-Blaze and Sauvage) a chance to cut some of the dialogue and to make some further musical adjustments. The press alluded to scenes being excised or shortened but was no more specific. And the published libretto (in the *Bibliographie de la France* on 25 December 1824, showing the cast for the 18 December performance) differs from the text as approved by the censor on 15 October.[40] In general, the dialogue is much

40. The censors' libretto is F-Pan F^{18} 613/149.

fuller in the October version, especially in the scenes between Tony (Max) and Richard (Caspar), and this is probably the version heard by the audience at the Odéon on 7 December, whereas the shorter version in the printed libretto reflects the abridgements heard at the second performance and thereafter.

The press reported that the repetition of the huntsmen's chorus at the end of act III was an addition made after the premiere by Castil-Blaze; although this is present in the published libretto, it is missing from the censor's libretto and suggests that Castil-Blaze, realizing that the huntsmen's chorus was one of the most successful numbers, did indeed choose to include it at the end.[41] A further report from the press criticized the end of the second act. "How, for example, was it possible to end act II with a feeble dialogue, after the monstrous effect of the infernal chorus? M. Castil-Blaze ought to have followed his inclination on such a propitious occasion and adapted here a finale suitable to the situation: no one would have accused him of wrongdoing."[42] Ending act II with a *dialogue débile* is exactly what the censor's libretto does.[43] Here Weber's music ends with the original shuddering F-sharp minor, but Sauvage's original libretto has only a couple of lines of dialogue. Castil-Blaze followed the advice offered by *Le Diable Boiteux* and added a chorus of demons at the end of the finale to balance the one at its beginning.

The act II finale created much of *Robin des bois*'s reputation, and regular attention was paid to renewing its scenery and enhancing its effect. Like most of the more successful stage designs in Restoration Paris, the sets were by Ciceri. The premiere was messy in this respect as well. The scenery was praised, but the bears and the bats were rated less highly.[44] One well-informed critic noted that, in German productions, the animals acted behind a semi-translucent screen and implied that the Odéon production should do the same.[45] As early as 8 January 1825, Bernard renewed the scenery for the wolf's glen scene, much to the delight of audiences and critics alike.[46] A year later, in January 1826, the scenery for the act II finale was entirely rejuvenated, again by Ciceri. One journal gave such a de-

41. *Le Diable Boiteux,* 10 December 1824.

42. Comment, par exemple, a-t-on pu finir le second acte par un dialogue débile, après l'effet monstrueux du choeur infernal? M. Castil-Blaze . . . aurait dû suivre son penchant dans une occasion aussi favorable, et adapter ici quelque final conforme à la situation: personne ne lui en eût fait un crime (ibid.).

43. F-Pan F^{18} 613/149.

44. *Le Diable Boiteux,* 10 December 1824.

45. *Le Courrier des Théâtres,* 9 December 1824.

46. *Journal de Paris,* 10 January 1825.

tailed report not only of the renovations, but also of what must have existed before:

> In order to reawaken the curiosity of the public that 150 performances had not entirely exhausted, Robin des bois has just made some additions to his Hell, which, indeed, greatly needed refurbishment. The devils, whose shabby coverings occasionally allowed a Christian nose or ear to appear, hardly generated any terror in young occupants of the galleries. Thanks to M. Ciceri, these agents of Lucifer have reappeared in all their splendor. The new set is very effective; the lovers of black magic have especially pointed out the horrendous ghost who appears to preside over the infernal assembly, and the colossal figure who arises in the middle of the theater at the end of the sorcery was greeted with a triple salvo of applause. As for the little bats who serve as assistants to the demons, they can hardly create an illusion as long as the wires that make them move are so clearly visible.[47]

In the same review, it was mentioned that the arrangers intended to reinstate some numbers that had previously been cut. Such claims were repeated throughout 1826 and culminated, in November 1826, in the reinstatement of the scene of the forging of the bullets in the act II finale.[48] None of the surviving sources for the music or the libretto preserve this reinstatement, but the melodrama that had been cut and replaced by spoken dialogue must have been reinstated, as well as the music for the forging of the first two bullets. In addition, the scene at the end where Robin (Samiel) hands three bullets to Richard (Caspar) must have been taken out, and the forging of the bullets put back into what for the previous two years had been an orchestral accompaniment to a tableau. Castil-Blaze's final chorus apparently remained however. It is significant that these moves back toward the integrity of the wolf's glen scene took place in 1826 and were perhaps

47. Afin de réveiller la curiosité du public, que cent cinquante représentations n'avaient pas entièrement épuisée, Robin des bois vient de faire quelques augmentations à son enfer, qui, à la vérité, avait grand besoin d'être un peu rafraîchi. Les diables, dont l'enveloppe usée laissait quelquefois apercevoir un bout de nez ou d'oreille chrétien, ne faisaient presque plus peur aux enfants des galeries. Grâce à M. Cicéri, ces agents de Lucifer ont reparu dans toute leur splendeur. La nouvelle décoration produit beaucoup d'effet: les amateurs de magie noire ont surtout remarqué l'horrible spectre qui semble présider à l'assemblée infernale, et la figure colossale qui s'élève au milieu du théâtre, à la fin de la conjuration, a été saluée par une triple salve d'applaudissements. Quant aux petites chauve-souris qui servent d'auxiliaires aux démons, elles ne peuvent guère produire d'illusion, tant qu'on apercevra aussi distinctement les fils d'archal qui les font mouvoir (*Le Frondeur,* 4 January 1826).

48. Unequivocal descriptions of the reinstated forging of the bullets are in *La Pandore,* 23 and 24 November 1825; and *Le Courrier des Théâtres,* 24 November 1825. Some references to reinstatement of suppressed material may also refer to Nancy's *romance* and aria "Un soir rêvant" (Ännchen's "Einst träumte meiner sel'gen Base").

triggered by Weber's visit to Paris in that year, and by his interest in the Odéon, its productions, and the possibility of mounting more of his works at the theater.

Response and Reputation

The critical response to *Robin des bois* was almost without precedent. After the difficulties of the first couple of performances, the press agreed on the work's success.[49] Audiences confirmed the critics' view. By mid-December 1824, the theater was full for all performances,[50] and by April 1825, the management was having to turn away numbers in excess of 300 each evening.[51] The work reached its 100th performance on 3 September 1825 and its 150th on the first day of the following year. Despite a scare in November 1825 that enthusiasm for the work was beginning to decline,[52] revivals in January 1826 and again in November 1826 meant that the work was still much in favor. Even on 2 December 1826, the audience forced the management to cancel a performance of another work in favor of *Robin des bois*.[53] There were consequences of such success. Throughout the early part of 1825, the management's reluctance to pass up chances to maximize profits from the work had held back productions that were ready to go into performance.[54]

Robin des bois was a massive financial success. The Odéon's maximum box, if all seats were sold at the usual price, was Fr 4,080 per performance.[55] In July 1825, takings of Fr 6,200 were reported, and figures in excess of Fr 6,000 were still being noted in November 1826.[56] When it was reported that the work had brought the theater Fr 80,000, this was shortly before the 150th performance and suggests that the average box over the previous year had been keeping up to the level of Fr 6,000 per performance every time *Robin des bois* was played.[57] Early in 1826, perhaps as a result of the lead of the duchesse de Berry who had heard *Robin des bois* on 8 January, an influx of *ultra-pontins* began to alter the structure of the Odéon's audience.[58] It can have been no accident that, whenever the opportunity for

49. E.g., *Le Courrier des Théâtres*, 16 and 17 December 1824; *Le Diable Boiteux*, 18 and 19 December 1824; *Journal de Paris*, 18 December 1824.
50. *Journal de Paris*, 10 January 1825.
51. *Le Diable Boiteux*, 13 April 1825.
52. *Le Frondeur*, 8 November 1825.
53. *Le Courrier des Théâtres*, 2 December 1826.
54. *Journal de Paris*, 7 February 1825.
55. *Le Diable Boiteux*, 22 July 1825.
56. *Le Courrier des Théâtres*, 24 November 1826.
57. Ibid.
58. *Le Diable Boiteux* 26 January 1825.

public display presented itself, the Odéon chose to mount *Robin des bois* to ensure a successful occasion; the coronation of Charles X is a case in point.

Castil-Blaze was right when he claimed that his actions in reworking *Der Freischütz* for the French stage had been the key to its success. Parisians were either perplexed by the complexity of Weber's music and what they saw as the intellectual demands it made on them, or they took exception to some of the longer numbers in the work, particularly the two scenes for Max and Agathe (reworked for their French counterparts, Tony and Annette).[59] The terms to which the critics frequently returned to describe Weber's music were *savant* and *compliqué*.[60] These were tropes that attached themselves to the music of both Meyerbeer and Mozart, as well as other "German" composers heard at the Odéon whether they were writing German or Italian music drama. The music's complexity could sometimes lead to jokes at its expense, as in the case of the occasion when the theater's management left a comma out of the playbill for one performance and advertised—rather than "*Robin des bois:* paroles de Castil-Blaze, Sauvage, musique de Weber"— a version that read in translation "*Robin des bois:* text by Castil-Blaze, savage music by Weber."[61]

The success of the work was associated with its drama. The supernatural, in the act II finale particularly, was regularly cited as reason for the work's popularity. The other recurrent thread in the response to *Robin des bois* was the conjunction of the evil with the innocent, especially in the wolf's glen scene and the bridal chorus in act III. Popular acclaim had *Robin des bois* on everyone's lips. In January 1825, Boieldieu's *Voitures versées* was mounted at the Opéra-Comique, and in the passage in which Dormeuil lists popular works from the time of the work's premiere (1820), Cassel added the name of *Robin des bois*—an addition that was greeted with good-natured whistling. Finally, Castil-Blaze and Sauvage could recognize the near immortality of *Robin des bois* when, in December 1825, the pâtissier Terrier, "Aux Palmiers, rue St-Honoré no. 254," announced his latest gastronomic treat: a patisserie entitled *Robin des bois*.[62]

Weber and Castil-Blaze

Weber's representations to Castil-Blaze at the end of 1825 and in early 1826 concerning the latter's use of his works in Paris are well known. They con-

59. *La Pandore*, 18 December 1824. The position was not improved by the fact that Agathe's *scena* was, in the view of at least one critic, taken too slowly at early performances (*Le Courrier des Théâtres*, 20 December 1824).

60. E.g., *La Pandore*, 8 December 1824.

61. *Le Diable Boiteux*, 21 December 1824.

62. *La Lorgnette*, 30 December 1825.

sist of two letters dated 15 December 1825 and 4 January 1826, both from Weber in Dresden. Having received no reply from Castil-Blaze, Weber asked Schlesinger to put his case to Castil-Blaze and to obtain a written declaration that none of Weber's music, especially numbers from *Euryanthe,* would appear in forthcoming productions at the Odéon; if Castil-Blaze declined the invitation to make such a written declaration, then Schlesinger was to publish Weber's two letters in all the Parisian newspapers. Castil-Blaze did not respond to Schlesinger's approach (if he ever made it), and the two letters were duly published in January 1826.[63] Castil-Blaze responded in the *Journal des Débats* of 25 January 1826, and Schlesinger responded in turn, on Weber's behalf, on 28 January the same year.[64] The correspondence exemplifies well the shifting attitudes to authorial rights in the 1820s and the particular problems of foreign authors in Paris.

Weber clearly realized that there was not a great deal he could do about *Robin des bois;* by December 1825, it was already a year old. He did however think that he could head off Castil-Blaze's plans to incorporate parts of *Euryanthe* into a pasticcio to be mounted at the Odéon in early 1826, *La forêt de Sénart.* Weber believed that Castil-Blaze had illegally obtained the scores of the two works. He set out his position in both open letters:

> You obtained the score [of *Der Freischütz*] in an entirely illegal manner (however legal it may have appeared to you); since my opera has been neither engraved or published, no music seller had the right to sell it [15 December 1825].

> I have not yet sold my score [of *Euryanthe*] and no one in France has a copy. You have perhaps taken the parts you wish to use from a piano-vocal score. You do not have the right to cripple my music by introducing into it pieces whose accompaniments are of your own making [4 January 1826].[65]

More important than the questionable legitimacy of Castil-Blaze's access to Weber's music was the question of fees. In the first of the two published letters, Weber referred clearly to Castil-Blaze's keeping the composer's fees for himself. Furthermore, in the letter that Weber wrote to Schlesinger asking

63. Weber's letters are published in Jullien, *Weber à Paris,* 27–29. Rather than being published in all Parisian newspapers, they were placed only in *Le Corsaire* and *L'Étoile* (see Heidlberger, *Weber und Berlioz,* 480–81).

64. Jullien, *Weber à Paris,* 33–34.

65. Vous vous procurez la partition sur un chemin tout à fait illégitime (pour légitime peut-être qu'il vous a paru), car mon opéra n'étant ni gravé ni publié, aucun maître ni marchand de musique n'avaient le droit de le vendre. . . .

Je n'ai point vendu ma partition, et personne ne l'a en France; c'est peut-être sur une partition gravée pour piano que vous avez pris les morceaux dont vous voulez vous servir. Vous n'avez pas le droit d'estropier ma musique en y introduisant des morceaux dont les accompagnements sont de votre façon (ibid., 27–28).

the latter to have the two letters to Castil-Blaze published, Weber returned to the question of remuneration: "The French nation is too sensitive to the idea of justice to allow rights to go unnoticed for any longer and to allow the works of an artist, who considers himself honored by the good feeling that [the French have] already shown him, to be disfigured."[66] Castil-Blaze's response to Weber's public complaints can have excited little comment in Paris. His responses reiterated the status quo, were echoed in the press, and were familiar to followers of contemporary theatrical business. He made the point that all French music drama that was produced outside France appeared in a version modified to suit local conditions, and that even his own works, *De l'opéra en France* and the *Dictionnaire de musique moderne,* had been translated by German publishers without payment of any fee. He continued, "I recognized this right that they [Stoeppel and Trautweins] had to pirate my works, and I was even flattered by the preference that they gave them. But, in a revenge as frank as it was just, I helped myself in turn to things that Germany had abandoned. I bought at Mainz forty kilograms of scores, from which I took the part that appeared the most useful."[67]

Castil-Blaze's account of the premiere of *Robin des bois* is as accurate as can be determined. He claimed that he "resolved to change nothing of the music; I kept my word as far as the conventions of our stage would allow me. And what happened? Everyone knows. The work was booed and booed again. Seeing that the opera could not stand alone, I thought to *cripple* it [Castil-Blaze adopts Weber's term *estropier*], and I did it with such goodwill that since then it has gone at such a pace that one no longer knows if it will ever stop, and 154 performances have justified the work of the arranger." Finally, Castil-Blaze pointed out that the authorship of *Robin des bois* had never been concealed, and that Weber's name had been useful in promoting the work. Castil-Blaze observed that practice in London, for example, was to mount the works of Grétry, Méhul, and Boieldieu under the names of the arrangers. In his own eyes, Castil-Blaze would have done wrong if he had followed that English example.

Weber and the Odéon

In many respects, the public disagreement between Weber and Castil-Blaze was an exercise in ground-clearing before the former's own visit to Paris at the end of February 1826. This visit is well known for Weber's enthusiasm for Boieldieu's *Dame blanche,* an inconclusive discussion with Fétis, Berlioz's futile attempts to meet the composer, and Weber's studied avoidance of the

66. Ibid., 29–30.
67. Ibid.

Odéon and Castil-Blaze.[68] Public posturing of this sort was greatly at odds with the fact that Weber had been in communication with Pierre Crémont, the music director of the Odéon, since October 1825 and had planned while in Paris to meet Crémont to discuss various operatic projects.[69]

Three surviving letters from Weber to Crémont allow the reconstruction of a correspondence stretching from October 1825 until 13 April 1826. On 3 December Weber acknowledged receipt of a letter from Crémont dating from 26 October.[70] Weber accepted the conditions laid down in Crémont's October letter and asked the latter to make known Weber's plans to the rest of the Parisian theatrical world in order to prevent anyone else from mounting Weber's works in Paris. He was particularly anxious to avoid the possibility of Castil-Blaze putting on a complete production of *Euryanthe*.[71] Weber's second letter to Crémont dates from 7 January and reveals that it had been Crémont who suggested that Weber should write to Castil-Blaze (as he had of course done).[72] The final exchange dates from 13 April 1826; Weber was still in London and writing the day after the premiere of *Oberon*.[73] Weber refers back to a letter received from Crémont on 2 December 1825 in which the latter had suggested abandoning Sauvage as a literary collaborator: "In speaking to you of M. Sauvage, I did not think that I had the right to impose him on us for all the works that you will put on at the Odéon; there are other men of letters who can do much better than he."[74] Crémont was clearly acting duplicitously with regard both to Sauvage and Castil-Blaze in this correspondence. The prizes were perhaps worth the risk: a collaboration with Weber at the Odéon (almost certainly the reworking of *Preciosa* as *Les bohémiens*) and, much more attractive to Crémont, a Parisian production of *Oberon*. The overall tone of the letter of 13 April is rather more frosty than that of the earlier ones (Weber had, in the meantime not come off as well as he had hoped in the dispute with Castil-Blaze over *Robin des bois* and *La forêt de Sénart*); Weber's closing comment states explicitly his intention of concluding arrangements on his return to Paris, and that "finally, everything will be perfectly arranged by word of mouth after

68. Summaries are in Warrack, *Carl Maria von Weber*, 345–49; and Jullien, *Weber à Paris*, 36–56.

69. Jullien claimed that Weber had indeed met Crémont during his brief sojourn in Paris (*Weber à Paris*, 58).

70. The draft of the letter of 3 December 1825 is D-Bds WFN Handschriftliches XVI, fol. 89a^v.

71. Castil-Blaze eventually made an arrangement of *Euryanthe*, which was premiered at the Académie royale de musique in 1831. The material survives in F-Po A.497.a.i–iii.

72. D-Bds WFN Handschriftliches XVI, fol. 89b^r.

73. F-Pn L.a. CXI, fol. 184^r.

74. Ibid.

my arrival in Paris."[75] At this point, Weber was still planning on returning to Paris. It was not until the end of May that he wrote to his wife, Carolina, finally agreed to bypass Paris and to return home via Frankfurt.[76] Weber's death on 5 June definitively ended the Odéon's hopes of mounting a work with the composer himself in attendance.

As early as October 1825, *Der Freischütz* was clearly a dead letter as far as Weber was concerned. Even his public anxieties were more with *Euryanthe* than anything else. Crémont was obviously interested in the new— especially *Oberon*—and in December 1825, although the work was nowhere near complete, Weber was promising a copy to Crémont when they met in February the following year.[77] As it turned out, the most important works of Weber discussed by the composer and Crémont were *Preciosa* and *Silvana*, the material that went to make up the centerpiece of the 1826 plan, *Les bohémiens*.[78]

Beethoven

Public recognition of Ludwig van Beethoven in France began with the founding of the Société des Concerts du Conservatoire in 1828, and much of the credit for this importation of Beethoven's music is attributed to Habeneck. The first public concert was given on 9 March 1828 and included the *Eroica* Symphony; subsequent concerts presented the Fifth Symphony and, in 1831, the ninth.[79] Beethoven's music had been known in Paris since 1800, however. The *Journal de Paris* for 9 September 1800 carried a publisher's advertisement for his music, and by 1810 over forty works were listed in Parisian publisher's catalogues. Although works by Beethoven were rare—indeed almost nonexistent—in public concerts during the period, the composer's works were receiving sympathetic performances in less formal environments.[80] Habeneck himself wrote in his memoirs (published in 1840) that it had been thirty-eight years ago (i.e., in 1802) that he got to know Beethoven's early quartets, and that informal performances of the first

75. Enfin, tout s'arrangera parfaitement bien *verbalement,* après mon arrivez [*sic*] à Paris (ibid.).

76. Carl Weber, *Reise-briefe von Carl Maria von Weber an seine Gattin Carolina* (Leipzig: Dürr, 1886), 213–15 (letter of 29–30 May 1826).

77. D-Bds WFN Handschriftliches XVI, fol. 89a[v].

78. "If you have any remarks to make to me on other subjects, for example *Silvana, Preciosa* etc., your letters will reach me here until February" (Si vous avez quelque remarque à me faire encore sur d'autres objets par e[xemple] *Silvana, Preciosa* etc., vos lettres me trouveront ici jusqu'au mois de février [ibid.]).

79. Jean Mongrédien, *La musique en France des Lumières au Romantisme* (Paris: Flammarion, 1986), 314.

80. Ibid., 311.

two symphonies followed shortly after.[81] The influential quartet player Pierre-Marie-François de Sales Baillot reported successful quartet sessions based presumably on Beethoven's op. 18 quartets in June 1805.[82] By the end of the first decade of the nineteenth century, Beethoven was regularly on the Conservatoire's programs of the annual *exercices publiques* of its pupils: the first symphony in 1807 and the *Eroica* in 1811.[83] A review of his compositions published by Simrock appeared in the issue of the *Journal de Paris* for 1 December 1814; Beethoven was considered a serious rival to the Parisians' ne plus ultra of *la musique allemande:* Daniel Steibelt.[84]

Six months before the *Journal de Paris*'s review of his music, Beethoven's only complete music drama, in its third incarnation as *Fidelio, oder die eheliche Liebe,* had been premiered at the Kärntnertortheater in Vienna; it was launched—finally as it must have seemed to Beethoven—on its international career.[85] By 1820, *Fidelio* had been produced on stages from Munich to Saint Petersburg and from Vienna to Danzig. Its first performance in Paris was not until 30 May 1829 as part of a touring season of German music drama in its original language that was given at the Théâtre italien. *Fidelio* was nevertheless an essential thread in the German tradition at the Théâtre-Royal de l'Odéon, even though it was never performed there. The reasons for its promotion at that theater and subsequent abandonment throw further light on the reception of German works at the theater and figure as well in the growth of interest in Beethoven's larger musical structures throughout the 1820s that would result in the 1831 performance of the Ninth Symphony. *Fidelio* was otherwise almost entirely ignored before 1829, when it was performed by Joseph August Röckel's Théâtre allemand, and the only other large-scale work given any exposure in Paris during the decade was the Mass in C, op. 86, the "Benedictus" and "Agnus Dei" of which had been performed during the *concerts spirituels* of April 1824.[86]

Only three weeks before the Odéon's opening, the *Journal des Débats* gave a preview of works that were destined for production there.[87] Castil-Blaze had written the article as one of his *Chroniques musicales;* given the subsequent prominence of his arrangements at the Odéon, it is no surprise that he was remarkably well informed about the forthcoming repertory. The

---

81. Ibid.

82. Ibid.

83. Ibid., 312.

84. Ibid., 312–13.

85. The literature on *Leonore* and *Fidelio* is enormous. The best up-to-date summary is Douglas Johnson, "Fidelio," in *GroveOpera*, 2:182–87.

86. These concerts all took place at the Académie royale de musique, and parts of the Mass in C were performed on 12 April 1824 ("Benedictus") and 15 April 1824 ("Agnus Dei").

87. *Journal des Débats*, 4 April 1824.

works to look forward to were *Le barbier de Séville, Le sacrifice interrompu,* then *La pie voleuse, La dame du lac, Les noces de Figaro, Don Juan, Otello,* and so on. Castil-Blaze's following comment is revealing: *"Der Freischutz* and *Fidello* [*sic;* recte *Der Freischütz, Fidelio*) were the only operas of the German school; only the latter can be mounted at the Odéon because the former belongs to the Gymnase dramatique as the *Le chasseur noir."* Castil-Blaze must have been aware of many of the decisions concerning the advance planning for the Odéon repertory, and every other work that he listed was indeed mounted at the theater. In April 1824, the theater had every intention of including Beethoven's *Fidelio* as part of its repertory.

By autumn 1825 a performance of *Fidelio* at the Odéon was the subject of speculation in the press but had been completely abandoned by the beginning of 1826. As early as 9 September 1825, the *Journal de Paris* was announcing it as a forthcoming attraction. Two months later, the same newspaper listed a number of new productions: Weber's *Preciosa, Fidelio, La nymphe du Danube, Le gnôme* [Spohr's *Berggeist*], *Agnès Sorel* [Paër's *Agnese*], *La veuve de Malabar* [Spohr's *Jessonda*], Meyerbeer's *Marguerite d'Anjou,* Mozart's *Don Juan* and *La flûte enchantée.*[88] Significantly less accurate than Castil-Blaze's 1824 list, it includes a number of ghosts: neither work by Spohr was produced at the Odéon, and neither was Paër's *Agnese* or Mozart's *Zauberflöte.* The claim that *Fidelio* was soon to be produced was repeated on 15 and 20 December. Four days later, it was announced that Castil-Blaze's pasticcio *La forêt de Sénart* would be played before *Fidelio.* By 4 January *Le Frondeur* could report that *Fidelio* had been set aside and that Gyrowetz's *Jeune aveugle (Der Augenarzt)* had been put into rehearsal. *La forêt de Sénart* was premiered on 14 January 1826, and *La jeune aveugle* followed on 2 March the same year. The decision to abandon *Fidelio* seems therefore to have been made during December 1825 and publicized in the New Year.

The surviving sources from 1825 to 1826 support the view that plans for a production of *Fidelio* were well advanced before they were abandoned. Both the 1806 and 1814 productions of *Leonore/Fidelio* had been followed by publications of vocal scores, the latter prepared by Ignaz Moscheles. Although manuscript full scores of the 1814 *Fidelio* must have been circulating all over German-speaking states in the decade after its premiere, the first published full score was associated with the aborted production at the Odéon. It was published by Farrenc, who was also responsible for at least part of the arrangement.[89] The title page of the piano-vocal score reveals

88. *Journal de Paris,* 14 November 1825.

89. *Fidelio: drame lyrique en trois actes* (Paris: Farrenc, n.d.). Farrenc also published a piano-vocal score made up of a series of extracts; their plate numbers are A.F.82 A to A.F.82 Q. In addition to a thematic catalogue, the composite publication contains a four-hand arrangement

the pseudonym of one of the translators—Camus, known as Merville—but is tantalizingly elusive about the author of the Italian translation supplied with the piano-vocal version of Farrenc's publication.

The publication history of Farrenc's scores ties in closely with what is known of the attempts to produce *Fidelio* in 1825 and 1826; an examination of the productions of Farrenc's publishing business from August 1825 to May 1826 shows that the extracts of *Fidelio* in piano-vocal score were advertised on 14 January 1826, in the wake of the feverish speculation about the production of the piece at the Odéon. They could not therefore have been published later than 14 January 1826, but (because the previous occasion on which Farrenc had advertised his publications was 29 October the previous year), the extracts could have been put on sale any time between the two dates. Farrenc usually did not wait until a large number of publications were ready before advertisement but rather promoted single works as they were published (the entries for 10 September 1825 represent an exception), so it is tempting to place the publication of the *Fidelio* extracts closer to 14 January 1826 than to 29 October 1825. Hence the publication of the extracts was probably planned, as was normal, to coincide with the production at the Odéon.

Farrenc's arrangement of the full score of *Fidelio* specifically mentions a premiere at the Odéon but leaves out the exact date.[90] It was therefore offered for sale at a time either when the Odéon production had not yet been abandoned (but the date for a premiere not yet set) or when the production had been aborted but after the printing of the title pages. The edition carries the plate number A.F.72 and was put on sale while the publisher was trading from the boulevard Poissonnière address; what must have happened is that the *Fidelio* full-score project was begun between 24 September 1825 and 8 October 1825, at which point the plate number was assigned. The project was many times larger than any of the others undertaken in the second half of 1825 or the first half of 1826 and would have taken much longer to complete. As in the case of the piano-vocal score, the full-score must have been prepared around the same time as the Odéon pro-

---

of the overture by Johann Nepomuk Hummel, another of Farrenc's published composers. For a partial account of the Farrenc full score see Jean Mongrédien, "À propos des premières éditions françaises de *Fidelio*," in *Musique, signes, images: liber amicorum François Lesure*, ed. Joël-Marie Fauquet (Geneva: Minkoff, 1988), 207–16. The claim that Castil-Blaze's arrangement of the work was conceived before 1825 and was associated with the Odéon (ibid., 209 and 213) rests on no evidence whatsoever but serves as a pretext for the author to traduce Castil-Blaze in just the way described earlier in this chapter.

90. This was not an uncommon practice. See Castil-Blaze's edition of *Le barbier de Séville* (discussed in my "Lindoro in Lyon: Rossini's *Le Barbier de Séville*," *Acta musicologica* 44 [1992]: 57–58).

duction and corroborates the chronological data offered by the contemporary press.[91]

It was relatively rare for a work to go quite this far at the Odéon and then to be abandoned. Reasons for the collapse of the *Fidelio* project lie not with the music or the translation of its texts but with the literary tradition of the libretto. No libretto printed either in 1825 or 1826 survives. Probably none was ever supposed to exist because the work was designed to use the text— or a close variant thereof—for the libretto of Beethoven's *Fidelio* and *Leonore*'s original source: Jean-Nicolas Bouilly's *Léonore;* this is the libretto that had been set by Pierre Gaveaux and first performed at the Théâtre Feydeau in 1798.[92] The evidence for the use of Bouilly's libretto in 1825–26 is slight but compelling. Of the two copies of the full score in the Bibliothèque nationale, one (F-Pn D.787) has manuscript *répliques* added at the beginning of each of ten numbers; of these, eight match Bouilly's libretto exactly. Given the regular inconsistency between the exact wording of the libretti and texting in full and piano-vocal scores, the fact that they do not all match has little significance. Given also the fact the next production in French of *Fidelio* was at the Théâtre-Lyrique in 1860 (in an entirely different translation by Jules Barbier and Michel-Florentin Carré), the Odéon production was the only opportunity to use Beethoven's score and Bouilly's libretto together.

The problem with Bouilly's libretto was that it was not in the public domain and therefore fell outside the Odéon license. Gaveaux had died as recently as the beginning of 1825 in the lunatic asylum at Charenton, where he had been incarcerated since 1819; Bouilly was not only still alive but was writing libretti throughout the 1820s; his last work was a collaboration with Scribe on Boieldieu's last staged work, *Les deux nuits,* and he did not die until 1842 at the age of eighty. The Odéon therefore had no automatic right to the libretto. Bouilly's longevity might explain the collapse of the Odéon project as well as the absence of a translation of *Fidelio* on the French stage until after mid century. It may even be responsible for the otherwise strange inclusion of an Italian translation in the piano-vocal score.

91. In describing the Farrenc full score of *Fidelio,* Georg Kinsky (*Das Werk Beethovens: thematisch-bibliographisches Verzeichnis seiner sämtlicher vollendeten Kompositionen,* completed and ed. Hans Halm [Munich, 1955], 186) cites an issue with the publication price of Fr 125 and a publication address of 21 rue St-Marc, incorrectly stating that it predates the issue discussed in this chapter (with the price of Fr 80 and the boulevard Poissonnière address).The price increase and Farrenc's occupancy of premises in the rue St-Marc from December 1831 until May 1836 (Devriès-Lesure, *Dictionnaire,* 2:169) confirm the sequence.

92. *Léonore ou L'amour conjugal: fait historique* (Paris: Barba, 1798). For the fullest account of the background to Bouilly's libretto, see David Charlton, "The French Theatrical Origins of *Fidelio,*" in *Ludwig van Beethoven: Fidelio,* ed. Paul Robinson (Cambridge: Cambridge University Press, 1996), 51–67.

The most curious part of this story is how the *Fidelio* project came about in the first place. In the wake of the popularity of French translations of German music drama and *Robin des bois* in particular, the project must have begun in ignorance of the relationship between Bouilly's libretto and Beethoven's music. If the work had been described as *Léonore,* the penny might have dropped sooner. Alternatively, Merville could well have been only the author of the text of the sung items, in which case the anonymity of the other translator listed on the title page of the piano-vocal score might have been an attempt to conceal the authorship of Bouilly himself. Once the existence of the original French libretto had been recognized, Bouilly could have been persuaded to collaborate with the Odéon on the *Fidelio* project by reworking the libretto so as to sidestep the theater's problem with its license. Sewrin would do something similar with *Emmeline ou La famille Suisse* in 1827, although this was a rather more complex case. Bouilly, for whatever reason, did not collaborate with Merville, Farrenc, and the administration of the Odéon. Whether it was for personal or contractual reasons is not known. Of Bouilly's three previous works, *Valentine de Milan* (Étienne-Nicolas Méhul, completed by Louis-Joseph Daussoigne-Méhul, 1822), *Jenny la bouquetière* (Frédéric Kreubé and Pradher, 1823), and *Agnès Sorel* (Auguste-Philippe-Marie-Ghislain Peellaert, also 1823), two had been for the Opéra-Comique and the third (*Agnès Sorel*) had been for a production in Brussels with music by a non-French composer; Bouilly's connections with the Opéra-Comique (the Odéon's main rival) may therefore have been behind his refusal to collaborate. Alternatively, his lack of sympathy with any music beyond French boundaries may also have prevented his collaboration.[93]

One can only speculate on the effect of a production of *Fidelio* at the end of 1825 or in early 1826. Certainly, composers from German speaking lands—Weber and all the composers discussed in this chapter—carried with them the automatic charge of writing *musique savante* and challenging the French tradition of melody with harmonic daring.[94] It is possible that Beethoven would have fared worse than his compatriots, especially his older contemporaries. In addition, once the production had been reviewed, the story would have suffered from its archaic (for 1825–26) rescue-opera plot. Yet the dialogue would at least have been based on a French model, unlike

---

93. Bouilly's memoirs illlustrate his preference for French music: "The skillful melodies of the Italian School could not make me forget the dramatic expression of French music, to which I owed my most worthy success" (La savante mélodie de l'école italienne ne pouvait me faire oublier l'expression dramatique de la musique française à laquelle je devais mes succès les plus honorables [Jean-Nicolas Bouilly, *Mes récapitulations* (Paris: Janet, 1836–37), 3:371]; translation quoted in David Galliver, "Jean-Nicolas Bouilly [1763–1842], Successor of Sédaine," *Studies in Music* 13 [1979]: 28). Bouilly does not mention the Odéon plans to mount *Fidelio* during his lifetime or German music in general.

94. Mongrédien, *Musique en France,* 312–13.

Robin des bois or *Le sacrifice interrompu*. Beethoven's music had to wait until after the composer's death before the Société des Concerts du Conservatoire put his orchestral music on the map. The prognosis for *Fidelio* in translation, as the Odéon put away their Farrenc vocal scores, looked bleak.

Viennese Musicians and the Kärntnertortheater

Conradin Kreutzer

Conradin Kreutzer was a Parisian resident during the years 1827–29 and was the only composer to write a successful new opéra comique for the Odéon.[95] Kreutzer had been musical director of the Kärntnertortheater in Vienna since December 1822; he had been given the appointment on the basis of the success of his *Libussa* earlier the same year by Domenico Barbaja, who in turn had become the lessee of the theater in December 1821. Fétis claimed that Kreutzer left Vienna for Paris after Barbaja's contract ran out,[96] although Kreutzer seems not to have left until 1827. Barbaja's contract had expired at the end of March 1825, the theater had been run by others for a year, and Barbaja was back as lessee from April 1826 onward.[97] It is more likely that the stimulus for Kreutzer to leave Vienna was the French season that ran from July 1826 to April 1827; this run of ballets, opéras comiques, and vaudevilles might have seemed a less congenial musical environment than the period up to the end of Barbaja's first period as lessee.[98]

Kreutzer was responsible for two works at the Odéon: the new one-act opéra comique, *L'eau de jouvence*, and an arrangement of an earlier romantic opera as *La folle de Glaris*. *La folle de Glaris* was premiered at the Odéon on 21 April 1827 and was an arrangement of Kreutzer's *Adèle von Budoy*, first given in Königsberg in 1821 and revived, as *Cordelia*, at the Kärntnertortheater in 1823. Unfortunately, no score (full or piano-vocal) survives of *La folle de Glaris*, so it is impossible to test the claims of the critic who said that the arranger of *Cordelia* had included music by another composer alongside

---

95. Much of the currently available biographical information concerning Kreutzer (Peter Branscombe, "Kreutzer, Conradin," *The New Grove Dictionary of Music and Musicians*, ed. Stanley Sadie [London: Macmillan, 1980] 10:262–64; Wolfgang Rehm, "Kreutzer, Conradin," *Die Musik in Geschichte und Gegenwart: allgemeine Enzyklopädie der Musik* [Kassel: Bärenreiter-Verlag, 1949–79], 7:1776) depends on the entry in *FétisB* 5:112.

96. Ibid.

97. Franz Hadamowsky, *Wien: Theater Geschichte von den Anfängen bis zum Ende des ersten Weltkriegs* (Vienna: Jugend und Volk, 1988), 264.

98. Ibid.; see also idem, *Die Wiener Hoftheater (Staatstheater), 1776–1966: Verzeichnis der aufgeführten Stücke mit Bestandsnachweis und täglichem Spielplan* (Vienna: Prachner, 1966–75), 2:ix.

Kreutzer's.[99] The libretto certainly mentions Jérôme Payer as one of the composers, and Fétis went as far as attributing the work to him. Payer had worked in Amsterdam during 1824 and had moved to Paris at the end of 1825; he worked as a concert artist, promoted the Physharmonica, and— again according to Fétis—directed the orchestra of the German theater's third season in Paris in 1831. Shortly after Kreutzer returned to the Kärntnertortheater in 1829, Payer returned to Vienna as director of music at the Josephstadttheater.[100] Whether Kreutzer had arrived in Paris by the time of the premiere of *La folle de Glaris* is difficult to judge, but he must have spent most of the central part of the year there because the product of that summer's work was *L'eau de jouvence,* premiered at the Odéon on 13 October 1827. Sources for *L'eau de jouvence* consist of a censor's libretto, a printed libretto, five printed extracts in piano-vocal score, and, most important, a manuscript full score of the complete work.[101] Now in the fonds du Conservatoire in the Bibliothèque nationale, this manuscript was acquired between April and June 1866.[102] It matches perfectly with the printed libretto: all the *répliques* correspond exactly, and the *rondeau* "Puissance invincible" (no. 7), which is crossed through and marked "passer" in the manuscript full score, is omitted from the printed libretto. *La folle de Glaris* received five performances and *L'eau de jouvence* ten. They were far from being the least successful works at the Odéon during the 1820s, but Parisian indifference may have been at least in part a reason for Kreutzer's subsequent return to Vienna.

Vienna

Connections between the repertory of German music drama performed at the Odéon during the 1820s and the Kärntnertortheater in Vienna are strong. In addition to the works already discussed in this chapter, Winter's *Das unterbrochene Opferfest* was translated as *Le sacrifice interrompu,* Gyrowetz's *Der Augenarzt* appeared as *La jeune aveugle,* and Weigl's *Die Schweizerfamilie* was given as *Emmeline ou La famille suisse* at the Odéon during the period 1824–28.

Three of the original composers of Odéon arrangements had been mu-

99. *La Pandore,* 22 April 1827.
100. *FétisB* 6:472–73.
101. The censors' libretto is F-Pan F^{18} 614/174; the work received the censors' visa on 4 October 1827. The printed libretto is *L'eau de jouvence: opéra-comique en un acte* (Paris: Duvernois, 1827). There are two surviving sources for the piano-vocal score containing four and five numbers respectively: F-Po ♭ 1629 and F-Pn Vm^5 1611. The title page of the first of the extracts in the copy in F-Po is no. 2/*L'eau de jouvence: opéra-comique en un acte* (Paris: Farrenc, n.d.).
102. F-Pn D.3100.

sical director at the Kärntnertortheater itself. Weigl had been assistant director from 1795–1804 and director from 1804 to 1805. He was succeeded by Gyrowetz, who in turn was succeeded by Kreutzer in 1821.[103] Both Winter's *Das unterbrochene Opferfest* and Beethoven's *Fidelio* had been written or rewritten specifically for the Kärntnertortheater.[104] Of the works not composed by residents of Vienna, *Der Freischütz* had been premiered at the Kärntnertortheater in 1821, and Kreutzer's *Cordelia* was a Viennese reworking of a Königsberg original.[105] Almost all the German music dramas mounted at the Odéon, if they had not been recently composed for, or premiered in, Vienna, were subject to revivals at the Kärntnertortheater during the 1820s and had been long-running successes. The only exception to this pattern is Weber's *Preciosa,* whose anomalous nature means that it could not have been mounted at the Kärntnertortheater in any case. Productions of Wolff's play with Weber's music had however taken place at the Theater an der Wien in July 1823 and at the Burgtheater in June 1825 (table 11).

Further works mentioned in connection with the Odéon included Mozart's *Zauberflöte.* It had been revived in Vienna in 1818[106] and, furthermore, was already well known in Paris. The two Spohr works were referred to by the titles by which they would have been known had they been produced at the Odéon: *La veuve de Malabar* (*Jessonda*) and *Le gnôme* (*Der Berggeist*); in the case of *La veuve de Malabar,* this was also the title of the original French source for the libretto. These last two works had been premiered in Kassel in 1823 and 1825 respectively but *Jessonda,* for example, would not receive a performance in Vienna until 1836. If the Viennese connection for all the German works performed at the Odéon is significant, it may well explain why the Spohr works never appeared in Paris in the 1820s.

Despite these close correlations, the search for a single conduit through which Viennese compositions passed to Paris is probably futile. Amalia Schütz had obtained a copy of the score of *Cordelia* to serve as the basis of *La folle de Glaris,* and she may have encouraged Kreutzer to move to Paris. She may also have been associated with the production of Weigl's *Schweizerfamilie* at the Odéon. However much Schütz may have had to do with French translations of German music drama at the Odéon in 1827, she clearly had nothing to do with them before then. Indeed, in the correspondence between Crémont and Sauvage concerning the transformation of *Preciosa* into *Les bohémiens,* it is clear that it was Sauvage who had obtained a full score of *Preciosa.* Such an ability must raise questions about the route by which other

103. Hadamowsky, *Wien: Theater Geschichte,* 358.

104. The 1805 and 1806 productions of *Leonore* had of course been mounted at the Theater an der Wien.

105. Hadamowsky, *Wiener Hoftheater,* 607 and 608.

106. Ibid., 606.

TABLE 11. Viennese compositions at the Théâtre-Royal de l'Odéon, 1824–28

Author, Title	Odéon Premiere	Vienna Premiere	Notes
Winter, *Das unterbrochene Opferfest*	21 October 1824	Kärntnertortheater, 1798	Revival in Vienna, October 1820
Weber, *Der Freischütz*	7 December 1824	Kärntnertortheater, 1821	Berlin premiere
Weber, *Preciosa*	17 November 1825 23 November 1826	—	Berlin premiere
Gyrowetz, *Der Augenarzt*	2 March 1826	Kärntnertortheater, 1811	
Weigl, *Die Schweizerfamilie*	6 February 1827	Kärntnertortheater, 1809	
Kreutzer, *Cordelia*	21 April 1827	Kärntnertortheater, 1823	As *Adèle von Budoy*, premiered in Königsberg
Kreutzer, *L'eau de jouvence*	13 October 1827	—	Original composition for Odéon
Beethoven, *Fidelio*	None, but a production planned	Kärntnertortheater, 1814	1805–6 productions of *Leonore* for Theater an der Wien
Mozart, *Die Zauberflöte*	None, but a production planned	Theater an der Wien, 1791	
Spohr, *Jessonda*	None, but a production planned	—	Kassel premiere, 1823
Spohr, *Der Berggeist*	None, but a production planned	—	Kassel premiere, 1825

Weber full scores found their way to the Odéon—*Der Freischütz* in particular. If Sauvage could have obtained copies of *Preciosa,* it seems entirely reasonable that he could just as easily have obtained the full score of *Der Freischütz* as could have, for example, Castil-Blaze.[107]

It is tempting to see the French seasons in Vienna as a corollary to the presence of German music drama at the Odéon and to draw conclusions about lines of transmission. The lines of connection between Vienna and the Odéon were strong, Kreutzer had worked there, and Weber had planned to. The reality is that, although the connections with Vienna certainly shaped the nature of the German repertory at the Odéon, they changed regularly and were the results of fortune and circumstance. The chronological range of the German works appropriated by the Odéon was narrow in comparison with that of Italian ones, and for all the success of music drama from beyond the Rhine, it was *Robin des bois* that forced German romanticism on the consciousness of Parisian opera audiences.

It is difficult to tell whether there was anything more than a fortuitous connection between the Odéon and the Kärntnertortheater: the evidence is allusive more than compelling. In striking contrast, *Fidelio* came very close to changing the reception of Beethoven in France. With music drama in the mix of genres under contemplation by Parisian romantics, alongside the symphonies and—to a lesser degree—the chamber music, the image of Beethoven might have looked very different by 1830. Critical responses since 1805 to *Leonore* and *Fidelio* have been contradictory, however, and it is by no means certain that a production of the latter at the Odéon in 1826 would have enhanced the composer's reputation by the beginning of the next decade. The impact of the work in German in 1829 to 1831 (it was played in all three of Röckel's seasons) was not as great as if it had been performed by a Parisian operatic institution and was much overshadowed by the works of Weber.

Music drama by Weber makes up half of the number of German works mounted at the Odéon, and *Robin des bois* has been a touchstone not merely for past misunderstanding of the theater's activities but also for the view that such works should be protected from rehabilitation to very different theatrical, dramatic, and musical conditions. The case of *Robin des bois* is so complex and so firmly entrenched in the musicological psyche, that its discussion requires the level of detail given here. What emerges is a more polychrome picture of the issue of musical autonomy than the black and

107. Yet it seems almost perverse to assume that Castil-Blaze's 40 kg of music bought in Mainz did not include *Der Freischütz.*

white image derived from Berlioz. Weber's enthusiasm for working at the Odéon—his best chance of getting some sort of performance in Paris—is clear from recently discovered correspondence, and his concerns—unlike those of Berlioz—were primarily financial. In the context of the commitment on the part of the Odéon management and its music staff to give a logical home to foreign music drama, Berlioz's complaints begin to look like the sort of intransigence that would have kept Weber out of Parisian musical and dramatic thinking for a generation. Indeed, he himself might not have encountered *Der Freischütz* before his visits to German-speaking states.

Conclusion

For a little over four years in the middle of the 1820s, the Théâtre-Royal de l'Odéon commanded a position in Parisian operatic culture that was second to none. The vogue for Rossini was beginning to diminish at the Théâtre italien, the Académie royale de musique had yet to receive a musical and aesthetic injection from *La muette de Portici, Guillaume Tell,* and *Robert le diable,* and the Opéra-Comique was suffering from severe financial and administrative problems that would result in intermittent closure at the end of the decade. Capitalizing on difficulties elsewhere in the city, the Théâtre-Royal de l'Odéon managed to carve out a position in Parisian stage music that was completely at odds with its disadvantageous geographical position in the faubourg St-Germain and its unfavorable administrative status as the Second Théâtre-Français. The Odéon successfully ran separate troupes for comedy, tragedy, and music drama and on several occasions—despite strict governmental control over its repertory—mounted performances that seduced audiences from the Théâtre italien and the Académie royale de musique.

The Odéon was a royal institution embedded in an administrative network that depended ultimately on the monarch; the regulation of this structure fixed the relations between all royal theaters in a way that controlled many aspects of their day-to-day running from the time that cleaners had to be out of a building right up to the sorts of music drama for each to perform and the amount of each subvention. It is difficult to overestimate the importance of the control exercised by the maison du Roi, most clearly expressed in the terms under which each of the Odéon's three managers worked. At one level the history of the theater from 1824 to 1828 consists of a series of attempts to renegotiate aspects of its license and contests with other theaters (most notably the Opéra-Comique) where the licenses of two theaters came close to overlap.

The operatic repertory of the Odéon in the 1820s fell into three categories: opéra comique in the public domain, occasional works and pasticci, and translated music drama. The theater put on fifty-six new operatic productions, at the rate of rather over one a month. This total included twenty-four opéras comiques that were already in the public domain and sixteen translations of complete foreign music drama; the rest of the new productions were of pasticci or works for such special occasions as the opening of the theater, the coronation of Charles X in 1825, or the monarch's name day. Artistic policy never swerved from its trust in novelty and vigorously promoted works by foreign composers unknown in the capital; Rossini, Weber, and Meyerbeer were the most successful beneficiaries of this policy. This search for novelty extended to opéra comique in the public domain as well; as soon as works fell into this category—usually as a result of the death of a composer or librettist—the Odéon would put in train plans to produce them.

Whatever the origins of the music drama mounted at the Odéon, works were all transformed—as contemporaries put it—*en opéra comique:* in other words, modified in order to alternate French-texted music with spoken dialogue in the same language. *Recitativo semplice* and the Italian and German languages were not permitted. To describe such works as Rossini's *Gazza ladra* or *Il barbiere di Siviglia,* Weigl's *Schweizerfamilie,* or Weber's *Freischütz* as opéras comiques merely because they were translated into French, offends against modern understandings of the conventions that govern *melodramma, commedia,* singspiel, or *romantische Oper.* Yet the absence of the equivalent of *la solita forma* within the compositional conventions of opéra comique meant that the transformation of foreign stage music in this way was largely unproblematic and the accommodation of both German and Italian models relatively straightforward. Nevertheless, the types of modification found are very much what might be expected: the simple strophic number from singspiel was merely translated whereas the complex Italian duet tended to lose its tempo di mezzo and repeats of its cabaletta. The most striking changes, however, resulted from a commitment on the part of most of the arrangers active at the Odéon to return to any French literary work that might have served as the basis for a foreign libretto; in these cases, the original French narrative was preferred to any translation of the Italian or German libretto, and the result was often a resequencing of the original music in addition to smaller-scale changes.

Two characteristics set the Odéon apart from other royal theaters. It was required to support troupes for comedy and tragedy as well as music drama and to perform all three types most nights of the week. True, the Académie royale de musique simultaneously mounted productions of grand opéra and ballet, but it was open only three nights out of seven. Its maximum number of works per week was six, as compared to the Odéon's twenty-one. Furthermore, the Odéon was located only just within the city walls and at a distance from the capital's main centers of operatic activity; it consequently served as a cultural focus for a neighborhood characterized by the large student population of the Schools of Medicine and Law. Artists lived locally for the most part and the theater offered both direct and indirect employment in the faubourg St-Germain. These qualities gave a particular flavor to audiences at the Odéon, and from a methodological point of view, make them easy to identify and differentiate from, for example, the audience at the Théâtre italien. The audiences were attentive and exhibited a high degree of musical and theatrical engagement. Perhaps the most striking illustration of this level of commitment is the collaboration between audience and manager that came close to banishing the claque from the theater's parterre, the first and only Parisian theater so to do. Attendance soared when the Odéon's management hit on a production that elicited more than purely local interest; *Robin des bois* is an excellent but by no means isolated example.

Many composers represented at the Odéon made little lasting impression on French operatic history. Winter, Gyrowetz, Weigl, and Conradin Kreutzer were rarely heard after the Odéon disbanded its opera troupe; when Röckel's itinerant German opera company gave three short seasons during the summers of 1829 to 1831, the 1830 season offered music drama by these composers but none of the productions were successful. The case of Mozart is perhaps the most difficult to judge; given the relatively slight impact that the composer's works made at the Odéon, his later success rests at least as much on his cultivation at the Théâtre italien or, however short-lived, at the Académie royale de musique. Although Rossini was a staple at the Odéon, it is difficult to make any claim that successes at the Odéon were of greater significance than those at the Théâtre italien or, for *Le comte Ory* and *Guillaume Tell,* at the Opéra. Weber's music, by contrast, had been put on the Parisian map for the first time by the success of *Robin des bois.* Less than a year after the Odéon's closure, Röckel's Opéra allemand began a series of seasons that would encompass *Der Freischütz, Oberon,* and—just after its production in French at the Académie royale de musique—*Euryanthe.* The subsequent fate of Weber in Paris was fitful: *Robin des bois* appeared at the Opéra-Comique in January 1835 in Castil-Blaze's arrangement but without the duet from *Euryanthe* and was followed by Berlioz's production of *Der Freischütz* at the Opéra in 1841; when the same work reappeared at the Théâtre-Lyrique in 1855 it was still in Castil-Blaze's and Sauvage's version known from the Odéon; although modified in a way that reinstated the major cuts and changes, it ran for nearly a decade before a new production attempted to return to Weber's original score and a new translation.

The greatest legacy that the Odéon offered Parisian stage music was the legitimacy of music drama in translation. It systematically promoted translation and evolved conventions governing its practice. Eventually other theaters would follow its lead: the Théâtre de la Renaissance in 1838–40 and the Théâtre-Lyrique in 1851–70. The Théâtre de la Renaissance gave a home to works by such indigenous composers as François-Louis Hippolyte Monpou and Albert Grisar, as well as laureates of the Prix de Rome, and proposed translations of Italian and German opera alongside new works by foreign composers. It put on a successful translation of Donizetti's *Lucia di Lammermoor* and was—at Meyerbeer's behest—considering a translation of Richard Wagner's *Liebesverbot*. Where it went beyond the Odéon was in actively encouraging new works by foreign composers. Friedrich Adolph Ferdinand Freiherr von Flotow was an important figure, both in collaborations with others and in his own *Naufrage de la Méduse*. Wagner's *Défense d'amour* was pretty well a new work when he proposed its translation (its composer would have been happy to swap the single catastrophic performance of *Das Liebesverbot* in Magdeburg in March 1836 with the sort of success Donizetti or Flotow enjoyed at the Théâtre de la Renaissance), Donizetti wrote *L'ange de Nisida* for the theater (it turned into *La favorite*) and there is evidence to suggest that Meyerbeer's projected completion of Weber's *Drei Pintos* might make an appearance there. Almost entirely absent from the repertory of the Théâtre de la Renaissance was the music of the past. Apart from a few fragmentary performances of Rossini's *Barbier de Séville* (in a French translation but presumably with accompanied recitatives, although the use of Castil-Blaze's translation or simply Beaumarchais's play cannot be ruled out), all the opera at the theater was new. There was not a note of Weber or Mozart, and its license forbade the production of opéra comique of any age. The resulting repertory was startling in its novelty but unsustainable in practice, and the theater abandoned music drama in early 1840.

By contrast, the Théâtre-Lyrique looked back to the past in much the same way as had the Odéon; its repertory mixed the new with works by Mozart, Beethoven, and Weber (Rossini, apart from the evergreen *Barbier de Séville,* was barely represented) as well as a smattering of opéra comique by Boieldieu, Carafa, Dalayrac, Devienne, Grétry, and Hérold. It also mounted productions of Verdi's *Rigoletto, La traviata, Macbeth,* and *Un ballo in maschera,* and of Wagner's *Rienzi,* eight years after the notorious Paris premiere of *Tannhäuser.* By the 1860s, when the licensing system was finally coming to an end, the Théâtre-Lyrique was probably better known for the premieres of such new works as Charles Gounod's *Faust* and *Roméo et Juliette,* Berlioz's *Troyens à Carthage,* and Georges Bizet's *Pêcheurs de perles.*

The Académie royale de musique started mounting translations of Rossini just two years after the Odéon had embarked on the same project. Such a tradition, of inviting foreign composers to mount French adaptations of their music drama at the Académie royale de musique, would continue with Donizetti's *Martyrs/Poliuto* (1840), Verdi's *Jérusalem/I lombardi alla prima crociata* (1847), and Wagner's *Tannhäuser* (1861). Both Italian composers would have a significant impact on the Parisian world of music drama, writing new works for the Académie royale de musique (*Dom Sébastien* in 1843) and the Académie impériale de musique (*Don Carlos* in 1867), but Wagner was unwilling to repeat the experiment of the 1861 *Tannhäuser*. The Odéon's influence could be seen in two productions from the decade after it closed: Weber's *Euryanthe* (1831) and Mozart's *Don Giovanni* (1834); it is no surprise that both involved—one way or another—Castil-Blaze. The 1831 production of *Euriante,* as it was called in translation, was the culmination of Castil-Blaze's efforts to get one of his arrangements mounted at the Académie royale de musique, and the 1834 *Don Juan* leaned heavily on his version of the work heard at the Odéon. In comparison with these two productions from the 1830s, the levels of arrangement found in works at the Odéon seems modest: in *Euriante,* most of the second act and all of the third is more or less rewritten, and four numbers from *Oberon* and one from Meyerbeer's *Crociato in Egitto* are interpolated into the musical fabric. *Don Juan* was configured as a five-act grand opéra (carrying the 1834 season in a way that Auber's *Gustave III* had in 1833 and Halévy's *Juive* would in 1835), with substantial cuts, and the inclusion of a chorus from *Die Entführung aus dem Serail,* entr'actes based on works as varied as the *Jupiter* Symphony, Symphony no. 39, and "Soave sia il vento" from *Così fan tutte;* the work closed with an epilogue based on "O voto tremendo" from *Idomeneo* and the "Dies irae" from the *Requiem* and featuring the corps de ballet.

The Odéon's bequest to Parisian operatic culture engendered a context for the reception of foreign music drama. Although there had been traces of attempts to acclimatize German stage music to Parisian operatic practice before 1824, most notably *Les mystères d'Isis,* the practice had never been institutionalized in the same way as it was at the Odéon. Similarly, although Italian music drama in its original language had its home at the Théâtre italien, earlier attempts at producing translations had been rare and did not benefit from the institutional structures that the Odéon and its successors enjoyed. The Odéon may have mounted operatic productions for only a little over four years, but it made a significant impact on the music drama of the Bourbon Restoration and set up institutional paradigms for music drama in translation that would be replicated throughout the nineteenth century.

Such productions as *Euriante* and *Don Juan* show that the friction between contrasting aesthetic standpoints—the adherence to textual authenticity and authorial coherence opposed to the free association of music-dramatic materials—continued well beyond the Odéon's demise in 1828. The theater's history of music drama gives ample evidence that large sections of the Parisian press and public did not share the judgments passed by Berlioz on the activities of the theater and *Robin des bois* in particular. But there is also a certain amount of evidence that interference with the work of composers who were rapidly becoming enmeshed in canonic discourses was deplored. In the field of instrumental music, where the status of a text is more easily identified than in music drama, these new aesthetic views gained ground quickly. Yet in productions of various sorts of music drama throughout the nineteenth century the aesthetic values of the Bourbon Restoration lasted far longer than many of their detractors would like to think.

The Odéon gave a home to music drama during the 1820s, and the decade saw its origins, rise, and fall as an opera house. The web of culture in which the theater and its activities rest allows not only an opportunity to consider such relations as those of the librettist and his career, or the orchestral player and the arrangement of works for the Odéon, but also a chance to explore how these relations changed within a closed diachronic frame. To an extent, this is true of individual regimes at the other theaters—Louis-Désiré Véron at the Académie royale de musique or Louis Viardot at the Théâtre italien—but changes of manager rarely involved the large-scale changes of personnel, repertory, and artistic policy that occurred at the Odéon in 1824 and 1828. Neither the Académie royale de musique at the beginning of the 1830s nor the Théâtre italien at their end offers a genuine point of departure for an institutional comparison.

APPENDIX ONE

The Théâtre-Royal de l'Odéon: Consolidated Repertory

Date of Premiere	Title	Composer/Librettist[a]	Category	Original Title; Composer/Librettist	Premiere
27 April 1824	Les trois genres	François-Adrien Boieldieu, Daniel-François-Esprit Auber/Eugène Scribe	occasional		
6 May 1824	Le barbier de Séville ou La précaution inutile	Castil-Blaze (François-Henri-Joseph Blaze)/Cesare Sterbini	translation	Il barbiere di Siviglia; Gioachino Rossini/Cesare Sterbini	20 February 1816, Rome, Teatro Argentina
13 May 1824	Le tableau parlant	André-Ernest-Modeste Grétry/Louis Anseaume	ancien répertoire		20 September 1769, Comédie-Italienne[b]
16 May 1824	La fausse magie	Grétry/Jean-François Marmontel	ancien répertoire		1 February 1775, Comédie-Italienne
18 May 1824	L'épreuve villageoise	Grétry/Pierre-Jean-Baptiste Choudard Desforges	ancien répertoire		24 June 1784, Comédie-Italienne
26 May 1824	Le tonnelier	Nicolas-Médard Audinot	ancien répertoire		28 September 1761, Opéra-Comique
27 May 1824	Richard Coeur-de-Lion	Grétry/Michel-Jean Sédaine	ancien répertoire		2 October 1784, Opéra-Comique
1 June 1824	Ambroise ou Voilà ma journée	Nicolas-Marie Dalayrac/Jacques-Marie Boutet de Monvel	ancien répertoire		12 January 1793, Comédie-Italienne
5 June 1824	Les folies amoureuses	Castil-Blaze	pasticcio		1 March 1823, Lyon, Grand Théâtre
18 June 1824	Zémire et Azor	Grétry/Marmontel	ancien répertoire		9 November 1771, Fontainebleau

(continued)

The Théâtre-Royal de l'Odéon: Consolidated Repertory (continued)

Date of Premiere	Title	Composer / Librettist[a]	Category	Original Title; Composer / Librettist	Premiere
22 June 1824	Sylvain	Grétry / Marmontel	ancien répertoire		19 February 1770, Comédie-Italienne
29 June 1824	Raoul, sire de Créqui	Dalayrac / Boutet de Monvel	ancien répertoire		31 October 1789, Comédie-Italienne
12 July 1824	Blaise et Babet ou La suite des "Trois fermiers"	Nicolas Dezède / Boutet de Monvel	ancien répertoire		4 April 1783, Versailles
23 July 1824	Philippe et Georgette	Dalayrac / Boutet de Monvel	ancien répertoire		28 December 1791, Comédie-Italienne
2 August 1824	La pie voleuse	Castil-Blaze	translation	La gazza ladra; Rossini / Giovanni Gherardini	31 May 1817, Milan, Teatro alla Scala
1 September 1824	Les fausses apparences ou L'amant jaloux	Grétry / Thomas d'Héle	ancien répertoire		20 November 1778, Versailles
19 October 1824	La rosière de Salenci	Grétry / Alexandre-Frédéric-Jacques Masson de Pezay	ancien répertoire		23 October 1773, Fontainebleau
21 October 1824	Le sacrifice interrompu	Auguste-Gustave Vogt and Pierre Crémont / comtes Joseph-Henri de Saur and Léonce de Saint-Geniez	translation	Das unterbrochene Opferfest; Peter von Winter / Franz Xaver Huber	14 June 1796, Vienna, Kärntnertor-theater
7 December 1824	Robin des bois	Castil-Blaze / Castil-Blaze and Thomas Sauvage	translation	Der Freischütz; Carl Maria von Weber / Friedrich Kind	18 June 1821, Berlin, Schauspielhaus

Date	Title	Type	Adaptation (arranger/librettist)	Original work / composer	Premiere
6 February 1825	*Les rêveries renouvelées des Grecs*	*ancien répertoire*	Félix-Jean Prot/Charles-Simon Favart, Claude-Henri de Fusée de Voisenon, and J.-N. Guérin de Frénicourt		26 June 1779, Comédie-Italienne
9 May 1825	*Les noces de Gamache*	pasticcio	Luc Guénée/Sauvage and Jean-Henri Dupin		
1 June 1825	*Raoul Barbe-Bleu*	*ancien répertoire*	Grétry/Sédaine		2 March 1789, Comédie-Italienne
7 June 1825	*Louis XII ou La route de Reims*	occasional pasticcio	Alphonse Vergne, Crémont [?], and Leroux/Jules-Henry Vernoy de Saint-Georges and Joseph-François-Stanislas Maizony de Lauréal		
30 June 1825	*Les Français au sérail*	*ancien répertoire*	François Devienne/Louis-François Picard		7 August 1792, Opéra-Comique
25 July 1825	*Othello ou Le More de Venise*	translation	Castil-Blaze	*Otello*; Rossini/Francesco Maria Berio, marchese de Salza	4 December 1816, Naples, Teatro del Fondo
16 August 1825	*La comédie à la campagne*	translation	Crémont/Félix-Auguste Duvert	*L'impresario in angustie*; Domenico Cimarosa/Giuseppe Maria Diodati	7 February 1786, Naples, Teatro Nuovo

(continued)

The Théâtre-Royal de l'Odéon: Consolidated Repertory (*continued*)

Date of Premiere	Title	Composer/Librettist[a]	Category	Original Title; Composer/Librettist	Premiere
31 October 1825	La dame du lac	Jean-Fréderic-Auguste Lemierre de Corvey/Jean-Baptiste Rose Bonaventure Violet d'Épagny, Edme-François-Antoine-Marie Miel, Sauvage, and Auguste Rousseau	translation	La donna del lago; Rossini/Andrea Leone Tottola	24 September 1819, Naples, Teatro San Carlo
17 November 1825	Preciosa	Crémont/Sauvage	translation	Preciosa; Weber/Pius Alexander Wolff	14 March 1821, Berlin, Hoftheater
14 January 1826	La forêt de Sénart ou La partie de chasse de Henri IV	Castil-Blaze	pasticcio		
2 March 1826	La jeune aveugle	Toussaint-René Poisson/Alexandre Chalas and Maurice Dufresne (Eugène-François Garay de Monglave)	translation	Der Augenarzt; Adalbert Gyrowetz/Johann Emanuel Veith	11 October 1811, Vienna, Kärntnertortheater
11 March 1826	Marguerite d'Anjou	Crémont/Sauvage	translation	Margherita d'Anjou; Giacomo Meyerbeer/Felice Romani	14 November 1820, Milan, Teatro alla Scala
13 June 1826	La fausse Agnès		pasticcio		
16 July 1826	Maison à vendre	Dalayrac/Alexandre-Vincent Duval	ancien répertoire		23 October 1800, Opéra-Comique

Date	Title	Authors	Type	Source	Premiere
22 July 1826	Les noces de Figaro	Castil-Blaze	translation	Le nozze di Figaro; Wolfgang Amadeus Mozart/Lorenzo da Ponte	1 May 1786, Vienna, Burgtheater
7 August 1826	Le neveu de Monseigneur	Luc Guénée/Jean-François-Alfred Bayard, Augusta Kernoc vicomtesse de Chamilly (pseud. François-Auguste Romieu), and Sauvage	pasticcio		
15 September 1826	Ivanhoé	Rossini and Antonio Francesco Gaetano Saverio Pacini/Émile Deschamps and Gabriel-Gustave de Wailly	pasticcio		
4 November 1826	L'école de Rome	Auguste Panseron and Pierre-Gaspard Rolle/Claude-Louis-Marie (pseud. Edmond) de Rochefort[-Lucay], Gustave Vulpian, and Espérance-Hippolyte Lassagne	occasional		
23 November 1826	Les bohémiens	Crémont/Sauvage	pasticcio		
22 January 1827	Le testament	Lemierre de Corvey/comtes de Saur and de Saint-Geniez	pasticcio		

(continued)

The Théâtre-Royal de l'Odéon: Consolidated Repertory *(continued)*

Date of Premiere	Title	Composer/Librettist[a]	Category	Original Title; Composer/Librettist	Premiere
6 February 1827	*Emmeline ou La famille suisse*	Crémont/Charles-Augustin-Bassompierre Sewrin	translation	*Die Schweizerfamilie;* Johann-Baptist Weigl/Ignaz Franz Castelli	14 March 1809, Vienna, Kärntnertor-theater
24 February 1827	*Monsieur de Pourceaugnac*	Castil-Blaze	pasticcio		
21 April 1827	*La folle de Glaris*	Sauvage	translation	*Adele von Budoy;* Conradin Kreutzer/Wolff	15 February 1823, Vienna, Kärntnertor-theater
14 May 1827	*Adolphe et Clara*	Dalayrac/Benoît-Joseph Marsollier des Vivetières	*ancien répertoire*		
20 August 1827	*La maison isolée ou Le vieillard des Vosges*	Dalayrac/Marsollier des Vivetières	*ancien répertoire*		
22 August 1827	*Les deux Figaro*	Aimé-Ambroise-Simon Leborne/Victor Tirpenne	translation	*I due Figaro, ossia il soggetto di una commedia;* Michele Carafa/Romani	6 June 1820, Milan, Teatro alla Scala
7 September 1827	*Tancrède*	Lemierre de Corvey/Édouard d'Anglemont and Jean-Pierre-François Lesguillon	translation	*Tancredi;* Rossini/Gaetano Rossi	6 February 1813, Venice, Teatro la Fenice
13 October 1827	*L'eau de jouvence*	Kreutzer/Duvert and Joseph-Xavier Boniface (pseud. Saintine)	new composition		

Date	Title	Composer/librettist[a]	Category	Original	Premiere[b]
23 October 1827	*Camille ou Le souterrain*	Dalayrac/Marsollier des Vivetières	*ancien répertoire*		19 March 1791, Comédie-Italienne
3 November 1827	*Charles V et Duguesclin*	Louis-Alphonse Gilbert, Jean-Baptiste-Louis Guiraud, Charles-Joseph Tolbecque/Pierre-François-Adolphe Carmouche and Sewrin	occasional		
24 December 1827	*Don Juan*	Castil-Blaze	translation	*Il dissoluto punito, ossia Il Don Giovanni*; Mozart/da Ponte	29 October 1787, Prague, National Theatre
1 February 1828	*Les deux aveugles de Tolède*	Étienne-Nicolas Méhul/Marsollier des Vivetières	*ancien répertoire*		28 January 1806, Opéra-Comique
18 February 1828	*Les brigands de Schiller*	Sauvage and Dupin	pasticcio		
4 May 1828	*Les deux mots ou Une nuit dans la forêt*	Dalayrac/Marsollier des Vivetières	*ancien répertoire*		9 June 1806, Opéra-Comique
18 May 1828	*Gulnare ou L'esclave persane*	Dalayrac/Marsollier des Vivetières	*ancien répertoire*		9 January 1798, Opéra-Comique
10 April 1828	*Le dernier jour de Missolunghi*	Louis-Joseph-Ferdinand Hérold/Jean-Georges Ozaneaux	incidental music		
28 May 1828	*Le déserteur*	Pierre-Alexandre Monsigny/Sédaine	*ancien répertoire*		6 March 1769, Comédie-Italienne

[a] In this column, those responsible for the musical construction of a pasticcio (Castil-Blaze, Guénée, for example) are listed as composers.
[b] The Comédie-Italienne was fused with the Opéra-Comique in 1762 and housed in the Hôtel de Bourgogne until 1783, when it moved to the Salle Favart. See Nicole Wild, *Dictionnaire des théâtres parisiens au XIXe siècle: les théâtres et la musique* (Paris: Amateurs des Livres, 1989), 101–2.

APPENDIX TWO

Letter from Prix de Rome laureates to the vicomte de La Rochefoucauld, [October] 1826 (F-Pan O³ 1792/I)

Les Ex-Pensionnaires du Roi, à Rome, / à Monsieur le Vicomte de Larochefoucault

Monsieur le Vicomte,

La munificence Royale a fondé a Rome une école où chaque année un peintre, un sculpteur, un architecte, un compositeur de musique vont se perfectionner dans l'étude de leur art.

A leur retour, le peintre, le sculpteur, l'architecte obtiennent de l'Administration un emploi ou des travaux. Ainsi le Grand Prix de l'Institut n'est pas seulement pour eux une récompense brillante, un moyen d'achever leurs études, c'est encore la base de leur fortune et de leur réputation.

Mais le compositeur, au retour de ses voyages d'Italie et d'Allemagne, lors qu'il pourrait mettre à profit ses observations et ses études, se trouve sans appui, sans protection, sans moyen d'aborder les deux théâtres lyriques de Paris, et obligé de se crier pour vivre des ressources étrangères à son talent.

Ainsi deviennent inutiles et les études qu'il a faites, et les sommes qu'il a coûtées au Gouvernement du Roi, pendant les cinq années qu'a duré sa pension.

Nous connaissons, Monsieur le Vicomte, les intentions généreuses et paternelles que vous avez manifestées envers les jeunes compositeurs. Ils n'ont d'espoir qu'en vous; et c'est avec confiance dans votre justice et dans votre amour éclairé pour les beaux-arts qu'ils viennent vous présenter un demande dont le succès assurera leur avenir.

Ils ont appris, Monsieur le Vicomte, que le Directeur de l'Odéon a demandé de votre bienveillance l'autorisation de jouer des opéras nouveaux. Ils vous supplient de vouloir bien lui accorder cette autorisation qui servirait à la fois les intérêts de son théâtre, et ceux de l'art qu'ils cultivent.

Les obstacles qu'ils rencontrent aux deux théâtres royaux sont presqu'insurmontables, puisqu'ils consistent d'abord dans le petit nombre d'ouvrages que ces théâtres peuvent représenter par an; ensuite dans la préférence bien naturelle que les directeurs, dans l'intérêt des établissements qu'ils dirigent, accordent aux compositeurs célèbres de notre école.

Le privilège que le Théâtre de l'Odéon obtiendrait de votre bienveillance pourrait seul tirer les jeunes compositeurs de l'état dans lequel ils languissent. L'Odéon ouvrirait pour eux une carrière où ils pourraient peut-être montrer que ce n'est point en vain qu'ils ont reçu les leçons des grands maîtres de l'école française et la récompense royale que décerne l'Académie des Beaux-Arts.

Ils espèrent donc, Monsieur le Vicomte, que vous voudrez bien prendre en considération leur demande, et leur accorder cette faveur qui leur sera bien précieuse et qui vous assurera toute la reconnaissance de jeunes artistes qui voient avec effroi leurs plus belles années condamnées à l'oisiveté.

Veuillez agréer l'expression du profond respect avec lequel ils ont l'honneur d'être,

Monsieur le Vicomte,

Vos très humbles et très obéissants serviteurs,

Dourien (1805); Blondeau (1808); Gasse (1805); Daussoigne (1809); Panseron (1813); Rolle (1814); Benoist (1815); Halévy (1819); Leborne (1820); Batton (1817); Chélard (1811); Paris (1826); Ermel (1823); Boilly (1823).

La demande des jeunes compositeurs à Monsieur de La Rochefoucauld est réellement basée, à la fois, sur l'intérêt général de l'art, sur celui d'un grand nombre de compositeurs que nos brillantes scènes lyriques attendent, et, de plus, sur l'intérêt même du Gouvernement qui, ayant payé l'éducation musicale par laquelle ils ont acquis leurs beaux talents, ne pourra qu'être satisfait d'en recueillir les fruits; car ce sera alors d'un père qui jouira du progrès de ses enfants. Aussi, c'est dans les sentiments de cette généreuse émulation, que naturellement, ils s'adressent avec confiance au Gouvernement auteur de leur éducation, pour en obtenir les moyens de lui marquer, avec éclat, leur vive reconnaissance. Le Sueur.

Je partage entièrement l'opinion de mon collègue, et puis vous assurer, Monsieur le Vicomte, qu'en faisaint droit à leur demande, vous acquérez de nouveaux droits, à la reconnaissance, de tous les amis de l'art musical. Berton.

Je joins mes sollicitations à celles de mes collègues, et je supplie avec insistance, Monsieur le Vicomte, de vouloir bien accueillir favorablement la demande des pensionnaires du Gouvernement. Catel.

BIBLIOGRAPHY

Primary Sources

Published Works

Almanach des bâtiments pour l'an 1828. Paris, 1828.

Almanach des spectacles pour l'an 1824. Paris: Barba, 1824 (and subsequent annual editions through 1828).

Almanach royal, pour l'année bissextile M. DCCC. XXIV. Paris: Guyot et Scribe, 1824 (and subsequent annual editions).

Beethoven, Ludwig van. *Fidelio: drame lyrique en trois actes*. Paris: Farrenc, n.d.

Bouilly, Jean-Nicolas. *Léonore ou L'amour conjugal: fait historique*. Paris: Barba, 1798.

———. *Mes récapitulations*. 3 vols. Paris: Janet, 1836–37.

Carrion-Nisas, André-Henri-François Victor de, and Thomas Sauvage. *Valérien ou Le jeune aveugle*. Paris: Pollet, 1823.

Castil-Blaze [François-Henri-Joseph Blaze]. *De l'opéra en France*. 2 vols. Paris: Janet et Cotelle, 1820; 2d ed. Paris: Sautelot, 1826.

———. *La pie voleuse*. Paris: Barba, 1822.

———. *Les folies amoureuses*. Paris, 1823.

———. *La fausse Agnès*. Paris, 1824.

———. *Robin des bois ou Les trois balles: opera-féerie en trois actes*. Paris: Barba, 1824.

———. *La forêt de Sénart*. Paris, 1826.

———. *Molière musicien: notes sur les oeuvres de cet illustre maître et sur les drames de Corneille . . . Beaumarchais, etc, où se mêlent des considérations sur l'harmonie de la langue française*. 2 vols. Paris, 1852.

———. *L'Opéra-Italien de 1548 à 1856*. Théâtres lyriques de Paris [2]. Paris, 1856.

Catel, Charles-Simon. *Traité d'harmonie*. Paris: Brandus, 1848.

Chassant les ennuis, je chante, je ris. Paris: Pacini, n.d.

Ciceri, Pierre-Luc, and Léger-Larbouillat. *Recueil des décorations théâtrales et autres objets d'ornement*. Paris: Léger-Larbouillat, 1830.

Collé, Charles. *La partie de chasse de Henri IV*. Paris: Gueffier, 1775.

Croizette, Armand, and Armand-François Chateauvieux. *Les aveugles de Franconville*. Paris: Barba, 1802.

Darmaing, Jean Jérôme Achille. *Relation complète du sacre de Charles X avec toutes les modifications introduites dans les prières et le cérémonies et la liste de tous les fonctionnaires publics qui ont été appelés au sacre par lettres closes.* Paris: Baudouin, 1825.

Destouches, Philippe. *La fausse Agnès ou Le poète campagnard.* Paris: Fages, 1802.

Duchatellier, Armand-René. *Essai sur les salaires et les prix de consommation de 1202 à 1830: demande d'une enquête à la Chambre des Députés.* Paris: Libraire du Commerce, 1830.

Duvert, Feliz-Auguste, and Saintine [Joseph-Xavier Boniface]. *L'eau de jouvence: opéra-comique en un acte.* Paris: Duvernois, 1827.

Gandini, Francesco. *Opere teatrali: traduzione.* 3 vols. Milan: Destefanis, 1813.

Garcia, Manuel. *École de Garcia: traité complet de l'art de chant.* 2 vols. Mainz: Schott, 1847. Translated by Beata Garcia as *Hints on Singing* (London: Ascherberg, 1894).

Gautier, Théophile. *Histoire de l'art dramatique en France depuis vingt-cinq ans.* 6 vols. Leipzig: Hetzel; Durr, 1858–59.

Hérold, Ferdinand. *Le dernier jour de Missolunghi.* Paris: Meissonnier, [1828].

Hoffmann, E. T. A. *Oeuvres complètes de E. T. A. Hoffmann, traduites de l'allemand par M. Théodore Toussenel et par le traducteur des romans de Veit-Weber.* 12 vols. [only vols. 5–12 appeared]. Paris: Lefebvre, 1830.

Jérôme Gâcheux à la représentation de Robin des bois: pot-pourri en trois actes. Paris: Vergne, 1825.

Journal historique des cérémonies et fêtes du sacre de Sa Majesté Charles X. Paris: Imprimerie royale, 1827.

Le Noble, Alexandre. *Relation du sacre de S. M. Charles X.* Paris: Pochet, 1825.

Lescot, Alphonse. *De la salubrité de la ville de Paris.* Paris: Huzard, 1826.

Mémoires de Mme du Hausset, femme de chambre de Mme de Pompadour, avec des notes et des éclaircissements historiques. Paris: Baudouin, 1824.

Mercier, Louis-Sébastien. *Tableau de Paris.* Neufchâtel: Fauch, 1781.

Meyerbeer, Giacomo. *Margherita d'Anjou: opera semiseria.* Paris: Schlesinger, n.d.

———. *Marguerite d'Anjou: drame lyrique.* Paris: Kretschmer, n.d.

Miel, Edme François Antoine Marie. *Histoire du sacre de Charles X dans ses rapports avec les beaux-arts et les libertés publiques de la France.* Paris: Panckoucke, 1825.

Monglave, Eugène-François Gary de [Maurice Dufresne, pseud.]. *Nouvelle biographie théâtrale.* Paris, 1826.

———. *Petite biographie théâtrale.* Paris, 1826.

Morogues, Pierre-Marie-Sébastien Bigot de. *De la misère des ouvriers et de la marche à suivre pour y remédier.* Paris: Huzard, 1832.

Mosè in Egitto. Paris: Pacini, n.d.

Ozaneaux, Jean-Georges. *Le dernier jour de Missolunghi.* Paris: Barba, 1828.

Picard, Louis-François. *Le pensionnat de jeunes demoiselles.* Paris: Barba, 1825.

Pixérécourt, René Charles Guilbert de. *Marguerite d'Anjou, mélodrame historique.* Paris: Barba, 1810.

———. *Ondine ou La nymphe des eaux.* Paris: Barba, 1830.

———. *Théâtre choisi.* 4 vols. Paris, 1841–43.

Plan routier de la ville et faubourgs de Paris divisé en 12 mairies, revu et corrigé en 1826. Paris: Jean, [1826].

Raguenet, Francis. *A Critical Discourse on Opera and Musick in England.* London: Lewis, 1709.

Recherches statistiques de la ville de Paris. 6 vols. Paris: Rignoux, 1821–60.

Règlement pour le second théâtre français. Paris: Ballard, [1819].

Regnard, Jean-François. *Les folies amoureuses*. Paris: Fages, 1806.

Robert [Louis Castel]. *Mémoires d'un claqueur contenant la théorie et la pratique de l'art des succès, des jugemens sur le talent de plusieurs auteurs, acteurs, actrices, danseurs, danseuses et un très-grand nombre d'anecdotes historiques toutes inédites*. Paris: Chantpie, Levasseur, 1829.

Romani, Felice. *Margherita d'Anjou: melodramma semiserio*. Milan: Pirola, [1820].

Rossini, Gioachino. *Armida*. Milan: Ricordi, n.d.

———. *Il barbiere di Siviglia*. Milan: Ricordi, 1969.

———. *Le barbier de Séville*. Paris: Petit, n.d.

———. *Bianca e Falliero*. Milan: Ricordi, n.d.

———. *La Cenerentola*. Paris: Pacini, n.d.

———. *La dame du lac*. 2 vols. Paris: Galignani, 1813.

———. *La gazza ladra*. Paris: Pacini, n.d.

———. *Ivanhoé*. Paris: Pacini, n.d.

———. *Semiramide*. Milan: Ricordi, n.d.

———. *Sigismondo*. Milan: Ricordi, n.d.

———. *Tancredi*. Paris: Pacini, n.d.

———. *Torvaldo e Dorliska*. Milan: Ricordi, n.d.

———. *Zelmira*. Paris: Picini, n.d.

Saint-Georges, Henri de, and Joseph-François-Stanislas Maizony de Lauréal. *Louis XII ou La route de Reims*. Paris: Bouquin de la Souche, 1825.

Scribe, Eugène. *Les trois genres*. Paris: Blosse, 1824.

Scribe, Eugène, and Mélesville [Anne-Honoré-Joseph Duveyrier]. *Valérie*. Paris: Ladvocat, 1822.

Second Théâtre-Français: Règlement. Paris: Ballard, [1822].

Siret, Charles Joseph Christophe. *Précis historique du sacre de S. M. Charles X*. Reims: Regnier, 1826.

Trollope, Fanny. *Paris et les Parisiens en 1825*. 3 vols. Paris: Fourier, 1836.

Véron, Louis. *Mémoires d'un bourgeois de Paris*. 6 vols. Paris: Gouet, 1853–56.

Weber Carl. *Reise-briefe von Carl Maria von Weber an seine Gattin Carolina*. Leipzig: Dürr, 1886.

Weber, Carl Maria von. *Der Freischütz*. Leipzig: Breitkopf und Härtel, n.d. Reprint, New York: Dover, 1977.

———. *Der Freischütz ou Le franc-chasseur*. Paris: Laffillé, n.d.

———. *Le chasseur noir/Freischütz: opéra romantique en trois actes*. Paris: Schlesinger, n.d.

———. *Les bohémiens*. Paris: Kretschmer, [1826].

Periodicals

Le Courrier des Théâtres, January 1824–August 1828.

Le Diable Boiteux, January 1824–June 1826.

Le Frondeur, August 1825–June 1826.

Gazette de France, December 1824–September 1827.

Journal de Paris, February 1824–September 1828.

Journal des Débats, April 1824–November 1825.

Journal du Gard, politique, administratif et littéraire, December 1818.

Königliche kaiserliche priviligierte Prager Zeitung, February 1816.

La Lorgnette, November 1825–January 1826.

L'Opinion, December 1825–December 1826.

La Pandore, January 1824–May 1828.

Manuscripts

Berlin, Staatsbibliothek zu Berlin—Preußischer Kulturbesitz, Musikabteilung mit Mendelssohn-Archiv [D-Bds]. N. Mus. Nachl. 97 X/47. Meyerbeer's notes for *La nymphe du Danube.*

———. N. Nus. Nachl. 97 E/51ᵃ. Letter from Pierre Crémont to Thomas Sauvage.

———. WFN Handschriftliches XVI, fol. 89aᵛ–bʳ. Letters from Pierre Crémont to Carl Maria von Weber.

London, British Library. MS Additional 30426, fols. 24ʳ–27ᵛ. Rossini's autograph sketches for linking material for *Ivanhoé.*

New York, Pierpoint Morgan Library. Cary Collection 142. Barbara Marchisio, "Cadenze e variante composte e eseguite dalle sorelle Marchisio."

Paris, Archives municipales. DQ7.9140. Purchase of Auguste Rousseau's interest in *La dame du lac,* May 1825.

Paris, Archives nationales [F-Pan]. AJ¹³ 125. Letter from Bernard to Duplantys, 16 February 1825.

———. AJ¹³ 1050. Dossier of materials relating to *Le dernier jour de Missolunghi.*

———. F¹⁸ 597ᴮ. Censor's libretto of *Le dernier jour de Missolunghi.*

———. F¹⁸ 613. Censors' libretti for *Le sacrifice interrompu, Robin des bois, Les noces de Gamache, Les Français au sérail, La dame du lac, Marguerite d'Anjou.*

———. F¹⁸ 614: Censors' libretti for *La jeune aveugle, Le neveu de Monseigneur, Ivanhoé, L'école de Rome, Le testament, Emmeline ou La famille suisse, Les deux Figaro, Tancrède, L'eau de jouvence, Les brigands de Schiller.*

———. F¹⁸ 615. Censors' libretto for *La folle de Glaris.*

———. F²¹ 967. Censors' reports for *Le sacrifice interrompu, Robin des bois, Les noces de Gamache, La folle de Glaris, Le dernier jour de Missolunghi.*

———. F²¹ 968. Censors' reports for *Emmeline ou La famille suisse, Les deux Figaro.*

———. F²¹ 980. Censors' report for *Le pensionnat de jeunes demoiselles.*

———. F²¹ 994. Censors' report for *Le neveu de Monseigneur.*

———. F²¹ 1099. Odéon: miscellaneous files.

———. F²¹ 1137–38. Gymnase dramatique (Théâtre de Son Altesse Royale, Madame, duchesse de Berry): miscellaneous files.

———. O³ 1742/134. Odéon: miscellaneous files.

———. O³ 1789/II. Odéon: reports, 1823–24.

———. O³ 1790/I. Odéon: contract with Bernard.

———. O³ 1790/VI. Odéon: general correspondence 1824.

———. O³ 1791/I. Correspondence: Lauriston to La Ferté, January–April 1824.

———. O³ 1791/II. Correspondence: Gimel to La Ferté, January–March 1824.

———. O³ 1791/III. Correspondence: Bernard to La Ferté and others, September 1823–November 1824.

———. O³ 1791/IV. Odéon: administration, 1823–28.

———. O³ 1791/V. Odéon: requests for free places, 1823–26.

———. O³ 1791/VI. Odéon: general files, 1823–24.

———. O³ 1791/VII. Odéon: finance files, 1823–26.

———. O³ 1791/VIII. Odéon: finance files, 1824–26.

———. O³ 1791/IX. Odéon: records of attendance, *jury de lecture,* 1824–28.

———. O³ 1792/I. Odéon: management of Frédéric du Petit-Méré, 1826–27.

———. O³ 1792/II. Odéon: management of Thomas Sauvage, 1827–28.

———. O³ 1792/III. Odéon: report on free places, 1825–27.

———. O³ 1792/IV. Odéon: payments to members of the *jury de lecture.*

———. O³ 1792/V. Odéon: miscellaneous requests, 1823–28.

———. O³ 1792/VI. Odéon: miscellaneous requests, 1824–26.

———. O³ 1793/I. Odéon: miscellaneous files, 1827–29.

———. O³ 1793/II. Odéon: submissions to the Maison du Roi by Frédéric du Petit-Méré.

———. O³ 1793/III. Odéon: miscellaneous files.

Paris, Bibliothèque nationale de France [F-Pn]. Lettres autographes XI, fols. 275ʳ⁻ᵛ: correspondence between Castil-Blaze and Boieldieu.

———. L.a. XVIII, fols. 98ʳ–100ʳ: correspondence between Castil-Blaze and Charles Laffillé.

———. L.a. XXIII, 311ʳ–19ʳ: correspondence between Crémont and Sauvage.

———. L.a. CXI, 184ʳ: correspondence between Carl Maria von Weber and Pierre Crémont.

———. Nouvelles acquisitions françaises 3042: papers relating to affaire Claude Bernard–Charlotte Kerckhoven.

———. N.a.f. 3042, fols. 109ʳ–20ᵛ: Ordonnance portant règlement sur la surveillance, l'organisation sociale et l'administration du Théâtre-Royal de l'Odéon.

———. Papiers divers de Berlioz: 1829 libretto of Berlioz, *Les francs-juges.*

———. Rés. Vm² 177: fragments of Berlioz, *Les francs-juges.*

———. Rés. 11837: copy of overture to Hérold's *Dernier jour de Missolunghi.*

———. Vm² 1341: autograph of Hérold's *Dernier jour de Missolunghi.*

———.Bibliothèque-Musée de l'Opéra [F-Po]. A.497.a: manuscript full score of the April 1831 version of Weber's *Euryanthe.*

———. A.796a²: manuscript addition of part of 54-bar entr'acte in *Le barbier de Séville.*

———. Arch. Th. Paris. Odéon.43: advertisement for shares in the Théâtre-Royal de l'Odéon, December 1825.

———. Registres TH 57. Odéon: summary of receipts and *droit des indigens,* 1828–29.

———. Rés. A. 500.a¹: Meyerbeer's musical sketches for *La nymphe du Danube.*

Secondary Sources

Adlung, Philipp. *Mozarts Opera Seria "Mitridate, rè di Ponto."* Hamburger Beiträge zur Musikwissenschaft 46. Hamburg: Wagner, 1996.

Allin, Michael. *Zarafa: A Giraffe's True Story, from Deep in Africa to the Heart of Paris.* New York: Walker, 1998.

Anderson, W. E. K., ed. *The Journal of Sir Walter Scott.* Oxford: Clarendon, 1972.

Angermüller, Rudolph. "'Les Mystères d'Isis' (1801) und 'Don Juan' (1805, 1834) auf der Bühne der Pariser Oper." In *Mozart-Jahrbuch 1980–83 des Zentralinstitutes für Mozartforschung der Internationalen Stiftung Mozarteum Salzburg,* 32–97. Kassel: Bärenreiter, 1983.

Azevedo, Alexis. *G. Rossini: sa vie et ses oeuvres.* Notice publiée par *Le Ménestrel.* Paris: Heugel, 1864.

Balzac, Honoré de. *Une double famille.* Vol. 3 of *Oeuvres complètes.* Paris: Conard, 1912.

Bara, Olivier. "Le Théâtre de l'Opéra-Comique entre 1822 et 1827: la difficile recherche d'un genre moyen." Ph.D. dissertation, Université de Paris III, 1998. Published as *Le Théâtre de l'Opéra Comique sous la restauration: enquête autour d'un genre moyen,* Musikwissenschaftliche Publikationen 14 (Hildesheim: Olms, 2001).

Barbier, Patrick. *Opera in Paris 1800–1850: A Lively History.* Translated by Robert Luoma. Portland Or.: Amadeus, 1995. Originally published as *La Vie quotidienne à l'opéra au temps de Rossini et de Balzac (Paris 1800–1850)* (Paris: Hachette, 1987).

Bartlet, M. Elizabeth C. "A Musician's View of the French Baroque after the Advent of Gluck: Grétry's *Les Trois Âges de l'Opéra* in Its Context." In *Jean-Baptiste Lully and the Music of the French Baroque: Essays in Honor of James R. Anthony,* edited by John Hajdu Heyer, 291–318. Cambridge: Cambridge University Press, 1989.

Baschet, Robert. *E.-J. Delécluze: témoin de son temps, 1781–1863.* Paris: Boivin, 1942.
———, ed. *Journal de Delécluze, 1824–28.* Paris: Grasset, 1948.

Becker, Heinz. "Eine *Undine*-Oper Meyerbeers für Paris." In *Festschrift Martin Ruhnke zum 65. Geburtstag,* 31–44. Neuhausen-Stuttgart: Hänssler, 1986.

Becker, Heinz, and Gudrun Becker. *Giacomo Meyerbeer: Briefwechsel und Tagebücher.* 5 vols. to date. Berlin: De Gruyter, 1960–.

Betzwieser, Thomas. "Der in Bewegung gesetzte Chor: Gluck und der *choeur dansé.*" In *D'un opéra à l'autre: hommage à Jean Mongrédien,* edited by Jean Gribenski, Marie-Claire Mussat, and Herbert Schneider, 45–54. Paris: Presses de l'Université de Paris-Sorbonne, 1996.

Blewer, Evelyne, et al., eds. *Victor Hugo raconté par Adèle Hugo.* Collection Les Mémorables. Paris: Plon, 1985.

Bohlman, Philip V. "On the Unremarkable in Music." *19th-Century Music* 16 (1992): 203–16.

Borgerhoff, Joseph-Léopold. *Le Théâtre anglais à Paris sous la restauration.* Paris: Hachette, 1912.

Börner, Wolfgang. "Die Opern von Daniel-François-Esprit Auber." Ph.D. dissertation, Universität Leipzig, 1962.

Boschot, Adolphe. *La Jeunesse d'un romantique: Hector Berlioz, 1803–1831.* Paris: Plon, 1906.
———. *Une Vie romantique: Hector Berlioz.* 2 vols. Paris: Plon, 1919.

Brandenburg, Daniel. "Musikdrama, das Traditionen änderte: zu Verdis *Macbeth.*" *Österreichische Musikzeitschrift* 55 (2000): 21–24.

Burke, Peter. "Unity and Variety in Cultural History." In *Varieties of Cultural History,* 183–212. Cambridge: Polity, 1997.
———. "The Microhistory Debate." In *New Perspectives on Historical Writing,* edited by Peter Burke, 115–17, 119. 2d ed. Cambridge: Polity, 2001.

Busk, Gorm. "Friedrich Kuhlau's Operas and Theatre Music and Their Performances at the Royal Theatre in Copenhagen (1814–1830): A Mirror of European Music Drama and a Glimpse of the Danish Opera Tradition." *Musik & Forskning* 21 (1996): 93–127.

Cagli, Bruno, and Sergio Ragni, eds. *Gioachino Rossini: lettere e documenti.* Vol. 2, *21 marzo 1822–11 ottobre 1826.* Pesaro: Fondazione Rossini, 1992.

Cairns, David. *Berlioz, 1803–1832: The Making of an Artist.* London: Deutsch, 1989. 2d ed. London: Penguin, 1999.

———, ed. and trans. *The Memoirs of Hector Berlioz, Member of the French Institute, Including His Travels to Italy, Germany, Russia and England.* London: Victor Gollanz, 1977.

Caron, Jean-Claude. *Générations romantiques: les étudiants de Paris et le quartier latin (1814–1851).* Paris: Colin, 1993.

Carse, Adam. *The Orchestra from Beethoven to Berlioz: A History of the Orchestra in the First Half of the 19th Century, and of the Development of Orchestral Baton-Conducting.* Cambridge: Heffer, 1948.

Castelvecchi, Stefano. "Walter Scott, Rossini e la *couleur ossianique:* il contesto culturale della donna del lago." *Bollettino del Centro Rossiniano di studi* 33 (1993): 57–71.

Caswell, Austin. "Mme Cinti-Damoureau and the Embellishment of Italian Opera in Paris, 1820–1845." *Journal of the American Musicological Society* 28 (1975): 459–92.

———. "Vocal Embellishment in Rossini's Paris Operas: French Style or Italian?" *Bollettino del Centro Rossiniano di studi,* n.s. 1–2 (1975): 5–21.

———. *Embellished Opera Arias.* Recent Researches in the Music of the Nineteenth and Early Twentieth Centuries 7 and 8. Madison, Wis.: A-R Editions, 1989.

Charlton, David. "The French Theatrical Origins of *Fidelio.*" *Ludwig van Beethoven: Fidelio,* edited by Paul Robinson, 51–67. Cambridge Opera Handbooks. Cambridge: Cambridge University Press, 1996.

Chevalier, Louis. *Classes laborieuses et classes dangereuses à Paris pendant la première moitié du XIXe siècle.* Paris: Librairie générale française, 1978.

Citron, Pierre, ed., *Hector Berlioz: correspondance générale.* Vol. 1, *1803–1832.* Paris: Flammarion [Nouvelle Bibliothèque romantique], 1972.

Claudon, Francis. "Meyerbeer: *Il crociato;* le grand opéra avant le grand opéra." In *L'opera tra Venezia e Parigi,* edited by Maria Teresa Muraro, 119–31. Studi di musica veneta 14. Florence: Olschki, 1988.

Conati, Marcello. "Between Past and Future: The Dramatic World of Rossini in *Mosè in Egitto* and *Moïse et Pharaon.*" *19th-Century Music* 4 (1980–81): 32–47.

Constant, Pierre. *Le Conservatoire national de musique et de déclamation: documents historiques et administratives.* Paris: Imprimerie nationale, 1900.

d'Almarès, Henri. *La Vie parisienne sous la restauration.* Paris: Michel, [1910].

Daumard, Adeline. *La Bourgeoisie parisienne de 1815 à 1848.* École pratique des hautes Études, VIe section, Centre de Recherches historiques: démographie et sociétés 8. Paris: S.E.V.P.E.N., 1963.

de Lassus, Lucien Augé. *Boïeldieu.* Les Musiciens célèbres. Paris: Laurens, 1908.

de Sauvigny, Guillaume de Berthier. *La Restauration, 1815–1830.* Nouvelle Histoire de Paris. Paris: Hachette, 1977.

de Van, Gilles. "Le grand opéra entre tragédie lyrique et drame romantique." *Il saggiatore musicale: rivista semestrale di musicologia* 3 (1996): 325–60.

del Litto, Victor, and Ernest Abravanel, eds. *Stendhal: Vie de Rossini suivie des Notes d'un dilettante.* Vols. 22–23 of *Stendhal: oeuvres complètes.* Geneva: Edito-Service, 1968.

Devriès, Anik, and François Lesure. *Dictionnaire des éditeurs de musique française.* 2 vols. (vol. 1 in 2 parts). Archives de l'édition musicale française 4. Geneva: Minkoff, 1979–88.

Drysdale, John. "Louis Véron and the Finances of the *Académie Royale de Musique, 1827–1835.*" Ph.D. dissertation, University of Southampton, 2000.

Dubech, Lucien, and Pierre d'Espeziel. *Histoire de Paris.* Paris: Payot, 1926.

Dudley, Sherwood. "Les premières versions françaises du *Mariage de Figaro* de Mozart." *Revue de musicologie* 59 (1983): 55–83.

Eigeldinger, Jean-Jacques. "Placing Chopin: Reflections on a Compositional Aesthetic." *Chopin Studies* 2 (1994): 102–39.

Ellis, Katharine. "Rewriting *Don Giovanni,* or 'The Thieving Magpies.'" *Journal of the Royal Musical Association* 119 (1994): 212–50.

Everist, Mark. "Lindoro in Lyon: Rossini's *Le Barbier de Séville.*" *Acta musicologica* 44 (1992): 50–85.

———. "Giacomo Meyerbeer and Music Drama at the Paris Odéon during the Bourbon Restoration." *19th-Century Music* 16 (1993): 124–48.

———. "The Name of the Rose: Meyerbeer's *opéra comique, Robert le Diable.*" *Revue de musicologie* 80 (1994): 211–50.

———. "Meyerbeer's *Il crociato in Egitto: Mélodrame,* Opera, Orientalism." *Cambridge Opera Journal* 8 (1996): 215–50.

———. "Gluck, Berlioz and Castil-Blaze: The Poetics and Reception of French Opera." In *Reading Critics Reading: Opera and Ballet Criticism in France, 1815–1848,* edited by Roger Parker and Mary Anne Smart, 86–108. Oxford: Oxford University Press, 2001.

———. "Translating Weber's *Euryanthe:* German Romanticism at the Dawn of French *Grand Opéra.*" *Revue de musicologie* 87 (2001): 67–104.

Favre, Georges. *Boïeldieu: sa vie, son oeuvre.* 2 vols. Bibliothèque de la Société des historiens du théâtre 21. Paris: Droz, 1944–45.

Fétis, François-Joseph [*FétisB*]. *Biographie universelle des musiciens et bibliographie générale de la musique.* 2d ed. 8 vols., with supplement in 2 vols. Paris: Firmin Didot, 1860–65.

Fulcher, Jane F. *The Nation's Image: French Grand Opera as Politics and Politicized Art.* Cambridge: Cambridge University Press, 1987.

Fuld, James J. *The Book of World-Famous Music: Classical, Popular and Folk.* New York: Crown, 1966. 3d ed. rev. and enlarged. 1966; New York: Dover, 1985.

Galliver, David. "Jean-Nicolas Bouilly (1763–1842), Successor of Sedaine." *Studies in Music* 13 (1979): 16–33.

Geertz, Clifford. "Thick Description: Toward an Interpretative Theory of Culture." In *The Interpretation of Cultures,* 3–30. New York: Basic Books, 1973.

———. "Art as a Cultural System." *Modern Language Notes* 91 (1976): 1473–99.

Gendron, Christian, ed. *Auguste Tolbecque: luthier et musicien.* Catalog of an exhibition held at Musée Ste-Croix, Poitiers, 6–24 June 1997 and Musée Bernard d'Agesci, Niort, 25 June–31 October 1997. Niort: Musées de Niort, 1997.

Genty, Christian. *Histoire du théâtre national de l'Odéon: journal de bord, 1782–1982.* Paris: Fischbacher, 1982.

Gerhard, Anselm. *The Urbanization of Opera: Music Theater in Paris in the Nineteenth Century.* Translated by Mary Whittall. Chicago: University of Chicago Press, 1998. Originally published as *Die Verstädterung der Oper: Paris und das Musiktheater des 19. Jahrhundert* (Stuttgart: Metzler, 1992).

Gille, Bertrand. *Histoire de la maison Rothschild.* 2 vols. Geneva: Droz, 1965–67.

Gilman, Todd S. "Handel's *Hercules* and Its Semiosis." *The Musical Quarterly* 81 (1997): 449–481.

Ginzburg, Carlo. *Il formaggio e i vermi: il cosmo di un mugnaio del '500.* Florence: Einaudi, 1976.

Girard, Henri. *Émile Deschamps dilettante: relations d'un poëte romantique avec les peintres, les sculpteurs et les musiciens de son temps.* Paris: Champion, 1921. Reprint, Geneva: Slatkine, 1977.

Gíslason, Donald Garth. "Castil-Blaze, *De l'opéra en France* and the Feuilletons of the *Journal des Débats* (1820–1832)." Ph.D. dissertation, University of British Columbia, 1992.

Gossett, Philip Edward. "The Operas of Rossini: Problems of Textual Criticism in Nineteenth-Century Opera." Ph.D. dissertation, Princeton University, 1970.

———, ed. *Tancredi: melodramma eroico in due atti di Gaetano Rossi, musica di Gioachino Rossini.* 2 vols. Edizione critica delle opere di Gioachino Rossini, Sezione prima 10. Pesaro: Fondazione Rossini, 1984.

Guichard, Léon. "Beaumarchais et Mozart: note sur la première représentation à Paris des Noces de Figaro." *Revue d'histoire littéraire de la France* 55 (1955) 341–43.

Guillaume, Jean, Claude Pichois, et al., eds. *Gérard de Nerval: oeuvres complètes.* 3 vols. Bibliothèque de la Pléiade, nos. 89, 117, 397. Paris: Gallimard, 1989–93.

Hadamowsky, Franz. *Die Wiener Hoftheater (Staatstheater), 1776–1966: Verzeichnis der aufgeführten Stücke mit Bestandsnachweis und täglichem Spielplan.* 2 vols. Museion: Veröffentlichungen der Österreichischen Nationalbibliothek 4. Vienna: Prachner, 1966–75.

———. *Wien: Theater Geschichte von den Anfängen bis zum Ende des ersten Weltkriegs.* Geschichte der Stadt Wien 3. Vienna: Jugend und Volk, 1988.

Heidlberger, Frank. *Carl Maria von Weber und Hector Berlioz: Studien zur französischen Weber-Rezeption.* Würzburger musikhistorische Beiträge 14. Tützing: Schneider, 1994.

Hemmings, Frederick William John. *The Theatre Industry in Nineteenth-Century France.* Cambridge: Cambridge University Press, 1993.

———. *Theatre and State in France, 1760–1905.* Cambridge: Cambridge University Press, 1994.

Henze-Döhring, Sabine. "E. T. A. Hoffmann-'Kult' und 'Don Giovanni'-Rezeption im Paris des 19. Jahrhunderts: Castil-Blazes 'Don Juan' im Théâtre de l'Académie Royale de Musique am 10 März 1834." *Mozart-Jahrbuch 1984–5 des Zentralinstitutes für Mozartforschung der Internationalen Stiftung Mozarteum Salzburg,* 39–51. Kassel: Bärenreiter, 1986.

Hibberd, Sarah. "Magnetism, Muteness, Magic: *Spectacle* and the Parisian Lyric Stage *c*1830." Ph.D. dissertation, University of Southampton, 1998.

Holoman, D. Kern. *The Creative Process in the Autograph Musical Documents of Hector Berlioz, c.1818–1840.* Studies in Musicology 7. 1975; 2d ed. Ann Arbor, Mich.: UMI Research Press, 1980.

―――. "Les Fragments de l'opéra perdu de Berlioz: *Les Francs-Juges.*" *Revue de musicologie* 63 (1977): 78–88.

―――. *Catalogue of the Works of Hector Berlioz.* Vol. 25 of *Hector Berlioz: New Edition of the Complete Works.* Kassel: Bärenreiter, 1987.

Hugo, Victor. *Choses vues, 1830–1846.* Paris: Gallimard, 1972.

Ierolli, Giuseppe. "*Mosè* e *Maometto:* da Napoli a Parigi." Tesi di laurea, Università degli studi di Bologna, 1989–90.

Isotta, Paolo. "Da *Mosè* a *Moïse.*" *Bollettino del Centro Rossiniano di studi* (1971): 87–117.

―――, ed. *Gioacchino Rossini: Mosè in Egitto, Azione tragico-sacra; Moïse et Pharaon, Opéra en quatre actes; Mosè, Melodramma sacro in quattro atti.* Opera 1a, no. 4. Turin: Unione tipografico-editrice torinese, 1974.

Jardin, André, and André-Jean Tudesq. *Restoration and Reaction: 1815–1848.* Translated by Elborg Forster. The Cambridge History of Modern France 1. Cambridge: Cambridge University Press, 1983. Originally published as *La France des notables* (Paris: Seuil, 1973).

Jean-Aubry, G. "A Romantic Dilettante: Émile Deschamps." *Music & Letters* 20 (1939) 250–65.

Johnson, James H. *Listening in Paris: A Cultural History.* Studies in the History of Society and Culture 21. Berkeley: University of California Press, 1995.

Johnson, Janet. "A Lost Rossini Opera Recovered: *Il viaggio a Reims.*" *Bollettino del Centro Rossiniano di studi* (1983): 5–57.

―――. "The Théâtre Italien and Opera and Theatrical Life in Restoration Paris." 3 vols. Ph.D. dissertation, University of Chicago, 1988.

Johnson, Lee. "The Last Scene of *Don Giovanni:* A Newly Discovered Delacroix." *The Burlington Magazine* 138 (1996): 605–7.

Jourbin, André, ed. *Journal d'Eugène Delacroix.* 3 vols., rev. and enlarged. Paris: Plon, 1950.

Jullien, Adolphe. *Weber à Paris en 1826, son voyage de Dresde à Londres par la France: la musique et les théâtres, le monde et la presse pendant son séjour.* Paris: A. Detaille, 1877. Reprinted in *Paris dilettante au commencement du siècle,* 7–66. Paris: Firmin-Didot, 1884.

Kern, Bernd-Rüdiger, and Reto Müller. "Originalwerk oder Machwerk? *Ivanhoé* mit Musik von Rossini." *Neue Zeitschrift für Musik* 151 (1990): 44–45.

Kinsky, Georg. *Das Werk Beethovens: thematisch-bibliographisches Verzeichnis seiner sämtlicher vollendeten Kompositionen.* Completed and edited by Hans Halm. Munich: Henle, 1955.

Krakovitch, Odile. *Les Pièces de théâtre soumises à la censure (1800–1830): inventaire des pièces (F^{18} 581 à 668) et les procès-verbaux des censeurs (F^{21} 966–995).* Paris: Archives nationales, 1982.

Kutsch, Karl-Josef, and Leo Riemens. *Großes Sängerlexikon.* 4 vols. Bern: Francke, 1987–94.

Larousse, Pierre [*LDD-NS*]. *Grand Dictionnaire universel du XIXe siècle français, histo-rique, géographique, biographique, mythologique, bibliographique, littéraire, artistique, sci-entifique, etc.* 15 vols. with supplements. Paris: Grand Dictionnaire Universel, 1866.

Leclercq, Yves. *Le Réseau impossible: la résistance au système des grandes compagnies fer-roviaires et la politique économique en France, 1820–1852.* Geneva: Droz, 1987.

Le Roy Ladurie, Emmanuel. *Montaillou, village occitain de 1294 à 1324.* Paris: Galli-mard, 1975.

Lever, Évelyne. *Louis XVIII.* Paris: Fayard, 1988.

Levi, Giovanni. "On Microhistory." In *New Perspectives on Historical Writing,* edited by Peter Burke, 97–115, 117–18. 2d ed. Cambridge: Polity, 2001.

Little, Ricky Ricardo. "A Comparative Study of *Le Barbier de Séville:* The Original Play, and the Two Operas, *Il barbiere di Siviglia* by Giovanni Paisiello and Gioachino Rossini." Doctor of Musical Arts dissertation, Ohio State University, 1985.

Loewenberg, Alfred. "Paisiello's and Rossini's 'Barbiere di Siviglia.'" *Music & Letters* 20 (1939): 157–67.

Longyear, Ray. "D. F. E. Auber: A Chapter in French Opera Comique." Ph.D. disser-tation, Cornell, 1957.

Loyer, François. *Paris au XIXe siècle: l'immeuble et la rue.* Paris: Hazan, 1987.

Malherbe, Charles. *Auber.* Les Musiciens célèbres. Paris: Laurens, 1911.

Mansel, Philip. *The Court of France 1789–1830.* Cambridge: Cambridge University Press, 1988.

Marchand, Bernard. *Paris: histoire d'une ville (XIXe–XXe siècles).* Paris: Seuil, 1993.

Martin-Fugier, Anne. *La Vie élégante, ou la formation du tout-Paris (1815–1848).* Paris: Fayard, 1993.

Mongrédien, Jean. "La musique aux fêtes du sacre de Charles X." *Recherches sur la musique française classique* 10 (1970): 87–100.

———. "*Les Mystères d'Isis* (1801) and Reflections on Mozart from the Parisian Press at the Beginning of the Nineteenth Century." In *Music in the Classic Period: Essays in Honor of Barry S. Brook,* edited by Allan W. Atlas, 195–211. New York: Pen-dragon, 1985.

———. *La musique en France des Lumières au Romantisme.* Harmoniques: la Musique en France. Paris: Flammarion, 1986.

———. "À propos des premières éditions françaises de *Fidelio.*" In *Musique, signes, images: liber amicorum François Lesure,* edited by Joël-Marie Fauquet, 207–16. Geneva: Minkoff, 1988.

———. "Les débuts de Meyerbeer à Paris: *Il crociato in Egitto* au Théâtre Royal Ita-lien." In *Meyerbeer und das europäische Musiktheater,* edited by Sieghart Döhring and Arnold Jacobshagen, 64–72. Thurnauer Schriften zum Musiktheater 16. Laaber: Laaber, 1998.

Montgomery, William. "The Life and Works of François Devienne, 1759–1803." Ph.D. dissertation, Catholic University of America, 1975.

Morel, Dominique, ed. *Achille Devéria: temoin du romantisme parisien 1800–1857.* Ex-hibition catalog, 18 June–29 September 1985. Paris: Musées de la ville de Paris, 1985.

Müller, Reto. "*Ivanhoé:* eine authentische Rossini-Oper?" *Mitteilungsblatt der Verein der Freunde der Musik Gaetano Donizettis* (May 1990) [unpaginated].

Die Musik in Geschichte und Gegenwart: allgemeine Enzyklopädie der Musik. 16 vols. Kassel: Bärenreiter-Verlag, 1949–79.

Neveu, Valerie. "Correspondance de Boïeldieu/état au 20 III 1991." Typescript, 1991.

Nicolodi, Fiamma. "Un *pastiche* di Rossini: *Ivanhoé* e il medioevo reinventato." In *49a Settimana Musicale Senese: 23–29 luglio 1992,* 135–57. Siena: Fondazione Accademia Musicale Chigiana, 1992.

Osborne, Richard. *Rossini.* The Master Musicians. London: Macmillan, 1986.

Ozanam, Yves. "Recherches sur l'Académie royale de musique sous la seconde restauration." Ph.D. dissertation, École nationale des Chartes, 1981.

Parakilas, James. "Mozart's Mad Scene." *Soundings* 10 (1983): 3–17.

———. "The Soldier and the Exotic: Operatic Variations on a Theme of Racial Encounter." *Opera Quarterly* 10 (1993–94): 33–56.

Parent-Lardeur, Françoise. *Les Cabinets de lecture: la lecture publique à Paris sous la restauration.* Bibliothèque historique. Paris: Payot, 1982.

Pendle, Karin. "*A bas les couvents!*": Anticlerical Sentiment in French Opera of the 1790s." *Music Review* 42 (1981): 22–45.

———. "The Boulevard Theaters and Continuity in French Opera of the 19th Century." In *Music in Paris in the Eighteen-Thirties,* edited by Peter Bloom, 509–35. La Vie musicale en France au XIXe siècle 4. Stuyvesant, N.Y.: Pendragon, 1987.

Phillips, W. Alison. "Greece and the Balkan Peninsula." In *The Restoration,* ed. A. W. Ward, G. W. Prothero, and Stanley Leathes. Cambridge: Cambridge University Press, 1934.

Pincherle, Marc. *Musiciens peints par eux-mêmes; lettres de compositeurs écrites en français (1771–1910).* Paris: Cornuau, 1939.

Pipers Enzyklopädie des Musiktheaters: Oper, Operette, Musical, Ballet. Edited by Carl Dahlhaus and Sieghart Döhring. 7 vols. Munich: Piper, 1986–97.

Porel, Paul, and Georges Monval. *L'Odéon: histoire administrative, anecdotique et littéraire du second théâtre français.* 2 vols. Paris: Lemerre, 1876–82.

Pougin, Arthur. *Hérold.* Les Musiciens célèbres. Paris: Laurens, 1906.

Price, Curtis Alexander. "Unity, Originality, and the London Pasticcio." *Harvard Library Bulletin,* n.s. 2–4 (1991): 17–30.

Prod'homme, Jacques-Gabriel."'Robin des Bois' et "le Freyschütz.'" *Le Ménestrel* 88 (1926): 437–40 and 449–51.

Pronteau, Jeanne. *Les Numérotages des maisons de Paris du XVe siècle à nos jours.* Ville de Paris: Commission des travaux historiques, sous-commission de recherches d'histoire municipale contemporaine 8. Paris: Préfecture de la Seine—Service des travaux historiques, 1966.

Proust, Jacques. "Beaumarchais et Mozart: une mise au point." *Studi francesi* 46 (January–April 1972): 34–45.

Radiciotti, Giuseppe. *Gioacchino Rossini: vita documentata, opere ed influenza su l'arte.* 3 vols. Tivoli: Chicca, 1927.

Revers, Peter. "Mozart und China: Henri-Montan Bertons Pasticcio *Le laboureur chinois:* Ein Beitrag zur französischen Mozart-Rezeption des frühen 19. Jahrhunderts." In *Mozart-Jahrbuch 1991 des Zentralinstitutes für Mozartforschung der Internationalen Stiftung Mozarteum Salzburg,* 777–86. Kassel: Bärenreiter, 1991.

Rice, John A. *W. A. Mozart: La clemenza di Tito.* Cambridge Opera Handbooks. Cambridge: Cambridge University Press, 1991.

Robert, Paul-Louis. "Correspondance de Boieldieu." *Rivista musicale italiana* 22 (1915): 520–59.

Roulleaux-Dugage, Jacques. "Un livret d'opéra inédit de Beaumarchais." *Nouvelles littéraires,* 3 November 1966, 12.

Sadie, Stanley, ed. *The New Grove Dictionary of Music and Musicians.* 20 vols. London: Macmillan, 1980.

———. *The New Grove Dictionary of Opera.* 4 vols. London: Macmillan, 1992.

Sala, Emilio. "Alla ricerca della *Pie Voleuse.*" In *Gioachino Rossini, 1792–1992: il testo e la scena; Convegno internazionale di studi, Pesaro 25–28 giugno 1992,* ed. Paolo Fabbri, 205–53. Pesaro: Fondazione Rossini, 1994.

Sauvage, Thomas. "Histoire de *Robin des bois:* opéra fantastique imité du *Freischütz,* représenté sur le Théâtre de l'Odéon le 7 décembre 1824." *Revue et gazette musicale de Paris* 33 (1866): 385–87 and 393–95.

Schneider, Herbert. *Chronologisch-thematisches Verzeichnis sämtlicher Werke von Daniel François Esprit Auber.* 2 vols. Musikwissenschaftliche Publikationen 1. Hildesheim: Georg Olms Verlag, 1994.

Servières, Georges. *Freischütz: opéra romantique en 3 actes, musique de Carl-Maria von Weber, traduction du poème de Friedrich Kind précédée d'une histoire de l'oeuvre et de ses adaptations françaises.* Paris: Fischbacher et Floury, 1913.

Slim, H. Colin, ed. *La donna del lago, melo-dramma in due atti de Andrea Leone Tottola, musica di Gioachino Rossini.* 3 vols. Edizione critica delle opere di Gioachino Rossini, Sezione prima 20. Pesaro: Fondazione Rossini, 1990.

Smith, Marian. "Music for the Ballet-Pantomime at the Paris Opéra, 1825–1850." Ph.D. dissertation, Yale University, 1988.

Stieger, Franz. *Opernlexikon.* 3 vols. Tutzing: Schneider, 1975–83.

Tartak, Marvin. "The Two 'Barbieri.'" *Music & Letters* 50 (1969): 453–69.

Théâtre de l'Odéon, 1782–1982. Catalog of exhibition held at the Théâtre de l'Odéon, October 1982–May 1983 and at the Mairie annexe du VIe arrondissement, 20 January–20 February 1983. Paris, 1982.

Tomlinson, Gary. "The Web of Culture: A Context for Musicology." *19th-Century Music* 7 (1984): 350–62.

Tyson, Alan. "Maurice Schlesinger as a Publisher of Beethoven: 1822–1827." *Acta musicologica* 35 (1963): 182–91.

Wagner, Roy. *The Invention of Culture.* 2d ed. Chicago: University of Chicago Press, 1981.

Walsh, Thomas Joseph. *Second Empire Opera: The Théâtre Lyrique, Paris, 1851–1870.* The History of Opera. London: Calder, 1981.

Waquet, Françoise. *Les Fêtes royales sous la restauration, ou l'ancien régime retrouvé.* Bibliothèque de la société française d'archéologie 14. Geneva: Droz, 1981.

Ward, A. W., G. W. Prothero, and Stanley Leathes. *The Restoration.* The Cambridge Modern History 10. Cambridge: Cambridge University Press, 1934.

Warrack, John. *Carl Maria von Weber.* 2d ed. 1968; Cambridge: Cambridge University Press, 1976.

Warrack, John, ed. *Carl Maria von Weber: Writings on Music.* Translated by Martin Cooper. Cambridge: Cambridge University Press, 1981.

Weber, William. "The Muddle of the Middle Classes." *19th-Century Music* 3 (1979): 175–85.

Weinstock, Herbert. *Rossini: A Biography.* London, 1968.

Wild, Nicole. *Dictionnaire des théâtres parisiens au XIXe siècle: les théâtres et la musique.* Paris: Amateurs des Livres, 1989.

————. "Fashioning Romanticism: Ciceri, a Stage Designer." Typescript.

Yvert, Benoît, ed. *Dictionnaire des ministres de 1789 à 1989.* Paris: Perrin, 1990.

Zedda, Alberto, ed. *Gioacchino Rossini: Il barbiere di Siviglia.* Milan: Ricordi, 1969.

Zimmermann, Reiner. *Giacomo Meyerbeer: eine Biographie nach Dokumenten.* Berlin: Henschel, 1991.

INDEX

Pasticci are listed under the name of the arranger; all other music dramas are listed under the name of the original composer.

Abbott, William, 67
Académie impériale de musique, 150–51
Académie royale de musique (Opéra): audiences, 127–28, 132, 133, 246; and Berlioz, 123, 216; composers, 3, 98, 99; genre, 2, 4, 209, 284–85; licensing, 29, 30; location, 22, 30, 42; management, 288; and Meyerbeer, 216–17, 246; occasional works, 152, 153, 158; orchestra, 95, 96, 110; personnel, 102, 103, 105; and politics, 151, 157, 168; rejuvenation, 29, 283; repertory, 30, 33, 34, 38, 40, 43, 63, 98, 209, 234, 248, 250, 283, 285, 287; and Rossini, 62, 63, 100–101, 174, 286–87; scenery, 41; singers, 37, 77–78, 80, 93, 94, 134, 217; and Weber, 255
Adam, Adolphe, 31, 50; *Giselle*, 107
Adélaïde Duguesclin, 158
Adrien (singer), 85
Advié (flutist), 94
Albertin, Hyacinthe, 205
Alissan de Chazet, André-René-Polydore, 112–13, 115, 119, 223; *Pauvre Jacques* (with Sewrin), 222–23
Allarde, Francis Leroi, baron d': *Les deux Jockos* (with Artois de Bournonville and Lurieu), 35; *La fête à la guinguette* (with Artois de Bournonville and Théaulon), 153

Allingham, John Till: *Fortune's Frolic*, 68
Ancelot, Jacques-Arsène: *Fiesque*, 135–36; *L'homme du monde* (with Boniface), 69; *L'important*, 69
Andrieux, François-Guillaume-Jean-Stanislas, 112–13, 114
Anglemont, Édouard d', 221–22, 296; *Le Cachemire* (with Lesguillon), 108
animals, 36
Anseaume, Louis, 199, 291
Antier, Benjamin: *Gustave ou Le napolitain* (with Laroche and Bourgeois), 35
Apel, Johann August: *Das Gespensterbuch* (with Laun), 222
arrangements, 53, 99, 102–4, 138, 139, 196, 218–26, 227–29, 242, 243, 250–51, 256, 274, 284, 288. *See also* pasticcio; translation
Artois, Charles-Philippe, comte d'. *See* Charles X
Artois de Bournonville, François-Victor-Armand d': *Les deux Jockos* (with Allarde and Lurieu), 35; *La fête à la guinguette* (with Allarde and Théaulon), 153; *Les vêpres odéoniennes* (with Simonin), 38
Auber, Daniel-François-Esprit, 2, 38, 47, 97, 98, 103, 110, 128, 144–45, 201, 291; *Le concert à la cour*, 34; *La fiancée*, 2; *Fra Diavolo*, 2; *Gustave III*, 2, 287; *Leicester ou*

Auber, Daniel-François-Esprit *(continued)*
    Le château de Kenilworth, 98–99, 178,
    208; *Lestocq,* 2; *Le maçon,* 32, 246; *La*
    muette de Portici, 2, 34, 38–39, 102, 105,
    283; *La neige ou Le nouvel Éginard,* 99,
    208; *Le philtre,* 2; *Le serment,* 2; *Les trois*
    genres (with Boieldieu), 6, 53, 55, 88, 96,
    98, 103, 105–6, 143–50, 156, 207, 291
audiences, 17–20, 43, 288. *See also* Acadé-
    mie royale de musique; Paris; Théâtre
    italien; Théâtre-Royal de l'Odéon;
    Théâtre-Royal de l'Opéra-Comique
Audinot, Nicolas-Médard, 291; *Le tonnelier,*
    55, 206, 291
Auguste (singer), 70, 109
Aumont, Louis-Marie-Céleste, duc d', 149,
    156, 208, 209, 210
Azevedo, Alexis, 225

Baillot, Pierre-Marie-François de Sales, 272
ballet, 2, 30, 33, 217, 285, 287
Balocchi, Luigi, 62
Balzac, Honoré de: *Une double famille,* 21
Barba (publisher), 136
Barbaja, Domenico, 277
Barbier, Jules, 275
Le barbier de Séville ou La précaution inutile
    (Rossini): performances of, 66, 69, 133,
    135, 177, 207, 227, 273, 286; premieres,
    9, 23, 54, 55, 126, 228, 291; process of
    adaptation, 218, 221, 229–38, 249, 284;
    publication of, 137; and singers, 42, 45,
    74–76, 79–80, 82, 84–87, 89–90, 133;
    success of, 56, 96, 126, 129, 194
Batton, Désiré-Alexandre, 225–26; *Le camp*
    du drap d'Or (with Leborne and Rifaut),
    105; *La fenêtre secrète,* 208, 225
Baudouin d'Aubigny, Théodore, 221
Bayard, Jean-François-Alfred, 106, 107, 191,
    295; *Anglais et français* (with de Wailly),
    69, 106; *Un dernier jour de folies* (with
    Romieu), 106; *Molière au théâtre* (with
    Romieu), 106; *L'oncle Philibert* (with de
    Wailly), 106; *Roman à vendre,* 106
Beaumarchais, Pierre-Augustin Caron de,
    6, 61, 229, 234, 248, 249; *Le barbier de*
    Séville, 32, 33, 218, 221, 229–34, 238,
    249; *Le mariage de Figaro,* 221, 234, 248
Beer, Michael, 242
Beethoven, Ludwig van, 3, 43, 98, 127, 138,
    172, 195–96, 215, 252, 271–77, 286;

Fidelio, 6, 108, 138, 224, 272, 273–77,
    279, 280, 281; *Leonore,* 273, 275, 281;
    Mass in C, 272; String Quartets, op. 18,
    272; Symphony No. 1, 272; Symphony
    No. 3 *(Eroica),* 271, 272; Symphony
    No. 5, 271; Symphony No. 9, 271, 272
Belle, Gabriel-Alexandre: *Le roi René ou La*
    Provence au quinzième siècle (with Sewrin),
    152
Belleyme, Louis-Marie de, 71
Bellini, Vincenzo, 3, 256; *I puritani,* 124
Belmont (Mlle) (singer), 120
Bercher, Jean (pseud. Dauberval), 32
Berlioz, Hector, 3, 5, 50, 122–24, 127, 171,
    181, 197, 213–18, 249, 252–55, 269,
    282, 285, 288; *Benvenuto Cellini,* 82;
    Le cri de guerre de Brisgaw, 216; *L'enfance*
    du Christ, 104; *Les francs-juges,* 213–18;
    Mémoires, 252; *La révolution grecque,* 117;
    Roméo et Juliette, 108, 181; *Les troyens à*
    Carthage, 286
Berlioz, Nanci, 215
Bernard, Claude, 5, 36, 44–59, 60, 61, 63,
    70, 71, 72, 73, 77, 85, 89, 113, 121, 134,
    143, 149, 168, 199, 206–10, 213, 240–
    41, 243, 263, 264
Berry, Charles-Ferdinand de Bourbon, duc
    de, 30, 157, 168
Berry, Marie-Caroline-Ferdinande-Louise,
    duchesse de, 30, 135, 151, 153, 168,
    186, 266
Bertati, Giovanni, 221
Berton, Henri-Montan, 210; *Aline, reine de*
    Golconde, 153; *Les deux mousquetaires,* 32,
    34; *Françoise de Foix,* 32; *Le laboureur chi-*
    nois, 172; *Montano et Stéphanie,* 32, 34;
    Pharamond (with Boieldieu and
    Kreutzer), 32, 33, 98, 158; *Virginie,* 34
Bertoni, Ferdinando, 222
Bertrand (publisher), 136
Bezou (publisher), 136
Bizet, Georges: *Carmen,* 104; *La jolie fille de*
    Perth, 107; *Les pêcheurs de perles,* 286
Blabis, Silvio Saverio, 222
Bloc, Nathan, 95, 138, 215
Bohrer brothers, 81
Boieldieu, François-Adrien, 47, 97, 98, 99,
    103, 110, 128, 143–49, 201, 269, 286,
    291; *La dame blanche,* 37, 57, 98, 145–
    49, 217, 246, 269; *Les deux nuits,* 98, 275;
    La marquise de Brinvilliers, 98; *Le petit*

chaperon rouge, 143, 208; *Pharamond* (with
Berton and Kreutzer), 32, 33, 98, 158;
Les trois genres (with Auber), 6, 53, 55, 88,
96, 98, 103, 105–6, 143–50, 207, 291;
Les voitures versées, 143, 267
Bonaparte, Napoléon, 26, 150–51
Boniface, Joseph-Xavier (pseud. Saintine
or Xavier), 108, 296; *L'homme du monde*
(with Ancelot), 69; *Picciola*, 108
Bonjour, Casimir: *Le mari à bonnes fortunes*,
32
Bonnechose, Émile de: *Rosamonde*, 186
Bonsignori (singer), 125
Borghi, Giovanni Battista, 195
Bouilly, Jean-Nicolas, 275, 276; *L'abbé de
l'épée*, 32
Boulard (singer), 109
Bouquin de la Souche (publisher), 136
Bourgeois, Anicet: *Gustave ou Le napolitain*
(with Antier and Laroche), 35
Boutet de Monvel, Jacques-Marie, 291, 292
Brice (singer), 109
Briffaut, Charles, 115–16, 119
Brisebarre, Jean-Bernard (pseud. Joanny),
134
Broussais, Casimir-Anne-Marie, 123
Broussais, François-Joseph-Victor, 122
Butler, Richard: *The Irish Tutor*, 68

Cagniez, Louis-Charles, 221
Camoin (singer), 73, 237
Camoin (Mme) (singer), 73
Campenaut (singer), 73, 74, 109, 262–63
Camus, Paul-Hippolyte, 95, 136
Camus, Pierre-François (pseud. Merville),
108, 274, 276; *Les deux Anglais*, 68;
La première affaire, 68
Carafa, Michele, 3, 39, 43, 100, 101–2, 105,
249, 286, 296; *Les deux Figaro*, 102, 104–
5, 116, 221, 296; *I due Figaro, ossia il
soggeto di una commedia*, 66, 102, 104,
105, 221, 296; *Jeanne d'Arc*, 101; *Jenny*,
102; *Masaniello*, 38–39, 101–2; *Le nozze
di Lammermoor*, 101; *Il paria*, 101; *Sangarido*, 102; *Le solitaire*, 101; *Le valet de
chambre*, 32, 34, 101, 208; *La violette*, 102,
105
Carmouche, Pierre-François-Adolphe, 106,
154, 297; *La dame jaune* (with Dupin and
Mazères), 37
Carré, Michel-Florentin, 275

Carrion-Nisas, André-Henri-François Victor
de: *Valérien ou Le jeune aveugle* (with
Sauvage), 223
Castel, Louis (pseud. Robert), 132; *Les mémoires d'un claqueur*, 130, 132
Castelli, Ignaz Franz, 222, 296
Castil-Blaze (pseud. of François-Henri-
Joseph Blaze): approach to arranging,
62, 218–21, 224–25, 245; journalism
and other writings, 99, 151, 212, 241–
42, 272–73; and Mozart, 248–49; and
Odéon, 99, 110, 138, 272–73; pasticci,
61, 99, 189, 193–97, 218, 291, 294,
296; publishing, 99, 136–38, 139; and
Rossini, 193–96, 218, 224–25, 227–39,
249; translations, 99, 218, 242, 286, 287,
291, 292, 293, 295, 297; and Weber,
100, 175, 195, 253, 254–71, 285; *De
l'opéra en France*, 269; *Dictionnaire de
musique moderne*, 269; *La fausse Agnès*, 60,
61, 138, 147–49, 193–94, 195, 196,
220–21, 294; *Les folies amoureuses*, 32, 35,
54, 55, 56, 90, 137–38, 193–95, 196,
197, 207, 219, 225, 291; *La forêt de Sénart
ou La partie de chasse de Henri IV*, 55, 57,
99, 100, 130, 138, 195, 196, 219, 268,
270, 273, 294; *Monsieur de Pourceaugnac*,
60, 61, 99, 134, 136, 195, 196, 221, 296;
Le répertoire d'opéras traduits, 137–38
Catel, Charles-Simon, 210; *Wallace ou Le
ménestrel écossais*, 208
Catrufo, Gioseffe, 43
Cayla, Mme du, 29
censorship. *See under* Théâtre-Royal de
l'Odéon
Cervantes, Miguel de: *Don Quixote*, 189, 190
Chabagnac, Adolphe-Gentil de, 46
Chabrol de Volvic, Gilbert-Joseph Gaspard,
comte de, 158
Chalas, Alexandre, 108, 223, 294
Champagne, Thibaut de, 196
Champein, Stanislas: *La mélomanie*, 32
Charbonel, Antoine, 123
Charles X, 28, 29, 64, 106, 118, 150–58,
168, 211; coronation of, 6, 33, 36, 56,
122, 124, 143, 151–52, 156–58, 170,
187, 267, 284
Chateaubriand, François-René, comte de,
196
La château de Robion (anonymous), 138
Chateauvieux, Armand-François, 223

Chelard, Hippolyte-André-Jean-Baptiste:
    Macbeth, 34
Chéron, François, 115–16
Cherubini, Luigi, 3, 43, 101, 172, 208; *Les
    deux journées,* 201; *Elisa ou Le voyage aux
    glaciers du Mont St-Bernard,* 208; *Lodoïska,*
    201
Chopin, Frédéric, 21, 124–25
Choron, Alexandre-Étienne, 82
Choudard Desforges, Pierre-Jean-Baptiste,
    291
Cibber, Colley, 253
Ciceri, Pierre-Luc-Charles, 40–41, 264–65
Cimarosa, Domenico, 3, 193, 195, 196, 249,
    293; *La comédie à la campagne,* 55, 56, 92,
    103, 107, 293; *L'impresario in angustie,*
    56, 92, 293; *Le mariage secret,* 137; *Il ma-
    trimonio segreto,* 68, 84; *I nemici generosi,*
    219
Cirque Olympique, 41, 135
Cléopâtre, 32
Codrington, Sir Edward, 118
Coeuriot (singer), 78, 79, 94
Collé, Charles: *La forêt de Sénart [La partie de
    chasse de Henri IV],* 219
Collin de Plancy, Clotilde-Marie: *Le chasseur
    rouge* (with Théaulon de Lambert), 38
Colman, George: *The Blue Devils,* 69
Comédie-Française. *See* Théâtre-Français
Comelli, Adelaide, 62
Compaignon, Léon, 213, 214, 215; *Richard
    en Palestine,* 214
Comte, Louis-Christian, 35
concerts spirituels, 80, 134, 272
Conservatoire, 96, 104, 105, 272. *See also*
    Société des Concerts du Conservatoire
Constant, Benjamin, 124, 196
Contat-Desfontaines, Joseph-Jean (pseud.
    Dormeuil): *La fête des marins ou La
    St-Charles à Dieppe* (with Théaulon), 153
Corbière, Jacques-Joseph-Guillaume-Pierre,
    comte de, 212
Cottenet, Émile, 256
Coupart, Antoine-Marie, 114–15, 116, 119
Courcy, Frédéric de: *La fée du voisinage ou La
    St-Charles au village* (with P.-J. Rousseau
    and Théaulon), 153
Crébillon, Prosper Jolyot de, 33; *Rhadamiste
    et Zénobie,* 32
Crémont, Pierre: arranger, 102, 103, 139,
    162–63, 173, 174–75, 242–47, 279;

conductor, 95, 96, 97, 292, 293, 294,
    295, 296; involvement in management,
    61, 72; negotiations with Weber, 270–
    71; *Les bohémiens,* 57, 60, 61, 83, 90, 102,
    103, 128, 135, 139, 173–77, 195, 222,
    270, 271, 279, 280, 295; *Louis XII ou
    La route de Reims* ([?] with Leroux and
    Vergne), 55, 56, 103, 106, 108, 136,
    158–67, 169, 187, 190, 293
Croizette, Armand, 223

Dalayrac, Nicolas-Marie, 8, 54, 187–88, 190,
    201, 286, 291, 292, 294, 296; *Adolphe et
    Clara,* 60, 61, 69, 83, 154, 187, 201, 296,
    297; *Ambroise ou Voilà ma journée,* 55,
    206, 291; *Camille ou Le souterrain,* 66,
    97, 201, 297; *Les deux mots ou Une nuit
    dans la forêt,* 39, 66, 201, 297; *Gulnare ou
    L'esclave persane,* 66, 201, 297; *Maison à
    vendre,* 60, 61, 294; *La maison isolée ou Le
    vieillard des Vosges,* 66, 201, 296; *Philippe et
    Georgette,* 32, 34, 55, 206, 292; *Raoul, sire
    de Créqui,* 55, 56, 292
La dame du lac (Rossini), 41, 214; at Opéra-
    Comique, 53; performances of, 55, 57,
    120, 135, 207, 227, 273, 294; process of
    adaptation, 100, 226, 238–42, 249; pub-
    lication of, 80, 138; and singers, 79–80,
    90, 94
da Ponte, Lorenzo, 221, 295, 297
Dauberval (pseud. of Jean Bercher), 32
Daussoigne-Méhul, Louis-Joseph, 276
Defauconpret, Auguste-Jean-Baptiste, 224
Delacroix, Eugène, 29, 117, 122, 124–26,
    127
Delaforest, A., 115
Delaunay (singer), 117
Delavau, Guy, 158
Delavigne, Casimir: *Les messéniennes,* 117;
    Les vêpres siciliennes, 35, 38, 54
Delavigne, Germain, 217
Delbouille (violinist), 94
Delécluze, Étienne-Jean, 126–27
Delestre-Poirson, Charles-Gaspard, 31, 257
Denohe (dramatist): *Frédigonde et Brunehaut*
    (with H. Franconi), 32
de Rancé: *Les trois cousins,* 32, 35
Derfeuille (Mme) (singer), 70
Déricourt (singer), 70
Deschamps, Émile, 108, 180–81, 182, 186,
    187, 224, 295

Destouches, Philippe: *La fausse Agnès*, 194, 219, 220

Devéria, Achille, 122, 124, 125, 126, 127

Devienne, François, 286, 293; *Les Français au sérail*, 55, 56, 79, 80, 202–6, 293; *Le pensionnat de jeunes demoiselles*, 202–3, 205–6; *Les visitandines*, 56, 57, 79, 202–3, 205, 207

Dezède, Nicolas, 291; *Blaise et Babet ou La suite des "Trois fermiers,"* 55, 56, 292

dilettanti, 128–29, 251

Diodati, Giuseppe Maria, 293

Donizetti, Gaetano, 3, 286, 287; *L'ange de Nisida*, 286; *Il campanello di notte*, 85; *Dom Sébastien*, 287; *La favorite*, 286; *La fille du régiment*, 106; *Lucie de Lammermoor*, 286; *Lucia di Lammermoor*, 82, 286; *Lucrezia Borgia*, 256; *Les martyrs*, 287; *Poliuto*, 287

Donzelli, Domenico, 32

Dorgebray, Amélie, 42, 94

Dormeuil. *See* Contat-Desfontaines, Joseph-Jean

Dormeuil (singer), 256, 267

Dormeuil (Mme) (singer), 256

Douesnel, 44

Drap-Arnaud, Prudent-Marc-Xavier-Victor: *La clémence de David*, 158

Droz, François-Xavier-Joseph, 112–13, 114

Ducis, Jean-François, 224–25

Ducray-Duminil, François-Guillaume, 105

Dufresne, Maurice. *See* Monglave, Eugène-François Garay de

Dupin, Jean-Henri: 37, 106, 189, 191, 293, 297; *Le bal champêtre ou Les grisettes à la campagne* (with Scribe), 257; *Les brigands de Schiller* (with Sauvage), 66, 106, 187–88, 190–93, 297; *La dame jaune* (with Carmouche and Mazères), 37; *Le mariage de raison* (with Varner), 186

Duplantys, Raphaël de Frédot, 77

Duport, Auguste: *Une journée de Charles V* (with P. Duport), 152, 153

Duport, Paul (pseud. Paulin): *Une journée de Charles V* (with A. Duport), 152, 153

Duprez, Édouard, 83

Duprez, Gilbert: 74–75, 82–83, 109, 117, 120, 189; *La cabane du pêcheur*, 83

Duprez (Mme) (singer), 83, 117

Durand (Mme) (singer), 70

Durand, Edme-Auguste, 29

Duval, Alexandre-Vincent, 294

Duvernois (publisher), 136

Duvert, Félix-Auguste, 107, 293, 296; *Le dernier des Romains*, 152

Duveyrier, Anne-Honoré-Joseph (pseud. Mélesville), 178, 257; *Le dîner sur l'herbe* (with Scribe), 257; *Valérie* (with Scribe), 223; *Les vêpres siciliennes* (with Scribe), 38

École royale [et spéciale] de chant, 75, 82

Édouard (singer), 44, 263

elephants, arrival of, 36

L'enfant trouvé, 32

Europarama, 36

Fabre, Auguste, 117

Farrenc, Jacques-Hippolyte-Aristide, 137, 138, 273–74, 276, 277

Favart, Charles-Simon, 293

Ferrand, Humbert, 213, 216, 217, 218

Fétis, François-Joseph, 252, 269, 277, 278; *Le bourgeois de Reims*, 158

Fieffé, Antoine-Marie, 25, 211

Fielding brothers (Théodore, Copley, Thalès, and Newton), 125

Florigny (Mlle [Mme Florigny-Valère]) (singer), 42, 73, 85–89, 90, 93, 256, 263

Flotow, Friedrich Adolf Ferdinand Freiherr von, 286; *Le naufrage de la Méduse*, 286

Fodor-Mainvielle, Joséphine, 235

Forbin-Janson, Louis-Nicolas-Philippe-Auguste, comte de, 29

Franconi, Henri: *Frédigonde et Brunehaut* (with Denohe), 32

Franconi brothers, 135, 136

Frédéric. *See* Petit-Méré, Frédéric du

Der Freischütz (Weber), 2, 8, 35, 56, 217, 279, 280, 285, 292; critical opinion of, 123, 124, 127, 267; translation of, 207, 212, 251, 255–56, 258, 259–61, 267, 268, 273, 281; and Weber, 252, 255–56, 259, 268, 271, 282; use in pasticci, 195

Frère (publisher), 156

Fulgence [de Bury], Joseph Désiré: *Les deux ménages* (with Picard and Wafflard), 32; *Le voyage à Dieppe* (with Wafflard), 32

Fusée de Voisenon, Claude-Henri de, 293

Gaillard de Murray (member of reading committee), 113

Garcia, Manuel, 43, 238

Gardet (publisher), 136

Gardi, Francesco, 222

Garrick, David, 253

Gautier, Théophile, 106–7; *Histoire de l'art dramatique,* 112

Gaveaux, Pierre, 201, 275; *Léonore,* 275

Geertz, Clifford, 8

Gehe, Eduard: *Heinrich IV, König von Frankreich,* 195

Generali, Pietro, 194

Géorama, 36

Georges-Weimer (Mlle) (actress), 130–31

Géricault, Jean-Louis-André-Théodore, 21

German music drama: Odéon repertory, 47, 53, 61, 71–72, 101–2, 212, 251–82, 284–85; pasticci, 173, 174–75, 195–96; publishing, 137, 138, 202; reception, 56, 127, 128–29; singers, 91; tradition in Paris, 6, 43, 250–51; translations, 31, 71, 100, 212, 218, 222–24, 226, 286, 287

Gherardini, Giovanni, 221, 292

Gignon (singer), 73

Gilbert, Ernest, 104

Gilbert, Louis-Alphonse, 104, 297; *Charles V et Duguesclin* (with J.-B.-L. Guiraud and C.-J. Tolbecque), 66, 103–4, 106, 153–54, 156, 297

Gimel, Michel-Ambroise de, 46, 113

Ginzburg, Carlo: *Il formaggio e i vermi,* 7

giraffe, arrival of, 36

Girard, Henri, 224

Gluck, Christoph Willibald, 3, 4, 34, 43, 56, 93, 117, 123, 133, 172, 248; *Armide,* 34; *Orphée,* 34, 153

Goldoni, Carlo, 221

Goldsmith, Oliver: *She Stoops to Conquer,* 68

Gosse, Étienne: *Le médisant,* 32

Gounod, Charles: *Faust,* 286; *Roméo et Juliette,* 286

grand opéra, 2, 4, 82, 106, 209, 216, 284, 287

Greek war of independence, 117–19, 179

Grétry, André-Ernest-Modeste, 34, 54, 56, 90, 91, 93, 133, 199–200, 206, 286, 291, 292, 293; *L'épreuve villageoise,* 55, 200, 291; *La fausse magie,* 55, 88, 200, 291; *Les fausses apparences ou L'amant jaloux,* 55, 292; *Raoul Barbe-Bleu,* 55, 56, 91, 93, 293; *Richard Coeur-de-Lion,* 55, 76, 91, 93, 200, 291; *La rosière de Salenci,* 55, 292; *Sylvain,* 55, 91, 93, 292; *Le tableau parlant,* 55, 76, 87, 200, 291; *Les

trois âges de l'opéra, 172; *Zémire et Azor,* 55, 56, 88, 91, 291

Grisar, Albert, 286

Grisi, Giulia, 124

Gros, Antoine-Jean, 29

Guénée, Luc, 102, 190, 191, 293, 295; *Le neveu de Monseigneur,* 60, 83, 90, 100, 102, 106, 108, 136, 156, 187–88, 190–93, 295; *Les noces de Gamache,* 32, 35, 55, 56, 69, 102, 106, 116, 138, 187, 189–92, 249, 293

Guérin de Frémicourt, J.-N., 293

Guiraud, Ernest, 104

Guiraud, Jean-Baptiste-Louis, 104, 297; *Charles V et Duguesclin* (with Gilbert and C.-J. Tolbecque), 66, 103–4, 106, 153–54, 156, 297

Gymnase dramatique, 22, 30, 31–33, 35, 37, 73, 75, 95, 99, 147–49, 153, 168, 186, 193, 209, 212, 255, 256–57

Gyrowetz, Adalbert, 98, 279, 285, 294; *Der Augenarzt,* 61, 104, 222, 223, 273, 278, 280, 294; *La jeune aveugle,* 60, 61, 104, 222, 223, 273, 278, 280, 294

Habeneck, François-Antoine, 209, 252, 255–56, 271–72; *Le page inconstant,* 32

Halévy, Fromental: *La juive,* 179, 287; *Le roi et le batelier* (with Rifaut), 153

Handel, George Frideric, 172

Harel, Charles-Jean, 71

Hasse, Johann Adolf, 172

Hausset, Mme de: *Mémoires,* 190

Haydn, Joseph, 127, 172

Héle, Thomas d', 292

Hensler, Karl Friedrich, 176, 177

Hérold, Louis-Joseph-Ferdinand, 2, 50, 97, 99, 110, 286, 297; *La clochette,* 208; *Le dernier jour de Missolunghi,* 66, 99, 108, 114, 116–19, 137, 297; *Marie,* 99; *Le muletier,* 208; *Le pré aux clercs,* 99; *Les rosiers,* 208; *Les troqueurs,* 208; *Zampa,* 99

Herz, Henri, 124

Hoffman, François-Benoît: *Le roman d'une heure,* 32, 35

Hoffmann, E[rnst] T[heodor] A[madeus], 224, 248

Holzbauer, Ignaz, 222

Huber, Franz Xaver, 222, 292

Hugo, Adèle (née Foucher), 124

Hugo, Victor, 5, 122, 124, 125, 180, 186, 224; *Cromwell*, 124, 181; *Hernani*, 124; *Les nouvelles odes*, 124; *Les odes*, 124; *Les orientales*, 124; *Le sacre de Charles X*, 124
Hummel, Johann Nepomuk, 138

Isouard, Nicolas (Nicolò), 201; *Aladin ou La lampe merveilleuse*, 34
Italian music drama: at Académie royale de musique, 62–63, 285, 286–87; aesthetics of, 124–27; and *dilettanti*, 128–29; and French literary sources, 6, 194–96, 218, 221–22, 224, 242–46; and French music drama, 6, 199, 200, 202, 206, 218, 229–38, 284; and Meyerbeer, 101, 173, 242–49; and Napoléon, 150–51; and Odéon license, 31, 47, 212; in Odéon repertory, 53, 56, 71–72, 100–102, 199, 218, 221–22, 224–26, 227–49, 251, 267, 284; and pasticci, 61, 171, 173, 188–98; and publishing, 137–39; and Rossini, 53, 56, 61, 62–63, 80, 100–101, 125–26, 128–29, 173, 188–89, 194–95, 196, 200, 224–26, 227–41, 284, 285, 286–87; and singers, 80, 83, 92–93; at Théâtre italien, 30, 43, 151, 239–41, 285; in translation, 50, 285, 286–87
Ivanhoé (Pacini and Rossini): creation of, 177–87, 188, 189, 224; and *dilettanti*, 129; and Pacini, 137, 156; performances of, 60, 61, 100, 168, 174, 295; and Rossini, 62, 63, 100, 173, 238; and singers, 76, 78, 83, 92

Janin, Jean-Marie (pseud. Mely-Janin), 112–13; *Louis XI à Péronne*, 13; *Oreste*, 113
Janin, Jules, 112
Joanny (pseud. of Jean-Bernard Brisebarre), 134
Jouy, Victor-Joseph-Étienne de, 62, 196
Jullien, Adolphe: *Weber à Paris*, 254
Jupin, Charles-François, 136

Kalkbrenner, Friedrich, 21
Kärntnertortheater (Vienna), 6, 83, 101, 272, 277–82
Kauer, Ferdinand: *Das Donauweibchen*, 176
Kenney, James: *Love, Law and Physic*, 68
Kerckhoven, Charlotte, 58
Kind, Friedrich, 259, 292
Klinger, Friedrich Maximilian, 108

Klingmann, August, 106; *Don Quijote und Sancho Panza, oder die Hochzeit des Camacho*, 189, 190
Kock, Paul de, 105
Kotzebue, August von, 108, 189
Kretschmer, H. A. (viola player and publisher), 137, 138–39, 247
Kreubé, Frédéric: *Jenny la bouquetière* (with Pradher), 276
Kreutzer, Conradin, 3, 100, 101, 138, 277–78, 279, 281, 285, 296; *Adèle von Budoy*, 61, 277, 280, 296; *Cordelia*, 61, 101, 277, 279, 280; *L'eau de jouvence*, 66, 101, 107, 108, 114, 138, 277, 278, 280, 296; *La folle de Glaris*, 41, 60, 61, 66, 84, 101, 116, 132, 277–78, 279, 280, 296; *Libussa*, 277
Kreutzer, Rodolphe: *La fête de Mars*, 150; *Jadis et aujourd'hui*, 32; *Pharamond* (with Berton and Boieldieu), 32, 33, 98, 158

Lablache, Luigi, 124
La Bouillerie, François-Marie-Pierre Roullet, baron de, 28, 64, 211–12
Lachnith, Ludwig Wenzel, 250; *Les mystères d'Isis*, 172, 250, 251, 252, 287
Lacretelle, Jean-Charles-Dominique de, 115–16, 118–19
Laennec, René-Théophile-Hyacinthe, 24
La Fayette, Marie-Jean-Paul-Yves-Roch-Gilbert du Motier, marquis de, 22
La Ferté, Louis-Victor-Xavier Papillon, baron de, 26, 28, 29, 46, 47, 48, 49, 50, 207
Laffillé, Charles, 137, 138, 139, 242, 243, 244, 258
Laffitte, Jacques, 21
Lainé, Étienne, 93
Lamartelière, Jean-Henri-Ferdinand: *Les francs-juges*, 123
Lamartine, Alphonse de, 224
Laroche, Philippe-Jacques (pseud. Létoile Hubert): *Gustave ou Le napolitain* (with Antier and Bourgeois), 35
La Rochefoucauld, Louis-François Sosthène de: and composers, 155, 214–15, 225, 301–2; at Département des beaux-arts, 24, 26, 28–29, 50; and finances of Odéon, 51, 52, 63, 64, 70; and repertory of Odéon, 199, 207–11, 213, 240–41; and singers, 77, 134; and Théâtre anglais, 67, 68

La Rochefoucauld-Doudeauville, Ambroise-Polycarpe, duc de, 27–28, 64, 65

Larousse, Pierre: *Grand dictionnaire universel du dix-neuvième siècle*, 28, 106

Lassagne, Espérance-Hippolyte, 106, 155, 295; *Le bourgeois d'Essonne* (with Rochefort and P.-J. Rousseau), 153; *Le théâtre dans la caserne* (with Vulpian), 152

Latappy (singer), 263

Laun, Friedrich: *Das Gespensterbuch* (with Apel), 222

Laurent, Émile, 67, 68

Lauriston, Jacques-Alexandre-Bernard Law, marquis de, 26–28, 46, 48, 49–50, 51, 52, 64, 149, 156, 207, 212

Laya, Jean-Louis, 115, 119

Leborne, Aimé-Ambroise-Simon, 104–5, 296; *Le camp du drap d'Or* (with Batton and Rifaut), 105

Lebrun, Louis-Sébastien: *Les aveugles de Franconville*, 223

Leclerc (singer), 70, 109, 189

Lecomte (singer), 17, 73, 75–78, 83, 94, 109, 133, 134, 241, 263

Lemaire (or Auguste Maire) (singer), 45, 73, 262–63

Lemercier, Népomucène, 107

Lemétheyer, Frédéric, 71

Lemierre de Corvey, Jean-Frédéric-Auguste, 100, 110, 188, 228, 239, 294, 295, 296; *Le testament*, 60, 83, 100, 187, 188–89, 239, 295

Lemontey, Pierre-Édouard, 115–16

Lemoule (Mlle [Mme Mondonville]) (singer), 70, 74, 89–90, 91, 92, 109

Léon-Bizot (singer), 73, 82, 263

Léon-Chapelle (singer), 74

Leroux (musician), 103, 293; *Louis XII ou La route de Reims* (with Crémont[?] and Vergne), 55, 56, 103, 106, 108, 136, 158–67, 169, 187, 190, 293

Le Roy Ladurie, Emmanuel: *Montaillou, village occitain de 1294 à 1324*, 7

Lescot, Alphonse: *De la salubrité de la ville de Paris*, 15

Lesguillon, Jean-Pierre-François, 107–8, 221–22, 296; *Le Cachemire* (with d'Anglemont), 108; *Les nouveaux Adelphes*, 107

Le Sueur, Jean-François, 210, 214; *Le triomphe de Trajan* (with Louis-Luc Louiseau de Persuis), 150

Letellier (Mme) (singer), 73, 76, 263

Liadières, Pierre-Chaumont: *Jane Shore*, 54

licensing, 30–33, 43, 209, 212, 213, 256, 257, 283–84, 286. *See also under* Académie royale de musique; repertory; Théâtre-Français; Théâtre italien; Théâtre-Royal de l'Odéon; Théâtre-Royal de l'Opéra-Comique

Liszt, Franz: 43, 124; *Dom Sanche*, 34

Loève-Veimars, François-Adolphe, 257

Louis XVI, 150

Louis XVIII, 50, 150–51, 152, 157, 168

Louiseau de Persuis, Louis-Luc: *Le triomphe de Trajan* (with Le Sueur), 150

Lourdouiex, Jacques-Marie Lelarge, duc de, 114–15, 116, 119

Lully, Jean-Baptiste, 172, 196

Lurieu, Joseph-Gabriel de (pseud. Gabriel): *Les deux Jockos* (with Allarde and Artois de Bournonville), 35; *Jocko ou Le singe de Brésil* (with Rochefort-Luçay), 35

Lyon, 23

Maire, Auguste. *See* Lemaire

maison du Roi, 25–29, 36, 77, 211, 283. *See also under* Théâtre-Royal de l'Odéon

Maizony de Lauréal, Joseph-François-Stanislas, 108, 165, 293

Margaillon (singer), 87

Marguerite d'Anjou (Meyerbeer): and Ciceri, 41; and Meyerbeer, 40, 61, 101, 173, 242; and other works, 175, 189; performances of, 60, 214, 249, 273, 294; process of adaptation, 103, 221, 242–47; publication of, 139; and singers, 17, 76, 78, 79, 82, 91; success of, 129, 249

Marianne, 32

Marivaux, Pierre Carlet de Chamblain de, 33; *Le jeu de l'amour et du hasard*, 32; *Le legs*, 32

Marmontel, Jean-François, 199, 291, 292

Mars (Mlle), 21

Marsollier des Vivetières, Benoît-Joseph, 201, 296, 297

Martelly, Honoré-Antoine Richaud: *Les deux Figaro ou Le sujet de comédie*, 66, 221

Martignac, Jean-Baptiste-Silvère Gaye, vicomte de, 25, 28, 119, 211–12

Martin, Nicolas-Jean-Blaise, 89

Masson de Pezay, Alexandre-Frédéric-Jacques, 292

Mazères, Édouard-Joseph-Ennemond:
   La dame jaune (with Carmouche and
   Dupin), 37; *Héritage et mariage* (with Pi-
   card), 69; *Le landau* (with Picard), 35
Méhul, Étienne-Nicolas, 172, 201, 208, 269,
   297; *Ariodante*, 208; *Bion*, 235; *Les deux
   aveugles de Tolède*, 66, 201, 297; *Joseph*, 32,
   34; *Le jugement de Paris*, 32, 33; *Le trésor
   supposé*, 32, 34; *Valentine de Milan*, 276
Meissonnier (publisher), 137
Mélesville. *See* Duveyrier, Anne-Honoré-
   Joseph
mélodrame, 2, 31, 213, 217, 221, 223, 244
Mely-Janin. *See* Janin, Jean-Marie
Mercadante, Saverio, 3, 35, 56, 98, 102,
   187, 189–92; *L'apoteosi di Ercole*, 189,
   190; *Elisa e Claudio*, 189, 190
Mercier, Louis-Sébastien, 14
Mercier-Dupaty, Louis Emmanuel Félicité
   Charles: *Félicie ou La jeune fille romanesque*,
   32
Méric-Lalande, Henriette, 256
Merville. *See* Camus, Pierre-François
Meyerbeer, Giacomo: at Académie royale
   de musique, 108, 216–17; at Odéon, 61,
   100, 173, 175–77, 181–82, 194–95,
   198, 221, 242–47, 249, 284, 294; in
   Paris, 3, 40, 43, 101, 110, 286; at
   Théâtre italien, 129; *Il crociato in Egitto*,
   32, 34, 40, 83, 84, 101, 117, 129, 176,
   242–47, 256, 287; *Emma di Resburgo*, 40,
   176, 189, 245; *L'esule di Granata*, 176;
   Les huguenots, 108; *Margherita d'Anjou*, 6,
   40, 176, 189, 243, 246, 294; *Marguerite
   d'Anjou* (see *Marguerite d'Anjou*); *La
   nymphe du Danube*, 61, 84, 89, 101, 103,
   173–74, 175–77, 181, 273; *Robert le
   diable*, 40, 101, 216–17, 244, 249, 283;
   Romilde e Costanza, 147–49, 176; *Semiramide rinconosciuta*, 176
Meyssin (Mme) (singer), 90, 91–93
Miel, Edme-François-Antoine-Marie, 294
Milen (Mme) (singer), 70, 109
Mocker (clarinetist), 95–96
Molière (pseud. of Jean-Baptiste Poquelin),
   6, 121, 195; *Don Juan*, 221, 273; *L'école
   des maris*, 32, 33; *Le misanthrope*, 32; *Mon-
   sieur de Pourceaugnac*, 195, 219, 221;
   Tartuffe, 32, 35, 68, 121
Mombelli, Ester, 88, 90
Mondonville (singer), 89, 109

Monglave, Eugène-François Garay de
   (pseud. Maurice Dufresne), 76, 81, 90,
   223, 294
Monnier (singer), 75
Monpou, François-Louis Hippolyte, 286
Monsigny, Pierre-Alexandre, 202, 297; *Le
   déserteur*, 66, 201–2, 297
Montano, Stéphanie, 23, 42, 74, 79–82, 85,
   87, 94, 134, 203, 238
Monval, Georges, 203
Morlacchi, Francesco, 191; *Tebaldo e Isolina*,
   68
Mosca, Luigi, 195
Moscheles, Ignaz, 273
Mozart, Wolfgang Amadeus: at Académie
   royale de musique, 250, 285; critical
   opinion of, 125, 126, 127, 285; at
   Odéon, 3, 8, 129, 159–167, 248–49,
   267, 285, 295, 297; pasticci, 159–167,
   172, 187, 194; at Théâtre italien, 126,
   285; translations, 247–49, 286; *La
   clemenza di Tito*, 160, 162–65, 172, 190,
   250; *Così fan tutte*, 172, 287; *Don Giovanni*, 6, 7, 34, 69, 76, 125, 126, 172,
   247–48, 250, 287, 297; *Don Juan*, 66,
   69–70, 89, 129, 137, 221, 247–48, 249,
   273, 287, 297; *Die Entführung aus dem
   Serail*, 6, 160–62, 190, 250, 287; *La flûte
   enchantée*, 137, 138, 273, 280; *Idomeneo*,
   160, 172, 287; *Les noces de Figaro*, 60, 61,
   89, 129, 137, 173–74, 176–77, 221,
   234, 247–48, 249, 273, 295; *Le nozze di
   Figaro*, 6, 61, 172, 186, 234, 247–48,
   295; *Requiem*, 287; Symphony No. 39,
   287; Symphony No. 41 (*Jupiter*), 287; *Die
   Zauberflöte*, 172, 250, 273, 279, 280
Murphy, Arthur: *Three Weeks after Marriage*,
   69
mutes, 39

Niedermeyer, Abraham Louis: *Stradella*, 108,
   181
Nodier, Charles, 124, 224
Notaris, François, 234
Nourrit, Adolphe (fils), 62–63, 77, 82
Nourrit, Adolphe (père), 77

occasional works, 3, 152–53. *See also under*
   Académie royale de musique; Théâtre-
   Royal de l'Odéon
Odéon. *See* Théâtre-Royal de l'Odéon

Opéra. *See* Académie royale de musique

Opéra-Comique. *See* Théâtre-Royal de
l'Opéra-Comique

opéra comique, 2, 6, 43, 66, 98–100, 102,
104–5, 106, 113, 153, 194, 246, 286;
and licensing at Odéon, 3, 6, 30–31, 47–
48, 50, 53, 54, 60, 71, 97, 149, 169; at
Opéra-Comique, 2, 3, 202, 205–6, 207–
13; as performed at Odéon, 6, 61, 66,
71, 93, 143–44, 199–226, 234, 277, 284

Orléans, Louis-Philippe, duc d', 135

L'orphelin de Bethléem (anonymous), 130,
131–32

Otway, Thomas: *Venice Preserved*, 69

Ozaneaux, Jean-Georges, 108, 116, 297

Pacini, Antonio Francesco Gaetano Saverio,
99–100, 110, 137, 156, 181–82, 184,
188, 193, 295; *Ivanhoé* (see *Ivanhoé*)

Paër, Ferdinand, 3, 43, 194; *Agnese*, 273

Paisiello, Giovanni, 230

Palais-Royal, 115, 119, 127

Panorama, 36

Panorama dramatique, 41

Panseron, Auguste, 104–5, 155, 156, 295;
L'école de Rome (with Rolle), 60, 61–62,
90, 105, 106, 153, 154–56, 295

pantomime, 31

Paris: boulevard du Temple, 17, 22;
chaussée d'Antin, 13, 21, 59, 144;
faubourg St-Germain, 13, 21–24, 50,
59, 80, 145, 151, 283, 285; faubourg
St-Honoré, 21–22; infrastructure, demography and topography of, 13–25,
42–43

Pasta, Giuditta, 80, 85

pasticcio, 171–73; and Castil-Blaze, 99, 138,
193–97, 218–21; and Mercadante, 189–
93; and Meyerbeer, 175–77; and Mozart,
159–67; at Odéon, 3, 6, 53, 56, 60, 61,
128, 132, 170, 173–98, 284; and Rossini,
62, 177–89, 227, 240; and Weber, 174–
75

Paulin. *See* Duport, Paul

Pavesi, Stefano, 194, 222

Payer, Jérôme, 101, 278

Peellaert, Auguste-Philippe-Marie-Ghislain:
Agnès Sorel, 273, 276

Penley, Samson, 67

Pepoli, Alessandro, 222

Perier, Joseph, 21

Peronnet (singer), 75, 89, 90–91, 93, 94,
120

Petit-Méré, Frédéric du, 52–53, 59–65, 70,
71–72, 78, 134, 135, 176, 177, 186,
209–11; and repertory, 66, 207, 247;
and singers, 77, 84

Petrosellini, Giuseppe, 230

Philidor, François-André, 47

Picard, Louis-François, 202–3, 213, 293;
Les deux ménages (with Fulgence and
Wafflard), 32; *Héritage et mariage* (with
Mazères), 69; *Le landau* (with Mazères),
35

Piccini, Niccolò, 3

pièces de circonstance. See occasional works

Pierret, Jean-Baptiste, 125, 126

Pixérécourt, René Charles Guilbert de,
210–11, 243–45; *Marguerite d'Anjou*,
242, 243–46; *Ondine ou La nymphe des
eaux*, 177

Plantade, Charles-Henri, 156

Poisson, Toussaint-René, 104, 294

Ponchard, Louis-Antoine-Eléonore, 90

Porel, Paul, 203

Pouilley (Mlle) (singer), 42, 81, 93, 109,
189, 263

Pradher: *Jenny la bouquetière* (with Kreubé),
276

Prix de Rome, winners of, 48, 104, 105, 123,
155–56, 207, 210, 215, 225, 226, 286,
301–2

Prod'homme, Jacques-Gabriel, 254

Prot, Félix-Jean, 293; *Les rêveries renouvelées
des Grecs*, 55, 56, 293

publishing, 136–39, 140, 156, 237, 274

Pucitta, Vincenzo, 194

Quincy, Antoine-Chrysostome Quatremère
de, 115–16

Racine, Jean: *Britannicus*, 32, 33; *Iphigénie en
Aulide*, 32, 33, 54

Radiciotti, Giuseppe, 225–26

Raguenet, François, 173, 185

Rameau, Jean-Philippe, 172

Raynouard, François-Juste-Marie, 112–13,
114

Regnard, Jean-François: *Les folies amoureuses*,
194, 219, 222

Reicha, Anton, 3, 43, 105; *Sapho*, 34

Reissiger, Carl Gottlob, 138

repertory, 31–43, 256, 286. *See also under*
  Académie royale de musique; licensing;
  Théâtre-Français; Théâtre italien;
  Théâtre-Royal de l'Odéon; Théâtre-
  Royal de l'Opéra-Comique
Richelieu, Armand-Emmanuel du Plessis,
  duc de, 28
Rifaut, Louis-Victor-Étienne: *Le camp du drap
  d'Or* (with Batton and Leborne), 105; *Du
  roi et du batelier* (with Halévy), 153
Rigel, Henri-Joseph: *Edmond et Caroline*, 32
Rivals (violinist), 94, 95
Robert. *See* Castel, Louis
Robert, Alphonse, 122
Robin des bois (Weber): and Castil-Blaze, 99,
  100, 175, 270; and Ciceri, 41; critical
  opinion of, 123, 124, 126–27, 287–88;
  performances of, 5, 32, 35, 50, 57, 158,
  168, 169, 175, 177, 241, 281, 292; premiere, 9, 38, 52, 55, 56, 97, 123; process
  of adaptation, 42, 65, 114, 116, 222, 224,
  255–69, 276–77, 284; publication of,
  137, 138; and singers, 42, 45, 73, 76, 83,
  84, 87, 88, 94; success of, 56, 69, 71, 128,
  135, 136, 195, 207, 209, 217, 246, 251,
  276, 285; and Weber, 100, 175, 217, 270
Rochefort-Luçay, Claude-Louis-Marie
  (pseud. Edmond [de] Rochefort), 106,
  155, 295; *Le bourgeois d'Essonne* (with
  Lassagne and P.-J. Rousseau), 153; *Le
  drapeau blanc* (with others), 1–6; *Jocko
  ou Le singe de Brésil* (with Lurieu), 35
Rocher, Édouard, 214
Röckel, Joseph August, 272, 281, 285
Roger, Jean-François: *L'avocat*, 32
Rolle, Pierre-Gaspard, 104–5, 155, 156,
  295; *L'école de Rome* (with Panseron), 60,
  61–62, 90, 105, 106, 153, 154–56, 295
Romanelli, Luigi, 222
Romani, Felice, 221, 243, 244, 245, 294, 296
Romieu, François-Auguste (pseud. Augusta
  Kernoc), 106, 108, 191, 295; *Code civile:
  manuel complet de la politesse, du ton, des
  manières*, 108; *Un dernier jour de folies*
  (with Bayard), 106; *Molière au théâtre*
  (with Bayard), 106
Rossi, Gaetano, 221–22, 296
Rossini, Gioachino, 1, 3, 200, 221, 247–48,
  285, 286; at Académie royale de musique, 43, 62–63, 174; arias inserted into
  other works, 79, 80, 88, 203; critical and

public reception of, 125–26, 128–29,
  133, 283; libretti, 224–26; and Odéon,
  56, 61, 100, 110, 173, 177–87, 227–42;
  248–49, 284, 291, 292, 293, 294, 295,
  296; pasticci, 99, 102, 172–73, 177–87,
  188–89, 193–98; and publishers, 137;
  and singers, 90, 91, 93; translations, 53,
  100, 207; *Armida*, 182–83, 185; *Aureliano
  in Palmira*, 183–85; *Il barbiere di Siviglia*,
  68, 84, 85, 218, 221, 229–38, 284, 291;
  Le barbier de Séville ou La précaution inutile
  (see *Le barbier de Séville ou La précaution
  inutile*); *Bianca e Falliero*, 183–84, 185;
  La Cenerentola, 32, 34, 83, 127, 182–85,
  193, 195; *Le comte Ory*, 63, 285; *La dame
  du lac* (see *La dame du lac*); *La donna del
  lago*, 53, 57, 83, 84, 100, 129, 178, 225–
  26, 239, 241, 294; *Elisabetta regina
  d'Inghilterra*, 1, 203; *La gazza ladra*, 23,
  34, 56, 120, 128, 182–85, 239, 284, 292;
  Guillaume Tell, 101, 283, 285; *L'inganno
  felice*, 188; *L'italiana in Algeri*, 34, 188–
  89; *Ivanhoé* (see *Ivanhoé*); *Maometto II*, 62,
  63, 183; *Moïse et Pharaon ou Le passage de
  la mer Rouge*, 34, 62, 63, 100–101, 137,
  138; *Mosè in Egitto*, 62, 63, 125, 137, 184,
  185; *Otello*, 32, 34, 90, 224–25, 228, 273,
  293; *Othello ou Le More de Venise*, 42, 55,
  56, 76, 84, 90, 96, 128, 129, 138, 224–
  25, 227, 228–29, 239, 293; *La pietra del
  paragone*, 195; *La pie voleuse*, 42, 55, 56,
  88, 90, 120, 128, 129, 137, 194, 196,
  221, 227, 228, 239, 273, 284, 292; *Semiramide*, 34, 83, 100, 126, 182–85, 188,
  189, 239–41, 249; *Le siège de Corinthe*,
  34, 62, 63, 100, 117, 248; *Sigismondo*,
  182–83; *Tancrède*, 66, 68, 100, 107–8,
  120–21, 133, 137, 221–22, 227, 239,
  296; *Tancredi*, 66, 68, 85, 94, 107, 126,
  184, 193, 221, 230, 235, 296; *Torvaldo
  e Dorliska*, 68, 184, 185; *Il turco in Italia*,
  195; *Il viaggio a Reims*, 63, 151, 158, 168,
  169; *Zelmira*, 83
Rothe de Nugent, D. (writer), 112
Rothschild, James, 21
Rousseau, Auguste, 138, 239, 294
Rousseau, Pierre-Joseph: *Le bourgeois
  d'Essonne* (with Lassagne and Rochefort),
  153; *La fée du voisinage ou La St-Charles au
  village* (with Courcy and Théaulon), 153
Rowe, Nicholas: *Jane Shore*, 69

Royer-Collard, Pierre-Paul, 196
Royou, Jacques-Corentin, 115–16, 118–19;
  La mort de César, 115–16, 134; *Phocion,*
  115; *Zénobi,* 115
Rubini, Giovanni Battista, 32, 124, 235

Sacchini, Antonio, 3, 34
Le sacrifice interrompu (Winter), 80, 102, 103,
  108, 116, 222, 251, 276–77, 278; per-
  formances of, 32, 35, 55, 56, 80, 135,
  168, 273, 292; and singers, 42, 80; suc-
  cess of, 128, 207, 251
Sainte-Beuve, Charles-Augustin, 112
Saint-Geniez, Léonce, comte de, 108, 188,
  292, 295
Saint-Georges, Jules-Henry Vernoy, comte
  de, 106–7, 165, 293
Saintine. *See* Boniface, Joseph-Xavier
Saint-Preux (singer), 17, 70, 109
Salle de la bourse, 30
Salle Favart, 30, 67, 128, 129
Salle Ventadour, 30
Salza, Francesco Maria Berio, marchese di,
  225, 293
Samson, Joseph-Isidore, 131; *La fête de
  Molière,* 130, 131
Sand, George (pseud. of Aurore Dudevant,
  née Dupin), 21, 126
Saur, Joseph-Henri, comte de, 108, 188,
  292, 295
Saurin, Bernard-Joseph: *Beverley ou Le joueur,*
  123
Sauvage, Thomas-Marie-François, 5, 61, 64,
  65–71, 109, 119, 135, 210; and closure
  of music drama at Odéon, 72; criticism,
  254–57; libretti and plays, 103, 106,
  108, 174, 175–77, 189, 191, 242–44,
  258, 259, 263–64, 267, 270, 279, 285;
  and Odéon repertory, 207, 211, 213,
  292, 293, 294, 295, 296, 297; and
  singers, 78, 89, 247; *Les brigands de
  Schiller* (with Dupin), 66, 106, 187–88,
  190–93, 297; *Valérien ou Le jeune aveugle*
  (with Carrion-Nisas), 223
Sauvo, François, 115–16
Schiller, Friedrich, 106; *Die Räuber,* 190
Schlesinger, Maurice, 137, 255–58, 268–69
Schubert, Franz, 43
Schütz, Amalia, 42, 66, 83–85, 94, 101, 109,
  121, 129, 132, 133, 134, 135, 177, 247,
  279

Scott, Walter, 57, 58, 178, 181, 186–87;
  Ivanhoe, 177, 179, 186–87, 224; *Kenilworth,* 178; *The Lady of the Lake,* 178,
  225–26
Scribe, Eugène, 2, 31, 105–6, 110–11, 143,
  178, 217, 244, 257, 258, 275, 291; *Le
  bal champêtre ou Les grisettes à la campagne*
  (with Dupin), 257; *Le dîner sur l'herbe*
  (with Duveyrier), 257; *Le plus beau jour
  de ma vie* (with Varner), 186; *Les trois
  journées,* 114, 143–50; *Valérie* (with Du-
  veyrier), 223; *Les vêpres siciliennes* (with
  Duveyrier), 38
Sédaine, Michel-Jean, 199, 293, 297
Seghers (violinist), 94, 95
Sémonville, Charles-Louis Huguet, marquis
  de, 48–49, 211
Servières, Georges, 254
Séveste, Edmond, 213
Séveste, Jules, 213
Séveste, Pierre-Jacques, 213
Sewrin, Charles-Augustin-Bassompierre,
  106, 154, 223, 276, 296, 297; *Pauvre
  Jacques* (with Alissan de Chazet), 222–23;
  *Le roi René ou La Provence au quinzième
  siècle* (with Belle), 152
Shakespeare, William, 5, 181, 253; *Hamlet,*
  68, 69; *King Lear,* 70; *Othello,* 68, 84,
  224–25; *Romeo and Juliet,* 68
Sheridan, Richard Brinsley: *The Rivals,* 68
Simonin, Antoine-Jean-Baptiste: *Les vêpres
  odéoniennes* (with Artois de Bournon-
  ville), 38
Sirand (singer), 70, 109
The Sleepwalker, 69
Smithson, Harriet, 84, 123
Société des Concerts du Conservatoire, 110,
  216, 271–72, 277
Sontag, Henrietta, 83–84
Sor, Fernando: *Cendrillon,* 32, 33
Soumet, Alexandre, 62, 224; *Saül,* 227
Spohr, Louis, 3, 279; *Der Alchymist,* 1; *Der
  Berggeist,* 224, 273, 279, 280; *Faust,* 1;
  Le gnôme, 273, 279, 280; *Jessonda,* 1,
  224, 273, 279, 280; *Pietro von Albano,*
  1; *La veuve de Malabar,* 224, 273, 279,
  280
Spontini, Gaspare, 3, 4, 34, 43, 172, 248;
  Fernand Cortez, 32, 33, 34, 151; *Olimpie,*
  34; *La vestale,* 32, 33, 34, 151
Steibelt, Daniel, 194, 272

Stendhal (pseud. of Henri Beyle), 235; *La vie de Rossini*, 126
Sterbini, Cesare, 218, 229–34, 237–38, 291
Stoeppel (publisher), 269

Talleyrand, Charles-Maurice de, 22
Talma, François-Joseph, 124
Tamburini, Antonio, 124
Terrier (pâtissier), 267
Terry, Daniel, 70
theaters, institutional structure and management of, 29–43
Théâtre allemand, 272, 285
Théâtre anglais, 5, 67–70, 84, 106, 124
Théâtre Bobino. *See* Théâtre du Luxembourg
Théâtre Comte, 35–36, 39
Théâtre de la Gaîté, 29, 31, 41, 59, 153, 243
Théâtre de l'Ambigu comique, 29, 31, 135
Théâtre de la Porte-St-Martin, 22, 29–30, 31, 35, 36, 39, 41, 70, 95, 136, 223
Théâtre de la Renaissance, 286
Théâtre de Madame. *See* Gymnase dramatique
Théâtre des arts. *See* Académie royale de musique
Théâtre des Jeunes Artistes, 109
Théâtre des Nouveautés, 41, 109, 123, 212
Théâtre des Variétés, 22, 29, 31, 35, 38, 39, 74, 109, 153
Théâtre du Luxembourg, 39, 213
Théâtre du Vaudeville, 29, 31, 37, 38, 39, 47, 109, 152, 153, 222
Théâtre Feydeau, 30, 40, 250, 275
Théâtre-Français (Comédie-Française): actors, 3, 37; claque, 130; licensing, 29, 30; location, 22; management, 36, 52; and Odéon, 31, 37, 47, 144, 145; performances, 33, 35, 158, 186; reading committee, 112; repertory, 115, 152, 153, 218, 219, 223, 238
Théâtre italien: audiences, 127, 128, 129, 132, 151, 246, 285; institutional structure, 4; licensing, 29, 30, 249; location, 22, 30, 42, 43; and Odéon, 88, 90, 128, 174, 209, 238, 239–41, 247, 249, 288; orchestra, 95, 96; performances, 35, 158, 168, 237; personnel, 103; repertory, 3, 30, 34, 69, 125–26, 168, 197, 241, 247, 283, 285, 287; singers, 80, 83–84, 85,

88, 90, 109, 235; and Théâtre allemand, 272; and Théâtre anglais, 67–68, 70
Théâtre Louvois, 30, 40
Théâtre-Lyrique, 4, 275, 285, 286
Théâtre-Royal de l'Odéon: artists (singers and actors), 5, 42, 63–64, 70–71, 73–94, 109, 110, 120, 133–36, 140, 262–63; audiences, 5, 6, 17–18, 20–25, 50–51, 119–33, 139, 140, 149–51, 168, 186, 214, 246, 252, 266–67, 285; benefit performances, 77, 133–36; box-office receipts, 50, 51, 63, 64, 65, 84, 133–36, 174, 246, 252, 266; and censorship, 6, 113, 114–19, 139, 140, 186, 243; claque, 6, 120, 129–33, 139, 140, 150, 285; command performances, 66, 152, 168–69, 170; composers, 5, 61, 97–105, 110, 198, 210, 214–15, 284; fines, 45; licensing, 3, 6, 30–31, 52, 60–62, 139–40, 143, 149, 169, 198, 207–12, 215, 240–41, 275, 283–84; literary collaborators, 5, 105–8, 110–11; and location, 21–25, 30, 51, 144–45, 283, 285; and maison du Roi, 5, 7, 45–46, 48–52, 64, 65, 71, 132, 134, 139, 207, 216–17, 226, 241, 249; management, 5, 44–72, 75, 77, 120, 127, 143, 207, 216, 226, 249, 266–67, 283–84, 285, 288; occasional works, 6, 111, 143–70, 207, 284; orchestra, 5, 94–97, 103–4, 109–10, 126, 215, 288; pension funds, 63–64; personnel, 45, 49, 67, 70, 71, 73–111, 288; reading committee, 6, 45, 112–14, 139, 144, 215; refurbishment, 65, 78; rehearsals, 42, 45, 50, 144, 177, 243, 262; repertory, 6, 31, 47–48, 50, 53–57, 60–63, 66–70, 73, 95, 137, 139, 141–282, 283–84, 288; salaries, 51, 64, 70, 78, 84, 134, 138; shares and shareholders, 52–53, 64; subvention, 47, 50, 51, 52, 64–65, 70, 208, 209. *See also under* Théâtre-Français; Théâtre italien; Théâtre-Royal de l'Opéra-Comique
Théâtre-Royal de l'Opéra-Comique: audiences, 127, 133; composers, 47–48, 98, 99, 103, 105; genre, 2, 3; institutional structure, 4; licensing, 29, 30, 48, 208, 212, 284; location, 22, 30, 42; management, 36, 52, 149, 244, 283; and Odéon, 48, 50, 57, 71, 103, 106, 144, 145, 149, 156, 169, 205–12, 225, 239, 276, 284;

Théâtre-Royal de l'Opéra-Comique *(cont.)*
orchestra, 95, 96; performances, 43, 158;
personnel, 222–23; repertory, 4, 30–31,
34, 37–40, 53, 98–99, 101, 143, 152–
53, 178, 202–3, 205–12, 267, 276, 285;
singers, 37, 53, 73, 75, 80, 85, 87, 89, 90,
109
Théâtre-Royal italien. *See* Théâtre italien
Théaulon de Lambert, Marie-Emmanuel-
Guillaume-Marguerite: *Le chasseur rouge*
(with Collin de Plancy), 38; *La fée du
voisinage ou La St-Charles au village* (with
Courcy and P.-J. Rousseau), 153; *La fête
à la guinguette* (with Allarde and Artois de
Bournonville), 153; *La fête des marins ou
La St-Charles à Dieppe* (with Dormeuil),
153
Tillmann (bass player, cellist), 94–95
Tirpenne, Victor, 221, 296
Tirso de Molina (pseud. of Gabriel Téllez),
221
Tolbecque, Charles-Joseph, 103–4, 297;
Charles V et Duguesclin (with Gilbert and
J.-B.-L. Guiraud), 66, 103–4, 106, 153–
54, 156, 297
Tolbecque, Isidore-Augustin-Joseph, 103
Tolbecque, Jean-Baptiste-Joseph, 103–4,
138
Tolbecque, Julien-Joseph, 103
Tottola, Andrea Leone, 225–26, 294
Tourterelle, Henri (pseud. Herdlizka),
222–23
tout-Paris, 21–25
translation, 53, 56, 165, 179, 286–87; at
Académie royale de musique, 62–63;
and Castil-Blaze, 54, 99, 197; of German
music drama, 250–82; of Italian music
drama, 227–49; and licensing, 3, 31, 47,
50, 60, 207, 212; and Odéon repertory,
53, 68, 71, 88, 90, 100–102, 129, 189,
218, 221–26, 284; and publishers, 137–
38, 139; and reading committee, 113–
14. *See also* German music drama; Italian
music drama
Trautweins (publisher), 269
Treitschke, Georg Friedrich, 172
Troupenas (publisher), 137

ultra-pontins, 119, 127–28, 266
University of Paris (schools of Law and
Medicine), 24, 50, 119–20; students,
132, 209, 285

Valère (singer), 45, 73, 85–87, 109, 124,
263
Vanderburch, Émile-Louis: *La salle de police*
(with Carmouche), 153
Varner, Antoine François: *Le mariage de raison* (with Scribe), 186; *Le plus beau jour
de ma vie* (with Scribe), 186
Varnhagen von Ense, Carl August, 108
Veith, Johann Emanuel, 294
Velluti, Giovanni Battista, 82
Vente (publisher), 136
ventriloquism, 35–36
Verdi, Giuseppe, 1, 2, 3, 287; *Un ballo in
maschera*, 286; *Don Carlos*, 287; *Jérusalem*,
82, 287; *I lombardi alla prima crociata*,
287; *Macbeth*, 286; *Rigoletto*, 286; *La tra-
viata*, 286
Vergne, Alphonse, 103, 162, 190, 293; *Louis
XII ou La route de Reims* (with Crémont[?]
and Leroux), 55, 56, 103, 106, 108, 136,
158–67, 169, 187, 190, 293
Vernet, Horace, 21, 29
Vernoy de Saint-Georges, Jules-Henry, 106–
7, 165, 293
Véron, Louis-Désiré, 288; *Mémoires d'un
bourgeois de Paris*, 28
Vial, Jean-Baptiste-Charles, 154
Viardot, Louis, 288
Viardot, Pauline, 21
Vigny, Alfred de, 224, 248
Villèle, Jean-Baptiste-Séraphin-Joseph,
comte de, 28, 64, 65, 119
Violet d'Épagny, Jean-Baptiste Rose Bona-
venture, 239, 240–41, 294; *Luxe et indi-
gence ou Le ménage parisien*, 32, 54
Viollet-le-Duc, Emmanuel-Louis-Nicolas,
113
Viollet-le-Duc, Eugène-Emmanuel, 113
Vivaldi, Antonio, 172
Vogt, Auguste-Gustave, 102–3, 292
Voltaire (pseud. of François-Marie Arouet),
126; *Mérope*, 69, 130–31; *Nanine*, 32;
Tancrède, 222
Vulpian, Gustave, 106, 155, 295; *Le théâtre
dans la caserne* (with Lassagne), 152

Wafflard, Alexis Jacques Marie: *Les deux
ménages* (with Fulgence and Picard), 32;
Le voyage à Dieppe (with Fulgence) 32
Wagner, Richard, 1, 2, 3, 286, 287; *La défense
d'amour*, 286; *Das Liebesverbot*, 286; *Rienzi*,
286; *Tannhäuser*, 286, 287

Wailly, Gabriel-Gustave de, 106, 182, 186, 224, 295; *Anglais et français* (with Bayard), 69, 106; *L'Oncle Philibert* (with Bayard), 106

Weber, Carl Maria von, 43, 135, 182, 215, 217, 276, 279; and Castil-Blaze, 138, 195–96; critical and public opinion of, 56, 57, 123, 124, 127, 128, 129, 133; and Odéon, 3, 100, 102, 103, 110, 114, 252–71, 281–82, 284, 292, 294; in Paris, 1–2, 285, 286; pasticci, 61, 99, 172, 173–75, 198; translations of, 35, 207; *Le chasseur noir*, 212, 256–58, 273; *Die drei Pintos*, 286; *Euriante*, 63, 285, 287; *Euryanthe*, 2, 63, 195, 252, 255, 259, 260, 268, 270, 271, 285, 287; *Der Freischütz* (see *Der Freischütz*); *Oberon*, 2, 102, 270, 271, 285, 287; *Preciosa*, 55, 57, 102, 103, 135, 174–75, 195, 222, 270, 271, 273, 279, 280, 281, 294; *Robin des bois* (see *Robin des bois*); *Silvana*, 174–75, 271

Weigl, Johann Baptist, 3, 98, 278–79, 285, 296; *Emmeline ou La famille suisse*, 60, 61, 103, 137, 177, 222–23, 276, 278, 279, 280, 284, 296; *Die Schweizerfamilie*, 61, 222, 278, 280, 284, 296; *La vallée suisse ou Pauvre Jacques*, 223

Winter, Peter von, 3, 98, 102, 285, 292; *Le sacrifice interrompu* (see *Le sacrifice interrompu*); *Das unterbrochene Opferfest*, 35, 56, 102, 103, 108, 207, 251, 278, 279, 280, 292

Wolff, Pius Alexander, 294; *Preciosa*, 174, 222, 279, 296

Xavier. *See* Boniface, Joseph-Xavier

Yates, Frederick, 67

Zingarelli, Nicola Antonio: *Giulietta e Romeo*, 68

Zuchelli, Carlo, 126

Compositor:	G&S Typesetters, Inc.
Music setter:	Mansfield Music Graphics
Text:	Baskerville
Display:	10/12 Baskerville
Printer and binder:	Malloy Lithographing, Inc.